# Management Operations in Education

## Guilbert C. Hentschke

The University of Rochester

McCutchan Publishing Corporation
2526 Grove Street
Berkeley, California 94704

© 1975 by McCutchan Publishing Corporation
All rights reserved

Library of Congress Catalog Card Number 75-9168
ISBN 0-8211-0757-7

Printed in the United States of America

*This book is dedicated to my Parents,*
*who view education as the most exciting profession on earth.*

# Acknowledgments

I am indebted to many for ideas and assistance. My primary obligation is to Robert A. Burnham (University of Illinois) and Frederick W. Hill (Hicksville Public Schools, New York), both of whom identified the need for a book like this, helped formulate its contents, and reviewed numerous outlines and drafts.

The following individuals aided me greatly by reading and commenting on various sections of the manuscript: Daniel J. Brown (State University of New York, Buffalo), Oliver S. Brown (Cambridge School Department, Massachusetts), Anthony M. Cresswell (Northwestern University), Robert Den Hartog (Lincoln Public Schools, Nebraska), Walter I. Garms (University of Rochester), Warren H. Hausman (University of Rochester), Michael Kirst (Stanford University), Paul L. Reason (City School District, Rochester, New York), Thomas E. Tellefsen (Coopers and Lybrand, Los Angeles), Richard Videbeck (University of Illinois), and Jerold Zimmerman (University of Rochester).

Several students have read drafts, contributed ideas for revision, and worked on quantitative problems to ensure that they are as error free as possible. Particular thanks go to Frederick Dembowski, George Kisha, Sa Koolrat Phoolsawat, Stephen Sumner, and Edwin Truax.

A special note of gratitude is extended to Sharon Monroe for her skillful typing of the manuscript.

Also, I thank the people at McCutchan Publishing Corporation: Frances Bowles, Mariam Kagan, Alice Klein, and John McCutchan.

Comments from readers are welcomed.

*Guilbert C. Hentschke*

# Preface

## Some Trends in Education Management

As the education sector of the economy has grown, so has the magnitude and complexity of the job of educational managers. Since the founding of the Boston Latin School in 1636, education has grown to become the nation's largest "industry." It has a current budget approximating $100 billion, about one-ninth of the GNP. Approximately three million instructional personnel are employed to teach approximately sixty million individuals and are supported or managed through the services of about eight million others.

The complexity accompanying this growth can be traced largely to three general factors: conflict among the goals of education, the state of knowledge about the learning process, and the evolution of the current form of educational organization. First, widespread agreement does not generally exist within or among educational organizations about the appropriate objectives to pursue, and educational managers often must determine organization priorities without clear guidelines as to the relative merits of programs. There are no unambiguous or apolitical methods for determining whether drop-out prevention is a better or worse objective for an educational organization than college preparation. In problematic situations such as this, the corporate yardstick of net profits is not meaningful, and the social science yardsticks of individual and social welfare are indeterminate.

Even in a context of general goal agreement, the process of learning is not clearly understood. Thus, for a given set of education goals, there is no totally unified body of education theory that both guides specific decisions *and* upon which a majority of educators can agree. This factor greatly increases the difficulty in determining the most appropriate means for a given end.

Finally, the current organizational structure of education serves to increase the complexity of management's task because the structure incorporates some of the least desirable characteristics of both highly centralized and highly decentralized organizations. The industry itself is divided up among about twenty-two thousand semiautonomous educational organizations, each with its own governing board. Because the average size of the "firm" is not large (average annual budget of $4.5 million), resources devoted to organizational planning and operations analysis within a single organization are limited, and often only rudimentary. Communication between these semiautonomous units, though highly desirable, is often haphazard. The existing structure also makes difficult the implementation of many state and federal education policies. On the other hand, these organizations enjoy little of the "freedom of movement" of separate organizational entities. Education organizations are quite permeable, in the sense that many groups that are not formally employed in those organizations have significant influence over decisions made in them. These include groups representing community interests, alumni, many governmental divisions, philanthropic agencies, and professional associations, whose influence ranges from advice to strict regulation.

Because of the increased size and complexity of education, the job of the education manager today is fundamentally different from the traditional one. The most basic changes have been shifts in emphasis from operation to analysis, from individual to collective management, and from human relations to technology.

## Operation vs. Analysis

The educational manager can no longer satisfactorily perform his duties by operating a system; he must also continually analyze and, when necessary, modify it. Even the most efficient operating system can become dysfunctional as the environment within which it exists changes.

The implication of this change in emphasis is that educational managers need to know more than how to operate a system as it is currently constructed; they need to know, in addition, the functional relationships in a system, how to evaluate an existing system in light of changing conditions, and how to recommend and implement modifications that will enhance the contribution of that operating system to the overall objectives of the educational organization. In short, the manager must also be the analyst. His or her work involves some of the central ideas of the scientific method: first, the objective investigation of a phenomenon; second, the formulation of a hypothesis; third, its repeated proof or modification by experiment; and, finally, its establishment as a working theory (even then, subject to reanalysis).

The notion of manager as analyst is not new. Frederick W. Taylor's famed shovel study (*Principles of Scientific Management*, New York: Harper & Bros., 1911, pp. 36-37) is an excellent example of the application of the scientific method to a management problem. In that case, the problem was to increase the productivity of men shoveling ore. Management had always assumed that the largest shovel a man could fill and carry was the size to maximize output. Even though this seemed to be a reasonable assumption, Taylor questioned it and designed a series of experiments to prove or disprove it. After testing all the relevant variables, Taylor determined that only one variable was really significant—the combined weight of the shovel and its load. Too much weight on the shovel, and the worker tired easily and moved slowly. Too little, and he had to make too many trips. For a "first-class man" the proper load turned out to be about twenty pounds. Since the density of ores differs greatly, a shovel was designed for each ore so that a correctly filled shovel would carry the proper weight. Productivity rose substantially after this change.

Although this example is from another era, the principle remains timely. Managers in educational organizations, no less than their counterparts in manufacturing and commercial organizations, consider their tasks in part as analyzable problems.

## Individual vs. Collective Management

Educational managers today are more dependent on the knowledge and opinions of specialists and other educational managers than they once were. There are at least two reasons for this. First, the technical complexity of operating systems requires increasingly specialized expertise, where a single well-trained generalist used to suffice. The "industry" of education has for a long time been influenced by psychology and sociology, especially as related to strictly pedagogic issues. In issues of management, educational organizations are being increasingly influenced by the emerging fields of accounting (e.g., nonprofit accounting, governmental accounting, cost accounting, auditing, cash flow, and risk management); operations research (e.g., inventory models, linear programming, and network models); economics (e.g., present values, production functions, cost-effectiveness analysis); and computer and information science (e.g., design, operation, and evaluation of management information systems).

Many of the techniques and principles developed in these fields are being applied to management problems in educational organizations. But managers cannot be expected to perform their daily tasks as well as keep current in any one, let alone all, of these major fields. On the other hand, they must know *enough* about the general issues in these fields to be able to work with and coordinate the work of account-ants, economists, operations researchers, and computer scientists. Consequently, the body of knowledge of educational managers must clearly extend beyond those dealing with teaching, learning, and the working of their particular organizations.

A second factor necessitating collective action is the increased interdependency of operating systems. Changes in the level of stu-dent transportation operations, for example, will affect personnel, maintenance, and purchasing operations, to name just a few.

## Technology vs. Human Relations

The ability to deal effectively with other people, especially to ac-complish work through others, has and will remain a fundamental ingredient in the management process. This is especially true where relatively complex problems are undertaken by management groups. Human relations skills are definitely necessary but, increasingly, not sufficient for managing complex educational organizations. Technical competence is also required for numerous and varied tasks. Activities that require scheduling, for instance, include courses, sports events, preventative maintenance, and counseling. Cost analysis is involved in such diverse areas as program and course costing, budgeting, purchas-ing insurance, planning new construction of buildings, and determin-ing the amount and kind of fringe benefits for employees.

These "business-related" activities clearly affect the quality and operation of seemingly purely pedagogic activities, just as pedagogic activities affect the nature and form of business-related decisions. It is for this reason that neither "instructional" nor "business" man-agers can work effectively in isolation from each other, and why business-related expertise is an important complement to educational competence.

## Overview of the Book

The general purpose of this book, then, is to acquaint the reader with (1) those activities in educational organizations requiring techni-cal, business-related competence and (2) those selected tools of man-agement that aid in the analysis of those activities. Although most of the examples used are from elementary-secondary education, much of the material applies equally to post-secondary education organizations. The book is divided into five major topical areas: fiscal systems, logistical systems, allocation systems, planning systems, and information systems.

The first part, *Fiscal Systems,* covers those operating information systems that deal primarily with financial data. Many aspects of accounting are included, and also the related problems of information handling and financial analysis. The aim of this part is to provide a perspective from which to view the operations of educational organizations.

The second part, *Logistical Systems,* covers the process by which human effort and facilitating resources are directed toward supporting the operation of the instructional programs. Four distinct but highly interrelated logistical systems are discussed: supply (or material) management, transportation, food service, and maintenance.

The third part, *Allocation Systems,* describes the process of allocating scarce resources to achieve organizational objectives. In developing and managing the budgeting process there are a number of considerations which affect the final allocation of resources. These factors include determining who is to be involved in budgeting and in what way, and then coordinating their efforts. They also include the development of decision rules for allocating blocks of resources, such as teaching positions to individual schools. The chapters included in this part describe some of the major allocation operations in educational organizations as well as some of the more commonly used methods for performing and analyzing these operations.

The fourth part, *Planning Systems,* deals with quantitative forecasting and planning models applicable to educational organizations. Many of the operations described in earlier parts imply either the assumption of or the need for planning. The term *planning* as used here describes a two-stage operation. One involves estimating factors over which management has little or no direct control but which significantly affect the form of the educational program (forecasting). Activities in this area include estimating further enrollments and amounts of expected revenue. The second stage involves developing programmatic alternatives (over which management exerts control) and examining them in the light of the constraints forecast in stage one.

The fifth part, *Information Systems,* focuses on management's role in the development, operation, and evaluation of information systems. This part affirms one of the fundamental premises of the book: that "hard" information is necessary in managing the operations of educational organizations.

Questions for review and discussion as well as references and related readings are provided at the end of each chapter. It is hoped that the book will stimulate further interest in one or more of the topics discussed.

# Contents

Preface      ix

**Part I. Fiscal Systems**      1

CHAPTER 1. ACCOUNTING CONCEPTS AND
     OPERATIONS      3
*Basic Accounting Concepts*
*Structure of the Accounting Operation*
*Questions for Review and Discussion*
*References*
*Related Readings*

CHAPTER 2. MANAGERIAL USES OF THE
     ACCOUNTING SYSTEM      32
*Managerial Accounting: Educational vs. Commercial*
     *Organization*
*Internal Control*
*Routine Decision Making*
*Nonroutine Decision Making*
*Questions for Review and Discussion*
*References*
*Related Readings*

CHAPTER 3. CASH PLANNING AND TEMPORARY
     INVESTMENTS      53
*Cash Planning Overview*
*Investment Instruments*
*Forecasting Cash Flows*
*Questions for Review and Discussion*
*References*
*Related Readings*

CHAPTER 4. RISK MANAGEMENT 68
*Theoretical Foundations*
*Methods for Controlling Risks*
*Developing Risk Management Policies and Procedures*
*Questions for Review and Discussion*
*References*
*Related Readings*

**Part II. Logistical Systems** 87

CHAPTER 5. SUPPLY MANAGEMENT 89
*Theoretical Foundations*
*Organizational Alternatives for Supply Management*
*Operating a Supply Management System in a School
    District*
*Questions for Review and Discussion*
*References*
*Related Readings*

CHAPTER 6. TRANSPORTATION 128
*Theoretical Foundations*
*Scheduling Bus Routes with the Aid of the Computer*
*Buy-or-Make Decisions*
*Suboptimization*
*Questions for Review and Discussion*
*Appendix A: Analyzing Means for Providing Student
    Transportation*
*References*
*Related Readings*

CHAPTER 7. FOOD SERVICE 171
*Analytical Prerequisites*
*Standard Costs*
*Cost Allocation*
*Factors Affecting Food Service Operations*
*Assessing the Interaction of Factors*
*Questions for Review and Discussion*
*References*
*Related Readings*

CHAPTER 8. OPERATIONS AND MAINTENANCE 205
*Theoretical Foundations*
*Maintenance Operating Policies*
*Questions for Review and Discussion*
*References*
*Related Readings*

**Part III. Allocation Systems**                                              231

   CHAPTER 9. BUDGET PLANNING USING PERT                     233
   *Listing Activities in the Budgeting Process*
   *Charting the List of Activities*
   *Developing a Time Estimate for Each Activity*
   *Scheduling Activities on a Calendar*
   *Analyzing the Structure, Sequence, and Timing of*
      *Activities*
   *Questions for Review and Discussion*
   *Appendix A: Estimating Durations of Project Activities*
   *References*
   *Related Readings*

   CHAPTER 10. ORGANIZING PERSONNEL FOR
      BUDGETING                                                     258
   *Traditional Methods of Relating People to Tasks*
   *Linear Responsibility Charting*
   *Using the Linear Responsibility Chart To Organize*
      *Personnel*
   *General Uses of PERT and LRC*
   *Questions for Review and Discussion*
   *References*
   *Related Readings*

   CHAPTER 11. CLASSROOM SCHEDULING                          276
   *Impact of Changing Curricula on School Scheduling*
   *Impact of School Schedules on Building Utilization*
   *Computer Assistance in Scheduling*
   *Questions for Review and Discussion*
   *References*
   *Related Readings*

   CHAPTER 12. FORMULAS FOR RESOURCE
      ALLOCATION                                                    295
   *Allocating State Financial Assistance to School Districts*
   *The Philosophical Bases of State Aid Formulas*
   *Allocating Resources to Schools Within a District*
   *Questions for Review and Discussion*
   *References*
   *Related Readings*

   CHAPTER 13. LINEAR PROGRAMMING                            323
   *Example 1: Mathematics Instruction in the Midville*
      *School District*
   *Example 2: Salary Schedules in Elementary-Secondary*
      *Education*

*Example 3: Higher Education Planning*
*Numerical Example of Goal Programming*
*Questions for Review and Discussion*
*Appendix A: Constraints and Objective Functions for*
    *Numerical Example of GP Model*
*References*
*Related Readings*

**Part IV. Planning Systems**                                          359

CHAPTER 14. ENROLLMENT FORECASTING                             361
*The Use of Assumptions in Forecasting*
*Forecasting Using Enrollment-Based Data*
*Forecasting Using Census-Based Data*
*Questions for Review and Discussion*
*Appendix A: Using Least Squares To Estimate Future*
    *Enrollments*
*References*
*Related Readings*

CHAPTER 15. PERSONNEL AND RESOURCE
    FORECASTING                                          382
*Computer Simulation*
*Modeling Demographics*
*Resource Forecasting*
*Questions for Review and Discussion*
*References*
*Related Readings*

**Part V. Information Systems**                                         405

CHAPTER 16. DEVELOPING INFORMATION
    SYSTEMS                                              407
*Analytical Prerequisites*
*Developing an Information System*
*Questions for Review and Discussion*
*References*
*Related Readings*

CHAPTER 17. INFORMATION SYSTEMS IN
    EDUCATIONAL MANAGEMENT                                433
*Information Requirements for Different Types of*
    *Management Decisions*
*Prevalent Attitudes of Managers about Information*
    *Generation*

*Impact of Computer-Based Information Systems*
*Questions for Review and Discussion*
*References*
*Related Readings*

Index                                                                                    453

# PART I

# FISCAL SYSTEMS

# 1

# Accounting Concepts and Operations

Accounting is concerned with providing certain kinds of information about the status and progress of an organization. It is analytical in the sense that it takes a great mass of data and, through classification and summarization, reduces that mass of data to a relatively small number of highly significant and interrelated items, which, if properly presented, tell much about that organization. In order for these analytical classifications to be meaningful to educational managers, the concepts underlying accounting must be understood.

To some people, accounting seems to be primarily procedural in nature. Recordkeeping and preparation of financial statements seem to be emphasized, rather than conceptually based analysis. This appearance is deceiving. Recording of financial transactions is actually preceded by an analysis of those transactions. From the development of a chart of accounts to preparation of financial statements (both discussed in this chapter), accounting is concerned primarily with analyzing the nature and effect of the transactions involved. Therefore, the recognition and development of the conceptual foundation of accounting is presented first in this chapter, followed by a section discussing basic accounting operations.

## Basic Accounting Concepts

*Accounting concepts* may be defined as those basic ideas that permit the identification and classification of phenomena or other ideas. As Mautz (1970, p. 20) states, "We must have a concept of an asset to separate assets from those items which are not assets. In turn, we must have a concept of current assets in order to separate current assets from noncurrent assets."

To be complete, a concept must state all that the given classification includes and all that it excludes, which is no small task. For example, one may start with a simple definition of an *asset* as "anything of value owned"—a satisfactory concept for simple situations. Yet there are numerous business situations in which, for example, certain types of leases grant the lessee rights to use property that, for some purposes, give him the equivalent of ownership. The rudimentary concept of an asset is thus accordingly modified to include such lease arrangements. Other arrangements will suggest other modifications of the basic concept until the once simple concept becomes quite complex.

Because so many of the concepts with which accounting deals are both abstract and potentially very complex, they are not easily stated in any complete sense. "We find it necessary to use broad, general terms to describe most concepts and rarely meet the requirements of a complete statement" (Mautz 1970, p. 20). Nonetheless, concisely stated concepts, even if incomplete, do aid in conveying fundamental understanding. It is in this sense that the following accounting concepts are presented and discussed.

Six major accounting concepts, when taken together, provide the foundation on which fiscal systems in educational organizations operate. In order to understand these six concepts some major subsidiary concepts (appended in parentheses) must also be understood:

1. Financial condition (asset, liability, fund balance)
2. Results of operations (revenue, expense, matching)
3. Enterprise (corporate entity, consolidated financial statements)
4. Continuity
5. Present fairly (generally accepted accounting principles, consistency, materiality, full disclosure)
6. Audit (standards, opinions)

## Financial Condition

As used by accountants, the term *financial condition* refers to the impression or conclusion one might draw from a balanced array of a company's assets and the claims against those assets. Although typically applied to profit-directed business enterprises, the concept is also applicable to both public and private educational institutions.

Assets and the claims against those assets are described in a semistandardized fashion. Without an understanding of the classification and measurement conventions applied in developing the descriptions, one could easily come to erroneous conclusions about their significance. Thus, in order to properly explain financial condition, it is necessary to explain *assets, liabilities,* and *fund balance.*

## Asset

An asset may be defined as anything of use to future operations of the enterprise, where the enterprise is seen to benefit from such use (Mautz 1970, p. 5). Assets may be monetary or nonmonetary, tangible or intangible, owned or not owned. As long as they can make a contribution to future operations of the organization, and the organization has the right to use them without expending additional cost in excess of the anticipated amount of that contribution, they constitute assets and are so treated in accounting.

One useful distinction among types of assets is that of current vs. noncurrent assets. For accounting purposes, the term *current assets* is used to designate "cash and other assets or resources commonly identified as those which are reasonably expected to be realized in cash or sold or consumed during the normal operating cycle [typically a fiscal year] of the business" (A.I.C.P.A. 1965, p. 38). Assets not meeting the terms of this definition are typically reported under a variety of headings (e.g., *general fixed assets*). Current assets are set off from noncurrent assets because of their importance in the organization's current position. *Current position* refers to the organization's ability to meet its impending financial obligations in the ordinary course of business with the assets at hand. Current assets typically include cash; bank deposits that are readily available; marketable securities about to be converted within an operating cycle; inventories; and any prepaid expense that, had it not been prepaid, would have been a drain on other resources within the next operating cycle.

Assets are generally measured by their *transaction price*—that is, the price of an "arm's-length" exchange transaction between independent parties in which the organization is one of the parties. ("Arms-length" here implies that the transaction was a simple exchange of goods or services for money.) This value may be reduced proportionately for observed and/or estimated consumption of its use value. If no stated price exists (as, for example, with donated goods), a price is inferred from surrounding circumstances. For instance, if foodstuffs are donated to an educational institution, a reasonable estimate of their worth may be what they would have cost in the marketplace.

There are, however, significant exceptions to this general rule for measuring assets. If the anticipated recovery from use or sale of an asset falls below the transaction price, accountants generally "write down" the carrying value of the asset to the anticipated recovery amount (i.e., record the lesser amount). However, they seldom do the opposite. That is, accountants are much less inclined to "write up" an asset to a higher anticipated recovery value. This practice is an example of the doctrine of *conversatism,* which holds that, given a situation in which exact measurement is not possible, accountants should err on the side of understatement of assets and overstatement of expenses, rather than vice versa. This doctrine is being increasingly challenged as continuing inflation (it is argued) makes transaction price data obsolete over short periods of time.

## Liability

The claims against the assets of an organization are typically classified under two headings: *liabilities* and *shareholders' equity.* Because of the nonprofit orientation and external funding arrangements of most educational institutions, the concept of *fund balance* effectively replaces that of shareholders' equity.

Liabilities are claims against an organization payable in cash, in other assets, or in service, on a fixed or determined future date (Mautz 1970, p. 8). Like assets, liabilities are generally classified as current or noncurrent. *Current liabilities* are those that will be paid from among the assets listed as current assets. Thus, a direct relationship exists between current liabilities and current assets (generally expressing the current position of the organization). *Noncurrent liabilities* in educational organizations would include such things as bonds for school construction, or site and large equipment purchases.

## Fund Balance

The concept of shareholders' equity is interpreted in a variety of ways, one of which is the arithmetic difference between the total of an organization's assets and the total of its liabilities. (Except in failing companies, this difference is positive.) Relying on this interpretation, then, equity is a balancing figure. In order to reinforce this interpretation of equity, educational institutions more often use the term *fund balance,* which is the balance of a specified group of accounts. (Funds are discussed in more detail later in this chapter.) It represents the excess of assets of a fund over its liabilities. The three concepts of assets, liabilities, and fund balance are related in the following manner:

$$\text{assets} = \text{liabilities} + \text{fund balance.}$$

## Results of Operations

In a profit-making organization, *results of operations* is a general term for the presentation of those accounting data that together indicate how well the organization has succeeded in fulfilling its profit-seeking purpose during a given period of time. The presentation attempts to show what the enterprise has accomplished and what costs have been expended in the process. The term takes on a slightly different meaning in a not-for-profit context: the concept of profit is replaced by the concept of *patterns of benefits* that result from the expenditure of revenues.

### Revenue

In profit-seeking businesses, *revenue* is generally defined as the monetary measure of the product or service transferred to customers during the period at the price paid or promised by those customers (Mautz 1970, p. 10). (It can also be derived by disposing of assets other than products or services.) Thus revenue generally represents the accomplishment of business. In not-for-profit organizations, such as educational organizations, the term is more usefully defined as "additions to assets which do not increase any liability, do not represent the recovery of an expenditure, and do not represent the cancellation of certain liabilities without a corresponding increase in other liabilities or a decrease in assets" (Roberts and Lichtenberger 1973, p. 138). Stated more simply, revenues are increases in assets and decreases in liabilities that increase the amount of the fund balance. Examples of revenue received by school districts include state aid, federal aid, and receipts from taxes and tuition.

### Expense

This is another term whose use differs according to context. In profit-seeking organizations, *expenses* is used to describe the efforts made by a company to obtain revenues. In this sense, expenses tend to fall into three groups: (1) the cost of goods or services sold to produce the revenues; (2) the costs of selling and administration; and (3) other costs of doing business that do not necessarily have any direct relationship to specific revenues. In educational institutions, especially public schools and colleges, expenses are viewed as decreases in assets or increases in liabilities that decrease the amount of the fund balance. Because educational spending is goal-directed, it is perhaps more useful to define expenses as charges incurred that are presumed to help achieve organizational objectives during the current fiscal year.

*Results of operations* is related to *financial condition* in the following way:

$$\text{current assets} = \text{current liabilities} + \text{fund balance} + \text{revenues} - \text{expenses}$$

Changes in one term affect other terms; for example, increases in revenue will bring about increases in assets. (For an extended discussion of this, see Adams 1967, pp. 22-24.)

## Matching

The term *matching* is used to describe the appropriate association of related revenues and expenses. Accounting presentations strive to associate data on an interpretive basis; that is, those items that are related to one another are presented together, and those that are not are separated. This concept leads to the establishment of separate funds in educational organizations.

A *fund* is an independent accounting entity (like a separate business) with its own assets, liabilities, and fund balances. Typically, educational institutions operate from three to ten separate funds, depending on specific needs. In school districts, for example, ordinary operations are financed through the *general fund*. Recorded here are taxes collected, state and federal aid, tuition, payment of teachers' salaries, costs of classroom supplies, utility costs, etc.

In addition to the general fund, school districts operate *special funds* for a variety of purposes. Two of the most common special funds are the capital project fund (used to account for all resources and for acquisition of capital facilities, including real property) and the school food service fund (used to record financial transactions related to food service operations). The most useful descriptions of special funds identify the function of the fund. *Revolving funds,* for example, describe those special funds that maintain an approximately steady level (of cash, receivables, inventory, or other assets) by restoring the amounts expended from the fund with earnings from operations or with transfers from other funds. *Sinking funds* are for setting aside money for a special use in the future (beyond the current year). Private educational organizations often have occasion to set up special *endowment funds,* where income from the principal may be expended, although the principal itself may not.

## Enterprise

Transactions are usually at least two-party propositions, but the accountant is interested in only one side of the transaction. That is, he is always concerned with a specific organization, largely ignoring the effects of the transaction on the other party or parties. It will be helpful to describe precisely what that "specific organization" is.

## Corporate Entity

Accounting concerns itself with the transactions of a *corporate entity*. What conditions must exist in an organization for it to be considered a corporate entity and, thus, for accounting to take place? The only requirements for the application of accounting are that a unit be identifiable and that it enter into transactions. Thus, a corporate entity may be defined as a legally constituted organization or some part of it.

## Consolidated Financial Statements

Even though separate accounting units may be usefully established within an educational organization, *consolidated financial statements* are also required of these organizations. Generally if a single economic entity includes more than one legal corporate entity, the financial statements of the legal entities must be consolidated into one set of statements to represent the total economic entity. While derived for use primarily in private for-profit enterprises, consolidation of financial statements also applies to the educational organizations with discrete legal subunits.

## Continuity

The concept of *continuity* applies to an assumption about the future of an organization: that the organization will continue in its present form, and with its present purpose, far enough into the future so that its assets will be used for the purpose for which they were acquired and the obligations against them will be paid in due course (Mautz 1970, p. 13). If this assumption could not be held in regard to an organization, it would be necessary to treat the organization as if it were about to go out of business (*liquidate*). To do so would fundamentally alter the valuation of assets, the treatment of liabilities, and the preparation of financial statements in general.

## Present Fairly

*Present fairly* is a term used by auditors to suggest that the financial statements examined are presented in a manner that is fair or just. In a broader context it represents a concept of "proper" or "appropriate" representation of financial information and includes a cluster of more specific concepts: *generally accepted accounting principles, consistency, materiality,* and *full disclosure.*

### Generally Accepted Accounting Principles

This term describes those practices and procedures that have been found over time to be most useful. Although they do not necessarily constitute the preferred treatment in every case, in combination they generally do present an agreed-upon method for arriving at a picture of the status and progress of an organization.

### Consistency

One of the primary purposes of accounting is to present reports on a comparable basis. By themselves, individual accounting figures are seldom informative; coupled with other figures (e.g., reports for the same organization for prior years), they become much more useful. If comparisons are to be made, however, it is imperative that reports be prepared in a consistent way over time. Thus great reliance is placed on consistency as a requirement for good accounting data.

### Materiality

It is not required that all transactions, however minor, be handled on a consistent basis; only transactions of material significance require such attention. A material transaction (or event or item) is one the knowledge of which might influence the judgment of an informed reader of the financial statements (Mautz 1970, p. 14). This definition, however logical, has been difficult to put into operation usefully.

### Full Disclosure

This means that the presented information includes everything that an informed reader should know to come to appropriate conclusions, nothing of substance having been concealed or omitted. Full disclosure does not necessarily mean that an overwhelming amount of detail need be included in financial statements; rather, that taken as a whole, the financial statements of an organization represent a satisfactory *overall* impression of its current position.

### Audit

A major factor in establishing and maintaining confidence in the financial reporting of organizations is the customary *audit*—an annual examination and report by independent certified public accountants (often required by law). The financial information of the organization is examined by an auditor, who applies previously determined *standards* and, on the basis of what is found, renders an *opinion*.

## Standards

Auditing standards cover general conditions of the auditing process as well as the result of auditing (i.e., the quality of the auditor's report). Standards applied to the auditing process relate to the competence and independence of the auditor, and the rigor and adequacy of the formal audit.

The standards applied to the result of auditing bear separate mention. The generally accepted standards of audit reporting adopted by the American Institute of Certified Public Accountants are:

1. The report shall state whether the financial statements are presented in accordance with generally accepted principles of accounting.
2. The report shall state whether such principles have been consistently observed in the current period in relation to the preceding period.
3. Informative disclosures in the financial statements are to be regarded as reasonably adequate unless otherwise stated in the report.
4. The report shall either contain an expression of opinion regarding the financial statements taken as a whole or an assertion to the effect that an opinion cannot be expressed. When an overall opinion cannot be expressed the reasons should be stated.

One of the most common means for presenting the results of auditing is the short-form report used in conjunction with basic financial statements. The usual short-form report consists of a representation as to the work performed, expressed in an opening paragraph, and a representation as to the independent auditor's conclusions, usually in a closing or "opinion" paragraph. An example of what this report might look like for a public school system is presented in exhibit 1.1.

## Opinions

The auditor's opinion is central to the auditing concept. In writing an opinion, the auditor is describing the nature of his examination of the organization and, equally important, the degree of responsibility he is taking for what he says about the organization. An unqualified opinion from an auditor represents in essence a certification of the appropriateness of the financial records of an organization. The short-form report in exhibit 1.1 is an illustration of an unqualified

## Exhibit 1.1: Prototypical Short-Form Report to a School District Board of Education

Members of the Board:

We have examined the balance sheets as of June 30, 19___, the related statements of revenue and expenditures, the statements of fund balance, and statements of changes in financial position for each fund and group of accounts used in financial administration of the _____ School System for the year then ended. Our examination was made in accordance with generally accepted auditing standards, and accordingly, included such tests of the accounting records and such other auditing procedures as we considered necessary in the circumstances.

In our opinion, the aforementioned financial statements present fairly the financial position of the _____School System at June, 19___, and the results of its operation and the changes in its financial position for the year then ended, in conformity with generally accepted accounting principles applied on a basis consistent with that of the preceding year.

> Very truly yours,
> /signature/

Source: Sam B. Tidwell, *Financial and Management Accounting for Elementary and Secondary School Systems* (Chicago: Research Corporation of the Association of School Business Officials, 1974), p. 424. Reprinted by permission.

opinion. Qualified opinions arise from conditions that represent departures from the statements in the short-form. For example, the auditor's scope of examination may be limited; the financial statements may not present fairly the financial position of the organization; accounting principles may not be consistently applied; unusual uncertainties may exist concerning future developments affecting the organization, etc.

While the concept of audit applies largely to an *independent* examination of an organization's financial data, it has more recently been expanded to include *internal auditing* and *governmental auditing* as well. As the term implies, internal auditing is conducted by personnel within an organization; the chief purpose is to test and improve financial operations. Governmental auditing deals with those funds supplied to organizations by various government agencies, typically state or federal. The primary objective of an audit by a governmental agency is to determine whether legal provisions prescribed by that agency are being adhered to. By definition, then, this type of audit is more limited in scope.

## Structure of the Accounting Operation

Any activity that changes the financial condition of the educational organization is referred to as a *transaction*. Such activities include buying supplies, paying teachers, receiving tuition, and selling bonds. Transactions are analyzed, recorded, and reported through the use of accounts. Accounts are, to a large degree, the building blocks of financial reports. There are two major classes of accounts: *proprietary accounts* (accounts for assets, liabilities, and fund balances) and *budgetary accounts* (accounts reflecting budgetary operations).

The term *single account* describes a record of "similar" financial transactions. In order to be able to increase the degree of similarity among transactions (and thus be more precise in recording transactions), it is necessary to describe each account in finer detail. This in turn requires the generation of more accounts. For example, one asset account may be labeled *cash,* which might be defined strictly as currency, checks, postal and express money orders, bankers' drafts on hand or on deposit with an official or agent designated as custodian of cash, and bank deposits. Although this is a rather precise description, an educational organization may wish to create an even more specific one, by making a distinction, for example, between *petty cash* and *cash.* Petty cash could be defined as a sum of money set aside for the purpose of paying small obligations for which the issuance of a formal voucher and check would be too expensive and time-consuming. It is evident from the definitions that petty cash is a form of cash. However, if the distinction between the two is deemed worthwhile, a separate account for petty cash would be created and the definition of the cash account would include a statement to the effect that "all cash except petty cash is in this account."

Each account is in the form of a *T*. The left side of the *T* is called the debit side, and the right side of the *T* is called the credit side.

| debit side | credit side |
|---|---|

Actually, account forms vary among organizations according to the complexity of the accounting system and the medium for record-keeping being used (e.g., manual vs. computer). All accounts, however, record the date of a transaction and give a brief description of it, as well as stating the amount of money debited or credited (see exhibit 1.2).

## Exhibit 1.2: Prototypical Account

ACCOUNT TITLE IN FULL          PAGE

| DEBIT SIDE | | | | CREDIT SIDE | | | |
|---|---|---|---|---|---|---|---|
| DATE | EXPLANATION | P.R. | AMOUNT | DATE | EXPLANATION | P.R. | AMOUNT |
| YEAR MONTH / DAY | | | | YEAR MONTH / DAY | | | |

Transactions are usually first recorded in a journal and then "posted" to separate accounts. In order to record a transaction in the journal, however, it is necessary to analyze the transaction and determine the accounts that will be affected by it. In order to understand how transactions get recorded in accounts, it will be helpful to take another look at an equation discussed earlier (p. 8):

assets = liabilities + fund balance + revenues − expenditures.

Assume for purposes of discussion that a single account is associated with each of the terms in this equation. (In an actual operating system each term would have many accounts associated with it.) The *T* accounts associated with each term would look like exhibit 1.3. A

**Exhibit 1.3: Basic Structure of Accounting Operations**

| assets | | = | liabilities | | + | fund balance | | + | revenues | | − | expenditures | |
|---|---|---|---|---|---|---|---|---|---|---|---|---|---|
| debit | credit | | debit | credit | | debit | credit | | debit | credit | | debit | credit |
| I | D | | D | I | | D | I | | D | I | | I | D |

transaction is analyzed in order to determine which of the accounts are affected, and whether an account is increased (I) or decreased (D), as a result of that transaction. Notice in the accounts in exhibit 1.3 that increases are not uniformly associated with credits. The particular conventions outlined above can be briefly summarized as follows:

1. To increase asset or expenditure accounts, debit
2. To decrease asset or expenditure accounts, credit
3. To increase liability, fund balance, or revenue accounts, credit
4. To decrease liability, fund balance, or revenue accounts, debit

These conventions are not founded on any theoretical basis. Rather they have been established with a very pragmatic purpose in mind: to create a situation in which (1) each transaction has at least one debit and at least one credit and (2) the total debits equal the total credits. These two facts act as built-in validity checks in the accounting system.

Perhaps the best way to understand the process of recording transactions in accounts is to look at a few examples. Nine transactions are presented in exhibit 1.4; note that in each transaction, the valid-

# Exhibit 1.4: Recording Transactions in Accounts

1. Assume that the assets of the New Hope School System's general fund, at the beginning of a year, are: cash in bank, $1,000; taxes receivable, $6,000; and temporary investments, $3,000. Assets total $10,000, and are shown on the debit side of the account. As these assets exist at the beginning of the period, no revenues are realized nor do liabilities exist. Therefore, fund equity exists in the amount of $10,000. These account balances at the beginning of the accounting period would be shown in the accounts as follows:

| Assets | | = | Liabilities | | + | Fund Equity | | + | Revenues | | − | Expenditures | |
|---|---|---|---|---|---|---|---|---|---|---|---|---|---|
| Increase | Decrease | | Decrease | Increase | | Decrease | Increase | | Decrease | Increase | | Increase | Decrease |
| Debit | Credit | | Debit | Credit | | Debit | Credit | | Debit | Credit | | Debit | Credit |
| $10,000 | | | | | | | $10,000 | | | | | | |

The debits of $10,000 equal the credits of $10,000 and the assets equal the liabilities plus fund equity.

2. Assume that taxes are assessed and levied in the amount of $30,000. This transaction increases assets by $30,000 and, at the same time, increases revenues by the same amount. Both transactions would appear as follows:

| | Assets | | = | Liabilities | | + | Fund Equity | | + | Revenues | | − | Expenditures | |
|---|---|---|---|---|---|---|---|---|---|---|---|---|---|---|
| | Increase | Decrease | | Decrease | Increase | | Decrease | Increase | | Decrease | Increase | | Increase | Decrease |
| | Debit | Credit | | Debit | Credit | | Debit | Credit | | Debit | Credit | | Debit | Credit |
| (1) | $10,000 | | | | | | | $10,000 | | | | | | |
| (2) | 30,000 | | | | | | | | | | $30,000 | | | |
| | $40,000 | | | | | | | $10,000 | | | $30,000 | | | |

Transaction (2) has equal debits and credits. By combining both transactions, debits of $40,000 equal credits of $10,000 plus $30,000. The equation, assets equal liabilities plus fund equity, plus revenues, minus expenditures, has been maintained.

3. Assume that the school system borrows $5,000 from the bank. When the cash is received, assets will be increased by $5,000 and will be recorded by debiting assets. At the same time an obligation is created by the debt owed to the bank. The obligation is recorded by a credit to the liability account. The transaction appears as follows:

| | Assets | | = | Liabilities | | + | Fund Equity | | + | Revenues | | − | Expenditures | |
|---|---|---|---|---|---|---|---|---|---|---|---|---|---|---|
| | Increase | Decrease | | Decrease | Increase | | Decrease | Increase | | Decrease | Increase | | Increase | Decrease |
| | Debit | Credit | | Debit | Credit | | Debit | Credit | | Debit | Credit | | Debit | Credit |
| (3) | $5,000 | | | | $5,000 | | | | | | | | | |

4. Assume that salaries are paid in the amount of $5,000. When cash is disbursed, assets are reduced and the reduction in assets is shown by a credit to the assets. Expenditures are increased by the same amount and are shown by a debit to expenditures. This transaction appears as follows:

| | Assets | | = | Liabilities | | + | Fund Equity | | + | Revenues | | − | Expenditures | |
|---|---|---|---|---|---|---|---|---|---|---|---|---|---|---|
| | Increase | Decrease | | Decrease | Increase | | Decrease | Increase | | Decrease | Increase | | Increase | Decrease |
| | Debit | Credit | | Debit | Credit | | Debit | Credit | | Debit | Credit | | Debit | Credit |
| (4) | | $5,000 | | | | | | | | | | | $5,000 | |

5. Assume that $8,000 is collected from the taxes assessed and levied in transaction (2). This is an illustration of a transaction in which a reduction in one asset results in the increase of another. Therefore, to record the transaction, assets are debited for $8,000—the amount of the cash received—and assets are credited for the same amount which represents the reduction in the asset, taxes receivable. The transaction appears as follows:

| | Assets | | = | Liabilities | | + | Fund Equity | | + | Revenues | | − | Expenditures | |
|---|---|---|---|---|---|---|---|---|---|---|---|---|---|---|
| | Increase | Decrease | | Decrease | Increase | | Decrease | Increase | | Decrease | Increase | | Increase | Decrease |
| | Debit | Credit | | Debit | Credit | | Debit | Credit | | Debit | Credit | | Debit | Credit |
| (5) | $8,000 | $8,000 | | | | | | | | | | | | |

6. Assume that the school system pays $4,000 to apply on the loan from the bank. The cash payment reduces assets and is recorded by crediting the assets account. The liability to the bank is reduced and a debit in the liabilities account records the reduction of $4,000. The transaction appears as follows:

| | Assets | | = | Liabilities | | + | Fund Equity | | + | Revenues | | − | Expenditures | |
|---|---|---|---|---|---|---|---|---|---|---|---|---|---|---|
| | Increase | Decrease | | Decrease | Increase | | Decrease | Increase | | Decrease | Increase | | Increase | Decrease |
| | Debit | Credit | | Debit | Credit | | Debit | Credit | | Debit | Credit | | Debit | Credit |
| (6) | | $4,000 | | $4,000 | | | | | | | | | | |

7. Assume that the school system lends $2,000 to the library fund. An investment creates a new asset, shown by a debit, and payment of cash reduces the asset, cash, and is shown by a credit to the asset account. The transaction appears as follows:

| | Assets | | = | Liabilities | | + | Fund Equity | | + | Revenues | | − | Expenditures | |
|---|---|---|---|---|---|---|---|---|---|---|---|---|---|---|
| | Increase | Decrease | | Decrease | Increase | | Decrease | Increase | | Decrease | Increase | | Increase | Decrease |
| | Debit | Credit | | Debit | Credit | | Debit | Credit | | Debit | Credit | | Debit | Credit |
| (7) | $2,000 | $2,000 | | | | | | | | | | | | |

# Exhibit 1.4 (continued)

8. Assume that the school system collects $6,500—representing $6,000 from taxes receivable assessed and levied in transaction (2) and $500 from interest and penalties. The asset, cash, is increased by a debit of $6,500. At the same time the asset, taxes receivable, is reduced by a credit of $6,000. In this transaction, $500 represents a source of revenue from interest and penalties. This revenue is recorded by a credit to the revenue account and the transaction appears as follows:

| Assets | | = | Liabilities | | + | Fund Equity | | + | Revenues | | — | Expenditures | |
|---|---|---|---|---|---|---|---|---|---|---|---|---|---|
| Increase | Decrease | | Decrease | Increase | | Decrease | Increase | | Decrease | Increase | | Increase | Decrease |
| Debit | Credit | | Debit | Credit | | Debit | Credit | | Debit | Credit | | Debit | Credit |
| (8) $6,500 | $6,000 | | | | | | | | | $500 | | | |

9. Assume that the school system pays salaries in the amount of $5,000. This is a repetition of transaction (4) and would be analyzed and recorded in the same way.
The following chart will show the combined effect of the preceding transactions on the accounts.

| | Assets | | = | Liabilities | | + | Fund Equity | | + | Revenues | | — | Expenditures | |
|---|---|---|---|---|---|---|---|---|---|---|---|---|---|---|
| | Increase | Decrease | | Decrease | Increase | | Decrease | Increase | | Decrease | Increase | | Increase | Decrease |
| | Debit | Credit | | Debit | Credit | | Debit | Credit | | Debit | Credit | | Debit | Credit |
| (1) | $10,000 | | | | | | | 10,000 | | | | | | |
| (2) | 30,000 | | | | | | | | | | 30,000 | | | |
| (3) | 5,000 | | | | 5,000 | | | | | | | | | |
| (4) | | 5,000 | | | | | | | | | | | 5,000 | |
| (5) | 8,000 | 8,000 | | | | | | | | | | | | |
| (6) | | 4,000 | | 4,000 | | | | | | | | | | |
| (7) | 2,000 | 2,000 | | | | | | | | | | | | |
| (8) | 6,500 | 6,000 | | | | | | | | | 500 | | | |
| (9) | | 5,000 | | | | | | | | | | | 5,000 | |
| | 61,500 | 30,000 | | 4,000 | 5,000 | | | 10,000 | | | 30,500 | | 10,000 | |

Source: Sam B. Tidwell, *Financial and Management Accounting for Elementary and Secondary School Systems* (Chicago: Research Corporation of the Association of School Business Officials, 1974), pp. 37-38. Reprinted by permission.

ity check rules have not been violated. In each case at least one debit and one credit has been affected, and the debits equal the credits.

Another very important, although less apparent, validity check in this system is that, for each transaction, the net change in assets equals the sum of the net changes in liabilities, fund balance, revenues, and expenditures. These validity checks, taken together, are not foolproof—for example, they would not flag an increase in the fund balance that should be posted as an increase in liabilities—but they do act efficiently to check many of the possible errors that can arise during the recording process.

These validity checks are applied to groups of transactions as well as to single transactions. The process of doing this is called *taking a trial balance,* and it entails summing and comparing the amounts of the transactions in each of the accounts. For example, the transactions described in exhibit 1.4 have been summed at the bottom of exhibit 1.4 and are presented separately in table 1.5. Notice in table

### Table 1.5: Trial Balance of Transactions Described in Exhibit 1.4 (gross figures)

| Transaction | Debits | Credits |
|-------------|--------|---------|
| Assets | $61,500 | $30,000 |
| Liabilities | 4,000 | 5,000 |
| Fund equity | | 10,000 |
| Revenues | | 30,500 |
| Expenditures | 10,000 | |
| Total | $75,500 | $75,500 |

1.5 that, for the sum of all nine transactions, debits equal credits, and assets equal liabilities plus fund balance, plus revenues, minus expenditures. These relationships are more apparent in table 1.6, where only the net differences in each account are reported.

### Table 1.6: Trial Balance of Transactions Described in Exhibit 1.4 (net figures)

| Transaction | Debits | Credits |
|-------------|--------|---------|
| Assets | $31,500 | |
| Liabilities | | $ 1,000 |
| Fund equity | | 10,000 |
| Revenues | | 30,500 |
| Expenditures | 10,000 | |
| Total | $41,500 | $41,500 |

As stated earlier, accounts are created to make distinctions between various transactions: similar transactions are clustered and separated from dissimilar transactions. The number of single accounts is proportional to the need for distinction among the various kinds of assets, liabilities, etc., in an organization. The need for creating these distinctions may stem from data requirements for improved decision making, from externally imposed reporting demands, or from other sources. Plausible distinctions among assets and within different funds are displayed in table 1.7; plausible distinctions among liabilities and fund balances are displayed in table 1.8; and plausible distinctions among types of revenue appear in table 1.9.

Plausible distinctions among expenditures are conceptually more complex than those relating to assets, liabilities, and sources of revenue. There are several reasons for this. First, expenditure information is more directly linked to an educational organization's activities and operations than are the other three. Organizational objectives are realized through expenditure. Because of this, classification schemes of one dimension are often inadequate. For example, classification of expenditures on the basis of the objects purchased, while totally inclusive, is not useful by itself in determining the costs of the different departments in a university.

A second complicating factor is that educational organizations are often subject to a variety of external mandates and restrictions from governmental bodies. Often such restrictions are monitored in large part by means of examining how an educational organization spends its money.

A single expenditure, then, may be classified along a number of different dimensions. One of these dimensions, which has already been mentioned, is *fund*. Another is *object of expenditure*. A third dimension is *function*. *Function* is a broad and somewhat eclectic classification scheme based on the different activities (or functions) for which expenditures are incurred. *Operational unit* or *site* is a useful expenditure dimension; it serves the purpose of distinguishing expenditures among physical locations. *Program* often refers to a classification scheme based on distinctions among subject matter, levels of instruction, or groups of students served. Additional dimensions may be added because of needs generated by internal decision making or external reporting. Eleven different dimensions for elementary-secondary schools are presented in table 1.10 along with examples of general distinctions among expenditures within each dimension.

Accounts are used to record and show the assets, liabilities, reserves, fund balances, revenues, and expenditures of an organization.

## Table 1.7: Plausible Distinctions Among Assets

| Balance sheet accounts | Funds and groups of accounts | | | | | | | | |
|---|---|---|---|---|---|---|---|---|---|
| | General fund | Special revenue fund | Debt service fund | Capital projects fund | Food service fund | Pupil activity fund | Trust and agency funds | General fixed assets | General long-term debt |
| **Current assets** | | | | | | | | | |
| Cash | X | X | X | X | X | X | X | | |
| Petty cash | X | | | | X | X | | | |
| Cash change funds | | | | | X | X | | | |
| Cash with fiscal agent | | | X | | | | | | |
| Taxes receivable | X | X | X | X | | | X | | |
| Estimated uncollectible taxes (credit) | X | X | X | X | | | X | | |
| Tax liens receivable | X | X | X | X | | | X | | |
| Estimated uncollectible tax liens (credit) | X | X | X | X | | | | | |
| Accounts receivable | X | | | X | X | X | | | |
| Bond proceeds receivable | | | | X | | | | | |
| Loans receivable | X | | | | | | | | |
| Due from _____ fund | X | X | X | X | X | X | X | | |
| Due from _____ government | X | X | X | X | X | X | X | | |
| Advance to _____ fund | X | | | X | | | X | | |
| Taxes levied for other governmental units | X | | | | | | X | | |
| Interest receivable on investments | X | X | X | X | X | X | X | | |
| Accrued interest on investments purchased | X | X | X | X | X | X | X | | |
| Inventory | X | | | X | X | X | | | |
| Inventory of stores for resale | | | | | X | X | | | |
| Investments | X | X | X | X | X | | X | | |
| Unamortized premiums on investments | | | X | X | X | X | | | |
| Unamortized discounts on investments (credit) | | | X | X | X | X | X | | |
| Deposits | X | | | | | | | | |
| Prepaid expenses | X | X | | | | | | | |
| Unamortized discounts on bonds sold | | | X | | | | | | |

**Table 1.7** *(continued)*

| Balance sheet accounts | General fund | Special revenue fund | Debt service fund | Capital projects fund | Food service fund | Pupil activity fund | Trust and agency funds | General fixed assets | General long-term debt |
|---|---|---|---|---|---|---|---|---|---|
| General fixed assets | | | | | | | | | |
| Land | | | | | | | | X | |
| Buildings | | | | | | | | X | |
| Improvements other than buildings | | | | | | | | X | |
| Equipment | | | | | | | | X | |
| Construction work in progress | | | | | | | | X | |
| Budgeting accounts and other debits | | | | | | | | | |
| Estimated revenues | X | X | X | X | | | | | |
| Revenues (credit) | X | X | X | X | | | | | |
| Bonds authorized—unissued | | | | X | | | | | |
| Amount available in debt service funds | | | | | | | | | X |
| Amount to be provided for payment of bonds | | | | | | | | | X |

Source: Adapted from Charles T. Roberts and Allan R. Lichtenberger, *Financial Accounting: Classifications and Standard Terminology for Local and State School Systems* (Washington, D.C.: U.S. Government Printing Office, 1973, OE 73-11800), pp. 5-6.

Table 1.8: Plausible Distinctions Among Liabilities, Reserves, and Fund Balances

| Balance sheet accounts | Funds and groups of accounts | | | | | | | | |
|---|---|---|---|---|---|---|---|---|---|
| | General fund | Special revenue fund | Debt service fund | Capital projects fund | Food service fund | Pupil activity fund | Trust and agency funds | General fixed assets | General long-term debt |
| **Current liabilities** | | | | | | | | | |
| Vouchers payable | X | X | X | X | X | X | X | | |
| Accounts payable | X | X | | X | X | X | | | |
| Judgments payable | X | X | X | X | X | X | | | |
| Contracts payable | X | X | | X | X | X | | | |
| Construction contracts payable | | | | X | | | | | |
| Construction contracts payable—retained percentage | | | | X | | | | | |
| Due to —— fund | X | X | X | X | X | X | X | | |
| Due to —— government | X | X | X | X | X | X | X | | |
| Advance from —— fund | X | X | X | X | X | X | X | | |
| Matured bonds payable | | | X | | | | | | |
| Matured interest payable | | | X | | | | | | |
| Payroll deductions and withholdings | X | X | | X | X | X | X | | |
| Accrued expenses | X | X | X | | X | X | | | |
| Deposits payable | X | X | X | X | | X | X | | |
| Due to fiscal agent | | | X | | | | | | |
| Unamortized premiums on bonds sold | | | | X | | | | | |
| Revenues collected in advance | X | X | | | | | X | | |
| Taxes collected in advance | X | | | | | | | | |

Table 1.8 (*continued*)

| Balance sheet accounts | General fund | Special revenue fund | Debt service fund | Capital projects fund | Food service fund | Pupil activity fund | Trust and agency funds | General fixed assets | General long-term debt |
|---|---|---|---|---|---|---|---|---|---|
| | | | Funds and groups of accounts | | | | | | |
| Long-term liabilities | | | | | | | | | |
| Bonds payable | | | | | | | | | X |
| Budgeting accounts and other credits | | | | | | | | | |
| Appropriations | X | X | X | X | X | X | | | |
| Expenditures (debit) | X | X | X | X | X | X | | | |
| Encumbrances (debit) | X | X | | X | X | X | | | |
| Reserves and fund balance | | | | | | | | | |
| Reserve for encumbrances | X | X | | X | X | X | | | |
| Reserve for inventory | X | | | | | | | | |
| Reserve for —— (special purposes) | X | X | X | X | X | X | X | | |
| Fund balance | X | X | X | X | X | X | X | | |
| Investment in general fixed assets | | | | | | | | X | |

Source: Adapted from Charles T. Roberts and Allan R. Lichtenberger, *Financial Accounting: Classifications and Standard Terminology for Local and State School Systems* (Washington, D.C.: U.S. Government Printing Office, 1973, OE 73-11800), pp. 6-7.

## Table 1.9: Plausible Distinctions Among Types of Revenue

---

Revenue from local sources
 Taxes
  Ad valorem taxes levied by LEA
  Ad valorem taxes levied by another governmental unit
  Sales and use taxes
  Income taxes
  Other taxes
  Penalties and interest on taxes
 Revenue from local governmental units other than LEAs
 Tuition
  Regular day school tuition
   Tuition from pupils or parents
   Tuition from other LEAs within the state
   Tuition from other LEAs outside the state
  Adult/continuing education tuition
   Tuition from pupils or parents
   Tuition from other LEAs within the state
   Tuition from other LEAs outside the state
  Summer school tuition
   Tuition from pupils or parents
   Tuition from other LEAs within the state
   Tuition from other LEAs outside the state
 Transportation fees
  Regular day school transportation fees
   Transportation fees from pupils or parents
   Transportation fees from other LEAs within the state
   Transportation fees from other LEAs outside the state
  Summer school transportation fees
   Transportation fees from pupils or parents
   Transportation fees from other LEAs within the state
   Transportation fees from other LEAs outside the state
 Earnings on investments
  Interest on investments
  Dividends on investments
  Gain or loss on sale of investments
 Food services
  Sales to pupils
  Sales to adults
 Pupil activities
  Admissions
  Bookstore sales
  Pupil organization membership
  Other pupil activity income
 Other revenue from local sources
  Rentals
  Contributions and donations from private sources
  *Sale and loss of fixed assets
   Sale of fixed assets
   Compensation for loss of fixed assets
  Services provided other LEAs
   LEAs within the state
   LEAs outside the state

**Table 1.9** *(continued)*

---

   *Refund of prior year's expenditures
   *Transfer from other funds
   *Sales of bonds
   Premium on bonds sold
   Miscellaneous
Revenue from intermediate sources
 Grants-in-aid
  Unrestricted grants-in-aid
  Restricted grants-in-aid
 Revenue in lieu of taxes
 Revenue for/on behalf of the LEA
Revenue from state sources
 Grants-in-aid
  Unrestricted grants-in-aid
  Restricted grants-in-aid
 Revenue in lieu of taxes
 Revenue for/on behalf of the LEA
Revenue from federal sources
 Grants-in-aid
  Unrestricted grants-in-aid received directly from federal government
  Unrestricted grants-in-aid received from federal government through the state
  Restricted grants-in-aid received directly from federal government
  Restricted grants-in-aid received from federal government through the state
 Revenue in lieu of taxes
 Revenue for/on behalf of the LEA

---

*Revenues with an asterisk are not revenues to a LEA (Local Education Agency).

Source: Charles T. Roberts and Allan R. Lichtenberger, *Financial Accounting: Classifications and Standard Terminology for Local and State School Systems* (Washington, D.C.: U.S. Government Printing Office, 1973, OE 73-11800), pp. 13-15.

# Table 1.10: Plausible Dimensions of Expenditure Accounts in Elementary-Secondary Educational Organizations

| Fund | Object | Function | Operational unit | Program | Source of funds | Fiscal year |
|---|---|---|---|---|---|---|
| 1 General fund | 1 Salaries | 1000 Instruction | 001 Friedley Elementary | Broad-based goals | 1 Local | 0 1969-1970 |
| 2 Special revenue | 2 Employee benefits | 1100 Regular programs | 501 McLune Middle | | 2 Intermediate | 1 1970-1971 |
| 3 Debt service | 3 Purchased services | 1200 Special | 701 Jones High | and | 3 State | 2 1971-1972 |
| 4 Capital project | 4 Supplies and materials | 1300 Adult/continuing education | 751 Chismore Vocational | subject matter | 4 Federal | 3 1972-1973 |
| 5 Food service | 5 Capital outlay | 2000 Support services | 781 Curtis Junior College | | | 4 1973-1974 |
| 6 Pupil activity | 6 Other objectives | 2100 Pupil support | 901 Central administration | and | | 5 1974-1975 |
| 7 Trust and agen. | 7 Transfers | 2200 Staff support | 911 Main warehouse | type of pupils | | |
| 8 Fixed assets | | 2300 General administrative support | 921 Main bus garage | combined with | | |
| 9 Long-term debt | | 2400 School administrative support | 990 — | | | |
| | | 2500 Business support | | level of instruction | | |
| | | 2600 Central support | | or | | |
| | | 3000 Community services | | age of learner | | |
| | | 4000 Nonprogrammed charges | | | | |
| | | 5000 Debt services | | | | |

| Instruction organization | Assignment | Term | Special cost center |
|---|---|---|---|
| 1 Elementary school | 1 Official/administrative | 1 Fall—day | 01 Girls' basketball |
| 2 Middle/junior high | 2 Professional-educational | 2 Fall—evening | 02 Drug abuse |
| 3 High school | 3 Professional-other | 3 Winter—day | 03 Special project |
| 4 Adult/continuing education school | 4 Technical | 4 Winter—evening | 99 Other special project |
| 5 Junior college | 5 Office/clerical | 5 Spring—day | |
| 9 Other school | 6 Crafts and trades | 6 Spring—evening | |
| | 7 Operative | 7 Summer—day | |
| | 8 Laborer | 8 Summer—evening | |
| | 9 Service work | | |

Source: Charles T. Roberts and Allan R. Lichtenberger, *Financial Accounting: Classifications and Standard Terminology for Local and State School Systems* (Washington, D.C.: U.S. Government Printing Office, 1973, OE 73-11800), pp. 63-64.

Accounts created for these purposes are referred to as *proprietary accounts*. Accounts are also used for budget planning and control; these are called *budgetary accounts* and are used to record and report the implementation of an adopted budget. Although the process of budgeting is discussed in chapters nine and ten, it would useful to briefly describe budgetary accounts here.

When an educational organization adopts a budget, it is committing itself to a rather detailed spending plan based on estimates of revenue from a variety of sources. Various amounts of money are appropriated for specified purposes; that is, specified sums are authorized to be used within a specified time frame (e.g., fiscal year). There are two general types of budgetary accounts: those dealing with estimated revenues and those dealing with appropriations.

Table 1.11 illustrates in a highly simplified manner how budget amounts and conditions are recorded in budgetary accounts. Table

## Table 1.11: Sample Budgeted Revenues and Appropriations in the General Fund

| | | |
|---|---|---|
| Estimated revenues from: | | |
| Taxes | $30,000 | |
| Tuition | 5,000 | |
| Rentals | 5,000 | |
| Total estimated revenues | | $40,000 |
| Appropriations: | | |
| Salaries | $28,000 | |
| Supplies | 8,000 | |
| Capital outlay | 2,000 | |
| Total appropriations | | $38,000 |

Source: Adapted from Sam B. Tidwell, *Financial and Management Accounting for Elementary and Secondary School Systems* (Chicago: Research Corporation of the Association of School Business Officials, 1974), pp. 130-31.

1.12 illustrates general journal entries that record the budget in the budgetary accounts.

If conditions under which estimates were made actually develop as anticipated, the budgetary accounts will remain unchanged until the end of the accounting period. If changes do occur, however, revisions must be made in the budget and recorded in the budgetary accounts. The following four conditions could develop, any one of which would require adjustments in the budget and budgetary accounts:

1. Estimated revenues are recorded for which no provision exists, such as an unrestricted grant-in-aid from the state.

Table 1.12: Sample Account Titles for Budgeted Revenues and
Expenditures

| | | |
|---|---|---|
| Revenue accounts in the general fund | | |
| Estimated revenue from taxes | $30,000 | |
| Estimated revenue from tuition | 5,000 | |
| Estimated revenue from rentals | 5,000 | |
| | | |
| Expenditure Accounts | | |
| Appropriation for salaries | | 28,000 |
| Appropriation for supplies | | 8,000 |
| Appropriation for capital outlay | | 2,000 |

Source: Adapted from Sam B. Tidwell, *Financial and Management Accounting for Elementary and Secondary School Systems* (Chicago: Research Corporation of the Association of School Business Officials, 1974), p. 130.

2. Estimated revenues, as recorded, are found to be in excess of all possible sources of revenue, such as from a tax levy.

3. Appropriations, as recorded, do not provide for an unexpected expenditure (e.g., destruction caused by a flood) and additional expenditures would be necessary to make replacement of the asset destroyed.

4. Appropriations, as recorded, are found to be in excess of required expenditures.

In each type of circumstance, budgetary accounts would be adjusted through entries that would have the effect of increasing or decreasing the fund equity in the account.

A system of encumbrances is used to avoid the possibility of overexpenditure of an appropriation. *Encumbrances* have been defined as "obligations or commitments in the form of purchase orders, contracts, salary commitments, etc., which are chargeable to an appropriation and for which a part of the appropriation is reserved prior to the actual expenditure of funds for that purpose" (Tidwell 1974, p. 137). Encumbrances are used to "earmark" some portion of the unexpected amount of appropriation.

Taken together, accounting concepts and operations such as those described in this chapter provide a means for ordering financial data. Financial data, systematically derived and organized, can be highly useful in managing educational organizations. It is to those managerial uses of financial data that we now turn in the following three chapters.

## Questions for Review and Discussion

1.   How does the concept of financial condition differ from the concept of results of operations?

2.   In what ways do educational organizations undertake profit-seeking activities? Are there any times when educational organizations expend resources in order to increase revenues? Describe them.

3.   Is the basic purpose of a fund designation any different from that of an account designation? If so, in what way?

4.   How do the purposes of proprietary accounts differ from those of budgetary accounts?

5.   What general criteria should be used in deciding whether or not to expand the number of accounts in a particular fund?

## References

Adams, Bert K. *Principles of Public School Accounting.* Washington, D.C.: U.S. Government Printing Office, 1967. OE 22025.

American Institute of Certified Public Accountants. "Inventory of Generally Accepted Accounting Principles for Business Enterprises," *Accounting Research Study No. 7.* New York: The Institute, 1965.

Mautz, R. K. "Basic Concepts of Accounting." *Handbook of Modern Accounting,* edited by Sidney Davidson, chap. 1. New York: McGraw-Hill, 1970.

Roberts, Charles T., and Lichtenberger, Allan R. *Financial Accounting: Classifications and Standard Terminology for Local and State School Systems.* Washington, D.C.: U.S. Government Printing Office, 1973. OE 73-11800.

Tidwell, Sam B. *Financial and Management Accounting for Elementary and Secondary School Systems.* Chicago: Research Corporation of the Association of School Business Officials, 1974.

## Related Readings

Palen, Jennie, M., ed. *Encyclopedia of Auditing Techniques.* Englewood Cliffs, N.J.: Prentice-Hall, 1974. Provides in its early chapters a nontechnical description of financial practices in general, and auditing practices in particular. See especially William S. Woodman's "Audit of a School District" (pp. 1257-86), which describes in a nontechnical manner the specific activities required of independent auditors engaged in the audit of a typical school district; and D. W. Edens's "Auditing of a University" (pp. 1466-1508), a nontechnical treatment of the required activities of auditing a university, which provides a rather comprehensive overview of the diverse financial dealings required of most universities.

Reason, Paul L., and White, Alpheus L. *Financial Accounting for Local and State School Systems: Standard Receipt and Expenditure Accounts.* Washington, D.C.: U.S. Government Printing Office, 1957. While updated by the Adams and Roberts references, this nevertheless provides a useful overview of school district accounting practices that is not at odds with many existing district accounting operations.

Samuelson, Everett V., and Tankard, George G., Jr. *Financial Accounting for School Activities.* Washington, D.C.: U.S. Government Printing Office, 1962. A guide for the financial accounting of money received by individual schools for school activities, including student clubs, student publications, the sale of merchandise through a school store, rental of textbooks, etc.

# 2
# Managerial Uses
# of the Accounting System

Now that the fundamental concepts of accounting systems have been described, the way has been paved for a discussion of their application to managerial decision making in education. The accounting system is the major quantitative information system in almost every organization. In educational organizations, as in others, it should provide information for three broad purposes:

1. Internal reporting to managers, for use in planning and controlling routine operations;
2. Internal reporting to managers, for use in making nonroutine decisions and in formulating major plans and policies; and
3. External reporting to outside parties (analogous to stockholders in for-profit concerns), such as government, granting agencies, etc. (Horngren 1972, p. 4).

In its attempt to provide information for these and other purposes, the accounting profession has developed specializations, the two most comprehensive of which are *financial accounting* and *managerial accounting*. Financial accounting has been characterized as "the branch of accounting that focuses on the general-purpose reports of financial position and results of operations known as financial statements" (A.I.C.P.A. 1970, p. 6). Financial accounting is the process that culminates in the preparation of financial reports *relative to the enterprise as a whole for use by parties both internal and external to the enterprise.* In contrast, managerial accounting pertains most directly to the accumulation and communication of information *relative to subsystems of the entity for use by internal parties* (American Accounting Association 1971, p. 9).

As implied, the distinctions in the field of accounting overlap to some degree with the organizational purposes of accounting. This operlap is illustrated in figure 2.1. It can also be said that financial

**Figure 2.1: Overlap of Accounting Specialties and Organizational Uses of Accounting**

|  | Managerial | Financial |
|---|---|---|
| Internal reporting: routine | XX | X |
| Internal reporting: nonroutine | XX | XX |
| External reporting | X | XX |

XX = heaviest emphasis

accounting concerns itself more with "how to do" accounting, while managerial accounting concerns itself more with "how to use" accounting in management. However, even this distinction is not entirely accurate, because there are things that managers *do* that can be properly termed managerial accounting.

While these accounting-related classification schemes are by no means mutually exclusive, they do provide a way for introducing the contents of this chapter and distinguishing this from the previous chapter. In the previous chapter, emphasis was placed more on financial accounting and on how it is done. In this chapter, the emphasis is more on managerial accounting and how to use accounting-related information. The first section describes the degree to which accounting in educational organizations differs in emphasis from accounting in for-profit organizations. Despite these differences, there are a far greater number of accounting concerns that are common across organizations. Three of these are discussed in this chapter: (1) internal control, (2) routine decision making, and (3) nonroutine decision making.

## Managerial Accounting: Educational vs. Commercial Organization

The accounting emphasis in not-for-profit educational organizations has been on internal control and external reporting and less on internal planning. There are several reasons for this. The financial activities of educational organizations—including accounting, reporting, and auditing—are governed by statutes to a much greater extent than those of commercial organizations. Compliance with statutory requirements is mandatory, even though they may, and frequently do, conflict with good accounting practices (Woodman 1974, p. 1258). Second, control of expenditures is considered of paramount importance, especially in those instances where public tax dollars are being spent. Ironically, however, internal control in educational organizations is often less effective than in commercial organizations because of the academic orientation of administrative personnel and overlapping statutory provisions.

Some of the differing emphases in accounting in educational organizations and other businesses can be traced to the relative complexity of each. Educational organizations generally engage in quite diversified activities, including large-scale sports programs; operation of transportation facilities, cafeterias, and bookstores; rental of facilities; and significant construction programs. Clientele and programs are diverse; for example, the basic instructional activities may involve day as well as night students and part-time as well as full-time students.

Although more complex and subject to greater external control than for-profit organizations, educational organizations attach relatively less importance to balance sheets and accounting for fixed assets (Woodman 1974, p. 1259). Balance sheets are less significant because the credit of the public educational organization is defined by its legal position (including, in the case of school districts, its taxing power) rather than by its recorded net worth. Assets are seldom pledged to secure debt, but the pledge of future revenues is common practice. (As a consequence, the statement of revenues and expenditures is of relatively more interest to educational managers than the statement of assets and liabilities.)

Since accounting for fixed assets is less important in educational organizations, it is quite common to find no formal accounting records of property accounts, whereas this is standard procedure in for-profit organizations. Motivation for keeping property accounts in educational organizations stems largely from insurance and external reporting requirements as opposed to taxation requirements (except with respect to those educational organizations devoted primarily to the production of income).

Despite these differences in emphasis, the managerial purposes for which accounting systems are used in educational organizations are much the same as in other organizations. These purposes involve the concepts of (1) internal control, (2) routine management decision making (both within the organization and by external sponsoring and regulatory agencies), and (3) nonroutine decision making.

## Internal Control

Internal control is defined by the American Institute of Certified Public Accountants as "the plan of organization and all of the coordinate methods and measures adopted within a business to safeguard its assets, check the accuracy and reliability of its accounting data, promote operational efficiency, and encourage adherence to prescribed managerial policies" (Committee on Auditing Procedure 1963, p. 27).

Accounting is an essential instrument for maintaining and enhancing internal control. Internal control is a management function, not an accounting function. There are, however, a number of management principles that will help to bring about accounting control and thereby minimize errors, fraud, and waste. *Minimize* is a more appropriate term here than *eliminate* because, as Horngren (1972, p. 668) says, "no framework for internal control is perfect in the sense that it can prevent some shrewd individual from 'beating the system' either by outright embezzlement or by producing inaccurate records."

A checklist for a good internal control system might include the ten items below (drawn from Horngren 1972, pp. 668-70, and Vatter 1950, chap. 11):

1. Reliable personnel. The accounting system, no matter how elaborate, is only as good as the individuals who operate it. This means that individuals should be given duties and responsibilities commensurate with their abilities, experience, interests, and reliability.

2. Separation of powers. Recordkeeping and the physical control of assets should not be in the hands of one person. For example, the bookkeeper should not handle cash, and the cashier should not have access to ledger accounts. This removes the temptation for a single person alter the ledger accounts to hide the theft of cash.

3. Supervision. The typical pyramid organization chart illustrates a common mode of supervision: everyone has a boss who oversees and appraises performance.

4. Responsibility. It is important to track actions as far down in the organization as is feasible, so that results may be related to particular individuals. This might mean, for example, having building-

level personnel sign for supplies received from a central warehouse, having workmen sign time cards, etc.

5. Routine and automatic checks. Establishing routine and automatic procedures for checking on operations is especially important in activities such as order taking, order filling, and dispersements. For example, no check should be written without an accompanying (signed) dispersement voucher that indicates who authorized the check. Forms should be designed so that the absence or incorrectness of key information is automatically uncovered and corrected on the spot. For example, the absence of a head custodian's signature prevents payments of overtime pay to custodians.

6. Document control. This term refers to measures that insure immediate, complete, and tamper-proof recording of transactions, especially those involving cash. This is encouraged, for example, by having all source documents prenumbered and accounted for.

7. Bonding, vacations, and rotation of duties. Key people who are subject to excessive temptation because of access to money should be bonded. Temptation is reduced when these people have understudies and are forced to take vacations. Improved control is also established by rotating clerks (e.g., those handling receivables and payables).

8. Independent checks. These include and extend beyond practices normally undertaken by independent auditors. Such practices should be undertaken by people who do not ordinarily have contact with the operation under review and would include reconciling bank statements with book balances and the physical counting of inventory.

9. Physical safeguards. This would cover all measures taken to physically protect cash, inventories, and records. Locks, safes, and watchmen fall in this category.

10. Cost feasibility. The complexity and costs of an internal control system have to be compared to the expected benefits. Unfortunately, "more" does not always mean "better." While difficult to quantify, these trade-offs must nonetheless be considered.

## Routine Decision Making

The word *routine* as used here does not imply mundaneness or triviality. Rather, routine finance-related decisions are those whose *form* is consistent over time. Many of the recurring, or routine, questions asked of the accounting system are answered via standard, basically unchanging, financial statements. There are at least four such general financial statements that together yield much information about the financial health of an educational organization. These financial statements provide the necessary information in a way that greatly condenses and organizes the mass of detail inherent in an accounting system.

The financial statements discussed here are: (1) the combined balance sheets, (2) the combined statement of revenues and expenditures, (3) the statement of changes in fund balances, and (4) the statement of changes in the overall financial position over time. The examples cited are drawn from elementary-secondary public education (Roberts and Lichtenberger 1973, pp. 167-74).

## Combined Balance Sheet

The combined balance sheet summarizes the assets, liabilities, and equity amounts for the entire educational organization. These figures are reported on a fund-by-fund basis and are usually backed up by more detailed statements of each fund. Table 2.2 shows the general form of a combined balance sheet for a school district.

It is possible to garner a wide range of information about the financial state of the organization from its combined balance sheet. In order to highlight different aspects of the combined balance sheet, school districts have started reporting various indices made up from the data. These include indebtedness indices (e.g., matured bonds and interest payable divided by total liabilities) and liquidity indices (e.g., cash divided by total assets and resources).

## Combined Statement of Revenues and Expenditures

This form yields a different but equally useful type of general information: it summarizes the major sources of revenue to the district (by fund) as well as the amounts spent in the major expenditure categories. This summary is often backed up by more detailed revenue-expenditure statements for each fund. Table 2.3 is an example of a combined revenue and expenditure statement. In a sense, this statement reflects the "activity" of each fund during the period. During the year past, the debt service fund, for example, received $300,000 from taxations and appropriations, other local and intermediate sources. The district earned $14,000 in interest on this money and spent $280,000 of the money on facilities.

Here, too, various indices can be helpful in gaining a more comprehensive picture of the financial condition of the organization— such as indices of the investment activity of the district (e.g., earnings on investments divided by total revenues).

# Table 2.2: Combined Balance Sheet for All Funds

| Balance sheet accounts | Total | Funds (end of year) | | | | | | | | |
| --- | --- | --- | --- | --- | --- | --- | --- | --- | --- | --- |
| | | General fund | Special revenue fund | Debt service fund | Capital projects fund | Food service fund | Pupil activity fund | Trust and agency funds | General fixed assets | Long-term debt |
| **Assets and resources** | | | | | | | | | | |
| Cash | $ 335,500 | $ 40,000 | $ 25,000 | $ 23,900 | $ 235,600 | $ 2,200 | $ 800 | $ 8,000 | | |
| Accounts receivable (net) | 18,000 | 15,000 | 3,000 | | | | | | | |
| Loans receivable (net) | 30,000 | | | | | | | 30,000 | | |
| Notes receivable (net) | 20,000 | | | 10,000 | | | | 10,000 | | |
| Interest receivable on notes | 3,200 | | | 2,400 | | | | 800 | | |
| Taxes receivable, current (net) | 140,000 | 80,000 | 30,000 | 30,000 | | | | | | |
| Interest receivable on taxes, current | 1,400 | 800 | 300 | 300 | | | | | | |
| Taxes receivable, delinquent (net) | 8,400 | 7,000 | 400 | 1,000 | | | | | | |
| Interest receivable on taxes, delinquent | 1,800 | 1,400 | 100 | 300 | | | | | | |
| Due from other units of government | 632,300 | 60,000 | 20,000 | 7,900 | 454,400 | 30,000 | 20,000 | 40,000 | | |
| Inventories | 17,700 | 1,300 | 6,400 | | | 7,000 | 3,000 | | | |
| Investments (including premiums and discounts) | 1,940,000 | | | 1,860,000 | | | | 80,000 | | |
| Bonds authorized and unissued | 310,000 | | | | 310,000 | | | | | |
| Amount available and to provide for retirement of bonds and interest | 2,400,000 | | | | | | | | | $2,400,000 |
| Land | 90,000 | | 8,000 | | | | 2,000 | | $ 80,000 | |
| Buildings | 3,553,000 | | 100,000 | | | 15,000 | | | 3,438,000 | |
| Improvements other than buildings | 98,000 | | 15,000 | | | 1,000 | | | 82,000 | |
| Machinery and equipment | 1,630,000 | | 20,000 | | | 140,000 | 70,000 | | 1,400,000 | |
| Total assets and resources | $11,229,300 | $205,500 | $228,200 | $1,935,800 | $1,000,000 | $195,200 | $95,800 | $168,800 | $5,000,000 | $2,400,000 |

| Liabilities | | | | | | | | | |
|---|---|---|---|---|---|---|---|---|---|
| Vouchers payable | $ 80,200 | $ 30,000 | $ 200 | | $ 2,000 | $ 20,000 | $10,000 | $ 18,000 | |
| Matured bonds and interest payable | 137,200 | 87,200 | | $ 50,000 | | | | | |
| Contracts payable | 370,000 | 75,000 | 22,000 | | 273,000 | | | | |
| Due to other units of government | 35,100 | 5,300 | 16,000 | | 5,000 | 8,000 | | 800 | |
| Interest payable in future years | 800,000 | | | | | | | | $ 800,000 |
| Bonds payable | 1,600,000 | | | | | | | | 1,600,000 |
| Total liabilities | $ 3,022,500 | $197,500 | $38,200 | $ 50,000 | $ 280,000 | $ 28,000 | $10,000 | $ 18,800 | $2,400,000 |
| Appropriations, reserves, and fund equities | | | | | | | | | |
| Appropriations | $ 300,000 | | | | $ 300,000 | | | | |
| Reserve for encumbrances | 421,000 | $ 6,000 | $ 15,000 | | 400,000 | | | | |
| Investment in general fixed assets | 5,000,000 | | | | | | | | $5,000,000 |
| Principal or capital | 360,000 | | | | | $160,000 | $50,000 | $150,000 | |
| Fund equity | 2,125,800 | 2,000 | 175,000 | $1,885,800 | 20,000 | 7,200 | 35,800 | | |
| Total appropriations, reserves, and fund equities | $ 8,206,800 | $ 8,000 | $190,000 | $1,885,800 | $ 720,000 | $167,200 | $85,800 | $150,000 | $5,000,000 |
| Total liabilities, appropriations, reserves, and fund equities | $11,229,300 | $205,500 | $228,200 | $1,935,800 | $1,000,000 | $195,200 | $95,800 | $168,800 | $7,400,000 |

Source: Charles T. Roberts and Allan R. Lichtenberger, *Financial Accounting: Classifications and Standard Terminology for Local and State School Systems* (Washington, D.C.: U.S. Government Printing Office, 1973, OE 73-11800), pp. 168-69.

Table 2.3: Combined Statement of Revenues and Expenditures

| | | Funds (end of year) | | | | | | |
|---|---|---|---|---|---|---|---|---|
| Revenue and expenditure accounts | Total | General fund | Special revenue fund | Debt service fund | Capital projects fund | Food service fund | Pupil activity fund | Trust and agency funds |
| **Revenues** | | | | | | | | |
| Taxations and appropriations | $2,561,000 | $1,521,000 | | $140,000 | | | | $800,000 |
| Tuition from patrons | 10,000 | 10,000 | | | | | | |
| Transportation fees from patrons | 14,000 | 14,000 | | | | | | |
| Revenue from other units of government | 50,000 | | | | | | | 50,000 |
| Earnings on investments | 68,000 | 20,000 | | 14,000 | $ 24,000 | $ 1,000 | | 9,000 |
| Revenue from food sales | 246,000 | | | | | 246,000 | | |
| Revenue from pupil activities | 314,000 | | | | | | 314,000 | |
| Revenue from other local sources | 2,735,000 | 1,000,000 | $ 175,000 | 60,000 | 1,400,000 | | | 100,000 |
| Revenue from intermediate sources | 143,280 | 43,280 | | 100,000 | | | | |
| Revenue from state sources | 2,480,000 | 1,380,000 | 1,100,000 | | | | | |
| Revenue from federal sources | 975,000 | 100,000 | 715,000 | | | 160,000 | | |
| Total revenues | $9,596,280 | $4,088,280 | $1,990,000 | $314,000 | $1,424,000 | $407,000 | $414,000 | $959,000 |
| **Expenditures** | | | | | | | | |
| Elementary programs | $1,890,000 | $1,240,000 | $ 197,000 | | | $138,000 | $ 15,000 | $300,000 |
| Middle/junior high programs | 1,740,000 | 1,070,000 | 188,000 | | | 110,000 | 97,000 | 275,000 |
| High school programs | 2,018,000 | 827,000 | 546,000 | | | 105,000 | 300,000 | 240,000 |
| Special education programs | 785,000 | 175,000 | 587,500 | | | 5,000 | 500 | 17,000 |
| Adult/continuing education program | 285,000 | 115,000 | 158,500 | | | 500 | | 11,000 |
| Administration | 122,000 | 107,000 | | | | | | 15,000 |
| Facilities acquisition and construction | 1,520,000 | | | $280,000 | $1,240,000 | | | |
| Transportation | 245,000 | 15,000 | 230,000 | | | | | |
| Community services | 178,000 | 175,000 | 3,000 | | | | | |
| Nonprogram charges | 214,000 | 214,000 | | | | | | |
| Total expenditures | $8,997,000 | $3,938,000 | $1,910,000 | $280,000 | $1,240,000 | $358,500 | $412,500 | $858,000 |

Source: Charles T. Roberts and Allan R. Lichtenberger, *Financial Accounting: Classifications and Standard Terminology for Local and State School Systems* (Washington, D.C.: U.S. Government Printing Office, 1973, OE 73-11800), p. 170.

## Changes in Fund Balances

Closely related to the combined statement of revenues and expenditures is the statement of changes in fund balances. Generally, this statement shows for each fund the net differences between revenues and expenditures, both at the beginning and at the end of the period; it reflects the degree of change in revenue-expenditure differences by fund in comparison with the previous year. In the example in table 2.4 all funds (except the general fund) show an increase in net revenue over the previous year.

## Changes in Financial Position

This statement describes in summary fashion (for all funds combined) the resources provided the district and to what they were applied. Resources are provided from revenues for each fund; from reduction in assets during the year; from increase of liabilities, appropriations, and reserves during the year; from collection of revenues from the prior year; and from expenditures being refunded. These funds are applied to the operations of the district via funds to increase assets during the year, decrease liabilities during the year, collect expenses for the prior year, and refund revenue collected in excess in the prior year.

An example of this statement appears in table 2.5. The changes in financial position statement is prepared using combined balance sheets at the beginning and end of the period (e.g., fiscal year) and the combined statement of revenues and expenditures. (Comparative balance sheets from which table 2.5 was prepared are presented in table 2.6.)

The financial statements described here provide a broad basis from which much of the financial condition of the organization can be inferred. While possibly indicating over time a wide variety of desirable and undesirable conditions in an organization, the financial statements rarely change in format and, as intended, are addressed to the recurring (routine) decisions facing management in educational organizations. They are also used by sponsoring and regulatory agencies as they formulate policy affecting the educational organizations.

## Nonroutine Decision Making

Generally, financial information that management knows will be routinely and frequently required should probably be generated through the transactions (accounting) system described above or

## Table 2.4: Changes in Fund Balances for All Funds (end of year)

| Balances | Total | General fund | Special revenue fund | Debt service fund | Capital projects fund | Food service fund | Pupil activity fund | Trust and agency funds |
|---|---|---|---|---|---|---|---|---|
| Beginning of year | $453,250 | $ 300,000 | $28,000 | $ 5,000 | $ 45,000 | $ 1,100 | $ (850) | $ 75,000 |
| End of year | 599,280 | 150,280 | 80,000 | 34,000 | 184,000 | 48,500 | 1,500 | 101,000 |
| Change | $146,030 | $(149,720) | $52,000 | $29,000 | $139,000 | $47,400 | $2,350 | $ 26,000 |

Source: Charles T. Roberts and Allan R. Lichtenberger, *Financial Accounting: Classifications and Standard Terminology for Local and State School Systems* (Washington, D.C.: U.S. Government Printing Office, 1973, OE 73-11800), p. 171.

# Table 2.5: Changes in Financial Position for All Funds (end of year)

## Resources provided from:

**Revenue for year**

| | |
|---|---:|
| General fund | $4,088,280 |
| Special revenue fund | 1,990,000 |
| Debt service fund | 314,000 |
| Capital projects fund | 1,424,000 |
| Food service fund | 407,000 |
| Pupil activity fund | 414,000 |
| Trust and agency funds | 959,000 |
| | $ 9,596,280 |

**Reducing assets during year**

| | |
|---|---:|
| Accounts receivable | $ 12,000 |
| Notes receivable | 20,000 |
| Taxes receivable, current (net) | 10,000 |
| Interest receivable on taxes, delinquent | 100 |
| Investments | 60,000 |
| Amount available and to be provided for retention of bonds and interest | 200,000 |
| | $ 302,100 |

**Increasing liabilities, appropriations, and reserves during the year**

| | |
|---|---:|
| Vouchers payable | $ 70,000 |
| Matured bonds and interest payable | 137,200 |
| Due to other units of government | 25,100 |
| Interest payable in future years | 500,000 |
| Appropriations | 300,000 |
| Reserves for encumberances | 401,000 |
| | $ 1,433,300 |

**Corrections of prior year**

| | |
|---|---:|
| Taxes receivable, delinquent | $ 39,000 |
| Interest receivable on taxes, delinquent | 87,000 |
| Inventories | 15,000 |
| | $ 141,000 |

**Expenditures refunded from prior year**

| | |
|---|---:|
| Elementary programs | $ 10,000 |
| Middle/junior high programs | 39,000 |
| Community services | 17,000 |
| | $ 66,000 |
| **Total resources provided** | **$11,538,680** |

## Resources allocated to:

**Operations**

| | |
|---|---:|
| General fund | $3,998,000 |
| Special revenue fund | 1,910,000 |
| Debt service fund | 280,000 |
| Capital projects fund | 1,240,000 |
| Food services fund | 358,500 |
| Pupil activity fund | 412,500 |
| Trust and agency funds | 858,000 |
| | $ 8,997,000 |

**Increase assets during year**

| | |
|---|---:|
| Cash | $ 266,800 |
| Loans receivable (net) | 20,000 |
| Interest receivable on notes | 1,000 |
| Taxes receivable delinquent (net) | 600 |
| Due from other units of government | 532,300 |
| Inventories | 3,700 |
| Bonds authorized and unissued | 310,000 |
| | $ 1,134,400 |

**Decreasing liabilities during year**

| | |
|---|---:|
| Contracts payable | $ 333,000 |
| Bonds payable | 652,000 |
| | $ 985,000 |

**Corrections of prior year**

| | |
|---|---:|
| Interest expense | $ 2,200 |
| Contracts payable | 73,080 |
| Due to other units of government | 92,000 |
| | $ 167,280 |

**Revenue rebates from prior year**

| | |
|---|---:|
| Revenue from taxes | $ 79,000 |
| Revenue from state sources | 87,000 |
| Revenue from federal sources | 89,000 |
| | $ 255,000 |
| **Total resources applied** | **$11,538,680** |

Source: Charles T. Roberts and Allan R. Lichtenberger, *Financial Accounting: Classifications and Standard Terminology for Local and State School Systems* (Washington, D.C.: U.S. Government Printing Office, 1973, OE 73-11800), pp. 172-73.

# Table 2.6: Comparative Combined Balance Sheets

| Balance sheet accounts | Beginning of year | End of year | Net changes Debits | Net changes Credits |
|---|---|---|---|---|
| **Assets and resources** | | | | |
| Cash | $ 68,700 | $ 335,500 | $266,800 | |
| Accounts receivable (net) | 30,000 | 18,000 | | $ 12,000 |
| Loans receivable (net) | 10,000 | 30,000 | 20,000 | |
| Notes receivable | 40,000 | 20,000 | | 20,000 |
| Interest receivable on notes | 2,200 | 3,200 | 1,000 | |
| Taxes receivable, current (net) | 250,000 | 140,000 | | 110,000 |
| Interest receivable on taxes, delinquent | 1,400 | 1,400 | | |
| Taxes receivable, delinquent (net) | 7,800 | 8,400 | 600 | |
| Interest receivable on taxes | 1,900 | 1,800 | | 100 |
| Due from other units of government | 100,000 | 632,300 | 532,300 | |
| Inventories | 14,000 | 17,700 | 3,700 | |
| Investments (including premiums and discounts) | 2,000,000 | 1,940,000 | | 60,000 |
| Bonds authorized and unissued | | 310,000 | 310,000 | |
| Amount available and to be provided for retirement of bonds and interest | 2,500,000 | 2,400,000 | | 100,000 |
| Land | 87,000 | 90,000 | 3,000 | |
| Buildings | 3,250,000 | 3,553,000 | 303,000 | |
| Improvements other than buildings | 95,000 | 98,000 | 3,000 | |
| Machinery and equipment | 1,800,000 | 1,630,000 | | 170,000 |
|   Total assets and resources | $10,258,000 | $11,229,300 | | |
| **Liabilities, reserves, and fund equity** | | | | |
| Vouchers payable | $ 10,200 | $ 80,200 | | 70,000 |
| Matured bonds and interest payable | | 137,200 | | 137,200 |
| Contracts payable | 703,000 | 370,000 | 333,000 | |
| Due to other units of government | 10,000 | 35,100 | | 25,100 |
| Interest payable in future years | 300,000 | 800,000 | | 500,000 |
| Bonds payable | 2,252,000 | 1,600,000 | 652,000 | |
| Appropriations | | 300,000 | | 300,000 |
| Reserve for encumbrances | 20,000 | 421,000 | | 401,000 |
| Investments in general fixed assets | 4,861,000 | 5,000,000 | | 139,000 |
| Principal on capital | 250,000 | 360,000 | | 110,000 |
| Fund equity | 1,851,800 | 2,125,800 | | 274,000 |
|   Total liabilities, reserves, fund equity, debits, and credits | $10,258,000 | $11,229,300 | $2,428,400 | $2,428,400 |

Source: Charles T. Roberts and Allan R. Lichtenberger, *Financial Accounting: Classifications and Standard Terminology for Local and State School Systems* (Washington, D.C.: U.S. Government Printing Office, 1973, OE 73-11800), p. 174.

through a system that operates directly off it. However, many decisions faced by educational managers differ in form over time. But it would be prohibitively expensive—if not virtually impossible—to design an accounting information system comprehensive enough to be adequate for all possible future financial information needs.

As a result, the financial information required as input for non-routine decisions cannot be provided directly by the accounting system. Accounting systems, for example, do not automatically report the cost of expanding an instructional program to serve 50 percent more pupils. In order to generate the information required for this type of decision, and many like it, the educational manager must be able to estimate costs (as well as income). To do this with any degree of validity requires an understanding of cost relationships in the organization.

The manager can use *cost analysis* to arrive at and to implement decisions made in the light of organizational objectives. Consequently, the structure and logic of cost analysis have a major impact on the decisions reached and on the ability of the organization to achieve its goals. It is therefore imperative that top management understand some of the more fundamental classifications of costs and how they are incurred. Among many types of costs that could be discussed, four of the most fundamental are discussed here. They are (1) variable vs. fixed costs, (2) direct vs. indirect costs, (3) total vs. unit costs, and (4) transfer pricing.

## Variable vs. Fixed Costs

A total cost may be either *variable* or *fixed* depending on whether or not it changes in relation to fluctuations in the activity of the program or quantity of the cost object under analysis. Many types of activity can be defined in this way: for example, man-hours worked, miles driven, students enrolled, gallons consumed, payroll checks processed. If a total cost changes in proportion to changes in activity, it is variable; if a total cost remains unchanged for a given period despite wide fluctuations in activity, it is fixed. A fixed cost is fixed only in relationship to a given period of time and a given, though wide, range of activity, called the *relevant range* (Horngren 1972, p. 24). For example, a school district may find that, over a 10 percent variation in enrollment, the variable costs include only teachers' salaries and instructional supplies. No additional administrative staff or facilities may be required; these may be considered fixed in this relevant range. Over a wider relevant range, however, these costs would vary. A significant increase in students would require additional facilities and support staff, whereas with a significant drop in existing levels in enrollment, schools may be closed. This is portrayed conceptually in figure 2.7. The likelihood of activities being outside the rele-

**Figure 2.7: Total Annual Fixed Costs—Conceptual Analysis**

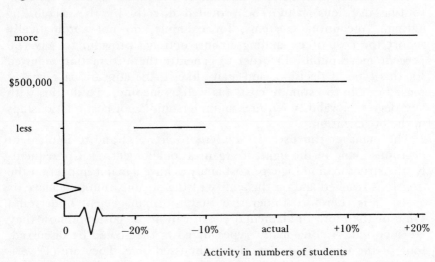

Activity in numbers of students

vant range is usually slight, so the $500,000 in figure 2.7 becomes the fixed cost level. The three-level refinement shown in this figure is not usually required because the chances are very remote that total enrollment will change more than 10 percent over the year (see figure 2.8).

Educational managers find this concept useful for a number of reasons. Most importantly it provides them with knowledge of their organization's cost behavior patterns (*cost functions*), which they can use to predict the impact of their decisions on costs and to formulate means for controlling cost incurrence.

Some costs are difficult to categorize as either strictly variable or strictly fixed. In fact, few costs are clearly one or the other. How a cost is identified depends largely on the activity base that is chosen. Central administration of a university, for example, may view telephones as a variable cost if the activity base is the number of professors on the faculty. However, such costs are fixed for an academic department that does not change in size and that uses as an activity base the number of calls made.

### Figure 2.8: Total Annual Fixed Costs as Plotted in Practice

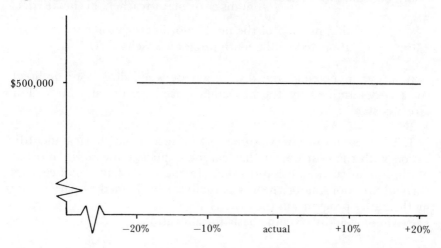

## Direct vs. Indirect Costs

Closely related to the concepts of fixed and variable costs are the concepts of *direct* and *indirect costs*. None of these terms has a useful meaning apart from its relation to a particular object of costing. The distinction between direct and indirect costs is made on the basis of *traceability*. The word *direct* refers to the obvious (traceable) relationship of a cost incurred with respect to an object of costing, whereas an indirect cost does not have this obvious relationship with an object of costing. For example, the salary of a mathematics curriculum coordinator who works at a school district central office would be a direct charge to the mathematics program of a school district. There is an obvious relationship between the math coordinator and the math program he coordinates. However, his salary would be an indirect charge to the various mathematics programs in each of the schools in the district. In order to allocate his salary among the various schools in the district, it will be necessary to determine some intervening allocation mechanism, such as the number of math teachers in each of the schools. The allocation of a portion of the math coordinator's salary to the math program at school A would be determined as follows:

$$\text{Math coordinator's salary} \times \frac{\text{number of math teachers in school A}}{\text{number of math teachers in the district}}$$

= that portion of the math coordinator's salary
allocated to the math program in school A.

In program costing, the distinction between direct and indirect costs is determined by the procedures used for the allocation. For direct cost:

1. There is almost always some sort of observable physical identification with the cost object that can be explicitly measured in terms of the quantity of the input used. (In the case of the mathematics curriculum coordinator, he has actually been defined as part of the mathematics programs in the district.)
2. There is no intervening basis for allocation.

For an indirect cost there would be an intervening basis for allocation. For example, the salary of the mathematics curriculum coordinator would be an indirect charge to the mathematics programs at each of the school sites, and such a cost would be determined on an allocation basis such as that described above.

The issue of determining direct and indirect costs is particularly crucial in educational organizations where external agencies often sponsor specific segments of the organization's operations (such as transportation and food service operations in elementary-secondary education and a wide variety of research and training programs in colleges and universities). In higher education the concern with increased indirect costs and the resulting growth in overhead rates is frequently expressed by sponsors but is shared by both higher education administrators and principal investigators. The impact of these costs on limited institutional funds and the resulting reduction in sponsors' funds available for direct costs are recognized by the college and university community as factors in the overall financial difficulty that has faced higher education since the late 1960s (National Association of College and University Business Officers 1974, p. 2).

In an effort to clarify indirect costing procedures used by the federal government in dealing with institutions of higher education, the American Council on Education summarized both the tentative nature of cost accounting as well as the impact of cost determination on organizational income (Commission on Federal Relations 1969, p. 2).

Depending upon how an institution organizes the management of its research, some cost may be considered either direct or indirect, *but not both*. These differences in organization for the management of research are the major reason for differing indirect cost rates among institutions, but such differences do not affect total costs. If indirect costs go up, direct costs come down correspondingly; total costs remain unchanged. But the amount of total costs recovered by the institution may be affected by a change in the mixture of indirect and direct cost elements.

A detailed example of indirect cost allocation is included in the discussion of food service in chapter seven.

## Total vs. Unit Costs

*Total cost* is a necessary but not sufficient piece of cost information for management decision making, especially in education. *Unit cost* information supplements total cost information and aids in selection and pricing decisions. For example, a particular reading program in a school district may cost $80,000 and serve 800 pupils. While it has a higher total cost than an alternative that costs $60,000 and serves 400 pupils, its unit (in this case, per-pupil) cost is less; therefore, if the programs are equally effective, the $80,000 alternative would be preferable. Similar examples in educational organizations might deal with those operations where student choice is a big factor (e.g., food service operations, elective programs). Alternative food service options, for example, will attract different numbers of pupils and reflect different unit costs. The volume of demand for a particular food service option (the denominator of our unit cost figure) may, in turn, be particularly sensitive to price. Consequently, in certain circumstances unit costs are important in pricing as well as in program selection decisions.

## Transfer Pricing

Goods and services are often exchanged between various departments and divisions of a company or an educational institution. In elementary-secondary education, for example, the maintenance department provides services to school buildings, the data processing department provides services to the accounting department, etc. These services are supplied at some cost. But the question immediately arises, at what price should these transfers of services and goods be valued?

Ideally, *transfer prices* should guide each manager to choose inputs and outputs in coordination with other subunits so as to maximize the effectiveness of the organization as a whole.

*Maximum effectiveness* in this context is defined as the best conceivable decision, given top-management objectives. There are at least three criteria that should be considered (simultaneously) when establishing transfer prices: goal congruence, performance evaluation, and autonomy (Horngren 1972, pp. 714-50). In other words, the aim is to design a transfer-pricing scheme that will point subunit managers (e.g., principals, department chairmen) toward top-management goals *and* provide incentive to reach these goals. While no simple pricing mechanism exists for achieving this, there is a general rule that may be applied in a particular situation: the transfer price should be (1) the incremental cost incurred in the transfer, plus (2) the opportunity costs for the organization as a whole. *Incremental cost* refers to the cash costs that are directly associated with the production and transfer of the goods or services. (Of course, these cash costs do not necessarily have to be made at a particular instant, but the action of the production and transfer will result sooner or later in some cost.) *Opportunity costs* are defined here as the maximum contribution to organizational goals foregone by the organization as a whole if the goods are transferred internally. The distinction between outlay and opportunity costs is made here because the accounting records ordinarily record the outlay costs of the best of the rejected alternatives (Horngren 1972, p. 734).

One of the more widely used bases for setting transfer prices is *actual cost*. This means that sending units charge the full cost of their services to the receiving units in the organization. If this is done, the performance of the receiving units would bear the accumulated efficiencies or inefficiencies of other divisions not subject to their control. Transfer prices that insure recovery of actual costs often fail to provide an incentive on the part of the sending unit to control their own costs. In higher education this issue bears most directly on the transfer prices affixed to various computing services. Computer rates vary significantly among universities, reflecting, at least in part, different attempts to encourage computer usage while controlling costs.

Viewed structurally, transfer pricing represents an attempt on the part of management to find some intermediate point between total centralization and total decentralization that will maximize the organization's objectives. Total centralization implies that purchasing functions take place at the top of an organization. Total decentralization in this context implies that units within an organization act as if they were independent of one another. Carried to the extreme, this would mean that each unit could act in its own self-interest, which could be dysfunctional to the organization as a whole. Transfer prices may be viewed as constraints on decentralization because they are designed to link subunits in an organization.

Management's ability to provide and interpret valid cost information for nonroutine decisions depends in large part on its ability (1) to assess costs that are valid and (2) to set prices and resulting levels of service in the subunits of the organization that best reflect the overall goals of that organization.

## Questions for Review and Discussion

1.   Why is accounting for fixed assets a more important function in for-profit organizations than in educational organizations?

2.   In what way do control measures to reduce human error differ from control measures to reduce instances of criminal acts?

3.   What particularly high (or low) values from the financial statements would indicate potential problems for the educational organization? On what basis would such values be judged high or low?

4.   In costing out a proposal of expanding an instructional program to serve 50 percent more students, which cost objects would be considered fixed costs? Which would be considered variable? Under what conditions would some of the fixed costs become variable costs?

5.   What goods and services in educational organizations typically have transfer prices associated with them? To what other goods or services in education could transfer prices be affixed?

## References

American Accounting Association. *Report of the Committee on Courses in Financial Accounting.* Evanston, Ill.: The Association, 1971.

American Institute of Certified Public Accountants. "Basic Concepts and Accounting Principles Underlying Financial Statements of Business Enterprises." *Statement of the Accounting Principles Board No. 4.* New York: A.I.C.P.A., 1970.

Commission on Federal Relations. *Direct and Indirect Costs of Research at Colleges and Universities.* Washington, D.C.: American Council on Education, 1969.

Committee on Auditing Procedure. *Auditing Standards and Procedures.* New York: American Institute of Certified Public Accountants, 1963.

Horngren, Charles T. *Cost Accounting: A Managerial Emphasis.* Englewood Cliffs, N.J.: Prentice-Hall, 1972.

National Association of College and University Business Officers. "Indirect Costs: A Problem in Communication." *Studies in Management* 4, no. 1 (1974): 1-4.

Roberts, Charles T., and Lichtenberger, Allan R. *Financial Accounting: Classifi-*

*cations and Standard Terminology for Local and State School Systems.*
    Washington, D.C.: U.S. Government Printing Office, 1973. OE 73-11800.
Vatter, William J. *Managerial Accounting.* Englewood Cliffs, N.J.: Prentice-Hall,
    1950.
Woodman, William S. "Audit of a School District." *Encyclopedia of Auditing
    Techniques,* edited by Jennie M. Palen, pp. 157-1286. Englewood Cliffs,
    N.J.: Prentice-Hall, 1974.

## Related Readings

American Council on Education. *College and University Business Administra-
    tion.* Washington, D.C.: The Council, 1968. See especially pp. 141-274.
    Treats financial reports and routine financial decisions commonly found in
    institutions of higher learning.
Anthony, Robert N. *Planning and Control Systems: A Framework for Analysis.*
    Boston: Harvard Business School, 1965. A classic text describing the scope
    of management activities in organizations and distinguishing between stra-
    tegic planning and operational control. Although written with the private,
    for-profit sector in mind, it is also relevant to educational organizations.
Dearden, John. "Interdivisional Pricing." *Harvard Business Review* 38, no. 1
    (1960): 117-25. Treats the fundamental issues involved in deciding upon,
    determining, and evaluating transfer pricing policies in organizations.
Hass, Jerome E. "Transfer Pricing in a Decentralized Firm." *Management Sci-
    ence: Application* 14, no. 6 (1968): B-310—B-317. Presents a technical
    model for ascertaining optimum pricing decisions.
Hungate, Thad L. *Finance in Educational Management of Colleges and Universi-
    ties.* New York: Teachers College, Columbia University, 1954. While some-
    what dated in a few technical details, this book describes the policy role of
    financial managers in higher education organizations as well as providing
    insight into a variety of technical tasks.
Taylor, Philip J., and Thompson, Granville K. *Financial Management of Higher
    Education.* New York: Coopers and Lybrand, Certified Public Account-
    ants, 1973. One of the most sophisticated yet readable volumes on the
    subject, it goes beyond descriptions of current practice in higher education
    financial management to assess weaknesses and trends in the field.

# 3
# Cash Planning and
# Temporary Investments

Three managerial uses of financial information were mentioned in the previous chapter: (1) routine controlling, (2) routine decision making, and (3) nonroutine decision making. This chapter and chapter four focus on the second use, and deal specifically with two kinds of routine decision making involving fiscal systems: *cash planning* and *risk management*. Cash planning is concerned with the problems and opportunities financial managers face in dealing with differences between revenues and expenditures over specified periods. Risk management concerns methods for identifying, evaluating, and hedging against potential financial loss.

Cash planning and risk management are fundamental operations of financial management in educational (and most other) organizations. Moreover, they introduce two concepts central to management and frequently referred to throughout this book: *constrained optimization* and *uncertainty*. Often the task of management is to achieve a maximum (or minimum) goal subject to externally imposed limitations. This, very generally, is constrained optimization. For example, a management objective might be to minimize heating and cooling systems costs subject to the constraint that a "significant" number of employees do not complain. Another hypothetical objective might be to minimize student transportation costs, subject to the limitation that students spend no more than forty minutes on the bus ride between home and school. (Although it is possible that the objective may be unconstrained by limitations, this rarely occurs without access to almost unlimited resources.)

While much of what managers pursue may be seen as constrained optimization, much of what they must cope with can be labeled uncertainty. If the following facts were known before their occurrence, educational management would be a less complicated task: the

*53*

number of admitted freshmen who actually enroll; the return on alternative investments of endowment; whether a large federally-funded program will be refunded; the number of faculty who will resign at the end of the year; which faculty will resign at the end of the year; the number of students who will purchase meals at different prices, etc. Management takes place in an environment of incomplete information, and many decisions are based on probability estimates of future events. Although planning the cash position of an educational organization involves a high degree of uncertainty, emphasis is placed in this chapter on constrained optimization under conditions of certainty. Probability concepts are then introduced in the following chapter dealing with risk management.

## Cash Planning Overview

Cash planning is a process of estimating all sources and uses of cash over a definite future period (Goodman 1973, p. 85). Cash planning is necessary because the inflow of resources (revenues) almost never exhibits the same pattern as the required outflow (expenditures). This is simplistically shown in figure 3.1, in which the revenue of a school district is plotted for one year. In this example, the school district receives revenues from four sources: local property taxes, state aid, federal aid, and receipts from charges for miscellaneous items such as tuition, sales of lunches, etc. The total amount of revenue flowing into the district during the year is $38 million, but it is not distributed evenly. Nine million dollars was received during each of the months of September and April. The bulk of this revenue comes from local taxes and federal aid. State aid is received in two installments, $5 million in October and an equal amount in March. Income from charges is evenly distributed throughout the year.

While the pattern of revenues for this district is variable over the months, the pattern of expenditures is less so. Figure 3.2 shows what the expenditure pattern might look like. To keep the example simple, only three general types of expenditures are considered: salaries of personnel holding twelve-month contracts (e.g., administrators, support personnel), salaries of personnel holding ten-month contracts (e.g., teachers), and all nonsalary expenditures (e.g., supplies, fuel). The expenditures in figure 3.2 equal the revenue in figure 3.1. However, as shown in figure 3.3, there are several times during the year when the organization will experience temporary cash surpluses and deficits. Some of the deficits will have to be covered by short-term borrowing, while some of the surpluses can be invested for short periods.

Figure 3.1: Flow of Revenue

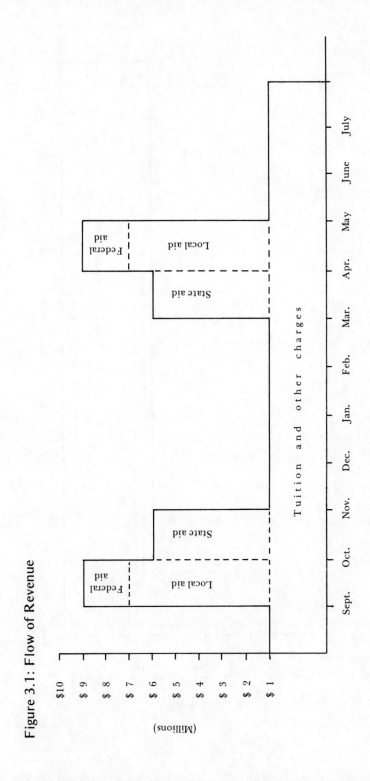

Figure 3.2: Flow of Expenditures

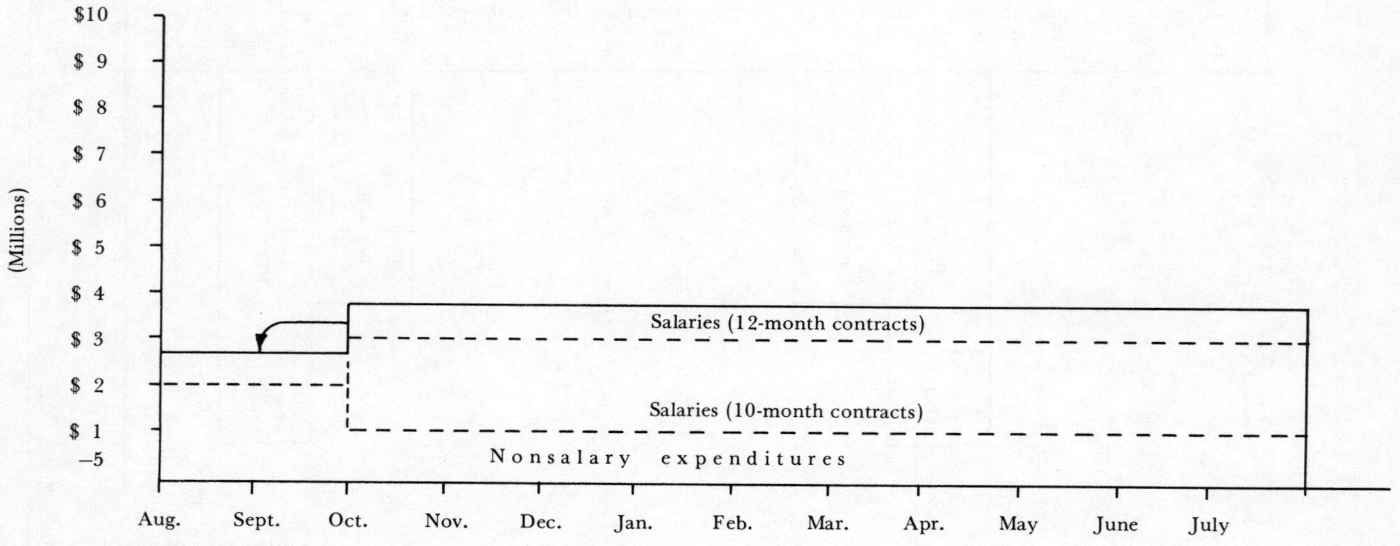

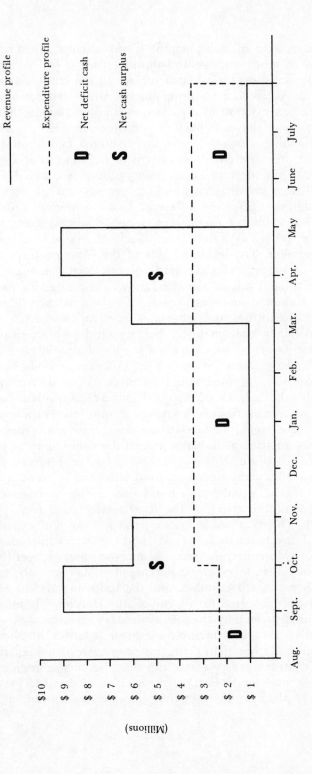

Figure 3.3: Cash Deficits and Surpluses

   The problem in cash planning is one of constrained optimization: earning as much as possible from investments (or paying as little as possible for short-term loans) subject to the constraint that all bills are paid. Accepted accounting practice stipulates that interest earned from the excess cash of a particular fund accrues to that fund. As a consequence, the cash planning problem applies to each fund, and cash planning is not the same for all funds. The amounts of money involved are different; the patterns of net deficits and surpluses are different; the degrees of certainty about estimated income and expenditures are different; and the periods of time over which cash planning takes place are different. Two examples of cash flow charts for different funds (and different school districts) illustrate this.

   Table 3.4 is a cash flow chart of a food service fund for the month of November. The left-hand side of the chart portrays estimates of outgoing funds, including dates, descriptions, amounts, and totals. The right-hand side of the chart shows anticipated income, including dates, amounts, and descriptions. The net balance between anticipated expenditures and income is listed in the extreme right-hand column. Daily changes in the balances and mid-month purchases of investments are shown. Generally, the chart indicates a policy of investing large sums (at least $100,000) for periods of at least 30 days. Smaller amounts could be invested for shorter periods. For example, the balance of $16,000 and $21,000 might have been invested on a daily basis in a savings account to return approximately $50 for the week. This relatively conservative investment policy is probably an attempt to hedge against the uncertainty of the forecast.

   Table 3.5 is a cash flow chart of a bond and interest fund. Sometimes called a capital projects fund, it is used to account for the proceeds of general obligation bond issues. The chart covers a longer period than the chart of the food service fund (one year vs. one month). This is possible because the income and expenditure patterns of the bond and interest fund can be estimated with greater accuracy. Moreover, the terms of investment are longer (90-270 days vs. 30-60 days). Investments purchased in May are to be sold at interest in November, December, and the following March. Although the fund is fully invested in November, the December bond and interest payment is covered by the sale of the May investment.

   Finally, the fund incurred negative balances in November and December. Rather than reflecting poor cash planning, this indicates that a central treasury exists and that the person in charge has analyzed all funds in developing its cash plan (Tidwell 1974, p. 363). He or she is planning to meet the temporary cash needs of the capital

Table 3.4: Monthly Breakdown of Daily Changes in the Balances and Mid-Month Investment Purchases (November)

| Date | Description of outgoing funds | Individual total | Gross total | Date | Anticipated income | Description of incoming funds | Balance |
|---|---|---|---|---|---|---|---|
| | | | | 1 | | Balance from September | 16,000 |
| | | | | 4 | 5,000 | Food service sales | 21,000 |
| 9 | October bills | 115,000 | 115,000 | 9 | 125,000 | Investment from 8/10/72 | 31,000 |
| 14 | 185,000 @ 6 percent Invest to 11/20/73 | 185,000 | | 13 | 161,000 | State aids | 192,000 |
| | | | | | | | 7,000 |
| 20 | Net October payroll | 296,000 | | 18 | 5,000 | Food service sales | 12,000 |
| | Payroll taxes | 46,000 | 342,000 | 19 | 351,000 | Invest from 9/20/72 | 363,000 |
| | | | | | | | 21,000 |
| 24 | 100,000 @ 6 percent Invest to 1/8/74 | 100,000 | | 24 | 83,000 | Federal aid | 104,000 |
| | | | | | | | 4,000 |

Source: James E. Law, "Manage Your Funds Properly!" *School Business Affairs* XL (February 1974), p. 79. Reprinted by permission.

Table 3.5: Cash Flow Chart—Bond and Interest Fund

| Date | Beginning balance | Tax receipts | Sale of investments | Total monies | Bond and interest payments | Purchase of investments | Term of investment | Ending balance |
|---|---|---|---|---|---|---|---|---|
| 1964 | | | | | | | | |
| May | $147,651 | $23,500 | $50,000 | $221,151 | $17,000 | $63,807 (a) | 180 days due 11/5/64 | $ 1,476 |
| | | | | | | 58,899 (b) | 210 days due 12/5/64 | |
| | | | | | | 79,969 (c) | 270 days due 3/31/65 | |
| June | 1,476 | 55,500 | — | 56,976 | | | | 44,876 |
| July | 44,876 | 18,180 | — | 63,056 | 12,100 | 61,456 | 90 days due 9/30/64 | 1,600 |
| August | 1,600 | — | — | 1,600 | — | | | 1,600 |
| September | 1,600 | — | 62,000 | 63,600 | 11,500 | | | 52,100 |
| October | 52,100 | 38,682 | — | 90,782 | — | 60,833 | 180 days due 4/8/65 | 52,100 |
| November | 29,949 | | 65,000(a) | 94,949 | 59,936 | 58,874 | 180 days due 5/6/65 | 29,949 |
| December | (23,861) | 9,000 | 60,000(b) | 45,139 | 52,554 | — | | (23,861) |
| 1965 | | | | | | | | |
| January | ( 7,415) | 12,500 | — | — | — | — | | ( 7,415) |
| February | 5,085 | — | — | — | — | — | | 5,085 |
| March | 5,085 | — | 81,000(c) | 86,085 | 44,100 | 37,100 | 90 days due 6/30/65 | 5,085 |
| April | 4,885 | — | 62,000 | 66,885 | — | 60,755 | 180 days due 10/8/65 | 4,885 |

Source: Eugene L. Moody, "How Lincolnwood, Illinois Earns $32,000 Annually." *Nation's Schools* 76, no. 3 (March 1965), p. 80. Reprinted by permission.

and interest fund using excess cash from another fund (via the central treasury). By consolidating cash planning in a central treasury, investments of larger amounts and longer durations can be made, yielding slightly higher earnings. This also reduces the need to go outside the organization to borrow money and incur interest.

Cash planning is complicated by two factors: selection of type and amount of investment and degree of certainty in forecasts. These are discussed separately below.

### Investment Instruments

Investment instruments differ in terms of risk, minimum purchase required, maturity dates, and yield. Generally, larger investments with longer maturities yield greater returns but, for a given profile of excess cash, there are many investment possibilities. Figures 3.6 and 3.7, for example, represent two quite different policies for the same profile of excess cash. In figure 3.6 large investments are held for

### Figure 3.6: Large Blocs of Cash Invested for Short Periods

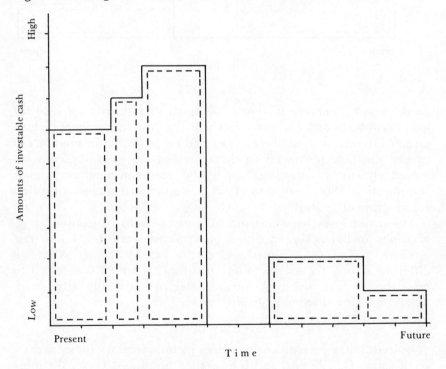

**Figure 3.7: Small Blocs of Cash Invested for Long Periods**

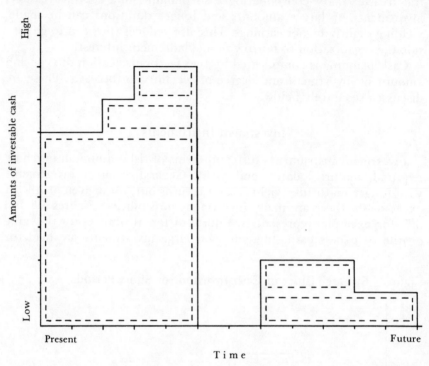

short periods, whereas in figure 3.7 small investments are held for long periods. In order to determine which of the two policies yielded greater interest, it would be necessary to know the actual amounts of money and time portrayed on the chart and the yield of each possible investment instrument as well as the minimum purchase amount and duration. (See Cozzolino (1971) for a detailed analysis of different investment strategies.)

The major investment instruments open to most educational organizations include: United States government securities, repurchase agreements, savings accounts, and certificates of deposit. Although differing among themselves, these instruments are all considered to meet the needs of investors who are concerned primarily with liquidity and safety and secondarily with yield.

### Treasury Bills

United States government securities include treasury bills, treasury certificates, U.S. bonds, and U.S. agency bonds. Of these, the most widely used are treasury bills. Treasury bills may be purchased through a commercial bank or by direct subscription from the federal treasury, and are usually three- to six-month investments.

On Thursday morning of each week the Federal Reserve issues a press release of the week's offering. It then receives competitive and noncompetitive tenders until the following Monday afternoon. The bids must be in writing and accompanied by a 2 percent down payment. The noncompetitive bids are all accepted. Their price is based on the average price of the competitive bids. The latter are then accepted, highest bid first, until the week's offering is sold (Scott 1965, pp. 31-39; Loll 1967, pp. 51-56).

The interest rates paid on government securities are determined by individual banks' needs for cash or bills as well as the basic fiscal policies of the Federal Reserve. The rates for treasury bills shift in units of one thousandth of 1 percent, but figuring the true interest rate is a rather complicated process. The complication exists because the yield is almost never based on a full year and .01 on a bill that has a year to run is not the same as .01 on a two-day bill. An example of this complexity is provided by Scott (1965, p. 90):

There is a mechanical reason for the fact that bill spreads widen as maturities become shorter. In order to explain this relationship, it is necessary to compute the dollar equivalent of a .01. Suppose that a one-year bill is bid 3.45. The price of a $1,000 denomination is then $965.50. Now suppose the bill sells down to 3.46. The price drops to $965.40. Thus the dollar equivalent of a .01 on a $1,000 bill which has one year to run is 1/100000 (= $0.10). Alternatively, if the bill is quoted at 3.45 and matures tomorrow its price is $999.903889. Therefore if a bill has only one day to run, a one basis-point change in the yield is equivalent to a change of $0.000278 in the price of a $1,000 instrument. In other words, the value of a .01 on a $1,000 denomination with 360 days to run is $0.10; with one day to run it is 1/360 of $0.10, or $0.000278.

Because of the complicated nature of determining this instrument's yield, most treasury bills are bought from banks on a 30-60-90-day basis at the particular discount available from the given trading bank on a given day. As investment instruments, the utility of bills depends on comparative rates between bills and other short-term instruments within the selected period.

## Repurchase Agreements

Repurchase agreements are contracts similar to a loan secured by collateral. The seller (or borrower) of the security continues to receive the interest while the security is owned by the buyer (or lender). At the same time, the seller pays the buyer (e.g., a school district) interest at a rate that is determined by money conditions when the "buyback" occurs. There is no risk of capital loss to the buyer since the repayment price plus interest is stipulated. Essentially the arrangement is a loan of money to the bank in return for a specified interest. Repurchase agreements can be useful for very short-term (including twenty-four hour) investments and can allow precise scheduling of maturities to coincide with the date on which money is needed.

## Savings Accounts

Savings accounts are probably the most common form of investment in our society. At one time many educational organizations held their money solely in demand deposit or checking accounts. This has changed and today many maintain at least small amounts of money in interest-bearing savings accounts.

## Certificates of Deposit

Certificates of deposit or "CDs" are bank instruments which usually have maturities of from one to twelve months although longer CDs are becoming common. They come in negotiable and non-negotiable forms and usually pay an interest rate similar to that of treasury bills. They are issued at face value and redeemed at maturity by the issuing bank.

The above list provides an introduction to the investments frequently used by educational organizations as part of cash planning. Usually interest increases as the riskiness of the investment and its length increase. This general rule can be upset by the rate of inflation and temporary conditions in the money market. The rates for 90-day bills, CDs, and repurchase agreements are similar as these are essentially cash investments. Federal agency bonds often pay more because their market is narrower and the risk is slightly higher (they are backed by the assumption that the treasury would not let them default rather than by the full faith and credit of the federal government). The rates of CDs and other government investments vary with seasonal fluctuations in the market and length of time of the investment. Because of regulatory requirements, selection is limited. It must be determined when idle funds will be needed and what conditions in the local money markets relate to interest on CDs and repurchase agreements.

## Forecasting Cash Flows

Revenue flows into most educational organizations from multiple sources, with varying degrees of uncertainty. State financial assistance for public schools provides an example. In some states, this source of revenue is predictable because districts are notified months in advance of the amount of aid they will receive or, at least, the amount per pupil. In other states, this is an uncertain source of revenue because of last-minute decisions emanating from the state capitol.

Revenues from charges must be estimated not only in terms of demand for the goods or services (e.g., tuition) but also the length of time it takes to turn an invoice into cash through the billing process. There is usually a positive relationship between gross revenue from charges for goods or services and gross expenditures. Consequently, assumptions underlying estimates of revenue also affect the pattern of expenditures.

The degree to which an educational organization is able to forecast large amounts of net cash surpluses depends on a number of related management operations, including billing procedures which speed cash into the organization, and cash handling procedures which speed the flow of cash from receipt to deposit. The speed with which an educational organization pays its bills reduces the amount of excess cash. Immediate payment, however, often entitles the payer to discounts in the bill.

The amount of effort that goes into the short-term investment program of an educational organization should yield its equivalent in financial gain. Because of this, cash planning decisions involve more than comparing investment costs with quoted yields, forecasting investable income, and plotting interest collection dates. Management must also decide whether a better cash planning system could be instituted (through more staff, etc.), whether the resources devoted to cash planning should be curtailed, or whether things are satisfactory the way they are. The answer will depend on whether the additional investment will be more than offset by commensurate gains, or, conversely, whether the advantages of curtailment more than offset the decreased interest.

Various studies on investment of idle funds in school districts report earnings ranging from .3 percent to 2.0 percent of the operating budget (McCanless 1952; Moody 1965; Rothrock 1972). Earning interest at the rate of 1.0 percent on an operating budget of $10 million yields $100,000 for the school district. If the district spent $10,000 in fees, staff time, etc. to earn that $100,000, it would be worth spending twice as much on cash planning if management could raise the average yield from 1.0 percent to at least 1.1 percent.

## Questions for Review and Discussion

1.   List five factors which constrain the amount of investable funds an organization has at its disposal. List three factors which constrain the rate of interest earned on idle funds.

2.   In what ways would cash planning for a private educational organization differ from cash planning for a public educational organization?

3.   Is there any reason to believe that, all other things being equal, educational organizations with large budgets would be able to earn more interest per budget dollar than organizations with small budgets?

4.   What conditions must exist to make it worthwhile to invest small sums of money for long periods?

5.   Which investment instruments are appropriate for investments of short duration?

## References

Cozzolino, John M. "Optimal Scheduling for Investment of Excess Cash." *Decision Sciences* 2, no. 3 (July 1971): 265-83.

Goodman, Sam R. *Financial Manager's Manual and Guide.* Englewood Cliffs, N.J.: Prentice-Hall, 1973.

Law, James E. "Manage Your Funds Properly!" *School Business Affairs* 40, no. 2 (February 1974): 45.

Loll, Leo M., Jr., and Buckley, Julian G. *The Over-the-Counter Securities Markets.* Englewood Cliffs, N.J.: Prentice-Hall, 1967.

McCanless, Clarence A. "The Investment of Idle School Funds." *Proceedings of the Association of School Business Officials of the United States and Canada.* Kalamazoo, Mich.: The Association, 1952.

Moody, Eugene L. "How Lincolnwood, Illinois Earns $32,000 Annually." *Nation's Schools* 76, no. 3 (March 1965): 80.

Rothrock, Paul D. "Results of National Survey of Handling of School Funds." *Report of the West Virginia Association of School Business Officials Legislative Committee* (August 14, 1972). Reported in Sumner, Stephen Isaac. "An Investigation into the Determinants of Rates of Returns on the Investment of Idle Funds in New York State." Ed.D. dissertation, Teachers College, Columbia University, 1974.

Scott, Ira O., Jr. *Government Securities Market.* New York: McGraw-Hill, 1965.

Tidwell, Sam B. *Financial and Managerial Accounting for Elementary and Secondary School Systems.* Chicago: Association of School Business Officials, 1974.

## Related Readings

Baumol, William J. "The Transactions Demand for Cash: An Inventory Theoretic Approach." *Quarterly Journal of Economics* (November 1952).

Hausman, Warren H., and Sanchez-Bell, Antonio. "The Stochastic Cash Balance Problem with Average Compensating-Balance Requirements." *Management Science* 21, no. 8 (April 1975): 849-57. A highly technical yet thorough treatment of a cash planning model. It includes formal consideration of uncertainty as well as costs associated with transferring assets from one form to another and with holding compensating balances.

Hulkover, William. "How to Turn Your Debt-Service Dollars into Profits." *School Management* 8, no. 4 (April 1964): 119. This article describes how to schedule the repayment of bonds in such a way as to earn maximum interest.

Matzer, John, Jr. "Determining Cash Available for Investment." *Municipal Finance* XLI, no. 41 (August 1968): 59-67. This nontechnical article describes the use of fixed ratios between active and inactive accounts which have been developed by municipal finance offices. These ratios provide benchmarks against which to evaluate an investment program.

Schaerer, Robert W. "How Gary, Indiana, Invests Idle Funds, Earns Thousands." *Nation's Schools* LXXVI, no. 76 (October 1965): 78-79. This nontechnical article describes how the district borrowed money by marketing an instrument called a tax anticipation note, and by reinvesting that money at a higher rate.

Sumner, Stephen Isaac. "An Investigation Into the Determinants of Rates of Return on the Investment of Idle Funds in New York State." Ed.D. dissertation, Teachers College, Columbia University, 1974. A study of factors that determine why some school districts earn large amounts of interest from idle funds while others earn little or none. It also provides a summary of similar studies of school districts.

# 4

# Risk Management

It is impossible to avoid completely the risk of unplanned financial loss. Educational managers should assess the probability of loss, estimate its consequences, determine the cost of hedging against loss, and, finally, minimize financial loss. It is seldom possible to make decisions consistently certain to yield the greatest financial gain. The first section of this chapter reviews some fundamental concepts about uncertainty and how they are incorporated into management decisions. The second section focuses on risks which could result in serious financial loss, and provides a general taxonomy of means for controlling them. The third section deals with the interface between high level management policies and operational level decisions affecting risk management programs.

## Theoretical Foundations

Many fundamental concepts of risk management derive from assessing probabilities and determining the impact of possible events on possible managerial acts. While the unit of measurement is often stated in dollars lost or gained, other criteria are also relevant. These concepts are discussed separately below.

### Probability

Probabilities fall into two basic categories, objective and subjective. *Objective probability* is based on historical evidence and common (objective) experience. For example, based on data showing the number of student lunches sold over the last two months, there is a 90 percent probability that between 520 and 580 lunches will be sold tomorrow.

Frequently, however, historical evidence is not available for decision making. In such cases the educational manager must assess the situation and the likelihood of the various possible outcomes. Such an estimate is known as *subjective probability.*

When probabilities are assigned to the possible outcomes of events, they must be mutually exclusive and collectively exhaustive. Consider, for example, the event of a budget election. The two possible outcomes of the budget election are that it passes or fails. These outcomes are mutually exclusive because the occurrence of one precludes the existence of the other; they are collectively exhaustive because no other outcome is possible.

In addition, probabilities can be classified as *independent* or *dependent.* When events are statistically independent, the occurrence of one event has no effect on the probability of the occurrence of another event. For example, the probability of a school bus being in a traffic accident is independent of the probability of a chemistry lab catching on fire.

Statistical dependence exists when the probability of one event is dependent on the occurrence of another event. For example, if Biology I is a prerequisite for Biology II, both are electives, and I is offered in the fall and II in the spring semester, the probability of a sufficient number of students electing Biology II is dependent on the probability that at least that number are previously enrolled in Biology I.

Statistically independent and dependent events both have three types of probabilities associated with them: *marginal, joint,* and *conditional* probabilities. Marginal probability is the simple probability of occurrence of an event. It is symbolized as $P(A)$, the probability of event A occurring, and is the same for independently and dependently occurring events.

Joint probability defines the probability of two or more events occurring together or in succession. The joint probability of two or more independent events is the product of their marginal probabilities. This is described symbolically as:

$$P(AB) = P(A) \times P(B).$$

In this equation $P(AB)$ is the probability of events A and B occurring together or in succession (joint probability), $P(A)$ is the marginal probability of event A occurring, and $P(B)$ is the marginal probability of event B occurring.

Returning to an earlier example, the probability of both a bus accident and a chemistry lab fire occurring within one year is the product of the probabilities of occurrence of each event. If the probability of a bus accident is .002 and the probability of a chemistry lab fire is .010, the probability of both occurring at the same time is:

$$.002 \times .010 = .00002.$$

The joint probability of dependent events is calculated differently with the following formula:

$$P(AB) = P(A/B) \times P(B).$$

This equation is read "the joint probability of events A and B equals the probability of event A, given that event B has occurred, times the probability of event B." Using the biology course example, assume that the probability of a sufficient number of students enrolling in Biology I is .60. Assume further that the probability of a sufficient number of students enrolling in Biology II is .70, if a sufficient number enrolled in Biology I, and only .10 if a sufficient number did not enroll in Biology I. The joint probability of a sufficient number enrolling in both courses is the probability that a sufficient number will enroll in Biology II, given sufficient enrollment in Biology I, times the probability of sufficient enrollment in Biology I:

$$.70 \times .60 = .42.$$

Conditional probabilities are different from both marginal and joint probabilities. Symbolically, conditional probability is written as $P(A/B)$ and is read "the probability of event A, given that event B has occurred." For statistically independent events, the conditional probability of event A given that event B has occurred is simply the probability of event A. However, for dependent events, the appropriate formula for conditional probabilities is:

$$P(A/B) = \frac{P(AB)}{P(B)} .$$

This is read "the probability of A given B equals the probability of both A and B occurring (joint probability) divided by the (marginal) probability of B." Using the biology courses example again, the probability of Biology II enrolling sufficient numbers (given that Biology I has enrolled sufficient numbers) equals the probability of both courses enrolling sufficient numbers (.42) divided by the probability of Biology I enrolling sufficient numbers (.70). The types of probabilities are summarized in table 4.1.

## Table 4.1: Probabilities Under Statistical Independence and Dependence

| Type of probability | Symbol | Formula under statistical independence | Formula under statistical dependence |
|---|---|---|---|
| Marginal | P(A) | P(A) | P(A) |
| Joint | P(AB) | P(A) $\times$ P(B) | P(A/B) $\times$ P(B) |
| Conditional | P(A/B) | P(A) | P(AB)/P(B) |

The ability to distinguish among types of probabilities is no less important than the ability to develop probability estimates when structuring many management decisions, especially those involving high risk. This point is illustrated by the following passage:

Most accidents in well-designed systems involve two or more events of low probability occurring in the worst possible combination. A typical aircraft-accident investigation, for example, might show that a mechanic forgot to install a safety washer so that the nut worked loose; that it happened to work loose during extremely bad weather which caused an excessive amount of fuel to be used; and that the pilot showed poor judgment. When people make predictions about the successful operation of a system, and the system then fails dramatically and embarrassingly in contradistinction to those predictions, the reason is usually that the predictor has not considered the combination of events which will cause the system to fail. Explicitly or implicitly, people multiply together probabilities of events of low probability and come out with impossibly small numbers when in fact the events are dependent. The reason that nut worked loose was because the airplane was buffeted by bad weather; the reason the pilot exercised bad judgment was because he was under an unusual amount of stress (Machol 1975, p. 53).

## Conditional Values

*Event* has been used so far to describe an occurrence of some type; a clearer distinction is needed now. An event may be an act of nature, over which management has no direct control, or it may be a management act. For example, an event may be the number of cases of milk purchased through the student cafeteria at a university (Bierman, Bonini, and Hausman 1973, pp. 45-54). Assume that available data make possible an objective determination of the probabilities of four levels of demand. These data are presented in table 4.2.

In this example, assume that the food service manager knows that

## Table 4.2: Demand for Cases of Milk in a University Cafeteria

| Event: total demand per day (cases) | Number of days each demand level was recorded | Probability of each event |
|---|---|---|
| 25 | 20 | 0.10 |
| 26 | 60 | 0.30 |
| 27 | 100 | 0.50 |
| 28 | 20 | 0.10 |
|  | 200 | 1.00 |

a $2 profit can be earned on every case that is sold, while an $8 loss is incurred on every case bought but not sold. From this information and the data in table 4.2 it is possible to construct a table of conditional profits as in table 4.3. Corresponding to each action taken by

## Table 4.3: Conditional Values (Profits for Different Stocking Decisions and Different Levels of Demand)

| Possible demand (in cases) | Possible actions | | | |
|---|---|---|---|---|
|  | Stock 25 | Stock 26 | Stock 27 | Stock 28 |
| 25 | $50 | $42 | $34 | $26 |
| 26 | 50 | 52 | 44 | 36 |
| 27 | 50 | 52 | 54 | 46 |
| 28 | 50 | 52 | 54 | 56 |

the food service director, and to each event that occurs, there is a conditional profit. If the manager stocks twenty-five cases of milk, he can sell only twenty-five cases, even if the demand is for twenty-eight cases. The food service manager can earn as much as $56 or as little as $26 profit, depending on what he chooses to do and what happens.

By considering the impact of the various interactions between acts and events as shown in table 4.3, the manager can assess the relative advantages of different decisions. How these impacts are calculated, however, can influence the decision. For example, instead of presenting the outcomes as conditional profits, they could be presented in terms of conditional opportunity losses. An *opportunity loss* can be defined as the amount of profit foregone by not choosing the best act for each event. For example, consider the act of stocking twenty-eight cases of milk. If demand turns out to be twenty-eight, the food service manager will make the maximum profit of $56. If he had stocked only twenty-seven, he would have made $54; this act would entail a $2 opportunity loss. If he had stocked twenty-seven with a demand of twenty-six he would have incurred an $8 opportunity loss. These opportunity losses are shown in table 4.4.

**Table 4.4: Conditional Opportunity Losses for Different Stocking Decisions and Different Levels of Demand**

| Possible demand (in cases) | Possible actions | | | |
|---|---|---|---|---|
| | Stock 25 | Stock 26 | Stock 27 | Stock 28 |
| 25 | $0 | $8 | $16 | $24 |
| 26 | 2 | 0 | 8 | 16 |
| 27 | 4 | 2 | 0 | 8 |
| 28 | 6 | 4 | 2 | 0 |

## Expected Monetary Value

Even though the conditional values and opportunity losses help characterize the problem facing the food service manager, he must do more with the existing data to determine an optimum solution. He would choose the best act if he knew how many cases of milk would be demanded tomorrow, but this information is not available. To forecast the event and then choose an act consistent with the forecast, he must analyze the assigned probabilities. This is accomplished by weighing the conditional values of each event in the conditional value table by the probability of the event occurring, and adding the products for each act. The resulting number is the expected monetary value of that act. The optimum act is the one with the highest expected monetary value. The calculations for the act of stocking twenty-six cases of milk are shown in table 4.5. The calculations for twenty-five, twenty-seven, and twenty-eight are similar.

**Table 4.5: Calculating Expected Monetary Value for the Act of Stocking Twenty-Six Cases**

| Possible demand (in cases) | Probability of the event | Conditional value (profit) | Expected value (conditional value times probability) |
|---|---|---|---|
| 25 | 0.10 | $42 | $ 4.20 |
| 26 | 0.30 | 52 | 15.60 |
| 27 | 0.50 | 52 | 26.00 |
| 28 | 0.10 | 52 | 5.20 |
| | Expected monetary value of stocking 27 cases = | | $51.00 |

The expected monetary values for all four acts are presented in table 4.6, where the act of stocking twenty-six cases is shown to be optimum. Using the same general procedure, it is also possible to calculate expected opportunity losses.

## Table 4.6: Expected Monetary Value of Each Act Under Consideration

| Act | Expected monetary value |
|---|---|
| Stock 25 | $50 |
| Stock 26 | 51 (Optimum act) |
| Stock 27 | 49 |
| Stock 28 | 42 |

## Expected Monetary Value vs. Utility

One of the reasons why expected monetary value is so often used in financial decision making is that it usually coincides with a manager's notion of utility. However, there are circumstances under which expected monetary value is not an adequate criterion for decision making. Greatest financial utility may not coincide with the decision yielding the highest expected monetary value. For example, consider a small college which has built a new facility worth $1 million. Suppose that there is only one chance in 1,000 (.001) that it will burn down this year. From these two figures we can compute the expected loss:

$$.001 \times \$1,000,000 = \$1,000 = \text{expected loss.}$$

Now suppose that the business manager of the college finds out that the building can be insured for no less than $1,250. Strict use of the notion of minimizing expected losses would dictate that the business manager refuse to insure the building. But, if the business manager felt that a million dollar uninsured loss would virtually wipe out the college, he would very probably discard monetary value as his decision criterion and buy the insurance at an extra cost of $250 per year per policy. He would choose not to minimize expected loss in this case but to maximize expected utility. In this sense, utility refers to the pleasure or displeasure anticipated from certain outcomes.

Whether expected monetary value or utility is the best criterion for a financial decision is not easy to determine; it depends in large part on the situation and the individual making the decision. This complex interaction is illustrated by an example drawn from Levin and Kirkpatrick.

The utility curves of three different businessmen for a decision are shown in figure 4.7. We have arbitrarily named these individuals

## Figure 4.7: Utility Curves of Three Businessmen

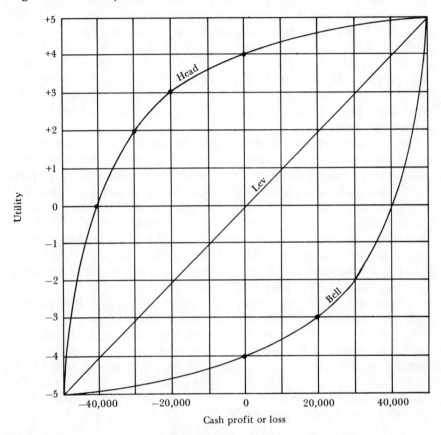

Cash profit or loss

Source: Richard I. Levin and Charles A. Kirkpatrick, *Quantitative Approaches to Management* (New York: McGraw-Hill, 1975), p. 138. Reprinted by permission.

Head, Bell, and Lev. Their attitudes are readily apparent from analysis of their utility curves. Head is a cautious and conservative businessman; a move to the right of the zero profit point increases his utility only very slightly whereas a move to the left of zero profit point decreases his utility rapidly. In terms of numerical values,

Head's utility curve indicates that going from $0 to $50,000 profit increases his utility by a value of 1 on the vertical scale, while moving into the loss range by only $20,000 decreases his utility by the same value of 1 on the vertical scale. Head will avoid situations where high losses might occur; he is averse to risk.

Bell is quite another story. We see from his utility curve that a profit increases his utility by much more than a loss of the same amount decreases it. Specifically, increasing his profits $10,000 (from $40,000 to $50,000) raises his utility from 0 to +5 on the vertical scale, but lowering his profits $10,000 (from $0 to −$10,000) decreases his utility by only .25, from −4 to −4.25. Bell is a player of long shots; he feels strongly that a large loss would not make things much worse than they are now but, on the contrary, that a big profit would be quite rewarding. He will take large risks to earn larger gains.

Lev, fairly well off financially, is the kind of businessman who would not suffer greatly from a $50,000 loss or increase his wealth significantly from a $50,000 gain. He would get about as much pleasure from making an additional $50,000 as he would pain from losing $50,000. Lev's utility curve is linear, he can effectively use expected monetary value as his decision criterion, whereas Head and Bell must use utility. In summary, Lev will act where the expected monetary value is positive, Head will demand a high expected value for the outcome, and Bell may act when the expected value is negative (Levin and Kirkpatrick 1975, pp. 137-39).

In addition to expected monetary value and utility, there are several other decision rules used by managers. One such rule is to determine the smallest possible gain for each act and pick the one for which the small gain is largest (a *maximin strategy*). Another is to determine the highest possible gain and select the action which results in that gain (a *maximax strategy*). A third is to determine the largest possible loss and pick the action for which the largest loss is the least (a *minimax regret strategy*).

## Methods for Controlling Risks

The number and kinds of risks resulting in loss are limitless. Fortunately the great majority are either trivial (e.g., the risk of getting caught in the rain without an umbrella) or have an extremely low probability of occurring (e.g., the risk of a giant fissure in the earth opening right under you). It would be just as uneconomical (and, of course, foolish) for management to concern itself with all possible risks as it would be to ignore all possible risks. In the middle ground there are risks that either occur often enough or are serious enough to require the attention of educational managers.

Most of these risks involve the possibility of loss of earning power or loss of property. Loss of property can result from a variety of causes including destruction or damage, dishonesty, failure of others, and legal liability. Just as there are a variety of risks (fire, liability, theft, etc.), there are a variety of methods for controlling them. Control strategies are designed to (1) avoid risk, (2) reduce risk, (3) assume risk, and (4) shift risk.

## Avoiding Risk

Educational organizations can avoid some risks that are too high in relation to the expected gain by means of substitution, screening, and elimination. For example, the risk of loss of breakable toys in a primary school can be avoided by providing suitable substitutes which are not breakable. The risk of damage to industrial arts machinery can be avoided by allowing only faculty to set up and start the machinery (screening). The risk of a giant post-football game bonfire burning down an adjacent dormitory can be averted by not permitting it to occur (elimination).

## Reducing Risk

Many unavoidable risks can be reduced. General methods for reducing risks might be termed "good management practices." Examples of such practices include the following:

(1) Perform regular inspections (see examples of building inspection forms in Hill and Colmey (1964, pp. 218-20));

(2) Work closely with the safety engineer and claims investigators of the insurance company if the organization carries liability insurance;

(3) Meet and work with safety committees;

(4) Maintain liaison with the health-services unit of the organization to check first-aid supplies and procedures;

(5) Coordinate activities with supplies and equipment personnel to prevent unsafe or unauthorized equipment being placed in use;

(6) Expedite corrective measures following reports of accidents;

(7) Supervise maintenance of accident records and statistics and the distribution of safety material to all personnel;

(8) Assist in the safety training of new personnel in all areas of school activity;

(9) Anticipate unusual hazards connected with "one-of-a-kind" construction or other activities, and set up special safety regulations affecting the particular activity;

(10) Assist in establishing standards governing the hiring and training of transportation and other personnel;

(11) Participate in review committees to evaluate all vehicle and other accidents (Allen 1965, p. 60).

Even if the risk of loss is shifted to insurance or elsewhere, management still has the opportunity to reduce risks in order to avoid excessive insurance premiums.

## Assuming Risk

Risks may be assumed by self-insurance. Funds may be set aside to cover certain potential risks. For example, educational organizations are sometimes permitted to establish a sinking fund to insure a building against fire and other losses. Such a strategy is feasible for an educational organization with many geographically separated facilities, but not one with a few buildings clustered together. For large multiplant educational organizations the amount of money set aside for replacing a single building may be sufficient, because the probability of more than one facility burning at the same time is slight.

## Shifting Risk

A fourth method for controlling risks in educational organizations is to shift them. While the most common method for shifting risks is through insurance, there are at least two additional strategies: hedging and subcontracting. One risk often encountered is unexpected changes in the prices of goods needed in the future. By agreeing to purchase a specified amount of goods at a specified future date at a given price (hedging), the organization is able to ensure that the price will not change. A similar end is gained by subcontracting at a fixed fee (e.g., for food service). (Hedging and subcontracting are discussed in greater detail in Pickle and Abrahamson (1974).)

Insurance is the most common means of shifting risks for several reasons. First, many educational organizations are required by local and state regulations to carry particular kinds of insurance in particular amounts. Second, there are large numbers of risks which insurance firms are willing to assume for a fee. In exchange for premiums, the insurance company agrees to sustain all or part of various losses. Each educational organization must analyze its risks and the cost of shifting the risks to insurance companies to decide what insurance coverage to buy and how much of the loss to shift.

The common categories of insurance are life, disability, fire, other property loss, transportation, liability, theft and fidelity, and surety. While most of these terms are self-explanatory, the last four require further explanation. The liability of an educational organization arises from claims against it resulting largely from accidents due to negligence, and is covered by liability insurance. Surety and fidelity coverage is often purchased in the form of bonds. Although bonds are not technically insurance, for purposes of administration they may be considered insurance against loss through larceny. These bonds share the basic principle of insurance, in that the surety (the insuring company) promises to recompense the beneficiary (the educational organization) if the principal (the employee or contractor) fails to perform his obligations.

Different types of insurance are provided for different types of risks because the odds associated with the risks and the amounts involved are different. The relationships between types of risks and the major types of insurance are shown in figure 4.8.

## Figure 4.8: Relationship Between Types of Risks and Types of Insurance

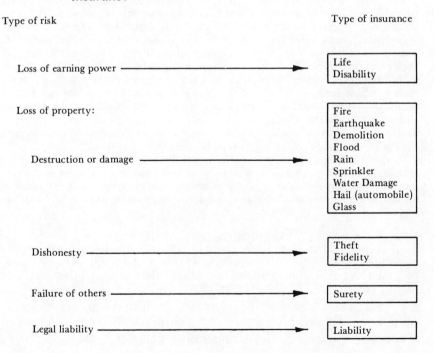

| Type of risk | Type of insurance |
|---|---|
| Loss of earning power ⟶ | Life / Disability |
| Loss of property: | Fire / Earthquake / Demolition / Flood / Rain / Sprinkler / Water Damage / Hail (automobile) / Glass |
| Destruction or damage ⟶ | |
| Dishonesty ⟶ | Theft / Fidelity |
| Failure of others ⟶ | Surety |
| Legal liability ⟶ | Liability |

## Developing Risk Management Policies and Procedures

Knowledge of the theoretical foundations of assessing risks as well as of the general strategies for controlling risks are necessary but not sufficient prerequisites for managing risks. Operations of this kind are governed by various sets of rules, three of which are discussed here: organizational policies, administrative guidelines, and professionally recognized procedures.

### Organizational Policies

The risk management policies of an educational organization will affix responsibility for carrying out the risk management program, and commit the organization to provide the necessary resources. An example of such a policy statement for a school district is provided below:

The governing board shall provide for a program of risk management for this school district consistent with all of the legal requirements pretaining thereto and consistent with the financial ability of the district to finance. The board shall purchase with district funds the type and amount of insurance necessary or shall set aside adequate reserves to self-insure in order to protect itself as a corporate body, its individual members, its appointed officers, and its employees from financial loss arising out of any claim, demand, suit or judgment by reason of alleged negligence or other act resulting in accidental injury to any person or in property damage within or without the school buildings while the above named insured are acting in the discharge of their duties within the scope of their employment and/or under the direction of the board.

Furthermore, within its program of risk management the governing board shall purchase from district funds the type and amount of insurance coverage to insure and/or self-insure all real and personal property of the district, to insure and/or self-insure the district from losses due to employee dishonesty, injury or death, and to provide a program of health and welfare benefits for employees to the limits established from time to time by the governing board.

Within the scope of this policy, the superintendent is directed to develop and maintain rules and regulations necessary for carrying out all aspects of this policy including the designation of the district employee responsible for administration and supervision of the risk management program. (Crockett 1975, pp. 131-32)

### Administrative Guidelines

Policy statements often do not provide a sufficient base on which to construct risk management operations that are unambiguous and comprehensive. In such cases, administrative regulations or guidelines are developed which describe in greater detail the scope and function of risk management operations. The precise differences between board-level policies and administrative guidelines are not always clear. The former are usually more goal oriented, while the latter define specific behaviors. As an analogy, a policy on safety in the use of book matches would read "safety first," whereas an administrative guideline might read "close cover before striking."

Administrative regulations deal with broad issues relating to managerial control of the risk management program, restrictions on methods of placing insurance, descriptions of the kinds of insurance authorized, determination of value to be insured, settlement of losses, and procedures for settling liability claims. An example of the specific clauses contained in administrative regulations for a school district's risk management program is included below:

Management and Control of District's Risk Management Program. The management and control of the district's risk management and any and all insurance authorized by the governing board shall be a function of the Business Division through such staff allocation of responsibilities as the assistant superintendent/ business services shall designate. The assistant superintendent for business services or his designated assistant shall be the risk manager for the district. The risk manager shall have authority to establish rules and procedures, consistent with board policy, to insure the safety and well being of pupils, employees and the public while on or in school district property that will aid in keeping the district's liability to a minimum and the premiums for insurance as low as possible consistent with the insurance requirements and the risks to be insured.

Placement of Insurance. The assistant superintendent for business services, through the superintendent, shall recommend to the governing board, and the governing board shall appoint a Broker-of-Record to assist and advise the district in the placement of insurance in each major line of insurance including fire, liability, fidelity, casualty and employee health and welfare benefits. Such appointment shall be effective until withdrawn or superseded by action of the board .... The risk manager shall report the need for insurance, together with all relevant information including statements of costs obtained by the broker-of-record from insurance companies, and his recommendation for the placing of such insurance to the superintendent who shall present his recommendations to the governing board. Upon authorization by the governing board, the risk manager, in cooperation with the broker-of-record shall place such insurance in accordance with said authorization and the relevant provisions of these rules and regulations.

In an emergency, the risk manager shall place insurance and the superintendent shall immediately report such placement for ratification by the governing board. Insurance carried by the governing board shall be obtained through negotiation, and when deemed necessary and to the best interests of the district, by competitive bids and shall be awarded to those insurance companies who agree to furnish the coverage required by the lowest and best price consistent with good service and security.

Kinds of Insurance Authorized. The following insurance shall be carried in accordance with applicable rules and regulations: fire and extended coverage insurance covering all buildings ... fidelity bonds ... workmen's compensation ... casualty, fire and theft insurance covering all vehicles ... burglary and robbery insurance ... boiler and pressure vessel property damage insurance ...

sprinkler leakage insurance . . . programs of insurance in the area of employee
fringe benefits . . . [and] such other insurance coverage as the governing board
may authorize. . . .
Settlement of Losses. When any property covered by insurance is lost, damaged,
or destroyed, a notice concerning the loss shall be sent immediately to all affected carriers to their representatives. The risk manager shall act as adjuster for
the governing board in the settlement of losses and he shall sign Proof of Loss as
authorized. The superintendent shall recommend to the governing board, as soon
as practicable, a basis for settlement and, upon adoption by the governing board,
the agreed amounts shall be collected from the insurance company(ies) and deposited to the credit of the district in accordance with the laws governing such
collection.
Liability Claims Procedure. A written notice of rejection shall be sent to the
claimant in all cases where a written claim has been filed in accordance with the
laws of the state governing the filing of such claims and the school district's liability insurance carrier has advised the district in writing that the claim has been
rejected. Such rejections shall be reported to the governing board by the superintendent for board approval. (Crockett 1975, pp. 132-33)

As is evident from this example, administrative regulations often
place great emphasis on establishing procedures for operations. Beyond broad procedural guidelines, however, top management must
rely on the technical competence of the risk manager. While able to
call on staff support from other departments, the risk manager usually assumes responsibility for determining the nature of that support.

## Professionally Recognized Procedures

A third set of general rules influences the nature of risk management. These emanate from the risk manager's professional peer group
and are the result of specialized practices and established conditions
in the profession. Two important procedures involve property valuation, and are used as examples here: insurable value vs. replacement
cost and co-insurance.

### Insurable Value vs. Replacement Cost

One of the basic tasks of the risk manager is to determine the
value of property in the organization. If the assessment is too high,
there is an unnecessary premium expenditure for excessive coverage.
If the assessment is too low and, for example, a fire loss occurs, the
insuring organization may not compensate the educational organization at the full amount of the policy (by invoking, for example, a
co-insurance penalty).

Most property depreciates. Various items depreciate at different
rates, for example, from six months to twenty-five years. While there
are many possible methods of calculating depreciation the accepted

practice in the profession is to average out the varying degrees of depreciation by taking a flat 25 percent depreciation on all personal property and insuring all equipment at 75 percent of the current replacement value (Allen 1965, p. 26). Since the insured equipment is used, it is not expected that the replacement cost can be recovered in full from the insurance carrier in the event of a loss. If the equipment is older than the average indicated, a correspondingly greater amount of depreciation should be taken. Recovery from the insurance carrier is in accordance with the amount of depreciation taken.

Similarly, the most common method of writing fire insurance is based on insurable value. This represents the replacement cost of the property less depreciation. For commercial properties this method is usually satisfactory, since depreciation is charged as a part of costs, and reserves may be set up to cover the cost. Many educational organizations, especially publically financed one, are faced with different constraints. Although properties should be depreciated each year, there is often no fund provided to cover depreciation or the added expense of replacing a building lost in a fire. Further, the utility of an older educational facility may represent greater value than that of a commercial structure. Consequently, one of the recommended practices in the profession is to insure at least part of the facilities on a replacement basis, without an allowance for depreciation (Allen 1965, p. 39).

## Co-insurance

Commonly accepted practices of the profession have been influenced by practices of insurance agencies. One example is the use of co-insurance penalties. This is a penalty that may be assessed by the insurance company in the settlement of a fire loss when fire insurance is not equal to a stated percentage of the total value of the insured property.

The mechanics of a co-insurance clause are summarized briefly as follows:

Fire-insurance rates are based on the assumption that insurance will be carried up to a reasonable proportion of the property value. It is recognized that most fire losses are partial losses, and many persons would be tempted to insure only that part of their property that they would expect to lose in a fire. This would leave them unprotected against the less likely, but always possible, severe or total loss, and would also act as a penalty to those persons who properly insure up to a reasonable proportion of value. Rating schedules have been set up to provide a sliding scale or decreasing charge per $100 of value according to the percentage of value insured. The rate per $100 of value under an average clause or co-insurance agreement of 90 per cent is less than that under an agreement of

70 per cent or less. Obviously, a greater amount of insurance must be carried, but the insured receives the added protection against the large loss along with the rate credit. The responsibility for deciding the total value of the property is generally left to the insured.

Except for providing a lower rate on the insurance, the average or co-insurance clause is inoperative until a loss occurs. At the time of a loss, the insurance carrier will determine the total value of the property insured and compare this with the amount of insurance carried and the co-insurance percentage. If the amount of insurance is not sufficient, a penalty is assessed based on the following formula:

$$\frac{\text{Amount of insurance}}{\text{Amount of insurance that should be carried}} \times$$

$$\text{Amount of loss} = \text{Liability of company}$$

(Allen 1965, p. 33)

Accepted operating procedures are another source of guidance (and constraint) in the operations of risk management. In addition to working within this loose network of rules and procedures, risk managers will occasionally need to reconcile differences arising from different perspectives of the risk management problem in a particular organization.

## Questions for Review and Discussion

1.   Under what conditions is it advisable to incur the cost of gathering historical information in order to assess the probable outcomes of a particular event?

2.   In assessing the potential risks of financial loss, are there situations where it would be difficult to determine whether the probabilities derived were independent or dependent? If so, give an example.

3.   List several decisions made by educational managers which would be more usefully modeled in terms of conditional profits as opposed to conditional opportunity losses. What factors enter into the decision to model a problem in terms of conditional opportunity losses instead of conditional profits?

4.   Would the concept of utility (as opposed to expected monetary value) ever enter into a decision situation where all the possible outcomes represented some net gain to the decision maker?

5.   What criteria would be useful in determining whether a risk was unavoidable?

6.   Are there any reasons to believe that, other things being equal, smaller educational organizations pay more in property insurance loss (per amount of property valuation) than larger ones?

7. In what specific ways do risk management policies, administrative guidelines, and accepted professional practices differ? How are the purposes of each different?

## References

Allen, Clifford H. *School Insurance Administration.* New York: Macmillan, 1965.

Bierman, Harold; Bonini, Charles; and Hausman, Warren. *Quantitative Analysis for Business Decisions.* Homewood, Ill.: Richard D. Irwin, 1973.

Crockett, James E. "Risk Management and School Insurance Policy Guide." *School Business Affairs* 41, no. 6 (June 1975): pp. 131-34.

Hill, Frederick W., and Colmey, James W. *School Business Administration.* Minneapolis: T. S. Denison, 1964, chap. 12.

Levin, Richard I., and Kirkpatrick, Charles A. *Quantitative Approaches to Management.* New York: McGraw-Hill, 1975.

Machol, Robert. "The Titanic Coincidence." *Interfaces* 5, no. 3 (May 1975): pp. 53-54.

Pickle, Hal B., and Abrahamson, Royce L. *Introduction to Business.* Pacific Palisades, Calif.: Goodyear Publishing Company, 1974.

## Related Readings

American Council on Education. *College and University Business Administration.* Washington, D.C.: The Council, 1968, chap. 7. Provides a general discussion on the kinds of insurance required in institutions of higher education.

Barkdull, Charles W. "Indirect Cost Rates: A New Tool for School Administrators." *School Business Affairs* 40, no. 10 (October 1974): pp. 243-46.

Barkdull, Charles W. "Indirect Costs—Part Two." *School Business Affairs* 40, no. 11 (November 1974): pp. 270-73. Describes how indirect costing techniques can be used to increase efficiency and reduce costs in school operations.

Jewell, William S. "Operations Research in the Insurance Industry, I, A Survey of Applications." *Operations Research* 22, no. 5 (September-October 1974): pp. 917-28. Provides an excellent review of how quantitative analysis has been applied in insurance operations, including an extensive bibliography.

Jewell, William S.; Johnston, Tom L.; and Leavitt, Stephen S. "Operations Research in the Insurance Industry, II, An Application in Claims Operations of Workmen's Compensation Insurance." *Operations Research* 22, no. 5 (September-October 1974): pp. 929-41. Describes the investigative studies and their conclusions; outlines the systems design and implementation; and gives a sample of the validation studies. Implementation of the "proprietary claims-management system" described has provided dramatic reductions in case durations and paid dollar losses, while returning the injured worker to his ultimate level of rehabilitation in a shorter time.

Linn, Henry H., and Joyner, Schuyler C. *Insurance Practices in School Administration.* New York: Ronald Press, 1952. Although limited in its treatment of analytical techniques and dated with reference to applicable regulations, this text provides a comprehensive treatment of insurance practices in public elementary-secondary schools and is replete with thought-provoking discussion of insurance issues.

Reason, Paul L., and Tankard, George G., Jr. *Property Accounting for Local and State School Systems*. Washington, D.C.: U.S. Government Printing Office, 1966. Provides a taxonomy for categorizing real property in school districts and discusses measures of property value.

Rossell, James H., and Frasure, William W. *Managerial Accounting*. Columbus, Ohio: Charles E. Merrill Books, 1964, chap. 6. Provides a comprehensive discussion of major issues and methods of property valuation, including methods of assessing depreciation.

# PART II

# LOGISTICAL SYSTEMS

# 5
# Supply Management

What does the term *logistics* mean, particularly when applied to the educational enterprise? The military provides a likely origin of the term. Together with tactics and strategies, logistics is one of the three major functions of the military mission. Military logistics has been defined as "the process by which human effort and facilitating resources are directed toward the objective of creating and supporting combat forces and weapons" (James L. Quinn, quoted in Heskett; Glaskowski; and Ivie 1973, p. 25). In adopting logistics management concepts from the military, business has also adapted such concepts to meet somewhat different needs. Logistics, as a function of the business enterprise, devotes primary attention to the movement and storage of products and supplies and is concerned only incidentally, if at all, with the movement of people. Indeed, business logistics has been defined as "all activities which facilitate product movement and the coordination of supply and demand in the creation of time and place utility in goods" (James L. Quinn, quoted in Heskett; Glaskowski; and Ivie 1973, p. 25).

As public enterprises, such as schools, have adopted logistics management concepts from business, the concept of logistics has evolved again. Its meaning in education is broader, as in the military. For purposes of this discussion, educational logistics can be defined as the process by which human effort and facilitating resources are directed toward the objective of supporting the operation of instructional programs.

In operating elementary-secondary instructional programs, four distinct, but highly interrelated, logistical subsystems serve to provide this necessary support: supply (or materials) management, maintenance, student transportation, and food service. (Educational logistics as a concept could be expanded to include an even wider range of management activities in education, such as staffing, budgeting, and capital planning. To do so, however, would have the effect of blurring the distinction between the activities that are supportive of operations and the large number of other management tasks.)

Supply management involves those processes whereby the materials required for operations are provided. Maintenance involves the processes of keeping the things required for operations in working order. Student transportation involves the processes of getting children to and from the sites of instructional programs, and food service, the processes for satisfying the nutritional needs of children while on site.

Supply management, once a relatively minor function in educational institutions, has increased greatly in size and importance. In New York State, for example, elementary-secondary purchasing costs rose from $92 million in 1955 to $360 million in 1968-1969. Given this increase in consumption patterns, enrollments, and purchase prices, it is estimated that costs will rise to $1 billion by 1980. This includes general fund, capital fund, and school lunch fund expenditures for equipment, supplies, materials, and school lunch food purchases. These figures exclude New York City (Peat, Marwick, Mitchell 1971, p. V-1).

Supply management includes or is otherwise heavily involved in a range of operations such as ordering, purchasing, bidding, warehousing, distributing, and accounting. Each of these operations is itself the subject of entire books. In a brief treatment of supply management in education, the most useful topics to discuss are those that best illuminate areas of relevant consideration for educational managers and that provide a basis for further inquiry elsewhere. Three such topics are discussed here: (1) theoretical foundations of supply management; (2) evaluating alternative organizational arrangements for supply management; and (3) operating supply management systems in education organizations.

## Theoretical Foundations

Much of the theory in supply management has stemmed from trying to answer two basic questions: *how much* to order at one time, and *when* to order it.

Management decisions are made within a context of competing goals and pressures, and inventory decisions are no exception. For example, one pressure is to order huge lots so as to minimize *order-*

*ing costs.* A counterveiling pressure is to order small lots so as to minimize *carrying costs.* If pushed too far, either of these courses will have an unfavorable effect on costs incurred in supply management. The optimum course of action is a compromise between the two extremes. By using some basic analytical tools (drawn mainly from operations research), it is possible to arrive at a model for deriving the *economic order quantity.* EOQ is that size order that minimizes total annual cost of ordering and carrying inventory. To discuss EOQ, ordering costs and carrying costs must first be described in more detail.

## Ordering Costs

Ordering costs are basically the costs of getting an item into a school district's inventory. They are incurred each time an order is placed and are expressed as a dollar-cost per order. Ordering costs start with the requisition sent to the purchasing office and include the costs of issuing the purchase order and of following it up; they continue with such steps as receiving the goods and placing them into inventory; and they end with the district paying the supplier. Salaries constitute the major ordering cost; stationery is another ordering cost.

To analyze ordering costs, *incremental costs* per order must also be known. This is the ratio of the additional dollar cost from one number of orders to another, larger number, divided by the difference between the two numbers of orders. (In the example discussed below, the numbers of orders examined are 3,000 and 5,000.) Securing incremental and ordering costs requires cost estimates from the purchasing department, from the receiving warehouse, and from the accounting office covering their operations on at least two different levels of operation. In the example in table 5.1, operational costs are estimated for 3,000 orders per year and for 5,000 orders per year. The additional 2,000 orders are estimated to cost an additional $38,500 (or $19.25 per *additional* or incremental order); whereas the *average* costs per order drop from $28.15 to $24.59. These two points of observation (estimates at 3,000 and 5,000 orders) yield an approximate relationship between number of orders and costs per order.

## Carrying Costs

Carrying costs are basically costs incurred because the school district owns or maintains inventories. Carrying costs include:

1. Foregone interest on money invested in inventory. Money tied

## Table 5.1: Calculating Average Cost/Order

|                          |                  | At 3,000 orders per year | | At 5,000 orders per year | |
| Expense category         | Annual salary    | Number required | Annual cost | Number required | Annual cost |
| ------------------------ | ---------------- | --------------- | ----------- | --------------- | ----------- |
| Purchasing department chief | $12,000       | 1               | $12,000     | 1               | $ 12,000    |
| Buyers                   | 7,000            | 3               | 21,000      | 5               | 35,000      |
| Assistant buyers         | 5,000            | 2               | 10,000      | 3               | 15,000      |
| Follow-up men            | 4,000            | 1               | 4,000       | 2               | 8,000       |
| Clerks                   | 3,000            | 3               | 9,000       | 4               | 12,000      |
| Typists                  | 2,800            | 2               | 5,600       | 3               | 8,400       |
| Supplies                 | —                | —               | 1,500       | —               | 2,500       |
| Receiving clerks         | 4,000            | 2               | 8,000       | 3               | 12,000      |
| Receiving supplies       | —                | —               | 300         | —               | 500         |
| Accounts payable clerks  | 4,200            | 3               | 12,600      | 4               | 16,800      |
| Accounting supplies      | —                | —               | 450         | —               | 750         |
| Total expenses           |                  |                 | $84,450     |                 | $122,950    |
| Average cost/order       |                  |                 | $28.15      |                 | $24.59      |

up in inventory could be invested in short-term securities. This is a major cost.

2. Obsolescence. This *can* be a major cost.

3. Storage-space rent. This may include heat, lights, or refrigeration, and can also be a major cost.

4. Stores operation, including recordkeeping, the taking of physical inventory, and protection.

5. Additional costs, such as insurance, depreciation, and deterioration.

Carrying costs are usually figured annually and expressed as a percentage of *average inventory* value. This percentage can be obtained in much the same manner as that used to get incremental cost per order, i.e., by estimating total carrying costs at two different inventory levels.

If a school district purchases only one amount or lot of a supply for the coming year, if the use of that item is constant, and if the last of the item is used on the last day of the year, then the district's average inventory equals one-half the amount bought (i.e., one-half the beginning inventory). Where inventory usage is not constant, the average inventory for the year will be greater or less than one-half the beginning inventory.

The simplest (and least satisfactory) method of arriving at a figure for average inventory is to add opening inventory on January 1 to closing inventory on December 31 and divide by two. A slightly better approach, for example, is to add three inventory figures (January 1, July 1, and December 31, for example) and divide by three. Probably the most common method is to add the beginning inventories of each of the twelve months and the closing inventory for December and divide by thirteen.

## Economic Order Quantity

To minimize inventory costs, management tries to minimize ordering costs *and* carrying costs. By determining incremental order costs, carrying costs, and average inventory, it is possible to estimate the economic order quantity (EOQ), the order that minimizes the total annual cost of ordering and carrying inventory. (Conditions of certainty are assumed for most of the discussions here; i.e., annual requirements are known or can be reasonably estimated. A discussion of strategies for ordering under uncertainty are included in most basic texts on operations research or management science. See, for example, Staff and Miller 1962.)

Assume that a school district uses $10,000 worth of an item during the year. Accountants in the district have determined that ordering costs amount to $25 per order and that carrying costs amount to 12.5 percent of average inventory. One approach to identifying the EOQ is to construct a table such as table 5.2.

Note that as the cost to carry the item declines, ordering costs increase. Note also that *total* costs, the figure we want to minimize, are lowest when carrying costs are equal to ordering costs. As such, it is the point to determine, because it is always the point of lowest total inventory costs for the year. Examination of table 5.2 shows that the educational manager should order that item five times during the year.

Note also that the total costs for ordering three, four, and five times a year (and also six if it has been calculated) are nearly the same. The practical significance of this fact is that the *approximate* answers in the situation are often very good ones, varying only slightly from ones that might be referred to as optimum answers. Figure 5.3 portrays graphically the data presented in table 5.2.

Obviously, EOQ formulas are only tools for use in decision making, and the answers derived from them are only as good as the data fed into the formula. Also, no educational institution will use the EOQ formulas to analyze the purchase of every item it buys and stocks. Some distinction must be made between items that account for a large part of the inventory value and those that are of minor

## Table 5.2: Identifying the Economic Order Quantity

| a | No. orders per year | | 1 | 2 | 3 | 4 | 5 | 10 | 20 |
|---|---|---|---|---|---|---|---|---|---|
| b | Dollars per order | ($10,000/a) | $10,000 | $5,000 | $3,333 | $2,500 | $2,000 | $1,000 | $500 |
| c | Average inventory | (b/2) | 5,000 | 2,500 | 1,666 | 1,250 | 1,000 | 500 | 250 |
| d | Carrying cost | (c × 12.5%) | 625 | 313 | 208 | 156 | 125 | 63 | 31 |
| e | Ordering cost | (a × $25) | 25 | 50 | 75 | 100 | 125 | 250 | 500 |
| f | Total cost per year to order and carry | (d + e) | $ 650 | $ 363 | $ 283 | $ 256 | $ 250* | $ 313 | $531 |

*Optimum

## Figure 5.3: Economic Order Quantity: Graphic Example

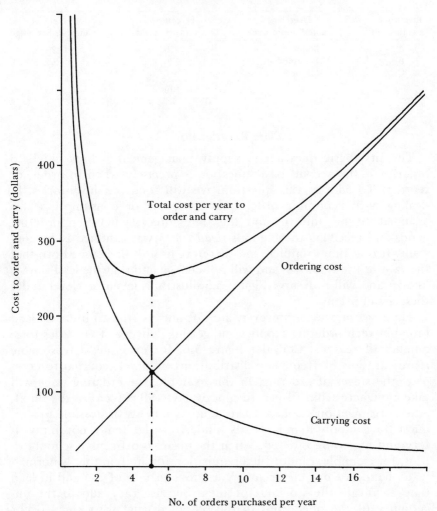

importance. The pattern indicated in table 5.4 is relevant to this discussion. In the case shown in that table, management would use formulas as an aid in controlling the A group because it is here that the cost consequences of mismanagement are greatest. Other tools, less technical, would be used for the B and C items. For example, management might set rule-of-thumb upper and lower inventory levels. Items B and C would seldom be controlled closely because they total only 20 percent of annual dollar usage.

## Table 5.4: Determining "Importance" of Inventory Items

| Inventory classification | Degree of capital importance | Percent of inventory items | Percent of annual dollar usage |
|---|---|---|---|
| A | Major | 10 | 80 |
| B | Intermediate | 20 | 15 |
| C | Minor | 70 | 5 |
| | | 100 | 100 |

### The Reorder Point

The first basic question in supply management is how much to order, and the second basic question is precisely when to order, or reorder. To address this question, we will focus on inventories. In dealing with economic order quantities, use or consumption was assumed to be uniform and the time intervals between ordering goods and receiving those goods (*lead time*) was assumed to be constant. It is at times simpler, and therefore useful, to assume both that the rate of use is known and will not change and that the lead time is known and will not vary. Figure 5.5 illustrates inventory level under these assumptions.

These assumptions, however, are not always true to life. The lead time between ordering supplies and getting delivery often varies for a number of reasons. Consider figure 5.6, for example, a reasonable representation of frequency distributions of times required to complete the stages of ordering. In this example, the ordering stage will take anywhere from fifteen to ninety days (99 percent of the time).

An organization's ability to respond as quickly as possible to a request for a supply item is greatly hindered if the item is not in inventory and has to be ordered. When the business office in a school district, for example, cannot fill a requisition for an item that is normally on hand, a *stockout* occurs. Variations in rate of use and in lead time aggravate the stockout problem because they add to the uncertainty of the operations in the school district. Stockouts occur when usage is normal but receipt of goods ordered is later than expected, or when delivery is on schedule but usage is greater than expected. (See figures 5.7 and 5.8.) The following discussion deals with ways to determine reorder points in such a way that the costs of being out of a stock are minimized.

The reorder point is the condition that tells the purchasing agent that it is time to place a buying order to replenish the stock of some item. Reorder points, therefore, reflect the two variables already

## Figure 5.5: Inventory Level with Constant Usage and Constant Lead Time (no safety stock)

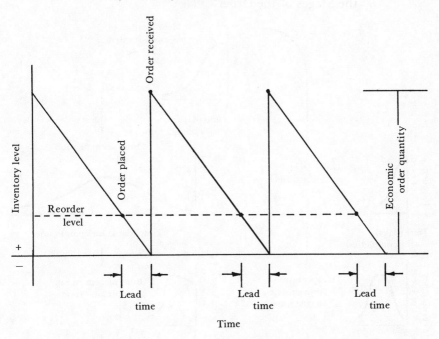

mentioned: rate of use and lead time. To determine the unadjusted point, multiply usage (number of units used per day) by lead time (in days).

The term *safety stock* refers to extra inventory held as a *hedge,* or protection, against the possibility of a stockout. It is obvious that a safety stock has two effects on costs in an educational organization: it will decrease the cost of stockouts, but it will increase carrying costs.

In many manufacturing situations the cost of stockouts can be calculated (using estimates of lost sales, lost customers, idle machines, employee ill will, etc.). These data can then be used in determining safety stocks. However, for a number of reasons, in educational organizations it is difficult, if not impossible, to determine the cost per unit of being out of stock. A more useful strategy in education is to adopt what is called a *service-level policy.* Organizations that use the service-level approach simply establish what probability of being out of stock they are willing to "live with." Then they take whatever

## Figure 5.6: Frequency Distributions of Times Required to Complete the Stages of the Order Cycle

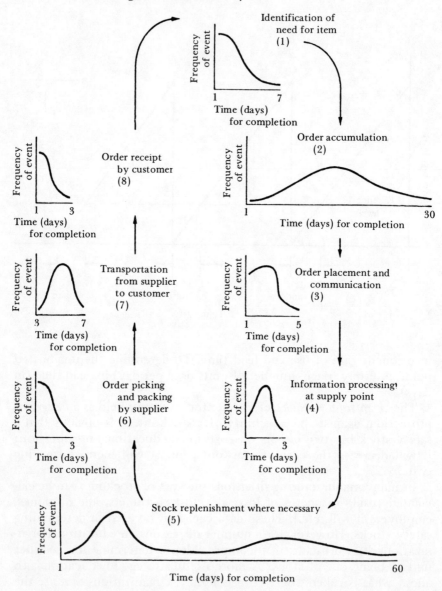

Source: James L. Heskett, Nicholas A. Glaskowsky, Jr., and Robert M. Ivie, *Business Logistics* (New York: Ronald Press, 1973), p. 246. Reprinted by permission.

### Figure 5.7: Inventory Level with Constant Usage and Excessive Lead Time (no safety stock)

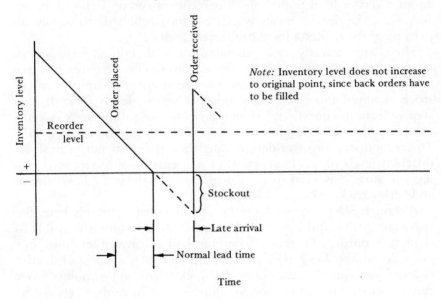

*Note:* Inventory level does not increase to original point, since back orders have to be filled

### Figure 5.8: Inventory Level with Excessive Usage and Constant Lead Time (no safety stock)

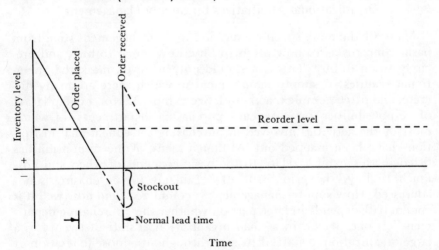

safety-stock action is required to keep the probability of being out of stock at or near this point. For example, a school district might adopt a service-level policy of 95 percent on certain items of inventory (i.e., the district business office wants to be able to supply 95 percent of the requests for those certain items).

There are basically two general steps in determining the safety stock required for any desired service level. The first step involves analyzing historical data to determine the number of units of safety stock required for each of the possible service levels desired. This step reflects the question, "How many units of safety stock would I need in order to fill $X$ percent of the order I received for that item?" The second step involves determining the total costs per year of the different levels of safety stock. (For a discussion of service-level policy and how it is used in the calculation of safety stock, see Levin and Kirkpatrick 1971, pp. 148-53.)

Although EOQ and reorder point are discussed separately here, the two concepts are quite related. An organization is more vulnerable to stockouts during the reorder period than at any other time. For example, as the EOQ rises (more units per lot), the school district orders fewer times a year. Thus the stock moves to low points fewer times a year, and the number of times it is vulnerable to stockouts diminishes. Conversely, as the EOQ falls (fewer units per lot), the district orders more times a year, the stock moves to low points more times a year, and the district finds itself in a vulnerable position more times a year.

## Organizational Alternatives for Supply Management

Many of the more specific issues in supply management stem from basic concerns as to how often to buy, how much to buy, and precisely when to buy. This fact should not, however, mask the operational realities of supply management in which there are many discrete, and often complex, activities. See exhibit 5.9 for a compilation of responsibilities for "typical" purchasing departments, in which most of the activities involved in purchasing for educational institutions have been mapped out. Although many of the responsibilities listed in this exhibit relate to the basic concerns of when and how much to buy, the prior issue of organizing for purchasing is not addressed. How supply management is conducted (and how well it is conducted) depends in large part on whether the "purchasing department" is one person in a small organization, a staff of twenty in a large organization, a staff of twenty throughout a loose federation of

## Exhibit 5.9: Responsibilities of a Typical Purchasing Department

*Records, data, and basic information*
 Maintaining general purchase records
 Maintaining price records
 Maintaining parts history records
 Maintaining vendor records, including financial and performance
 Maintaining specification files
 Maintaining standards file, including MIL/JAN specifications
 Maintaining catalog files

*Purchasing research, analysis, and studies*
 Conducting market studies and trends
 Conducting material studies
 Conducting make-or-buy studies
 Conducting price/cost analysis
 Investigating supply sources
 Conducting supplier-plant visits and inspections
 Developing new supply sources
 Developing alternate materials and sources
 Participating in value studies

*Purchasing*
 Checking authorized requisitions
 Obtaining capital appropriations
 Issuing requests for bid
 Determining bidders list
 Preparing request for bids
 Conducting pre-bid briefings
 Receiving all bids
 Analyzing quotations and/or proposals
 Determining nonresponsive bids
 Evaluating suppliers
 Selecting suppliers
 Determining quantity to buy
 Scheduling purchases and deliveries
 Determining mode of transportation and carrier
 Interviewing salesmen
 Determining type of contractual instrument
 Negotiating contracts
 Writing and issuing contractual agreement (purchase order, subcontract, blanket order, lease, rental agreement, etc.)
 Developing legal conditions of contracts
 Determining applicable federal, state, and local taxes or foreign duties
 Following up for delivery, i.e., expediting and updating open-order status reports
 Checking receipt of materials
 Checking and approving invoices
 Corresponding with suppliers
 Negotiating adjustments with suppliers
 Negotiating contract changes
 Terminating contracts

*Inventory management*
 Developing inventory classifications
 Maintaining minimum stocks
 Establishing economic order levels
 Maintaining inventory balance
 Improving inventory turnover
 Establishing stock and parts numbering system
 Transferring materials
 Consolidating requirements

**Exhibit 5.9** *(continued)*

---

Avoiding excess stocks and obsolescence
Declaring surplus inventory
Standardizing packages and containers
Accounting for returnable containers
Accounting for demurrage charges
Making periodic reports of commitments
Maintaining property records
*Managerial*
Preparing and updating purchasing manuals
Assisting in department audits and reviews
Evaluating purchasing performance
Evaluating personnel performance
Performing merit reviews and salary determination
Making reports to management
Conducting training and job enrichment programs
Conducting cost improvement programs
Participating in quality and zero defects programs
*Shared with other departments*
Contracting for services
Purchasing consultants' and special services
Purchasing construction contracts
Determining whether to make or buy
Negotiating leases for real property and equipment
Purchasing vehicles, trucks, and off-the-road equipment
Operating garage and fleet maintenance
Operating janitorial and custodial services
Operating and maintaining record archives
Supervising reproduction equipment
Purchasing exhibit material
Conducting scrap and surplus sales
Establishing employee purchase program
Operating cafeteria, in-plant feeding, and vending services
Purchasing computer time sharing and special outside test facilities

---

Source: George W. Aljian, *Purchasing Handbook,* 3d ed. (New York: McGraw-Hill, 1973), pp. 1-18–1-19. Reprinted by permission.

organizations, a staff of five in one of many organizations in a federation of organizations, etc. Consequently, it is this prior issue that must be addressed first (i.e., the organizational structure through which supplies are managed).

Determining the "best" organizational arrangement for supply management is a process that requires consideration of feasible organizational arrangements as well as alternative costs, delivery times, etc. Assuming that an existing organizational arrangement is in operation, the search for a possible alternative arrangement is motivated by the feeling on the part of management that a better organization could provide a means for improving supply management. In this section the search for alternative organizational arrangements is discussed as a process involving (1) analysis of the current system, (2) listing of the problems perceived to exist in the current system, (3) generating plausible alternatives to the current system, (4) generating criteria for evaluating each of the proposed alternatives, and (5) the selection of an alternative that appears to meet the criteria best. The process is more realistically described in figure 5.10, where these seemingly separate activities are seen as highly interactive. While attention here is focused on supply management, the activities described could be applied to a wide range of planning/analysis activities in a wide range of organizations.

**Figure 5.10: Process of Search for Organizational Alternatives in Supply Management**

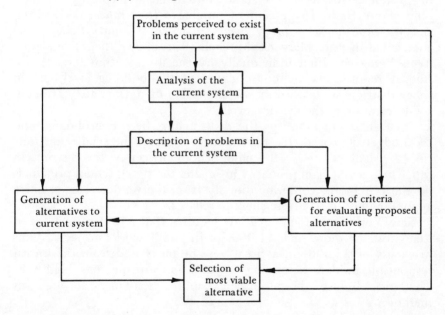

The data used in the following analysis are drawn largely from a report prepared for the New York State Commission on the Quality, Cost, and Financing of Elementary and Secondary Education (Peat, Marwick, Mitchell 1971). This study is instructive from two standpoints. First, it presents a concise picture of current problems and future prospects in school district supply management. Second, it represents a particularly practical application of "rational management" processes in searching for alternatives.

This example presumes that problems have been perceived to exist in supply management.

## Analysis of the Current System

Current operations of supply management in the school districts may be divided into areas of requisitioning, purchasing, storage, and distribution. Submitting requisitions is part of the budget preparation process in that during the prior year each unit within the education system (teacher, department, etc.) submits a budget requisition indicating its needs for the next school year. Some of the items are specified on districtwide "standard items" lists generated by the business office of the school district. This is done in order that a need common to many requisitioners may be satisfied by a single service of product. However, this standard-item group typically includes only about 10 to 15 percent of purchases (*Centralized Purchasing and Warehousing Feasibility Study*, Rockland County School District, cited in Peat, Marwick, Mitchell 1971, p. 23), the remainder of items being specified individually by the units within the system. Budget requisitions are consolidated at the building level, and in those districts with centralized purchasing operations they are consolidated again at the district level.

Once all requisitions for the district have been consolidated and the budget approved, the purchasing begins. In the smaller districts this is usually done by the chief school officer of the district. In other instances (again primarily in smaller districts), school principals do the purchasing, ordering directly from the vendor. This practice applies mainly to relatively small purchases.

New York State municipal law requires that any item or class of items totaling more than $1,000 (or in public works projects, items in excess of $2,500) in a fiscal year be purchased from the lowest responsible bidder responding to public advertising for sealed bids. The largest bulk of the purchase expenditures are made through this method.

In addition to these standard purchasing procedures, school districts in New York State can use several others. One alternative is purchasing through the state's Office of Governmental Services. The OGS Standards and Purchasing Group awards contracts for a wide variety of commodities required by the various state agencies. As an accommodation to political subdivisions, some of the contracts have been "extended" to enable school districts to purchase at the contract price, terms, and conditions if they desire. New York State contracts presently account for approximately 15 percent of school pur-

chases, primarily in the area of fuel, buses, furniture, and maintenance and transportation supplies.

A second alternative to standard purchasing procedure in New
York State is cooperative bidding. Cooperative bidding requires that
participating districts agree in advance on the specifications of items
to be purchased. One district assumes the responsibility of writing
the specifications, advertising for bids, analyzing the bids, and award-
ing the contract. Each of the other districts then places orders directly with the successful vendor for direct shipments to the district's
schools. Most cooperative bidding has focused on purchasing food
items.

The first alternative, purchasing through the state, has the advantages of generally lower prices and savings in purchasing effort. The
second alternative has the same general advantages though mani-
fested in different ways.

Storage and distribution of school district purchases entail three
activities: (1) receiving purchases from vendors, (2) storing purchases
until needed, and (3) distributing purchases to the points of consumption. In most school districts, the bulk of purchased items are
received and stored in individual school buildings.

## Problems with the Current System

Briefly stated, supply management practices in New York State
school districts were seen as functioning adequately but the process
was excessively expensive.

Overall, the present [supply management] system provides an acceptable level of
service. For a variety of reasons, however, the cost is excessive. The function
receives only part-time attention; no incentive exists to consolidate needs; the
system ignores the vendors' own economics; and the [supply management] function's tie to the budget cycle prevents districts from working with the market for
better prices. (Peat, Marwick, Mitchell 1971, p. V-5)

In over 40 percent of the districts, the chief school officer has
direct responsibility for the activity and spends only about 10 percent of his or her time on purchasing. In another 40 percent of the
districts, purchasing falls under the business manager, who spends an
average of 15 to 20 percent of his or her time on it. Fewer than 20
percent of the districts employ a full-time professional purchasing
agent. (See Pasnik 1960, p. 61. It is likely that the percentage of full-
time purchasing agents has increased since this study was completed.)
These facts raise questions about the ability of most districts to
design appropriate specifications, identify the best markets, negotiate

the best price, etc. These questions are especially germane considering that (1) only 8 percent of the districts operate with an up-to-date purchasing procedure manual, (2) fewer than 33 percent routinely request user evaluation of product performance, and (3) only 25 percent use testing facilities to check quality (Pasnik 1960, p. 68).

School districts have no incentive to consolidate needs, and indeed are reluctant to do so, despite favorable experience of savings through cooperative bidding on food. Reluctance stems largely from (1) fear of loss of control (agreement among districts on specifications is a necessary prerequisite to consolidating needs), and (2) local pressure to keep expenditure of funds in the local area.

Inadequate consideration of the vendors' cost factors manifests itself in several ways. Peak-season purchasing on the part of school districts requires many school-oriented vendors to take on part-time seasonal help. This additional cost is often passed on to the districts in the form of a "premium" price schedule during the peak season. (In New York State approximately 75 percent of school district purchase orders are placed within the two-month period following budget approval. Peat, Marwick, Mitchell 1971, p. V-6.) In addition, by doing this, districts forfeit seasonal savings for those commodities for which purchase could be staggered to their cost-opportune buying season. The problem is compounded by districts requesting one-time deliveries of the total annual requirements.

Most school buildings cannot store the total amount of materials safely, and an undetermined amount of shrinkage occurs. Further, the school district's resources are not being used as effectively as they might be. Every dollar and square foot of space tied up in inventory is a resource that could be put to an alternative use; i.e., reduced inventory levels could free funds to be invested for a return to the district and could free space to further the educational program. (Peat, Marwick, Mitchell 1971, p. V-7)

Because very few districts maintain a central receiving facility, vendors are often requested to make deliveries to individual school buildings and even to individual teachers. The somewhat ironic result is that even though deliveries are made only once a year, quantities that might otherwise qualify for bulk discount prices are priced at higher rates.

Finally, a number of payment practices in school districts tend to delay payments beyond the deadline for cash discounts. In some districts, for example, invoice payment approval must await the meeting of the school board. Also, a number of districts do not have a policy of partial payments to vendors on receipt of partial shipments. This might require a vendor to finance an entire purchase for up to several months at a cost that is ultimately passed along to the district.

## Alternatives for Improving Supply Management in School Districts

Six alternatives were generated, ranging from slight modifications in the existing system to a large-scale restructuring of it. The alternatives differ in the degree of centralization of supply management activities and in the size of the centralized entity. The initial appeal of all alternatives stems from economies of scale and/or increased professionalism. (These alternatives are described in greater detail in Peat, Marwick, Mitchell 1971, pp. V-8—V-20.)

1. Expanded New York State contractual system.
2. State purchasing-specialist service. (The state education department would provide training and other assistance in supply management to school districts.)
3. Expanded cooperative bidding.
4. Regional purchasing and distribution. (Regional agencies are established throughout the state to purchase for the component districts. These agencies then receive bulk purchases, which they redistribute immediately to various drop-points.)
5. Regional purchasing, storage, and distribution. (Individual schools or districts requisition their current needs from the regional agency, which distributes the requisitioned item from its warehouse stock.)
6. State purchasing for school districts. (The "region" described in alternative 5 becomes, in effect, the entire state.)

## Criteria for Evaluating Alternatives

After a systematic search has commenced for alternatives, criteria are established that will aid in developing (and subsequently evaluating) them. Taken together, the criteria should point out the *differing* dimensions that are deemed important in the various alternatives. The five criteria developed for the study reported here were economy, service, simplicity, responsiveness and flexibility, and acceptability (Peat, Marwick, Mitchell 1971, pp. I-3—I-5).

1. Are the economics of the alternative favorable? Is the cost to design the system, establish it, and possibly fulfill capital needs reasonable? Do the expected operating savings justify this cost of implementation?
2. Will the alternative provide a minimum optimum level and

breadth for service? For example, will purchases match requirements and can they be delivered on time?

3. Is the alternative simple to implement and operate? Can it be installed within a reasonable length of time?

4. Is the alternative flexible enough to be responsive? Can the system meet both routine and special needs? Can the system accommodate future development?

5. Would the alternative be acceptable to the affected parties? Could the legislature mandate the change without undue public pressure against it? Is the alternative nonthreatening and does it coincide with the personal needs of professionals? Does the alternative result in any inconvenience or harm to the public?

The results of evaluating the alternatives described in this example are outlined in exhibit 5.11. Note that adjectives (and not numbers) are deemed adequate here for describing most variations in meeting of the criteria.

### Exhibit 5.11: Evaluating Alternatives Against Established Criteria

Alternative 1: Expanded New York State contract system
    Economics
        Implementation: Insignificant
        Operation: Favorable ($13,500,000 savings per year)
        Change: Insignificant
    Service
        Matching of purchases to requirements: Good
        Reliable deliveries: Probably not as good as at present
    Simplicity
        Implementation: Very simple
        Operation: Simple
    Responsiveness and flexibility
        Routine requirements: Fair
        Special needs: Poor
        Future environment: Unknown—but probably difficult
    Acceptability
        Legislature: Good
        Professionals: Good
        Public: Some pros and cons
    *Conclusion:* Appropriate to implement
Alternative 2: State purchasing-specialist service
    Economics
        Implementation: Insignificant
        Operation: Highly favorable ($3,450,000 savings per year)
        Change: Insignificant
    Service
        Matching of purchases to requirements: Very good
        Reliable deliveries: Good

Simplicity
  Implementation: Simple
  Operation: Simple
Responsiveness and flexibility
  Routine requirements: Good
  Special needs: Very good
  Future environment: Good
Acceptability
  Legislature: Good
  Professionals: Good
  Public: Neutral
*Conclusion:* Obviated by more appropriate alternative
Alternative 3: Expanded cooperative bidding
  Economics
    Implementation: Low
    Operation: Favorable ($13,200,000 savings per year)
    Change: Insignificant
  Service
    Matching of purchases to requirements: Good
    Reliable deliveries: Good
  Simplicity
    Implementation: Somewhat difficult
    Operation: Can be complex
  Responsiveness and flexibility
    Routine requirements: Good
    Special needs: None
    Future environment: Unknown factor
  Acceptability
    Legislature: Good
    Professionals: Good
    Public: Neutral
  *Conclusion:* Obviated by more appropriate alternative
Alternative 4: Regional purchasing and distribution
  Economics
    Implementation: High ($5,000,000)
    Operation: Highly favorable ($23,900,000 savings per year)
    Change: Insignificant
  Service
    Matching of purchases to requirements: Good
    Reliable deliveries: Good
  Simplicity
    Implementation: Difficult and time-consuming
    Operation: Relatively simple
  Responsiveness and flexibility
    Routine requirements: Good
    Special needs: Good
    Future environment: Good
  Acceptability
    Legislature: Good
    Professionals: Apprehensive
    Public: Not favorable
  *Conclusion:* Obviated by more appropriate alternative
Alternative 5: Regional purchasing, storage, and distribution
  Economics
    Implementation: High ($10,000,000)

**Exhibit 5.11** *(continued)*

      Operation: Most favorable ($28,100,000 savings per year)
      Change: Insignificant
   Service
      Matching of purchases to requirements: Good
      Reliable deliveries: Excellent
   Simplicity
      Implementation: Difficult and time-consuming
      Operation: Simple
   Responsiveness and flexibility
      Routine requirements: Very good
      Special needs: Good
      Future environment: Good
   Acceptability
      Legislature: Good
      Professionals: Apprehensive
      Public: Not favorable
   *Conclusion:* Appropriate to implement
Alternative 6: State purchasing for school districts
   Insufficient data available
   *Conclusion:* Rejected

Source: Adapted from Peat, Marwick, Mitchell and Company, "Non-Instructional Services: A Study of Alternatives" (New York: New York State Commission on the Quality, Cost, and Financing of Elementary and Secondary Education, 1971), p. V-21.

## Selection of the Most Viable Alternative

Based on evaluations against the criteria, alternative 1 appeared to be the most viable alternative under consideration. The precise nature of alternative 1 is then described, along with procedures for implementing it. The proposed operation of the alternative is portrayed in figure 5.12.

From a management perspective, the form of the alternative is perhaps less important than the form of the process used to arrive at that alternative. Strategies inherent in this particular process have increased the probability of some things happening and reduced the probability of other things happening. For example, by considering a relatively wide range of alternatives, it is probable that the cost of searching for alternatives has increased, while the probability of not including a potentially worthwhile alternative has been reduced. By determining evaluation criteria independent of the actual evaluation, it is most probable that alternatives will be evaluated uniformly, and perhaps less probable that all important evaluative criteria will have been generated (on the assumption that some alternatives will suggest unique strengths or weaknesses not thought of ahead of time).

This particular search for alternatives (organizational alternatives for supply management) was, for several reasons, an especially wide-

Figure 5.12: Proposed Operation of Regionalized Supply Management System

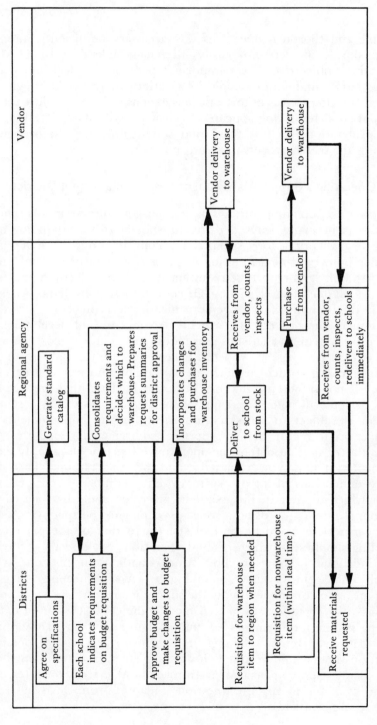

Source: Peat, Marwick, Mitchell and Company, "Non-Instructional Services: A Study of Alternatives" (New York: New York State Commission on the Quality, Cost, and Financing of Elementary and Secondary Education, 1971), p. VI-4.

ranging and thorough one. This was necessary because the alternatives considered were not easily interchangeable over time. Also, extensive "objectivity" was important because the decision would affect large numbers of people in a variety of ways. Although the search for alternatives in this case was expensive in an absolute sense, the potential for saving appeared to clearly justify its undertaking. It is considerations such as these that should influence the particular form of the search process in an organization.

### Operating a Supply Management System in a School District

How to set up an operating supply management system in a school district is in many ways a different subject from purchasing and inventory theory. More specifically, considerations of EOQ and reorder point will be a function of prior considerations of information-gathering-and-reporting requirements, shared decision making, and overall operating efficiency. Of course, these considerations exist within the framework of a given organizational setting.

As such, the process of "search" becomes one of developing an operating system that satisfies user requirements at least cost. (A *user* in this case is a person who has a need for information in supply management in order to perform part of his job.) Operating efficiency is not something that can be determined and then ignored for long periods of time. The supply management system in a school system is subject to necessary modifications and improvements as changes occur in cost factors, reporting requirements, size, etc.

It is a truism that before the operating efficiency of a supply management system can be evaluated it must be "understood." There are many dimensions of supply systems and a number of perspectives from which to view it. For example, attention could be focused on personnel interaction using a social-psychological perspective. A second perspective could be limited strictly to that of the person requesting supplies, in which case all operations not directly involving that individual become obscure. "Understanding" in this context of supply management takes on a highly specific meaning; that is, attempting to comprehend how the supply management system operates *as an information system.* (A more complete discussion of determining system requirements is found in chapter sixteen, "Developing Information Systems.") This greatly narrows the range of possible questions that would be asked about the system. In determining how an existing supply management (information) system operates, the following kinds of specific questions (adapted from Davis 1969, p. 468) would be asked:

*Related work:*
What work related to supply management is being done?
How is it being done?
*Preparation and processing:*
Who originates source data?
Who prepares documents?
How often is processing performed?
How long does it take?
Where is the processing performed?
Who performs it?
What equipment and supplies are used?
How many copies of documents are prepared? Who receives them?
Is there unused process capacity?
What is the volume of documents (maximum, minimum, and average)?
What has been the historical growth rate?
*Form and timeliness of documents:*
Is the document in useful form?
What are the specific limitations of the various forms?
Can two or more documents be combined?
Is greater accuracy needed?
Can lesser accuracy be tolerated?
Is faster reporting desired? Is it needed?
*Use of documents:*
Who receives the various documents?
Does a document initiate decision? What decision? By whom?
Is there a part of the document that is ignored or rarely used?
What additional information is needed?
What processing is performed by the user of the document?
What is the flow of the document?
*Storage and retrieval:*
Is the document retained? How? For how long?
What are the procedures for retention and purging?
How often is data purged and updated?
How often is it retrieved?
What are the procedures for retrieval?
How many different records are kept?
What is the average size per record?
What is the growth rate of each record?
Is there a need for integrating different files? Which files?
*Cost:*
What is the cost of processing the document?

What is the change in cost resulting from a change in the frequency or accuracy of processing?

How much of present costs of processing could be eliminated by computer processing?

What is the cost of storage and retrieval?

Answers to these questions are not uniformly easy to come by. In fact, something as "objective" as the cost of processing a document can vary greatly depending upon the cost-accounting conventions used. The validity of the answers to these questions should improve over time if managers of supply systems set about asking the questions from the day they first occupy the position. The implication is that answers to the questions will change over time, and no supply management system can be safely cast in concrete on the assumption that it will always be the best possible.

These questions, then, describe a general approach to understanding and, hopefully, improving a supply management system. Additionally, they point up the fact that, *for purposes of evaluation*, a supply management system cannot be usefully described outside its specific organizational context. For purposes of general description, however, it can.

Precise operating details of supply management systems vary among educational organizations, depending on such diverse and interrelated variables as geographic size and wealth, purchasing policies of the organization, number of buildings. Keeping this in mind, we can attempt a general description of operating procedures.

The example described below is summarized in table 5.13, "Linear Responsibility Chart of School District Supply Management." (See chapter ten for a more detailed description of linear responsibility charting.) The example (1) shows purchasing as an activity involving interactions among a variety of roles, (2) clarifies the distinction between "business" and "instructional" decision responsibilities, and (3) indicates the kind of support functions that electronic data processing can provide in a medium-sized school district. (This case was prepared with the assistance of Dr. Robert Den Hartog, Associate Superintendent for Business Affairs, Lincoln [Nebraska] Public Schools.)

The Case Public School District has an enrollment of 30,000 students, in thirty-two elementary, ten junior high, and four senior high schools; and an instructional supply budget of $900,000. Each school is allocated funds for the purchase of general classroom supplies on a per-pupil basis, according to enrollment. In special areas,

# Table 5.13: Linear Responsibility Chart of School District Supply Management

| Activity | Department heads | School principals | Purchasing department | Data processing | Business office | Instructional division | Vendors | Duplicating office |
|---|---|---|---|---|---|---|---|---|
| Allocates funds to purchase general classroom supplies | | N | | | M | | | |
| Prepares catalog of nonstock supplies (as per curriculum guides) | | | | N | | M | | N |
| Catalogs printed | | | | M | | | | A |
| Printed catalogs are duplicated | | | | | | | | M |
| Verified catalogs stored on disk | | | | A | | | | |
| Completed catalogs are distributed to schools (including order blanks) | | N | | | | | | |
| Principals issue order sheets to department heads | N | M | | | | | | |
| Teachers fill out forms and return to principals for authorization | M | N | | | | | | |
| Principals submit collected forms to business office for first verification | | M | | | N | | | |
| Requisitions are fed into computer, where order sheets are printed | | | | A | | | | |
| Order sheets and first verification are returned to schools to verify | | N | | M | | | | |
| Principal returns order sheet indicating changes if necessary | | M | | N | | | | |
| Final verification is fed into computer | | | | A | | | | |
| Order printed for district total of each item and sent to purchasing | | | N | M | | | | |
| Group items for special bidding | | | A | | | | | |
| Grouped items are printed on bid forms | | | N | A | | | | |
| Bid forms are addressed to vendors, but sent in bulk to purchasing | | | M | M | | | N | |
| Purchasing reviews bid forms and sends them out | | | N | | | | | |
| Vendors return bids | | | | N | | | M | |
| Purchasing (with instructional division) reviews and awards bids | | | M | | | N | | |
| Computer prints purchase orders and encumbers appropriate school accounts | | N | | M | | | | |
| Total amount (and kind) purchased by school is printed and distributed | | N | N | M | | | | N |
| Summary of district orders is printed and distributed | | | N | M | N | N | | |
| Items received are inventoried and checked against purchase list | | | A | | | | | |
| Items grouped for distribution to schools | | | A | | | | | |
| Items distributed to schools | N | N | M | | | | | |

A initiates activity not immediately affecting another unit
M initiates activity affecting another unit
N is affected by activity initiated by another unit

such as home economics or industrial education, such allocations are made on the basis of program enrollment. These allocations are made in the fall of each year on the basis of each school's fourth-Friday registration. Table 5.14 is an example of the budget allocation and monthly report for one high school.

To assist principals and teachers in deciding what instructional supplies are suitable, each central office consultant in the instruction division prepares a catalog of nonstock supplies that are acceptable and outlined in curriculum guides. Consultants recommend items to be stocked in the supply distribution center that are needed with regularity throughout the school year. The purchasing department then places these items in stock according to their estimated annual usage and consequently obtains the price advantages of volume purchasing. The office of business affairs does not determine items to be included in the catalogs.

Exhibit 5.15 is a page from the food services catalog. Separate catalogs exist for most types of items used in the school district, including textbooks, industrial arts supplies, general stockroom supplies, and standard forms. As can be noted, the catalogs are printed from the computer and printed by offset in the central office duplicating center. The item descriptions in the catalogs are complete and will be used in writing the purchase orders. Through this phase, the item description has been written by the consultant, keypunched, printed by data processing, and verified by office personnel for final writing on the disk file. As will be noted, this information will not be "typed" again by clerical staff in schools or central office, but will be "typed" from the computer seven additional times for the complete cycle.

The completed catalogs are distributed to the schools, each item having its own unique six-digit number (which was assigned by the computer according to disk address). Special order blanks (exhibit 5.16) are sent with the catalogs. The basic control system involves three factors: (1) accounting code for items to be ordered, (2) school number for distribution and accounting purposes, and (3) a catalog page number. School and page numbers are of prime importance through this phase since all control is based on these figures.

The principal issues the order sheets to department heads. The teacher or other person using any catalog merely places the quantity and item number of articles wanted in the appropriate spaces, makes the price extension, and places that amount in the teachers' work area. As a page is completed, the total amount for the page is placed in the appropriate space; the principal, by his or her signature,

Table 5.14: Budget Allocation and Monthly Report for One High School*

| Budget | Account description | Budget allowance | Current expenditure | Y.T.D. expenditure | Budget balance | Encumbrance | Percent unencumbered | Unencumbered balance |
|---|---|---|---|---|---|---|---|---|
| | PRIN ALLOC 01 LINCOLN HIGH | | | | | | | |
| 023233601 | Alloc Gen LHS | $10,723.00 | $1,368.72 | $ 6,336.72 | $ 4,386.28 | $ 679.61 | 034.6 | $ 3,706.67 |
| 023273601 | Alloc Art Sup LHS | 2,370.00 | 405.25 | 899.94 | 1,470.06 | 35.46 | 060.5 | 1,434.60 |
| 023283601 | Alloc AV Sup LHS | 1,865.00 | 702.54 | 1,583.37 | 281.63 | 42.15 | 012.8 | 239.48 |
| 023303601 | Alloc Bus Ed LHS | 932.00 | 41.41 | 208.63 | 723.37 | | 077.6 | 723.37 |
| 023403601 | Alloc Home Econ LHS | 1,220.00 | 57.10 | 822.25 | 397.75 | | 032.6 | 397.75 |
| 023413601 | Alloc Ind Ed LHS | 4,285.45 | 222.70 | 1,651.10 | 2,634.35 | 200.90 | 056.8 | 2,433.45 |
| 023503601 | Alloc PE Sup LHS | 1,250.00 | 252.68 | 361.81 | 888.19 | 40.00 | 067.9 | 848.19 |
| 023563601 | Alloc Sci Sup LHS | 1,865.00 | 6.12 | 300.79 | 1,564.21 | | 083.9 | 1,564.21 |
| 023583601 | Alloc Sup Books LHS | 3,543.00 | 80.21 | 1,082.94 | 2,460.06 | 3,402.72 | 026.6 | 942.66— |
| | *TOTAL* | 28,053.45 | 3,136.73 | 13,247.55 | 14,805.90 | 4,400.84 | 037.1 | 10,405.06 |

*Case Public Schools financial statement of May 31, 1970.

# Exhibit 5.15: Example from Nonstock Supplies Catalog: Food Services

| ITEM# | | UNIT | PAGE 001 PRICE | |
|---|---|---|---|---|
| 000001 | PARING KNIFE, DEXTER, #42411G - 3 IN BLADE | EA | .74 | 46 |
| 000002 | FRUIT & SALAD SLICER, #B6476SC-6 IN BLADE | EA | 2.60 | 6 |
| 000003 | LUNCH SLICER, W.E., #B6478SC - 8 IN BLADE | EA | 3.15 | 13 |
| 000004 | BUTCHER KNIFE, W.E., #6448 - 8 IN BLADE | EA | 2.85 | 4 |
| 000005 | FRENCH KNIFE, W.E., #6424 - 10 IN BLADE | EA | 3.35 | 6 |
| 000006 | FORK, KITCHEN W.E., #6440S - 10 IN HANDLE | EA | 1.75 | |
| 000007 | FORK, KITCHEN W.E., #6143 - 14 IN HANDLE | EA | 2.15 | 3 |
| 000008 | PEELER, ECKO, #5-KP - 3 IN KNEE ACTION | EA | .40 | 20 |
| 000009 | SPREADER, DEXTER, #S-2493-1/2 - 3 3/4 IN BLADE | EA | .97 | 16 |
| 000010 | SERVER, W.E., "69632, 2-1/4 x 2-1/4 | EA | .75 | 7 |
| 000011 | TURNER, OFF SET W.E., #6537S, 4-1/4 x 2-1/4 | EA | 1.50 | 11 |
| 000012 | SPATULA, CHROME, VANADIUM W.E., #6348, 8 IN x 1-1/4 IN | EA | 1.95 | 4 |
| 000014 | SPATULA, CHROME VANADIUM W.E., #6350, 10 IN x 1-1/4 IN | EA | 2.35 | 1 |
| 000016 | SERVING SPOONS, VOLRATH, METAL HANDLE, SOLID #6012 - 11 3/4 IN | EA | .68 | |
| 000018 | SERVING SPOONS, VOLRATH, METAL HANDLE, SOLID #6016 - 15 1/2 IN | EA | .90 | 3 |
| 000020 | SERVING SPOONS, VOLRATH, METAL HANDLE, SOLID #6021 - 21 IN | EA | 1.85 | |
| 000022 | SERVING SPOONS, VOLRATH, METAL HANDLE SLOTTED #6111 - 11 3/4 IN | EA | .67 | |
| 000024 | SERVING SPOONS, VOLRATH, METAL HANDLE SLOTTED #6115 - 15 1/2 IN | EA | .78 | |
| 000026 | SERVING SPOONS, VOLRATH, METAL HANDLE PERFORAT #6112 - 11 3/4 IN | EA | .67 | |
| 000028 | SERVING SPOONS, VOLRATH, METAL HANDLE PERFORAT #6116 - 15 1/2 IN | EA | .90 | 5 |

# Exhibit 5.16: Supply Order Forms

**LINCOLN PUBLIC SCHOOLS**

**ANNUAL SUPPLY ORDER 1974-75**

Total Dollars This Page    $ _____    P48 [ ] [ ] [ ] [ ]   [ ] [ ]   [ ] [ ]   [ ] [ ]

ACCOUNT        PROGRAM      LOCATION      REQ. NO.

1. PRINCIPAL'S SIGNATURE          DATE   P41 [ ] [ ] [ ] [ ]   [ ] [ ]

CORRECTED ACCOUNT    PROGRAM      SCHOOL NAME

2. PRINCIPAL'S SIGNATURE          DATE

TEACHER'S NAME

NOTE: PRINCIPAL'S SUPPLY ACCOUNT NUMBERS    | 0 | 2 | 3 | 5 | 6 |  INSTRUCTIONAL MATERIALS

| 0 | 2 | 3 | 7 | 8 |  SUPPLIES--Office & Classroom

| Teachers Work Area | Quantity | Item Number | Corrected Quantity In Red | Teachers Work Area | Quantity | Item Number | Corrected Quantity In Red |
|---|---|---|---|---|---|---|---|
| 1 | | | 1 2 3 4 5 6 7 | 5 | | | 1 2 3 4 5 6 7 |
| 2 | | | 1 2 3 4 5 6 7 | 6 | | | 1 2 3 4 5 6 7 |
| 3 | | | 1 2 3 4 5 6 7 | 7 | | | 1 2 3 4 5 6 7 |
| 4 | | | 1 2 3 4 5 6 7 | 8 | | | 1 2 3 4 5 6 7 |

White - Business Affairs    Green - School Copy

8000/SH-300/JH-150/E-100

authorizes the page for return to the central office with all other order pages for a first verification.

As pages are received, data cards are punched and the order sheet numbers are now "typed" with quantity, description, prices extended, and pages totaled. The order sheet and first verification are returned to the school for their verification. (Exhibit 5.17 shows in detail how corrections are to be made on the order sheet.)

The principal returns the order sheet with a second signature, authorizing changes as shown or indicating that the sheet was correct. (The page must be signed if correct and returned to verify the original accuracy.) As order sheets are returned, the data processing department makes corrections and types a final verification, which is returned to the school with the original order sheet.

At this phase, when all sheets are returned and corrected, all data for the total district (number of each item, by account number, by school) are stored on disk and sorted into item-number sequence. A district total of each item and description ordered is then typed and sent to the purchasing department.

While the aforementioned steps are being executed, the purchasing department is busy determining items to be ordered from specific vendors or to be grouped for special bidding. Exhibit 5.18 is a completed form by the purchasing department, which shows how many items are to be gathered on bids numbered and sent to vendors as listed. This data is keypunched and the computer types an original bid in two parts for each vendor listed; the vendor name is pulled from disk in the process by using the proper vendor name.

These bid sheets (exhibit 5.19) are returned to the purchasing department and mailed to the appropriate address. The name of the school district buyer is listed here, in the event that information is needed by the bidder, and the bid due-date is included.

The purchasing department analyzes the bids and, after reviewing them with instructional consultants, makes the award by placing the item number, vendor number, unit price, and alternate description, if necessary, on the form shown in exhibit 5.20. Then the form is returned to data processing, where it is punched.

The computer now types the purchase order by vendor and items with school distribution as shown in exhibit 5.21. The bid price is extended; the specific item to be delivered is typed, and accounting cards are punched that are used to encumber, to the appropriate school accounts, the total dollars per purchase order. This encumbrance will first be shown to the principal in the monthly statement.

## Exhibit 5.17: Order Verification Sheet

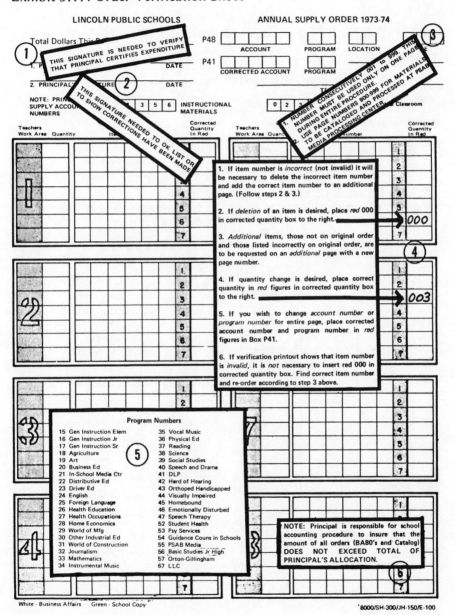

# Exhibit 5.18: Gathering Requests on a Bid Sheet Form

**FORM NO. PD050**

Punched ____
Verified ____

## PURCHASING PROCEDURES — PREPARE BID SHEET

REQUESTED BY_____ PHONE EXTENSION _____ DATE _____ PAGE_____

**HEADER** *(one card per quote)*

| **1** | CTL P23 *1-3* | SET 1 *4* | QUOTE NO. /_/_/_/ *5  6  7  8* | DATE DUE /_/_/_/_/_/ *9  10  11  12  13  14* | BUYER'S NAME /_/_/_/_/_/_/_/_/_/_/_/_/_/_/ *15  16  17  18  19  20  21  21  23  24  25  26  27  28* |
|---|---|---|---|---|---|

| **2** | ITEMS ON ABOVE QUOTE *(Item numbers are inclusive)* |
|---|---|

| CTL *1-3* | SET *4* | QUOTE *5-8* | ITEM 5 digits  9-13 | TO | ITEM 5 digits  14-18 |
|---|---|---|---|---|---|
| P29 | 2 | /  /  /  / | | | |
| D | | | | | |
| U | | | | | |
| P | | | | | |
| L | | | | | |
| I | | | | | |
| C | | | | | |
| A | | | | | |
| T | | | | | |
| E | | | | | |
| | | | | | |
| | | | | | |
| | | | | | |
| | | | | | |
| | | | | | |
| | | | | | |

| **3** | VENDORS FOR THIS QUOTE *(All vendors must be on file) To add vendors use FORM BD040* |
|---|---|

| CTL *1-3* | SET *4* | QUOTE *5-8* | VENDOR 6 digits  9-14 | OFFICE USE |
|---|---|---|---|---|
| P39 | 3 | /  /  /  / | | |
| D | | | | |
| U | | | | |
| P | | | | |
| L | | | | |
| I | | | | |
| C | | | | |
| A | | | | |
| T | | | | |
| E | | | | |
| | | | | |
| | | | | |
| | | | | |
| | | | | |
| | | | | |
| | | | | |

Lincoln Public Schools

## Exhibit 5.19: Bid Request Sheet

```
079600 HENKLE & JOYCE                      PURCHASING DEPARTMENT
       800 Q STREET                        P. O. BOX 82889
       LINCOLN    NE  68505                 LINCOLN, NEBRASKA  68501

                                           REQUEST FOR QUOTATION # 2222
                                           DUE DATE 01/15/74      PAGE 2
                                           REFER TO BUYER  CUSICK
```

<u>ALL QUOTATIONS WILL BE F.O.B. LINCOLN.</u>

| | QTY. NEEDED UNIT | UNIT PRICE | TOTAL QUANITY PRICE | OUR NUMBER |
|---|---|---|---|---|
| DESCRIPTION | | | | |
| PEELER, ECKO, #5-KP - 3 IN KNEE ACTION | 2-EA | * .45 * | .92 | *00008 |
| SPATULA, CHROME, VANADIUM W.E., #6350, 10 IN x 1-1/4 IN | 11-EA | *2.50* | 27.50 | *00014 |

```
   PREPARED BY - -           DATE -          TELEPHONE -
............................................................................
```

```
138200 PEGLER AND CO                       PURCHASING DEPARTMENT
       1700 CENTER PARK ROAD               P. O. BOX 82889
       LINCOLN    NE  68512                LINCOLN, NEBRASKA  68501

                                           REQUEST FOR QUOTATION # 2222
                                           DUE DATE 01/15/74      PAGE 2
                                           REFER TO BUYER  CUSICK
```

<u>ALL QUOTATIONS WILL BE F.O.B. LINCOLN.</u>

| QTY. NEEDED UNIT | UNIT PRICE | TOTAL QUANITY PRICE | OUR NUMBER |
|---|---|---|---|
```
...........................................................................
```

```
131910 OFFICE c/D. HICKEY                  PURCHASING DEPARTMENT
       720 SOUTH 22nd STREET               P. O. BOX 82889
       LINCOLN       NE  68510             LINCOLN, NEBRASKA  68501

                                           REQUEST FOR QUOTATION # 2222
                                           DUE DATE 01/15/74      PAGE 2
                                           REFER TO BUYER  CUSICK
```

<u>ALL QUOTATIONS WILL BE F.O.B. LINCOLN.</u>

| | QTY. NEEDED UNIT | UNIT PRICE | TOTAL QUANITY PRICE | OUR NUMBER |
|---|---|---|---|---|
| DESCRIPTION | | | | |
| PEELER, ·ECKO, #5-KP - 3 IN KNEE ACTION | 2-EA | * | * | *00008 |
| SPATULA, CHROME, VANADIUM W.E., #6350, 10 IN x 1-1/4 IN | 11-EA | * | * | *00014 |

```
   PREPARED BY - -
                        DATE -          TELEPHONE -
```

# Exhibit 5.20: Purchasing Procedures: Updates for Purchase Orders

FORM NO. PD 060

Punched _____
Verified _____

REQUESTED BY _____ PHONE EXTENSION _____ DATE _____ PAGE _____

| C.C. 1-3 | C.C. 5-50 | C.C. 51-56 | C.C. 61-67 | C.C. 71-75 |
|---|---|---|---|---|
| Control | Alternate Description (if any) | Vendor No. | New Price (if any) | LPS Catalog Item No. |
| 3 Digits | 46 Digits | 6 Digits | 7 Digits | 5 Digits |
| P 21 | | | | |
| D | | | | |
| U | | | | |
| P | | | | |
| L | | | | |
| I | | | | |
| C | | | | |
| A | | | | |
| T | | | | |
| E | | | | |

# Exhibit 5.21: Purchasing Procedure Claim Voucher

F 12130

**CLAIM VOUCHER**

## LINCOLN PUBLIC SCHOOLS
### LINCOLN, NEBRASKA
An Affirmative Action Plan Equal Opportunity Employer.

DATE ___2/08/74___

ORDER NO. ___00002___

1. Make changes as required to correct name and address.
2. Extend prices, sign and return immediately at time of complete or partial shipment.
3. MAIL TO: LINCOLN PUBLIC SCHOOLS BUSINESS AFFAIRS OFFICE  P.O. BOX 82889 LINCOLN, NEBRASKA 68501

**SHIP TO**

| | |
|---|---|
| [X] | LINCOLN PUBLIC SCHOOLS — DIST. CTR.<br>505 SOUTH STREET<br>LINCOLN NEBRASKA 68502 |
| [ ] | LINCOLN PUBLIC SCHOOLS — O & M BLDG.<br>800 SOUTH 24th STREET<br>LINCOLN, NEBRASKA 68510 |
| [ ] | LINCOLN PUBLIC SCHOOLS — FOOD STORES<br>2420 RANDOLPH<br>LINCOLN, NEBRASKA 68510 |
| [ ] | _____ |

FOR ACCOUNTING PURPOSES ONLY

082100    HOCKENBERG & CO
          1024 FARNAM
          OMAHA          NB 68102

PAGE  001

YOUR INVOICE NO. →

| QUANTITY | UNIT | DESCRIPTION | UNIT PRICE | TOTAL |
|---|---|---|---|---|
| 4 | EA | FORK, KITCHEN W.E., #6440S- 10IN HANDLE<br>DISTRIBUTIONS FOR OFFICE USE ONLY<br>    4  LEFLER            001-7133005-15       7.00 | 1.750 | 7.00 |
| 2 | EA | SPREADER, DEXTER, #S-2493-1/2 - 3 3/4IN BLADE<br>DISTRIBUTIONS FOR OFFICE USE ONLY<br>    2  LEFLER            001-7133005-15       2.00 | 1.000 | 2.00 |
| 10 | EA | SERVING SPOONS, VOLRATH, METAL HANDLE, SOLID<br>    #6012 - 11 3/4IN<br>DISTRIBUTIONS FOR OFFICE USE ONLY<br>    3  LEFLER            001-7133005-15       2.10<br>    7  ARNOLD            001-7133005-20       4.90 | .700 | 7.00 |
| 2 | EA | SERVING SPOONS, VOLRATH, METAL HANDLE, SOLID<br>    #6021 - 21IN<br>DISTRIBUTIONS FOR OFFICE USE ONLY<br>    2  LEFLER            001-7133005-15       4.40 | 2.200 | 4.40 |

| QUOTE NO. | | F.O.B. | | TERMS | TOTAL COST | |
|---|---|---|---|---|---|---|
| 1111 | SIGN AND RETURN AT ONCE | LINCOLN | | NET | $ | 20.40 |

PRICES AND TERMS CORRECT.
AUDITED AND PASSED FOR PAYMENT

| | ASSISTANT SUPERINTENDENT<br>IN CHARGE OF BUSINESS AFFAIRS | |
|---|---|---|
| AUDITOR | | REC. COPY<br>ATTACHED |
| DATE  MATERIALS RECEIVED, CHECKED AND AGREES WITH ORDER | | |
| RECEIVING CLERK | | |

| | | | |
|---|---|---|---|
| GENERAL FUND | ____WARRANT NO.____ | $_____ |
| ADULT FUND | ____WARRANT NO.____ | $_____ |
| BUILDING FUND | ____WARRANT NO.____ | $_____ |
| LUNCHROOM FUND | ____WARRANT NO.____ | $_____ |
| GOVERNMENT FUND____WARRANT NO. ____ | | $_____ |
| ____FUND____WARRANT NO. ____ | | $_____ |
| | | $ |
| | TOTAL | |

**THIS CLAIM VOUCHER MUST BE SIGNED IN INK AND RETURNED
BEFORE IT WILL BE CONSIDERED FOR PAYMENT**
THIS IS TO CERTIFY THAT THE ABOVE CLAIM IS A JUST, TRUE AND COM-
PLETE STATEMENT OF ABOVE CLAIMANT, AGAINST THE SCHOOL DISTRICT
OF THE CITY OF LINCOLN, NEBRASKA, WITH ALL JUST CREDITS ALLOWED,
AND THAT THE SAME IS UNPAID.

X _____

CLAIMANT OR AUTHORIZED AGENT          AUTHORIZED AGENT'S TITLE

When computer purchasing is completed, a detailed report is "typed" and sent to each principal for all catalog orders for his or her school; this report may be used for reviewing purposes and must be used for further inquiries. The purchase order number is used in all follow-up procedures in case of nonreceipt of specific items in the school.

Now the computer types for the eighth, and last, time a complete copy of all catalogs showing the number of each item ordered and the actual unit price paid. One copy is sent to the instruction division for analysis and future reference by instructional consultants and the carbon to the purchasing department for back-up information.

The purchasing system is seen and described in this particular instance as a flow of information among people. While it describes the system in general detail, not enough data has been presented here to enable an evaluation of the system to be made.

Supply management, which is grounded in widely acknowledged (if abstract) theories of purchasing and inventory control, encompasses a variety of discrete activities. Two general types of such activities have been discussed here: (1) the search for alternative organizational arrangements and (2) the generation of description and evaluation of internal efficiency. Two assumptions lie behind the discussions of these activities. First, supply management operates within and is shaped by an organizational environment containing a variety of sometimes conflicting values and goals. Consequently, supply management can be "improved" only within the constraints of this broader environment. Second, the process of improvement nevertheless is enhanced through systematic and objective procedures.

## Questions for Review and Discussion

1.  How might the concept of economic order quantity be modified by the existence of discounts for purchases above a certain quantity?

2.  What other departments in educational organizations would be likely to deal directly with the purchasing department on a routine basis?

3.  What conditions should exist before management undertakes a systematic examination of alternative ways of providing supplies?

4.  How could the school district purchasing system described in this chapter be altered to allow for greater autonomy in purchasing decisions at lower levels in the organization? How would that new organizational form affect the costs of supply management?

# References

Aljian, George W. *Purchasing Handbook.* 3d ed. New York: McGraw-Hill, 1973.

Davis, G. B. *Computer Data Processing.* New York: McGraw-Hill, 1969.

Heskett, James L.; Glaskowsky, Nicholas A., Jr.; and Ivie, Robert M. *Business Logistics.* New York: Ronald Press, 1973.

Levin, Richard, and Kirkpatrick, Charles. *Quantitative Approaches to Management.* New York: McGraw-Hill, 1971.

Pasnik, Marion. "A Survey and Evaluation of Purchasing Procedures of Selected New York State Public School Districts." Ph.D. dissertation, Teachers College, Columbia University, 1960.

Peat, Marwick, Mitchell and Company. "Non-Instructional Services: A Study of Alternatives." New York: New York State Commission on the Quality, Cost, and Financing of Elementary and Secondary Education, 1971.

Staff, M. K., and Miller, D. W. *Inventory Control: Theory and Practice.* Englewood Cliffs, N.J.: Prentice-Hall, 1962.

# Related Readings

Burns, H. Spilman. *Supply Management Manual for School Business Officials.* Evanston, Ill.: Association of School Business Officials, 1962.

Hart, Anthony. "Determination of Excess Stock Quantities." *Management Science* 19, no. 12 (August 1973): 1444-51. Describes a procedure for solving the following problem: Given an excess stock of an inventory item, how much should be disposed at a scrap price, and how much should be retained for regular sale, in order to minimize the present value of all the relevant costs?

Inglehart, Donald L., and Morey, Richard C. "Inventory Systems With Imperfect Asset Information." *Management Science* 18, no. 8 (April 1972): B-388—B-394. Describes in relatively technical language optimum inventory counting strategies, given that an inventory stock record is often not in agreement with the physical stock. (Such discrepancies may be introduced because of time lags between flow of information and material, pilferage, incorrect unit of issue, inaccurate physical inventory counts, etc.)

Ritlershamp, J. J.; Abbot, F. L.; and Ahrens, B. C., eds. *Purchasing for Educational Institutions.* New York: Columbia University Press, 1961.

Westing, J. H.; Fine, I. V.; and Zenz, G. J. *Purchasing Management.* New York: John Wiley & Sons, 1969. A basic text on the subject covering in depth many of the topics briefly touched in this chapter, with an extensive section devoted to actual cases and related discussion questions.

# 6

# Transportation

## Theoretical Foundations

On first analysis, transportation management seems to be one of the most straightforward operations in education. This is largely because the main management objective often appears deceptively simple: to move people (mainly students) and things from place to place as efficiently as possible. Although transportation is complicated by many of the management tasks required of other operations (such as accounting), at least it can be said that the objective is clear.

What makes transportation objectives relatively clear? One factor is that output measures, such as student travel time or distances traveled, can be reliably and objectively measured. A second, and perhaps more important, reason is that the relationships between inputs and outputs can be relatively clearly determined. For example, the "causes" of student travel time are more easily assigned than the "causes" of student achievement. Student time on a bus can be described as a function of the distance a student traveled on that bus. Therefore, if a management objective is to reduce student travel time, one of the most effective ways to do this is to reduce the distance a student must travel. This sounds circular or definitional, perhaps, until we consider the much more elusive objective of (for example) improving student achievement in arithmetic.

It is because the relationships between inputs and outputs are relatively clear in transportation that useful mathematical models have been developed (outside education), which are applicable to transportation problems in education. The general forms of two such models are described here: the linear programming solution to the transportation problem (an analytical model), and the routing, or "traveling salesman," problem (a numerical model).

*128*

## The Transportation Problem

The transportation problem is approached here with the use of a special form of *linear programming*. (Linear programming is treated separately in the chapters on allocation systems, and only those aspects useful for analyzing transportation are discussed here.)

Since the development of quantitative models of transportation in the early 1940s, a number of approaches have been developed (see Thierauf and Grosse 1970, pp. 296-330). However, the general form of the problem itself has remained the same. The pieces of the general model include shipping sources (e.g., factories), destinations (e.g., warehouses), and a given cost for transportation between each source and each destination. Both the shipping source and the destination are associated with various constraints. For example, a shipping source such as a warehouse is constrained by its capacity: no more can be shipped at any one time than can be stored. Further, no more can be shipped to a destination such as a retail outlet than is ordered by that outlet. The goal (the *objective function*) sought is to minimize total transportation cost while satisfying the constraints of the shipping sources and the destinations.

This general model applies in a number of ways to transportation in educational institutions, especially in elementary-secondary school systems. Shipping sources may be defined as neighborhoods that yield "supplies" of children. They must be transported to destinations (school sites) that have specific capacities or "demands." The "cost" of shipping in the educational setting may be defined in one of several ways: (1) as the calculated cost of shipping between each source and destination; (2) as the physical distance between them; or (3) as the transport time required for each trip. (These measures are usually highly correlated, but they do reflect different concepts of cost.)

The transportation problem, then, is a construct involving sources, destinations, and transport costs. Perhaps the best way to illustrate this is by examining two transportation problems that are solved using linear programming. Since the purpose here is not to describe how linear programming problems are actually solved, but to show how linear programming is applied to school transportation, only the initial set up of the problem and the resulting solution are discussed.

### Example 1: Placing Students in Work-Study Programs

A county school district has seventeen students at four high schools who are seniors, trained in secretarial skills, and eligible for a half-day work-study program. Six major corporations in the county have indicated a willingness to hire various numbers of these students.

Students from the different schools need to be assigned to the different corporations (*decision variables*). All things being equal, we want to minimize the students' round-trip travel time between school and work (*objective function*).

The number of eligible students at each school is shown in table 6.1; the number of openings at each business, in table 6.2; and the round-trip travel time between the schools and the businesses, in table 6.3. The "measure of effectiveness" in this case is the total travel time of the students expressed in minutes.

## Table 6.1: Eligible Work-Study Students at Each School

| School | Number of eligible students |
|--------|------------------------------|
| 1 | 3 |
| 2 | 4 |
| 3 | 2 |
| 4 | 8 |

## Table 6.2: Work-Study Openings at Each Business

| Business | Number of openings |
|----------|---------------------|
| 1 | 3 |
| 2 | 3 |
| 3 | 6 |
| 4 | 2 |
| 5 | 1 |
| 6 | 2 |

## Table 6.3: Round-Trip Travel Time Between Schools and Businesses (in minutes)

| School | Business | | | | | |
|--------|----|----|-----|----|-----|-----|
|        | 1  | 2  | 3   | 4  | 5   | 6   |
| 1 | 50 | 30 | 70  | 30 | 80  | 50  |
| 2 | 50 | 60 | 120 | 50 | 70  | 110 |
| 3 | 20 | 80 | 30  | 40 | 80  | 20  |
| 4 | 90 | 60 | 100 | 50 | 100 | 90  |

Let $X_{ij}$ represent the number of students to be assigned from school $I$ to business $J$. Thus $X13$ represents the number of students to be assigned from school 1 to business 3; $X32$ represents the number of students to be assigned from school 3 to business 2, etc.

The objective function should be written in such a way that total round-trip time is minimized. That is,

$$
\begin{aligned}
\text{Minimize } Z &= 50X11 + 30X12 + \ldots + 50X16 \\
\text{(total round-} &+ 50X21 + 60X22 + \ldots + 110X26 \\
\text{trip travel} &+ 20X31 + 80X32 + \ldots + 20X36 \\
\text{in minutes)} &+ 90X41 + 60X42 + \ldots + 90X46.
\end{aligned}
$$

Notice that all constraints deal with numbers of students (numbers at each school, openings at each business). For example, the numbers of students available from school 1 (three students) can be expressed as follows:

$$X11 + X12 + X13 + X14 + X15 + X16 = 3 \text{ (school 1)}.$$

And the same can be done for the students from the other schools:

$$
\begin{aligned}
X21 + X22 + X23 + X24 + X25 + X26 &= 4 \text{ (school 2)}; \\
X31 + X32 + X33 + X34 + X35 + X36 &= 2 \text{ (school 3)}; \\
X41 + X42 + X43 + X44 + X45 + X46 &= 8 \text{ (school 4)}.
\end{aligned}
$$

Additionally, the constraints on students can be looked at from the perspective of the receiving organizations (businesses). For example, the three openings in business 1 can be expressed as follows:

$$X11 + X21 + X31 + X41 = 3 \text{ (business 1)}.$$

Similarly for the other businesses:

$$
\begin{aligned}
X12 + X22 + X32 + X42 &= 3 \text{ (business 2)}; \\
X13 + X23 + X33 + X43 &= 6 \text{ (business 3)}; \\
X14 + X24 + X34 + X44 &= 2 \text{ (business 4)}; \\
X15 + X25 + X35 + X45 &= 1 \text{ (business 5)}; \\
X16 + X26 + X36 + X46 &= 8 \text{ (business 6)}.
\end{aligned}
$$

With the problem thus formulated the next step would be to feed the data into a library or "canned" computer program. The solution to this problem is shown in table 6.4. The total round-trip travel time of the students has been minimized at 1,030 minutes.

## Table 6.4: Number of Students Assigned from School I to Business J

|        | Business |   |   |   |   |   |
|--------|---|---|---|---|---|---|
| School | 1 | 2 | 3 | 4 | 5 | 6 |
| 1      | 0 | 0 | 1 | 0 | 0 | 2 |
| 2      | 3 | 0 | 0 | 0 | 1 | 0 |
| 3      | 0 | 0 | 2 | 0 | 0 | 0 |
| 4      | 0 | 3 | 3 | 2 | 0 | 0 |

As in most problems of this type, student travel time is simply one of many criteria that will enter into the decision about where to assign students. Although the solution to this linear programming problem may well influence the final decision, it will not necessarily determine it.

### Example 2: Busing Students for Integration (adapted from Van Dusseldorp, Richardson, and Foley 1971, pp. 76-79)

A school district has some schools that are racially imbalanced. The board has decided to bus students in order to bring about a better balance. The present enrollment is shown in table 6.5.

## Table 6.5: Racial Composition of Schools in District

|        | Number of Students |       |
|--------|-------|-------|
| School | Black | White |
| A      | 74    | 531   |
| B      | 190   | 442   |
| C      | 611   | 0     |
| D      | 556   | 12    |
| E      | 287   | 314   |
| F      | 36    | 504   |
| G      | 0     | 528   |

The following decisions have been made:

1. Each school shall have at least ninety black and ninety white students.
2. The total enrollment of each school shall remain at the present number.
3. In the morning all students will go to the school they now attend. Those assigned elsewhere will then be bused to those schools.

4. The total mileage traveled by bus by all students is to be kept to a minimum.

The mileage between the schools is charted in table 6.6.

**Table 6.6: Distances Between Schools**

| School | A | B | C | D | E | F | G |
|--------|-----|-----|-----|-----|-----|-----|-----|
| A | – | | | | | | |
| B | 3.1 | – | | | | | |
| C | 2.7 | 3.7 | – | | | | |
| D | 4.6 | 3.8 | 2.4 | – | | | |
| E | 5.9 | 3.9 | 4.4 | 2.1 | – | | |
| F | 6.2 | 7.3 | 3.6 | 4.1 | 6.1 | – | |
| G | 8.8 | 8.2 | 6.0 | 4.3 | 5.1 | 4.1 | – |

Thus, the problem is to determine, within the above constraints, how many black and white students are to be bused from each school to each of the other schools (*decision variables*), so that the total distance traveled by all students is minimized (*objective function*). The measure of effectiveness in this problem is expressed in terms of total miles traveled by all bused students.

Before we begin to set up this problem, which is similar in form to the last problem, it would be useful to discuss it with an eye toward finding the most economical and simple solution. What general observations can we make? First, two of the seven schools under consideration (schools B and E) are superfluous to the problem because both already have sufficient quantities of black and white students. In addition, neither would serve as a school from which to send students into other schools because one of the constraints (2) dictates that the school populations remain the same. So if we bused students out of schools B and E to fill quotas in other schools, we would have to bus in an equal number from other schools. Even if schools B and E were on a direct path between two other schools, it would be easier to by-pass these schools rather than to exchange one group of students for an equal number. Therefore, we have already eliminated two schools from the problem.

Essentially, two schools will be sending black students (schools C and D), and three schools will be sending white students (schools A, F, and G). Black students will be bused to schools that are busing white students, and vice versa. Consequently, there need be only twelve terms in the objective function (instead of the much larger number required if all sending and receiving possibilities were to be included). The objective function can then be stated as

Minimize $Z = 2.7Xca + 3.6Xcf + 6.0Xcg + 4.6Xda + 4.1Xdf +$
(total one-  $4.3Xdg + 2.7Yac + 4.6Yad + 3.6Yfc + 4.1Yfd +$
way travel  $6.0Ygc + 4.3Ygd,$
in miles)

where $X$ represents numbers of black students to be bused to pre-dominantly white schools, and $Y$ represents numbers of white students to be bused to predominantly black schools. The subscripts *ca*, *cf*, and *cg* represent travel from school C to schools A, F, and G respectively. In like manner *da*, *df*, and *dg* represent travel from school D to school A, F, and G respectively, and so on.

What about constraints? Ten constraints are required in this prob-lem. By referring back to table 6.5 we see, for example, that the number of black students bused into school A must be at least six-teen (to equal the minimum quota of ninety) and that these students are going to come from schools C and D. This can be expressed as the following constraint:

$$Xca + Xda \geqslant 16.$$

Also, in order that school populations not be changed, the number of white students bused from school A (to schools C and D) must equal the number of black students bused into school A. This is rep-resented as the following constraint:

$$Yac + Yad - Xca - Xda = 0.$$

The same kinds of constraints must be constructed for white stu-dents being sent to school C, white students being sent to school D, black students being sent to school F, and black students being sent to school G. The following eight functions represent these con-straints:

(white students sent to school C)
$$Yac + Yfc + Ygc \geqslant 90$$
$$Xca + Xcf + Xcg - Yac - Yfc - Ygc = 0;$$
(white students sent to school D)
$$Yad + Yfd + Ygd \geqslant 78$$
$$Xda + Xdf + Xdg - Yad - Yfd - Ygd = 0;$$

(black students sent to school F)
$$Xcf + Xdf \geqslant 54$$
$$Yfc + Yfd - Xcf - Xdf = 0;$$
(black students sent to school G)
$$Xcg + Xdg \geqslant 90$$
$$Ygc + Ygd - Xcg - Xdg = 0.$$

The methodology whereby this problem is solved is discussed in greater detail in chapter thirteen. It is sufficient to say here that using linear programming this problem can be solved. The solution is shown in table 6.7.

### Table 6.7: Number of Black and White Students Bused Between Schools

|  |  | Number of students | |
| --- | --- | --- | --- |
| From school | To school | Black | White |
| A | C |  | 24 |
| C | A | 24 |  |
| C | F | 54 |  |
| C | G | 12 |  |
| D | G | 78 |  |
| F | C |  | 54 |
| G | C |  | 12 |
| G | C |  | 78 |

The minimum number of miles traveled by all bused students is 1333.2.

### The Traveling Salesman Problem

The traveling salesman problem is different from the transportation problem in that it deals with routing vehicles among a number of stops as opposed to determining quantities to be shipped between sources and destinations. This routing problem is commonly referred to as the traveling salesman problem because it is usually formulated as follows: "A salesman has a certain number of cities he must visit. He knows the distance (or time, or cost) of travel between every pair of cities. His problem is to select a route which starts at his home city, goes through each city only once, and returns to his home city in the shortest possible distance (or time or cost)" (Ackoff and Rivett 1963, p. 46). In applying the traveling salesman problem to a school setting, the "salesmen" are defined as buses and the "cities" are defined as bus stops. At first glance this problem may appear trivial. If only two bus stops are involved there is, of course, no choice. If three bus stops are involved, one of which is the home base (A), there are two possible routes (ABC and ACB). For four bus stops there are six possible routes. The problem, however, gets complex quickly: with eleven bus stops, for example, there are approximately 3,700,000 possible routes!

Additional factors may complicate the problem. In the most simplified version (the symmetrical case), it is assumed that the distance (or time or cost) between any two bus stops, A and B, is the same regardless of the direction of travel (A to B, or B to A). This may not always be the case. A number of factors may have the effect of requiring more cost or time to go from A to B than to go from B to A (e.g., one-way streets, steep grades, time of day). In this case (the asymmetrical case), calculations are obviously more complicated.

While it is possible to find a single best solution to the traveling salesman problem, the method required is very different from the linear programming solution to the transportation problem. The linear programming solution represents an *analytical* solution, whereas the solution to the traveling salesman represents a *numerical* solution. (The difference between these two types of solutions can perhaps best be explained by using the analogy of calculating a square root. We are most familiar with the *analytical* approach, in which the process starts out by pairing digits, determining the largest square root for the pair of digits furthest to the left, etc. A *numerical* approach to calculating the square root of a number, say 15, is to take a number, say 3.01, which when squared is less than 15, add .01 and square repeatedly until you get as close to 15 as possible.)

One of many possible numerical approachs to solving the traveling salesman problem is to add bus stops to the itinerary (one at a time in random order) until all cities are included in the problem. As each bus stop is added, evaluate all the alternative ways it could be incorporated into the current network. This is done by calculating the effect of inserting the bus stop between every other pair of bus stops. You would then choose the most desirable point on the bus route to insert the stop, given that the balance of the routing remains unchanged. Using a computer, this task could be repeated many times in order to find a satisfactory solution.

In solving this problem numerically, we have used some simple rules of thumb, called *heuristics*. The solution obtained is likely not to be the best one, but generally good enough. The heuristic technique is used whenever time and money do not allow for a better solution or whenever the problem is so hopelessly complex that better solutions are nearly impossible. Much of the analytical work done in school bus routing and scheduling is heuristic in nature.

## Scheduling Bus Routes with the Aid of the Computer

Because school bus routing and scheduling are essentially heuristic activities, a plausible management objective is to develop "acceptable" or "good" bus routes and not optimal routes. A "good" set of bus routes could mean, for example, routes that keep the total bus fleet mileage relatively low, with the constraint that no pupil is kept on a bus longer than an agreed number of minutes. It is virtually impossible to know when, for example, total fleet mileage is at a *minimum,* because there are simply too many combinations of variables to consider, including all bus stops, all possible routes, and different sizes of buses.

By learning from many modifications of a system over a long period of time, it would be possible to develop a highly efficient school transportation system, if there was no change in student population in terms of numbers or locations. Unfortunately, in most school districts this is simply not the case. Many school districts report a complete turnover of students during the course of a school year in some of their schools. This problem is magnified several times in transporting students with physical or educational handicaps. Changes in road conditions require route changes. A further complicating factor is that some transportation reimbursement formulas in some states constrain the most efficient routing of buses. (This is discussed separately at the end of the chapter.) The net impact of these facts is that transportation officials in medium- and large-size school districts are forced to make daily changes in routes and schedules.

In order to maintain or improve efficiency in the midst of rapidly changing constraints, it is necessary to develop a generalized method for scheduling transportation, rather than one specific to a unique setting at one point in time. What are the information requirements necessary to schedule and route student transportation? In most school settings there are at least eight discrete points of information required by transportation supervisors for each designated bus route:

1. The bus capacity, i.e., the maximum number of children who would normally be allowed to travel on the bus (for any given bus, the figure will vary depending on the ages of the students);
2. The bus stops (in the order of pickup);
3. The arrival times at the bus stops and at the school;
4. The actual number of students on the bus;
5. The duration of the trip from the first pickup to the school (usually in minutes);
6. The sum of the traveling times of every student on the trip (ob-

tained by multiplying, for each pickup point, the number of students at the point and the time these students will be on the bus);

7. The interstop travel times, in minutes; and

8. An array of numbers of students by travel distances, i.e., the numbers of students using the bus tabulated by given ranges of distances.

The general strategy for determining the system of student transportation is:

1. Divide the district into sub-areas for routing purposes;

2. Determine pickup points or bus stops;

3. Within each sub-area determine the route of the bus among the pickup points; and

4. Determine the time of the pickups and deliveries.

Because it is probable that pickup points, routes, schedules, and even bus capacities within each sub-area will change continually, the transportation management system must, above all else, be amenable to inexpensive and rapid change. It is for that reason that the computer can be well utilized.

Traditionally, the key tool for scheduling and routing school buses has been a large district map, repleat with pins and, sometimes, strands of yarn connecting pins. The pins represent pickup points or students, while the yarn represents bus routes. (In settings with relatively very low density and highly stable student populations, this may still be the most efficient system.)

For many of the reasons cited above the "pin map" is increasingly difficult and ultimately costly to operate. It becomes difficult as alternative routes and schedules must be considered. It becomes costly because of the man-hours consumed in updating it and the excess transportation costs incurred by less frequent updates.

It is in the area of improving the pin map that the computer has been especially helpful. The general process whereby the pin map is recreated on a computer is described below. Figure 6.8 shows the road system of a sub-area in a school district. The dots and corresponding numbers represent the current pickup points and the number of students at each pickup point in that area. The distances between the pickup points would be measured using an odometer along the most direct set of roads connecting each pair of pickup points.

This information is modified for input into a computer by means of a coordinate system. A grid network is superimposed on the map,

Figure 6.8: Road System of a Sub-Area in a School District

and each grid line is given a number. See figure 6.9. The students can now be located by means of the coordinate system formed by the grid line numbers. The lines must be numbered consecutively but need not start with 1.

Near the far left-hand side of the map is a single stop for two students. Using accepted conventions, that stop can be identified as "1513." The scale of the grid system used in any particular setting will be determined largely by the size of the district and the density of the population. Increased precision is paid for with increased complexity and cost. The probable size of one side of a grid will range from one-half mile to a mile.

Distances between points on the coordinate system are calculated as straight lines. In order to determine interstop travel times, a factor must be calculated for converting distance (in miles) to time (in minutes). This conversion factor is calculated as follows:

$$F = (P) \times (Q) \times (R),$$

where $F$ = the conversion factor; $P$ = the size of the coordinate grid (in miles) selected; $Q$ = the conversion of straight line miles to road miles between points; and $R$ = the average time (in minutes) taken for a bus to travel one mile.

As an example, assume a 1/2 mile grid is used, and let one straight-line mile be equivalent to 1 1/8 road miles. If the average speed of the school bus is 30 miles per hour, it will travel 1 mile in 2 minutes. Thus $P = 1/2$, $Q = 1\ 1/8$, and $R = 2$. The conversion factor is 1.125 minutes per half mile grid. This procedure is useful in deriving average travel times, but there are often cases in a sub-area where actual distances are far greater than the theoretical average (e.g., if two bus stops are not directly connected by road).

The computer program is capable of handling a wide variety of specific conditions, and can reference all possible pairs of points in the coordinate system. However, we are concerned only with those points where bus stops are located. Consequently, it is necessary to specify those locations separately. To accomplish this, various methods have been used; one developed by Tracz and Norman (1969) is described here. Those grid squares that contain a bus stop are given a number in addition to the coordinate reference and the number of students at the coordinate reference. In using the program written by Tracz and Norman, these new numbers must start at 1 and be consecutive. It is necessary to start with the lowest occupied square in the farthest left column containing any occupied squares, and have

Figure 6.9: Grid Network Superimposed on Map

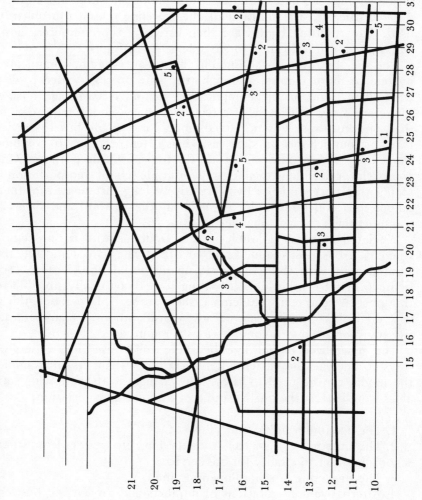

subsequent numbers follow up that column, then the adjacent column, and so forth. (See figure 6.10.)

Once the occupied squares have been identified, and a procedure for determining the travel times between the coordinates has been established, it is possible to determine the shortest route among the pickup points. To determine the route among pickup points a procedure identical to the solution of the traveling salesman problem is used. The resulting routes are then listed by the computer, along with interstop travel times, total student travel time, etc.

The specific routes established in the sub-area may be complicated by one or more factors, although the same process is used to deal with them. One of the complicating factors is two-stage busing. There are many districts where few elementary schools require more than one bus, and it is not uncommon for a single bus to service three or four schools. In such cases it is often necessary to combine elementary schools into one group for transportation purposes. One approach for dealing with single bus/multiple school transportation is to (1) transport students living relatively long distances from their school to a collection point (usually another school) and then (2) transport them to their final destination.

A related approach is double-seating. Double-seating is a procedure whereby a bus drops some children off at one school and fills the vacated seats with children picked up further along the route. (See figure 6.11.) By using double-seating it is theoretically possible to transport twice as many students as there are seats. In practice, this is very difficult to accomplish, because consideration of many alternative transportation area combinations is required.

The generalized model described here can be used in a variety of ways to analyze the current transportation system. As an example, the model can be used to assess how changes in the following variables would affect the quality and cost of pupil transportation:

1. The maximum riding time allowed;
2. The minimum distance students have to reside from their schools in order to qualify for bus service;
3. The staggering of school-opening times;
4. Alternative configurations of numbers and capacity of buses in the fleet;
5. Safety regulations.

To perform such tests by hand would be impractical because of the computation time required, but the introduction of a computer-

Figure 6.10: Identifying Bus Stops on the Grid System

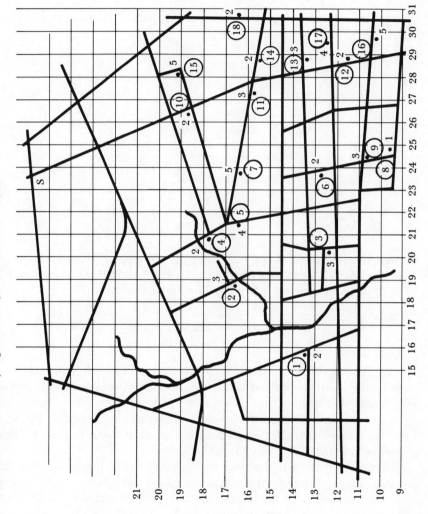

## Figure 6.11: Example of a Double-Seating Bus Route

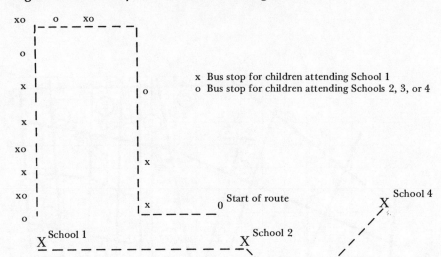

based model provides the necessary capability. (A listing of the computer program described here is available from Dr. George Tracz at the Ontario Institute for Studies in Education.)

## Buy-or-Make Decisions
### (adapted from Elwood 1971, pp. 1-14)

While scheduling and routing bus service to and from school is easily the most important transportation function in schools, managing student transportation is greater in scope than the foregoing discussion implies. This section deals with some other considerations in transportation planning and operations within the context of a decision-making problem: buy vs. make.

What are buy-or-make decisions? Every educational organization makes many fundamental decisions about whether to use its own production skill and resources to make needed items or to purchase those items from some supplier. These "items" include goods (e.g., cabinets, buildings, curriculum) and services (e.g., instructional, maintenance, transportation). Fundamental ingredients in arriving at a buy-or-make decision include:

1. Determination of the good or service needed, including potentially desirable alternatives (quality and quantity);

2. Determination of alternative means of providing the good or service, including cost and benefit data; and

3. Comparison of cost/benefit relationships among selected alternatives.

### Determination of the Need for Transportation

This phase can be broken down into sub-activities:

1. Analysis of the present need for basic service (getting students from home to school);

2. Analysis of the present need for extra service (field trips, etc.);

3. Short-term projection of the need for basic service;

4. Short-term projection of the demand for extra services in order of importance.

The present need for basic service can be analyzed by making a survey of current transportation operations. For each area the requisite data would include (1) number of buses; (2) total seating capacity; (3) total number of students transported; (4) route mileage; and (5) cost per day. In some cases, data can be usefully organized by current attendance areas and by method of service (board-owned vs.

### Table 6.12: Sample Data Collection Sheet: Basic Service

| | | Daily service detail | | | | |
|---|---|---|---|---|---|---|
| | Method of service | Number of buses | Total seating capacity | Students transported | Route mileage | Cost/ day |
| Elementary | 1. Contractor A | 7 | 400 | 600 | 400 | $210 |
| | 2. Contractor B | 1 | 60 | 60 | 50 | 33 |
| | 3. Board fleet | 2 | 140 | 260 | 120 | 70 |
| | 4. | | | | | |
| Total elementary | | 10 | 600 | 920 | 570 | $313 |
| Secondary | 1. Contractor A | 14 | 1000 | 900 | 800 | 600 |
| | 2. Contractor B | 3 | 180 | 150 | 200 | 60 |
| | 3. | | | | | |
| | 4. | | | | | |
| Total secondary | | 17 | 1180 | 1050 | 1000 | $660 |

Source: Bryan C. Elwood, *Student Transportation: Comparing Alternative Methods of Providing the Service* (Toronto: The Ontario Institute for Studies in Education, 1971), p. 6. Reprinted by permission.

contracted). Table 6.12 shows a simple data collection sheet containing sample data.

The analysis of the present need for extra service closely relates to the program-planning activities going on in a district. Basic data required for the analysis include the frequency of trips in various programs and their respective time and mileage averages. Table 6.13 shows a sample data collection sheet.

## Table 6.13: Sample Data Collection Sheet: Extra Service

|  | | | Annual service detail | |
| --- | --- | --- | --- | --- |
|  | Program | Number of trips | Average mileage (miles/trip) | Average duration (hours/trip) |
| Elementary | Extracurricular | 30 | 50 | 2.5 |
|  | Excursions | 25 | 75 | 5.0 |
| Secondary | Extracurricular | 75 | 60 | 3.0 |
|  | Excursions | 50 | 97 | 5.5 |

Source: Bryan C. Elwood, *Student Transportation: Comparing Alternative Methods of Providing the Service* (Toronto: The Ontario Institute for Studies in Education, 1971), p. 6. Reprinted by permission.

### Basic Service

In projecting the need for basic service, the planning period should be sufficiently short so that operational decisions can keep pace with changing conditions and objectives (e.g., roughly three years). Clearly, program plans and enrollment estimates need to be periodically updated.

Before future needs can be projected, three basic questions must be answered.

1. What unit of measure will be used to indicate the need for transportation? If number of buses is the unit of measure, a working average capacity would have to be determined.

2. What constitutes the amount of "work" the buses do? Two units are applicable: the loading ratios (the number of students carried by each bus each day) and route lengths.

3. How can the proportion of future student population be determined?

Basically, changes in enrollment patterns need to be projected by grade level within each attendance area. (See chapter fourteen for an extended discussion of how this might be done.) If this cannot be done it will be necessary to make several assumptions about uniform change throughout the district, which may be simplistic and affect the estimates adversely. Assumptions would include, for example: (1) that student population will increase uniformly throughout the district and (2) that the proportion of students requiring basic service will remain constant over the planning period. Once these data have been obtained, basic service can be predicted in terms of the number of buses required each year over a three-year period.

Next, average loading ratios (ALR) are found by dividing the number of transported students by the total bus seating capacity, then multiplying by the standard bus capacity used to measure basic service demands.

Finally, the demand for basic service over the three-year period is projected simply by dividing enrollment projections by the average

## Exhibit 6.14: Projection of Basic Service Needs

| | Current year | Planning year 1 | Planning year 2 | Planning year 3 |
|---|---|---|---|---|
| *Area i enrollment projection* | | | | |
| Elementary | 5,000 | 5,313 | 5,625 | 5,938 |
| Secondary | 4,000 | 4,400 | 4,800 | 5,200 |

| | Current year | Planning year 1 | Planning year 2 | Planning year 3 |
|---|---|---|---|---|
| *Projection of daily basic service demand* | | | | |
| Elementary | 920 | 978 | 1,035 | 1,043 |
| Secondary | 1,050 | 1,057 | 1,262 | 1,368 |

*Loading ratios (average bus capacity = 60)*

Elementary (920 students ÷ 600 seats) $\times$ 60 = 92.0 students per bus

Secondary (1,050 students ÷ 1,180 seats) $\times$ 60 = 54.3 students per bus

| | Current year | Planning year 1 | Planning year 2 | Planning year 3 |
|---|---|---|---|---|
| *Projection of buses needed* | | | | |
| Elementary | 10.0 | 10.6 | 11.3 | 11.9 |
| Secondary | 19.7 | 21.7 | 23.6 | 25.6 |
| Total | | | | 38 buses |

From a survey of Area i it is known that 5,000 elementary and 4,000 secondary students are currently in attendance. Projections have been made for the district by attendance area. Also, from survey data it is known that 920 elementary and 1,050 secondary school students (18.4 percent and 26.3 percent of Area i enrollment respectively) are bused to school each day. We assume that these percentages will remain the same throughout the forecast period, and the resulting projection of demand for busing are the products of these percentages times the enrollment projections. Next the average loadings are found. Finally, the need for basic service over the planning period is projected by dividing the student demand projections by the average loading factors.

loading ratios calculated above. The resulting projections for all attendance areas are then summed to obtain the projection for the entire district. An example of these steps is shown in exhibit 6.14.

## Extra Service

The need for extra service usually arises in connection with such extracurricular activities as musical or dramatic presentations, athletic competitions, and excursion or enrichment programs. Also, the need for such service in a particular year is usually not known well in advance, and actual arrangements are usually made on several weeks notice. Since the amount of extra service is largely determined by district administration (i.e., not mandated), it is useful to analyze several probable levels of service for cost comparisons.

To project the need for basic service, demand is stated in terms of the numbers of buses required. This can be done because the service is regular. Extra service, however, is not regular. The trip parameters that affect cost (time and mileage) can vary widely. Consequently, it is necessary to state demand for extra service in terms of groups of trips that have similar parameters. Elwood (1970) groups trips by instructional program. Other classifications could include length of trip and number of students. In this discussion, extra service trips are grouped by program. The average trip parameters are estimated for each program. The operational measure for projecting extra service then becomes the *number* of trips for each program along with its average trip parameters.

Basically, data from several sources must be pieced together in order to broadly specify those programs requiring extra service. Within a program budgeting context, it is possible that such data could be readily built in and extracted, thereby eliminating the need to piece together data from various sources. These sources could include (1) specific board policy and budget statements on programs and activities; (2) program plans; (3) transportation records from previous years; and (4) surveys.

Although there are several ways that extra service can be estimated (e.g., by curve fitting or by analyzing budget requests), Elwood recommends a three-stage process:

1. Develop appropriate categories of trips and estimate the annual number of trips in each category;
2. Estimate the average mileage and time per trip for each category;

3. Rank the categories by priority according to interpretation of board policy and curriculum planning groups. The resulting list should reflect the probable range of need for extra service. See the example in table 6.15.

## Table 6.15: Projection of Need for Extra Service

| Program | Trips/Year | Miles/Trip | Hours/Trip | Priority |
|---|---|---|---|---|
| Extracurricular | | | | |
| Elementary | 30 | 50 | 2.5 | level |
| Secondary | 75 | 60 | 3.0 | 1 |
| Excursion* | | | | level |
| Secondary | 173 | 97 | 5.5 | 2 |
| Middle | 44 | 75 | 5.0 | level 3 |
| Elementary | 154 | 75 | 5.0 | level 4 |

*Figures for excursions are based on one trip per class per year, with an assumed average class size of 30.

The categories of programs listed above describe the range of extra service from minimum (level 1) to maximum (level 4). These categories and parameters are the same as those listed in table 6.13.

For the extracurricular program, the number of trips from the transportation survey shown in table 6.13 is adjusted upward to year 3 after consideration of all relevant information—enrollment projections, the number of new schools to be added to the system, the future composition of the extracurricular program, etc. (In this example we have assumed for the sake of simplicity that no growth occurs in the program.) Average trip parameters are also taken from table 6.13.

For the excursion programs, the number of trips in year 3 is estimated from the enrollment projections developed earlier (table 6.14) assuming, for this example, 30 students per class.

## Selections of Alternative Systems

In projecting the need for transportation the *amount* of service required must be established. At this point then, one task is to generate alternative means for providing that level of service. School boards have two general alternative methods for transporting students: they can contract the services of one or more private operators ("buy") or they can purchase or lease and operate their own fleet of buses ("make"). In reality they have many alternatives, which are various combinations of the two methods. For example, figure 6.16 shows graphically the range of alternatives that exists if the known or estimated demand is for 200 school buses. One of these examples is shown, i.e., a system composed of 150 board-owned buses and 50 contracted buses. Although consideration of many alternatives appears to be necessary, many can be eliminated

**Figure 6.16: The Contract-Purchase Mix**

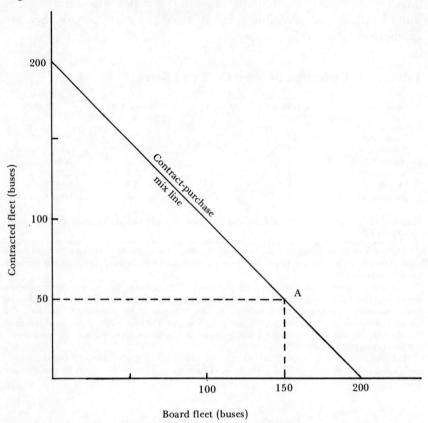

Board fleet (buses)

because they are not desirable or feasible. Consequently, once the overall range of alternatives has been established (the contract-purchase mix), the next step is to select those alternatives that are acceptable.

How does the selection process work? In essence it is designed by consensus:

The transportation planner makes a preliminary selection of the more reasonable alternatives. The people who are directly or indirectly concerned with student transportation are then consulted. These include board officials, staff members responsible for coordinating transportation at the schools, trustees, parents and students, contractors, and other experts in local transportation systems. Through consultation and discussion, the list of alternatives is narrowed down and the proposed system designs are revised. During this process of selecting the reasonable alternatives the transportation planner functions as both a catalyst and synthesizer. He proposes a number of transportation systems and tries them out on various advisory groups. He uses their feedback to eliminate and revise until, through compromise and consensus, the four or five most practical and acceptable alternatives emerge. These are the alternatives that will subsequently be compared by cost to determine the best system overall. (Elwood 1971, p. 10)

During this process of selecting acceptable alternatives, a range of qualitative issues should emerge that have the effect of ruling out many alternatives. Several of these considerations are discussed briefly below.

*Feasibility* deals with the physical requirements and constraints associated with the actual implementation of a proposed system. Unless a transportation system can be readily implemented, it is not feasible.

The remaining alternatives must also be judged according to how well they satisfy *user requirements.* Examples of specific questions that can be asked here include: "Is the system flexible enough to meet current user programs? Can the required degree of safety be met and maintained?"

Alternative proposals must be *compatible* with board policies. Criteria for compatibility would deal with questions of taxpayer reactions, moral obligations to present operators and employees, etc.

Additional considerations in the design of alternative transportation systems include fleet size, fleet maintenance and repairs, and staffing. Two factors related to *fleet size* that may reduce the range of realistic alternatives are the resources available to local contractors.

The desired method of *fleet maintenance* for alternative systems that include board buses should be decided on early, since maintenance is a basic design consideration. (Bus maintenance itself can be seen as a class of buy-or-make decisions.) Factors to be analyzed include cost, standard of upkeep, and availability of facilities. The total cost of in-house and contracted bus upkeep for each of the alternative systems should be estimated. Factors affecting total cost of alternatives will be influenced by possible variances in standards of upkeep among alternatives as well as the presence or absence of maintenance facilities.

Another important variable requiring analysis is *staffing.* It will be necessary to generate staff requirements for supervising and operating each of the alternative systems. The precise staffing configurations of the various alternatives will depend upon many factors.

(Each of the general considerations discussed above would have to be pursued in much greater detail in an actual analysis.)

Once established, the alternative programs would have to be *costed out.* That is, cost estimating would be made of each system alternative for each of the possible levels of total service (basic service and different levels of extra service). These cost data are then incorporated into an overall evaluation of alternatives. Appendix A is an example of such an analysis.

## Suboptimization

Much has been said about the benefits of efficiency resulting from systematic analysis. Rigorous efforts to organize, schedule, and route bus fleets will yield dollar savings while providing better service. One implicit assumption is that if two education agencies (e.g., the school district and the state) share the costs of transportation, both agencies will benefit from district efforts to reduce transportation costs. Many states reimburse school districts for certain student transportation costs. Other states merely provide general operating aid, with no specific allocation for transportation costs.

This assumption can be stated another way: If each school district in a state operated its transportation system in a "nearly optimal" manner, the reimbursement costs of the state (and the total costs of student transportation) would be near minimum (optimum). Ironically, this assumption is not necessarily true.

The methods of reimbursement by the state may be such that the minimization of their costs by school districts may result in a less than optimum situation from the perspective of the state. This is a form of *suboptimization.* How this state of affairs can occur is perhaps best illustrated by a specific case, New York State.

In theory, New York State reimburses 90 percent of district-incurred approved school transportation costs. *Approved costs* are basically those that arise from providing daily transportation for students living more than one and one-half miles from school. If the district contracts a bus fleet to provide this transportation, the state finances 90 percent of the cost of the approved contract. If the district operates its own fleet, a complicated state aid formula is used to determine the approved operating expenses.

There are certain irregularities of the reimbursement system that can provide incentive for school districts to suboptimize, i.e., to operate inefficiently in order to minimize district costs, increase state reimbursement, and thereby increase the total cost of transportation.

One is that some expenses included in an approved contracted system are not included as approved expenses in a district-owned system. These nonreimbursable expenses include bus collision insurance, bus driver fringe benefits, and the salary of a district-employed transportation director. The total reimbursement to districts operating their own fleet is therefore less than the reimbursement for the same service provided by a contracted fleet. As a result, the district might choose to contract for bus service, which would be less costly for the district than running its own fleet, but more costly to the state. If both district and state costs were added together, it could be more costly in total. To put it another way, districts are encouraged to be inefficient whenever their costs in operating their own system (the 10 percent not reimbursed by the state plus any unapproved costs as described above) are greater than their outlay for contracting a more expensive privately operated system.

Here is a second, more complex, illustration. Many districts transport pupils who live less than the minimum one and one-half miles from school, and the way in which the state deducts the costs of busing such nonallowable pupils tends to promote inefficiency. This deduction is computed according to the following formula:

$$\text{deduction for transport of nonallowable students} = \frac{\dfrac{\text{nonallowable}}{\text{pupil miles}} \times \dfrac{\text{total operating}}{\text{expenditures}}}{\text{total pupil miles}}.$$

Each bus driver must keep a count of the number of allowable and nonallowable pupils on the bus for each run. A record of the total mileage of the run is also maintained. Total pupil miles is the sum of allowable and nonallowable pupil miles.

Two basic situations can arise in the calculation of pupil miles. If all the pupils on a run are classified as either allowable or nonallowable, then the number of pupil miles is the product of the number of pupils and the total miles traveled by that bus. However, if a run contains both types of pupils the allowable pupil miles are calculated as above, but the nonallowable pupil miles are calculated by multiplying a constant one and one-half times the number of nonallowable pupils. These situations are illustrated in table 6.17.

If a district transports a large number of nonallowable pupils, the formula can encourage it to inefficiently route its buses so as to ensure the presence of at least one allowable pupil on every bus. This results in a decrease in the number of nonallowable pupil miles and a corresponding increase in the amount of state aid received. The

## Table 6.17: Calculation of Pupil Miles

|  | Bus number | Total daily miles | Allowable pupils | Non-allowable pupils | Allowable pupil miles | Non-allowable pupil miles |
|---|---|---|---|---|---|---|
| All allowable | 1 | 10 | 20 | | 200 | |
| All nonallowable | 2 | 10 | | 20 | | 200 |
| Mixed | 3 | 10 | 10 | 10 | 100 | 15 |

following example illustrates the effect on state aid received by a district that reroutes to pick up one allowable pupil on a bus transporting primarily nonallowable pupils: A school district operates two buses, each making twenty runs and costing the district a total of $1,000. Bus 1 carries fifty allowable pupils ten miles per run. Bus 2 transports fifty nonallowable pupils ten miles per run. If there are no other deductions, the approved aidable expenditure for the forty runs is:

$$\$1,000 - \frac{10,000 \times \$1,000}{20,000} = \$500 \text{ (state pays 90 percent of this).}$$

If bus 2 altered its route by two miles to pick up one allowable pupil at an increase of $100, the following would occur:

| Bus number | Total daily miles | Allowable pupils | Nonallowable pupils | Allowable pupil miles | Nonallowable pupil miles |
|---|---|---|---|---|---|
| 1 | 10 | 49 | | 490 | |
| 2 | 12 | 1 | 50 | 12 | 75 |

The aidable expenditure for the forty runs is now:

$$\$1,100 - \frac{1,500 \times \$1,100}{11,540} = \$957.02.$$

The increased cost to the state is $411.32 (.9(957.02 − 500)). The $100 increased cost to the district is more than offset by the increased aid. Here again the formula can encourage inefficient (from the state's perspective) transportation policies among districts that transport large numbers of nonallowable pupils and can indirectly create inequities between districts that choose to bus nonallowable pupils and those that do not or cannot.

The illustrations are included to point out that whether an operating system is "best" or "most efficient" depends in part on one's perspective. Most often managers will proceed (probably rightly) in such a way as to improve operations under their personal responsibility even though this may not necessarily improve (and may reduce) the efficiency of the total operation.

## Questions for Review and Discussion

1. Are the goals of student transportation programs clearer than the goals of, for example, the supply management system or the financial accounting system? If so, what makes them clearer?

2. The merits of busing to achieve racial balance constitute one of the most controversial educational issues of our time. How would the transportation planner go about determining the constraints of this problem?

3. In racial busing, which part of the linear programming problem has the potential for generating the most controversy: the objective function or the constraints? Why? Can the two parts of a linear programming problem really be separately evaluated this way?

4. What general conditions would have to exist before it would become economical to use a computer for transportation scheduling?

5. In what ways could the method of state-level financial aid for transportation affect the buy-or-make decisions of a school district? In what ways could it affect the amount of extra transportation service provided by a school district?

## Appendix A:
## Analyzing Means for Providing Student Transportation
### (adapted from Elwood 1971, pp. 14-24)

In District X, transportation services are currently provided by three contractors who operate a total of fifty-eight buses and by a small board fleet of twenty-two buses, supplemented by two spares. Regular maintenance of the board fleet is handled by one full-time driver in between his regular morning and afternoon routes; however, bus repairs and major maintenance jobs are contracted out to local repair shops. As a preliminary step in the contract-purchase analysis, this method of fleet upkeep (in-house maintenance and contracted repairs) has been evaluated and found to be both adequate and economical. It has therefore been decided to continue with this method of upkeep for any alternative system that involves board buses.

The full-time driver can handle the number of currently projected excursion trips in addition to his regular duties, but these trips are usually handled by twenty-one part-time drivers. It is planned to continue with the present policy of using board buses for extra service, pending results of the cost comparison.

Supervision of the entire operation rests with the staff of the transportation department. The head of this department is thoroughly experienced in all phases of passenger transportation and is a competent administrator as well. His supervisors and supporting personnel include an inspector, a dispatcher, and a part-time clerk-stenographer. Both the board and the administration consider the department's organizational structure to be minimal for adequate supervision of student transportation, whatever the alternative system proposed.

Transportation demand has been projected for the three transportation areas in the district and is summarized in table 6A.1. Of the range of possible alternative systems of transportation, four have been selected for final consideration. The essential ingredients in each are outlined below.

## Table 6A.1: Projected Daily Basic Service Demand in Year 3 by Area

| Area | Elementary | Secondary | Total |
|------|-----------|-----------|-------|
| 1 | 11.9 | 25.6 | 37.5 |
| 2 | 14.1 | 16.2 | 30.3 |
| 3 | 16.0 | 16.2 | 32.2 |
| Total | 42.0 | 58.0 | 100.0 |

(The contract-purchase mix is defined by basic service demand in year 3, i.e., 100 buses.)

The four alternatives vary in a number of ways. As far as staffing, for example, each represents a departure from the present system: but for each alternative, decisions about retention, hiring, firing, and promotion would be different. The staffing requirements of the alternatives are presented in table 6A.2.

Consideration of driver staff first requires an estimation of the number of full-time drivers needed for maintenance and extra service. The number of part-time drivers will then correspond to the number of board-owned buses *not* operated by full-time drivers.

## Table 6A.2: Staffing Requirements of Alternative Systems

| Alternative system | A | B | C | D |
|---|---|---|---|---|
| Board fleet | 24 | — | 105 | 34 |
| Elementary | 10 | — | 42 | 16 |
| Secondary | 12 | — | 58 | 16 |
| Spares | 2 | — | 5 | 2 |
| Repairs | contracted | — | contracted | contracted |
| Maintenance | in-house | — | in-house | in-house |
| Contracted fleets | 78 | 100 | — | 68 |
| Elementary | 32 | 42 | — | 26 |
| Secondary | 46 | 58 | — | 42 |
| Administrative staff | | | | |
| Managers | 1 | 1 | 1 | 1 |
| Route supervisors | — | — | 3 | 1 |
| Inspectors | 1 | 1 | — | 1 |
| Dispatchers | 1 | 1 | 3 | 1 |
| Clerk-stenos | 1/2 | 1/2 | 2 | 1 |
| Mechanics | — | — | 1 | — |

It is known that a trained driver, working between his scheduled routes, can service approximately fifty buses a month. Since all buses are serviced monthly, the number of full-time drivers assigned to this operation will depend on the size of the boards' fleet—there should be one full-time driver for every sixty buses. Table 6A.3 shows the full-time drivers required to maintain buses in each of the alternative systems being considered.

## Table 6A.3: Full-time Drivers Required for Basic Service by the System

| | System | | | |
|---|---|---|---|---|
| | A | B | C | D |
| Board buses | 24 | 0 | 105 | 34 |
| Full-time drivers* | 1 | 0 | 2 | 1 |

*The number of full-time drivers is obtained by dividing the number of board buses by 60 (the number of buses one man can service monthly).

In District X it happens that the extracurricular program involves short trips that are generally handled by part-time drivers before and after their regular route duty. Most of the excursion programs planned, however, will take place during the school day. They will be scheduled evenly over 160 days of the school year and will not interfere with regular route service.

Because the trip averages five to five and one-half hours, each trip requires one bus and a driver for an entire day. As a result, the complement of full-time drivers required for excursions will correspond to the number of trips scheduled daily, and this in turn will depend on the excursion component of each level of extra service and will hold for each of the alternative systems. For example, at extra service level 4, the projected number of excursion trips is 435 + 145 = 490, or 1,070 annually. If the excursion trips are spaced evenly over 160 days, then roughly seven must be scheduled each day. Therefore, seven full-time drivers will be needed to handle extra service excursions at level 4. Table 6A.4 shows the full-time staff required at each level of extra service.

### Table 6A.4: Full-time Drivers Required for Extra Service by Level

| Level | Excursion: Trips/Year | Full-time drivers* |
|-------|----------------------|--------------------|
| 1**   | 0                    | 0                  |
| 2     | 435                  | 3                  |
| 3     | 580                  | 4                  |
| 4     | 1070                 | 7                  |

*The number of full-time drivers is obtained by dividing the number of excursion trips by 160 (the number of school days available for excursions).
**Level 1 (extracurricular) is handled by part-time drivers.

Table 6A.5 gives a complete summary of the composition of the board driving staff for each of the systems, by level of service. Here the total number of drivers remains constant. The number of part-time drivers is simply the difference between the number of full-time drivers and the number of board-owned buses in the system proposed.

### Table 6A.5: Total Drivers Required by System and Quantity of Service

| Quantity of service | System | | | |
|---------------------|--------|---|---|---|
|                     | A      | B | C | D |
| Basic               | 1(21)  | 0 | 2(98) | 1(31) |
| Basic + Level 1     | 1(21)  | 0 | 2(98) | 1(31) |
| Basic + Level 2     | 4(18)  | 0 | 5(95) | 4(28) |
| Basic + Level 3     | 5(17)  | 0 | 6(94) | 5(27) |
| Basic + Level 4     | 8(14)  | 0 | 9(91) | 8(24) |

*Note:* The number of part-time drivers is shown in parentheses following the number of full-time drivers.

In developing cost estimates of the alternative systems, three cost categories are used: capital costs, operating costs, and indirect costs.

Capital costs include:

1. Bus acquisition—the purchase cost or depreciation on board-owned vehicles.
2. Land and buildings—the purchase cost or depreciation on operating and office facilities.
3. Equipment—the purchase cost or depreciation on all tools, service vehicles, and other equipment used to support the transportation operation.
4. Interest—all interest charges incurred in the purchase of all the above.

Operating costs include:

1. Administration—the salaries of the transportation department's administrative and supporting staff.
2. Labor—the wages of the operating staff, including drivers, mechanics, and helpers.
3. Benefits—the board's contribution to fringe and statutory benefits for all members of the transportation department.
4. Bus operation—the cost of actually running board buses, such as parts and supplies, licenses, insurance, and maintenance and repair contracts.
5. Transportation contracts—the fees paid to private operators who provide transportation services to the board.
6. Rent—charges for rental of buses, lands and buildings, and equipment.

Indirect costs, or general overhead (the portion of the total board budget that is spread over all operating departments), include the cost of senior administration, general supporting services (e.g., accounting and purchasing), utilities, heat, office supplies, etc. They are distributed proportionately among the operating departments according to their budgets.

### Application of the Cost Model: System D

In system D, the specifications for basic service are as follows:

Board fleet
    Elementary—16
    Secondary—16

Spares—2
TOTAL—34 buses
Contracted fleets
Elementary—26
Secondary—42
TOTAL—68 buses
Staff
Manager—1
Route supervisor—1
Inspector—1
Dispatcher—1
Clerk-stenographer—1
Full-time driver—1
Part-time drivers—31
Average routes
Elementary—11,000 miles/year
Secondary—12,000 miles/year

## Costing Basic Service

The first steps in establishing the cost of basic service are to determine the appropriate items in the costing structure and to collect the necessary data.

### Capital costs

1. Bus acquisition (in this case bus replacement is a continuing program, so that the annual repayment schedule will remain constant)
   a. Size of board fleet: 34 sixty-passenger school buses
   b. Net purchase price, including trade-in: $8,100/bus
   c. Financing: five-year debentures yielding 7 1/2 percent; the principal to be repaid in five annual installments of $1,620/bus
   Annual cost of bus acquisition = 34 buses × $1,620/bus = $55,080
2. Land and buildings
   a. Value of garage and property: $80,000
   b. Method of costing: straight-line depreciation over 40 years
   Annual cost of land and buildings = $80,000 ÷ 40 = $2,000
3. Equipment
   a. Value of tools and other equipment for servicing buses: $10,000
   b. Method of costing: straight-line depreciation over 10 years
   Annual cost of equipment = $10,000 ÷ 10 = $1,000

4. Interest
   a. Interest repayment schedule: 7 1/2 percent paid annually on outstanding principal balance of debentured investment
   b. Method of costing: total interest averaged over five-year repayment period (approximately $350/bus/year)
   Annual interest charges on bus acquisition = 34 buses × $350 = $11,900

*Operating costs*

1. Administration (annual salaries)
   a. Manager: $10,000
   b. Route supervisor: $8,000
   c. Inspector: $7,400
   d. Dispatcher: $7,000
   e. Clerk-stenographer: $5,200
   Annual cost of administration = $37,600

2. Labor (annual wages)
   a. Full-time driver: $6,300
   b. Part-time drivers (31): $1,900/driver
   Annual cost of labor = $6,300 + (31 × $1,900) = $65,200

3. Benefits
   a. Fringe benefits for full-time employees: 11 percent of gross earnings
   b. Statutory benefits for part-time employees: 6 percent of gross earnings
   Annual cost of benefits = (0.11 × $37,600) + (0.11 × $6,300) + (0.06 × $58,900) ≈ $8,360

4. Bus operation
   a. Number of basic service routes and average annual mileages: 16 elementary school routes at 11,000 miles/year; 16 secondary school routes at 12,000 miles/year
   b. Bus operating costs (from adjusted historical data): gasoline (5.4¢/mile), other supplies and parts (2.0¢/mile), and repair contracts (7.0¢/mile); total = 14.4¢/mile
   c. Vehicle insurance and licenses: $160/bus
   Annual cost of bus operation = (16 routes × 11,000 miles/route × 14.4¢/mile) + (16 routes × 12,000 miles/route × 14.4¢/mile) + (34 buses × $160/bus ≈ $58,430)

5. Transportation contracts
   a. Number of basic service routes and lowest annual average prices tendered: 26 elementary school routes at $5,500/route; 42 secondary school routes at $6,000/route
   Annual cost of transportation contracts = (26 routes × $5,500/route) + (42 routes × $6,000/route) = $395,000

*Indirect costs*
1. General overhead rate calculated by accounting department: 5 percent
2. Sum of capital and operating costs above: $634,570
   Annual indirect costs = 0.05 × $634,570 ≈ $31,730

All the applicable costs for operating basic service transportation using System D have now been calculated. They work out to a total of $666,300 per year (see table 6A.6).

**Table 6A.6: Estimated Yearly Cost of Basic Service: System D**

| | |
|---|---:|
| Capital costs | |
| Bus acquisition | $ 55,080 |
| Land, buildings, and equipment | 3,000 |
| Interest charges | 11,900 |
| Operating costs | |
| Administration (salaries) | 37,600 |
| Labor (wages) | 65,200 |
| Benefits | 8,360 |
| Bus operation | 58,430 |
| Contract fees | 395,000 |
| Indirect costs | 31,730 |
| Total | $666,300 |

*Costing Extra Service*

When the additional expenditures required for each level of extra service have been calculated, they can be combined with the cost of basic service to derive the range of transportation costs for System D. Table 6A.6 specifies the levels of this variable component of the transportation demand.

Since it is board policy to handle extra service with a board-owned fleet whenever possible, the cost of contracting out extra service would normally be obtained only if System B, which is an entirely contracted service, were costed. In this example, we have calculated the cost of extra service by both basic methods for the sake of completeness and as an illustration of the similarities and differences in the procedures for costing each method.

Essentially, the cost of extra service boils down to those direct operating expenses that are associated with either the number of miles driven or with contractors' service charges, plus a proportionate increase in indirect overhead. It is assumed here that the extra administrative burden can be absorbed by the same staff. Below are the pertinent items and unit costs for extra service.

*Operating costs*
1. Labor wage and benefits
   Level 1 of extra service, which involves only the extracurricular program, is handled entirely by part-time drivers who are paid at an hourly rate. Levels 2, 3, and 4 of extra service, which involve excursion trips, are handled by an increasing number of full-time drivers; here, the net additional expense increases in proportion to the number of drivers shifting from part- to full-time work, and is simply the difference between the wages and benefits in the two classifications.
   a. Annual bus operating time at level 1 (see table 6A.6): 850 hours.
   b. Part-time drivers' wages and benefits: $3.33/hour
   c. Net additional expense when a driver shifts from part- to full-time work: $4,980/driver
   d. Additional full-time drivers required for extra service (see table 6A.4): level 1—0; level 2—3; level 3—4; level 4—7
   Annual cost of labor wages and benefits:
   level 1 = 850 hours × $3.33/hour = $2,830
   level 2 = $2,830 + (3 × $4,980) = $17,770
   level 3 = $2,830 + (4 × $4,980) = $22,750
   level 4 = $2,830 + (7 × $4,980) = $37,690
2. Bus operation
   Since insurance and licenses are already paid for, they do not add to the cost of providing extra service and the costs of bus operation rise in direct proportion to the mileage driven. However, there is a slight reduction in unit cost for extra service attributable to the improved gasoline mileage that results from decreased idling time.
   a. Bus operating costs, including gasoline, parts and supplies, and repair contracts (from adjusted historical data): 13¢/mile
   b. Annual mileage for extra service (see table 6A.6): level 1—17,000 miles; level 2—59,195 miles; level 3—70,070 miles; level 4—106,820 miles
   Annual cost of bus operation:
   level 1 = 13¢ × 17,000 miles ≈ $2,210
   level 2 = 13¢ × 59,195 miles ≈ $7,700
   level 3 = 13¢ × 70,070 miles ≈ $9,110
   level 4 = 13¢ × 106,820 miles ≈ $13,890

3. Transportation contracts

In order to compare the cost of contracted with board-operated extra service, the three local contractors were asked to submit per-trip quotations for each extra service program given in table 6A.5. They were also asked to indicate the extent to which they could handle the expected demand. Contractor B's per-trip quotations were lowest for all programs, and he had sufficient capacity to operate all levels of extra service.

a. Annual number of trips and unit prices quoted for extra service programs: extracurricular (elementary)—100 trips at $30/trip; extracurricular (secondary)—200 trips at $36/trip; excursions (secondary)—435 trips at $60.80/trip; excursions (senior elementary)—145 trips at $50/trip; excursions (junior elementary)—490 trips at $50/trip

Annual cost of transportation contracts:

level 1 = (100 trips × $30/trip) + (200 trips × $36/trip) = $10,200

level 2 = $10,200 + (435 trips × $60.80) ≈ $36,650

level 3 = $36,650 + (145 trips × $50/trip) = $43,900

level 4 = $43,900 + (490 trips × $50/trip) = $68,400

*Indirect costs*

As with basic service, all direct extra service costs must be increased by five percent to cover general overhead. Direct operating costs for board-run extra service are obtained by adding the cost of labor wages, benefits, and bus operation at each level; direct operating costs for contracted extra service are simply the cost of the contracts at each level.

1. Annual indirect costs for board-run extra service:

level 1 = 0.05 × ($2,830 + $2,210) ≈ $250

level 2 = 0.05 × ($17,770 + $7,700) ≈ $1,270

level 3 = 0.05 × ($22,750 + $9,110) ≈ $1,590

level 4 = 0.05 × ($37,690 + $13,890) ≈ $2,580

2. Annual indirect costs for contracted extra service:

level 1 = 0.05 × $10,200 = $510

level 2 = 0.05 × $36,650 ≈ $1,830

level 3 = 0.05 × $43,900 ≈ $2,200

level 4 = 0.05 × $68,400 ≈ $3,420

All the applicable costs for operating extra service transportation using both board-owned and contracted buses have now been calculated. The total annual cost at each level of extra service is shown in table 6A.7.

## Table 6A.7: Estimated Yearly Cost of Extra Service by Level

| Level | Board-run service | Contracted service |
|-------|-------------------|--------------------|
| 1 | $ 5,290 | $10,710 |
| 2 | 26,470 | 38,480 |
| 3 | 34,450 | 46,100 |
| 4 | 54,160 | 71,820 |

### Costing Total Service

The basic service costs have been calculated for System D. When these basic service costs are combined with the cost of each of the four levels of extra service shown in table 6A.7, the entire range of transportation service costs can be established.

Suppose now that basic service costs for the three other alternatives have been derived and combined with the extra service costs. The costs derived for board-operated extra service apply to Systems A, C, and D (the alternatives that included board-owned buses); the costs derived for contracted extra service apply to System B. Table 6A.8, which summarizes all the cost data, shows the total annual cost of the four alternative systems at the basic service level and at each of the four levels of extra service.

## Table 6A.8: Costs by System and Quantity of Service

| Quantity of service | System | | | |
|---------------------|-----------------|-----------------|----------------|------------------|
| | A (combination) | B (contracted) | C (board-run) | D (combination) |
| Basic | $649,030 | *$639,420* | $703,370 | $666,300 |
| Basic + level 1 | 654,320 | 650,130 | 708,660 | 671,590 |
| Basic + level 2 | *675,770* | 677,900 | 730,110 | 693,040 |
| Basic + level 3 | *683,480* | 685,520 | 737,820 | 700,750 |
| Basic + level 4 | *703,190* | 711,240 | 757,530 | 720,460 |

In figure 6A.9, the same information is presented graphically. The vertical axis represents the overall cost of transportation services; the horizontal axis, the quantity of transportation, scaled according to bus mileage. For each system, the calculated cost/quantity-of-service points have been joined by straight lines to show a cost "curve." Under the assumptions on which this model is based, the actual relationship between cost and quantity of service will be a step function. However, the "curves" that are obtained by this series of linear

**Figure 6A.9: Costs by System and Quantity of Service**

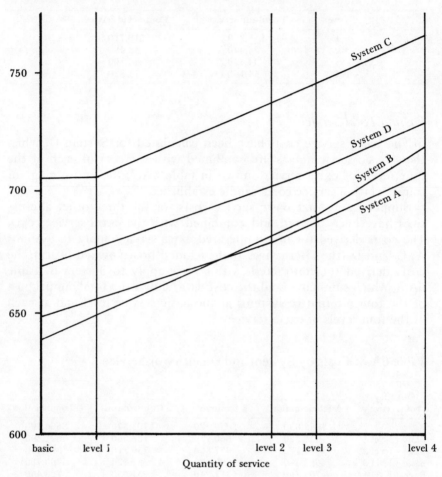

interpolations give a reasonable approximation. These curves permit visual comparison of the general cost trends of the alternative systems.

## Analysis of Costs

Analysis of the results provides both insight into the operation of the student transportation system and a good indication of the alternative best suited to the needs of the district. The transportation planner can use the following procedure in carrying out the analysis:

1. Examine the two systems that most closely approximate the two basic methods of service for differences in the cost of basic service and extra service. (Remember, the cost estimates will contain some error; ±3 percent is not unusual in this kind of analysis.)

If there is a significant difference at the basic service level, determine whether the combination systems reflect a progressive difference related to the board/contract fleet ratio. If they do, then there is probably a fundamental difference between the two basic methods in either the quality of the service or the efficiency of the operation. For example, if costs for basic service increase according to the number of board buses in the various alternatives, then the board-run operation is qualitatively superior, operationally inferior, or both.

In the extra service range, note should be taken of the slopes of the cost curves. If they converge or intersect, this indicates a change in the relative efficiency of the systems with type of service (basic as opposed to extra). If they diverge or parallel one another, this indicates that the systems retain their relative advantage or disadvantage for both types of service. Again, look at the combination systems to see if the difference in cost trends is proportionate to the board/contract fleet ratios.

2. Look next for the system that shows an overall cost advantage at the level at which transportation services will most likely be provided. This system, according to the major selection criterion—overall cost—will be the best system; however, the behavior of its cost curve in relation to the expected growth rates of basic and extra service should also be considered. For example, suppose a completely contracted system is cheapest at the most probable level of operation, but its cost curve converges rapidly on that of a combination system providing extra service with board buses. The "break-even" point— the level of service at which the combination system overtakes the all-contract system—will soon be reached if extra service increases at a faster rate than basic service. And once this level has been surpassed, it is the combination system that will have the overall cost advantage. In a situation of this kind, it is wise to select the system that includes at least some board buses to provide for a gradual transition to the one that is eventually expected to offer the advantage.

3. Identify, if possible, the difference in efficiency between the two basic systems. The effects of operational factors are reflected in various costs:

    a. Capital costs, with the possible exception of those for land and buildings, should be equivalent in board-operated and contracted systems.

b. Operating costs will differ according to the system. Differences in administration costs may result from differences either in the quality of service or in administrative efficiency. Differences in bus operation costs may reflect differences in mileage, the number of stops and starts, road condition, fleet condition, etc. Unfortunately, most operating costs for contracted fleets are irretrievably buried in the contract fee, making item-by-item comparison with the board fleet difficult. (The exception here is licenses, which cost the board $2 per bus, and the contractor $150 to $200 per bus.)

c. Indirect costs will differ in proportion to the differences in the totals of the other costs.

4. Finally, review the entire analysis in light of the results, reassessing assumptions and conditions as well as qualitative criteria in relations to costs. The key personnel involved in the final selection should also have an opportunity to reconsider their decisions. Minor adjustments may be indicated during this stage.

The following example shows the analysis of costs for alternative systems in our hypothetical district:

In the costs for the four systems summarized in table 6A.8, the one with the lowest cost at each quantity-of-service level is shown in italic type.

If we look at basic systems, System C (the all-board system and the most expensive one) costs almost 10 percent more than System B (the all-contract system and the cheapest one). In the two combination systems, the costs rise according to the number of board-owned buses in the system. From these figures, it is fairly obvious that for basic service the contracted operation has a significant economic advantage over board operation under present conditions in the district.

However, if we look at costs over the extra service range, we would draw quite the opposite conclusion. As table 6A.7 shows, board-operated extra service programs are considerably cheaper than contracted ones. The costs for System B rise far more quickly than for the other systems, which handle extra service with board buses, and, as is shown in figure 6A.9, between levels 1 and 2 System B becomes more costly overall than System A. The intersection of their respective cost curves indicates the break-even point.

The administration estimates that extra service programs in the coming year will be expanded to include secondary excursions, so that most transportation will operate close to level 2. At this level, Systems A, B, and D are all economically competitive, although System A has a nonsignificant (less than 3 percent) advantage. In view of the expected increase in extra service programs in the near future, and the clear cost advantage obtainable through providing extra service with board buses, System A is probably the best choice.

After reviewing the entire analysis with senior officials, the transportation manager recommends to the board that System A be adopted. Implementation will be easy; the present system will be augmented by contracted buses over the next three years as basic service demand increases. Meanwhile the board operation will be examined to find out how efficiency can be improved to the point where it is competitive with contracted basic service operations.

## References

Ackoff, Russell L., and Rivett, Patrick. *A Manager's Guide to Operations Research.* New York: John Wiley & Sons, 1963.

Elwood, Bryan C. *Student Transportation: Comparing Alternative Methods of Providing the Service.* Toronto: The Ontario Institute for Studies in Education, 1971.

Thierauf, Robert J., and Grosse, Richard A. *Decision Making Through Operations Research.* New York: John Wiley & Sons, 1970.

Tracz, George S., and Norman, Michael J. *A Computerized System for School Bus Routing.* Toronto: The Ontario Institute for Studies in Education, 1969.

Van Dusseldorp, Ralph A.; Richardson, Duane E.; and Foley, Walter J. *Educational Decision-Making Through Operations Research.* Boston: Allyn & Bacon, 1971.

## Related Readings

Bayliss, Edward T. *Cost Analysis for Regional Transportation System.* Bedford, Mass.: Concord Research Corporation, 1974. ERIC, no. ED098693. Describes a project to develop a model for sharing the transportation of the special education children of nine contiguous school districts. Also describes some of the benefits of a centralized transportation system and suggests legislation which would facilitate cooperative action among school districts.

Delahanty, Joseph F.; Cerrelli, Enzio C.; Gordy, Nelson; and Soule, David H. *Pupil Transportation Safety Program Plan.* Washington, D.C.: National Highway Traffic Safety Administration, U.S. Department of Transportation, 1973. ERIC, no. ED083678. Focuses specific attention on three areas the authors feel need improvement: vehicle brakes, the "structural integrity" of the vehicle, and the seats. A series of recommendations relative to these problems is included.

Larsen, Robert A. *School Bus Ridership Orientation and Training.* Minneapolis: Minneapolis Public School System, 1973. ERIC, no. ED085860. Designed to assist those people who are responsible for child safety on school buses. It includes suggested safety procedures covering the different phases of student transportation (e.g., going to the bus stop and loading at the school for the take-home trip). It also includes an annotated bibliography on child behavior.

Richards, Thomas C. "A Survey of Computerized School Bus Routing." ERIC, no. ED087451, 1973. Presents a survey of the different routing systems that have been developed, including: (1) manual schemes, (2) punched card systems, (3) systems based on shipping, (4) computerized systems, and (5) randomly generated routing systems. The problems of borrowing another district's routing system are discussed.

Wells, Thomas L. *Managing School Transportation. A Handbook.* Toronto: Ontario Department of Education, School Business and Finance Branch, 1973. ERIC, no. ED084644. Provides information and guidelines on the management of school transportation systems, including transportation policies, information system requirements, route design and planning, and contracted vs. board-owned operations.

# 7

# Food Service

## Analytical Prerequisites

In order to discuss food service operations from a management perspective, it is useful to first discuss two concepts relating to cost analysis, *standard costs* and *allocation of costs and expenses*. While these concepts are more or less applicable to all management operations in education, they are discussed here because they apply particularly well to food service management.

Food service operations in educational organizations exhibit many of the characteristics of private manufacturing concerns. First, goods (varieties of food) are produced. Second, pricing and customer tastes are important factors in determining the volume of production. Third, in many instances, educational institutions have determined that food service operations should operate on a self-sustaining basis, that is, not operate at a net loss.

Because they exhibit many of the characteristics of private manufacturing concerns, school food service operations are also subject to many of the same management problems. A manufacturer takes raw materials and, by applying direct labor and factory overhead, converts them into finished products. These are the three general factors involved in production. Although cost data are important for effective management in virtually all areas of educational organizations, they take on particular importance in the management of production processes because decisions must be made continually about the appropriate mixes of these three factors. Therefore, it is important to consider some fundamental areas of cost determination before we embark on an analysis of food service operations.

## Standard Costs

Very generally, *standard costs* may be defined as objectively determined costs that are used as a basis for comparison with actual costs. Standard costs were initially developed as a means of reducing or minimizing cost. As standard cost systems evolved, they were used for other purposes—for example, as an aid to product pricing and as a convenience in accounting for inventories. The most common uses of standard costs are (1) for controlling cost; (2) for costing inventories; (3) for ascertaining interim and annual profits; (4) for planning and budgeting; (5) for studying alternatives; and (6) for pricing present or prospective products. Standard costs are applied in all these ways to the management of food service in educational organizations.

The comparison of the actual and standard costs of an organization, especially by detailed operations, represents a basic objective of a standard of cost system. Consequently, when possible, costs are activity-oriented; that is, they are measured and related to specific operations and responsibility units of an organization.

Different concepts of *standard* are in use. *Past standards,* for example, refer to standards developed entirely from historical data. *Currently attainable standards,* on the other hand, involve analysis of material and work methods, in order to express (in standards) what can be attained by individuals and groups working at high levels of efficiency. Most other definitions of standard differ in terms of time (past, present, future) and level of performance (average, optimum). Unless otherwise indicated, "standard costs" will be used here to refer to average costs derived from current empirical data.

In order to apply concepts of standard costs to food service, three additional concepts must be introduced: *standard hour, operation,* and *cost center.*

## Standard Hour

If the production facilities of a manufacturing organization were devoted to the manufacture of a single product, all production costs, both on a standard and actual basis, could easily be established by units of product. However, food service in an educational organization is not necessarily usefully analyzed as a single-product enterprise. Not only may types of meals vary significantly but the ingredients that go into each meal vary as well.

Comparing actual with standard costs is more complex in a multi-product firm. In order to compare the actual and standard costs of operations and cost centers (organizational entities), some unit must be established as a common denominator of production. Because all production takes time, a common way of expressing the achievement of diverse production is in *time allowed*. Standard time is expressed in terms of machine time or labor time, depending on which is the more suitable expression for a particular operation. A *standard hour* is defined, therefore, as the output that should be accomplished in a particular operation in one clock hour.

## Operation

Although *operation* may be used in a general way simply to express activity, in standard cost accounting it has a technical meaning as well. It refers to the lowest practical subdivision of manufacturing activity. By *practical* we mean that significant costs can be traced to the defined activity and that control efforts of management can be aided by a comparison of actual and standard costs at this level.

## Cost Center

Because the words *department* and *program* have been used ambiguously to refer to areas of analytical interest as well as to areas of responsibility of varying scope, the more restrictive term *cost center* has come into favor in standard cost accounting. It refers to "an area of responsibility under the jurisdiction of an individual at the lowest level of management" (Benninger 1970, p. 39-40). A cost center, therefore, does not necessarily refer to a stipulated amount of space to be occupied or to the accomplishment of some distinct and unified function. In fact, space occupied by different cost centers may vary widely, and the operations under the command of a particular supervisor may be diverse and not amenable to logical classification under some general heading. In general, to determine the scope of a cost center, it is necessary for top management to determine which specific operations are the responsibility of a particular supervisor.

## Constructing Standard Costs

Costs of production factors (materials, labor, and overhead) are standardized in different ways. For material goods *price standards* are commonly used. In dealing with material goods, it is possible to account for the usage of the item in physical units or in the aggregate cost of the usage. Those who advocate the use of dollar standards (as opposed to standards in physical terms) are essentially arguing for a monetary weighting to guide the analyst as to the significance of costs and variance. At the same time they want to avoid the confusion that results from comparing different quantities in terms of different prices per unit of measurement. For example:

| | |
|---|---|
| January excess usage: 400 lbs. @ $5.00 per lb. | $2,000 |
| February excess usage: 500 lbs. @ $4.00 per lb. | 2,000 |
| Change in efficiency | 0 |

Instead, the standard cost accountant often states that price standards are used as a filter to arrive at differences in quantity usages from standard (see Benninger 1970, pp. 39-10–39-13). In the foregoing illustration the cost accountant would use standard prices as a filter in order to obtain more meaningful information concerning usage. For example:

| | |
|---|---|
| January excess usage: 400 lbs. @ $5.00 per lb. | $2,000 |
| February excess usage: 500 lbs. @ $5.00 per lb. | 2,500 |
| Unfavorable change in efficiency | $  500 |

A second production factor is *labor*. Standard labor rates may be computed by reference to labor budgets. Alternatively, rates may be computed by reference to union contracts or to existent levels of rates in the locality modified by anticipated adjustments. It is desirable from a standard costing point of view to establish a single rate for each task in an organization. However, this may be impractical because of differential rates arising from a seniority schedule or from a wage incentive plan. Despite these problems, a single rate can be obtained by using a weighted average approach. Where an operation is construed as embracing several individuals working at different rates, some standard composition of hours and applicable rates can be computed, as shown in table 7.1.

*Direct labor* may be defined as labor that has an obviously traceable relationship to the manufacture of a specific product. The creation of a product is significantly and causally related to this type of labor. A standard direct labor hour may not take place without the appearance of a product. Thus, in the establishment of direct labor hours, a careful investigation is made of the interrelationship of labor and the creation of a product.

## Table 7.1: Calculating Composite Standard Labor Costs

| | |
|---|---|
| 12 labor hours @ $2.75 per hour | $33.00 |
| 8 labor hours @  3.50 per hour | 28.00 |
| 2 labor hours @  4.75 per hour | 9.50 |
| 22 labor hours @ $3.20 per hour | $70.50 |

Such relationships are usually ascertained by one or more of the following methods: time-and-motion studies; motion studies using tables of motion times; test runs; and the use of past experience. The time-and-motion study involves a careful investigation of the movements required by a worker to accomplish a designated task. After a determination of proper motions and subsequent education of the employee, an operation is time-studied. The second approach, similar to the time-and-motion study, involves reviewing an operation to ascertain the proper motions, and, once these are determined, consulting standard motion-time reference works. Under test runs, the conditions of work, the type of worker, and the operation itself are all carefully controlled. Past experience may be used as the sole basis for the establishment of labor time standards, or it may supplement other methods.

The third, and most complex, factor in the production process may be termed *overhead*. In addition to direct materials and direct labor costs, a host of other expenses are incurred in production operations, such as the costs of indirect materials and supplies, indirect labor, utilities, and depreciation of equipment. Because such costs by their nature are activity-oriented and generally subject to supervisory control, rates for these are determined on an individual basis by operations of cost centers. Fixed overhead costs, on the other hand, include costs that are not activity-oriented in the short run. These costs arise in part from the general circumstances of having a plant (in this case, food service facilities) in a position to produce. These costs are of interest largely because of the convention of assigning them to products. Standard overhead costs are calculated as a function of activity standards such as the standard hour. Overhead will be discussed in greater detail in the section on cost allocation.

## Using Standard Costs in Variance Analysis

Essentially, *variance analysis* is the comparison process inherent in standard cost accounting; it focuses explicit attention on active control and feedback considerations demanding the attention of the accountant and management. There are several ways that variances from standard costs can be interpreted. For example, they may indicate (1) variation in efficiency; (2) changes in market prices established primarily to facilitate usage analysis; (3) differences between actual and standard costs indicating incorrectly established standards; and (4) a cost differential arising from anticipated fluctuations in activity from some given measurement called "normal" or "average" (therefore not requiring management attention). (For an extended discussion of this, see Henrici (1960).)

## Standard Costs in Food Service

When applying standard costing techniques to school food service, each of the three factors of production (materials, labor, and overhead) should be reduced to the most *practical* level of detail.

In one large district, for example, labor costs have been divided into the following categories: (1) on-site, (2) central kitchen, (3) field supervision, and (4) fringe benefits (McKinsey 1970). On-site personnel prepare and serve food in the schools. Their cost is the most variable and therefore the most difficult to compute. Accurate standard labor costs in this case must be calculated as a function of the number of lunches served (by dividing total labor costs by the number of lunches served).

In schools served by a central kitchen (food is prepared centrally and distributed to the schools where it is heated, etc., before serving), costs can differ from those in other schools even when the number of lunches served is consistent. Figure 7.2 indicates that, in this

**Figure 7.2: Labor Costs Per Meal for Different Levels of Average Daily Service (Schools with Central Kitchen Facilities)**

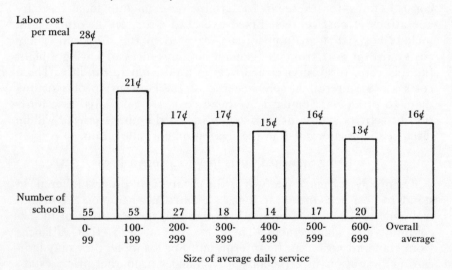

particular example, average cost per meal drops significantly as volume increases. This is another way of saying that the overall standard labor cost per meal in the district (sixteen cents) has great variance and that it is useful for management to calculate standard costs as a function of volume. Figure 7.3 indicates that the strength of the cost-volume relationship is weaker at higher volume and, further, that there is a fixed daily labor cost of approximately thirteen dollars.

## Figure 7.3: Calculating Standard Daily Labor Costs (Schools with Central Kitchen Facilities)

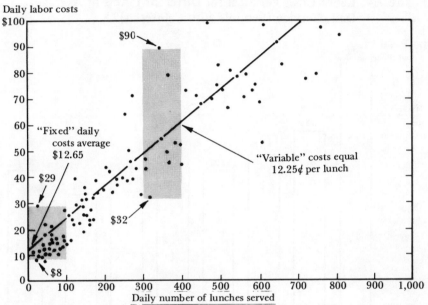

Source: McKinsey and Company, *Managing the School Lunch Program* (New York: Board of Education of the City of New York, 1971), p. 47.

The reasons for these findings are relatively straightforward. Fixed costs exist because even the smallest lunch program requires some personnel, and for such schools the cost per meal tends to be higher because labor costs incurred must be distributed over fewer lunches. Moreover, when many lunches are served, labor productivity is often higher since personnel tend to specialize more, thereby increasing the rate at which individual operations are performed and decreasing the number of employees needed per lunch. Thus, while per-meal costs decrease with increasing volume, total daily costs generally increase as volume rises. The heavy line drawn through the dots in figure 7.3 shows this relationship of the volume of lunches served to daily costs. The upward slope of the line indicates that after the $12.65 in fixed labor costs, each meal served costs an additional $0.1225 in labor.

How do these cost figures compare with alternative means for providing food service? In schools with cafeterias, for example, where food is prepared on site, costs are determined by many things, and the statistics presented in figure 7.4 are idiosyncratic. Nevertheless,

**Figure 7.4: Labor Costs Per Meal for Different Levels of Average Daily Service (Schools with Cafeterias)**

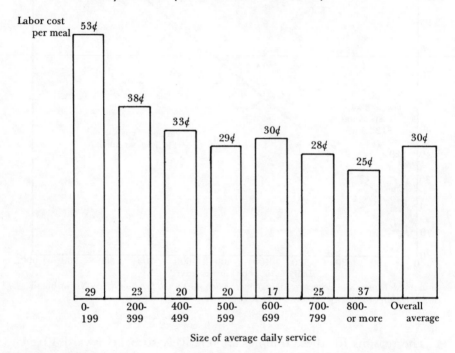

Size of average daily service

they do indicate some of the relative differences in costs that can be expected when considering alternative food service options. The data presented in figure 7.4 indicate decreasing per-meal labor costs as volume increases. Figure 7.5 indicates that the on-site personnel costs for cafeteria schools are high, since a full complement of cooks, helpers, dishwashers, etc., is needed. Fixed costs in this case are reported at $42.78 and variable costs are $0.2177 per lunch.

Other kinds of labor costs may better be determined by different methods, depending in large part on the nature of the labor. A food

**Figure 7.5: Calculating Standard Daily Labor Costs (Schools with Cafeterias)**

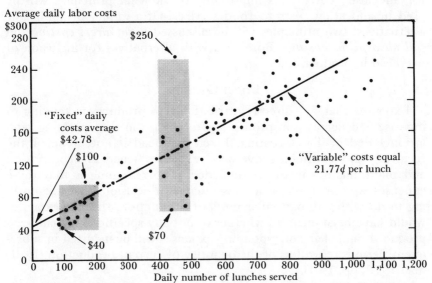

Source: McKinsey and Company, *Managing the School Lunch Program* (New York: Board of Education of the City of New York, 1971), p. 53.

service field supervisor, for example, usually provides overall supervision and administrative support to the school programs within specified areas. In many districts these people oversee a number of school sites, including central kitchen and cafeteria schools. The costs for supervisors cannot be identified by type and volume of service, as can costs for on-site personnel. Therefore, one objective way of allocating supervisory costs is simply to assign an equal portion of total supervisory costs to each meal served. An alternative would be to assign an equal portion of supervisory costs to each of the school sites. The allocation formula chosen will depend in large part on whether supervisors spend more time at schools serving more lunches.

## Cost Allocation

Closely related to the concept of standard costs is the concept of *cost allocations*. Cost allocation is the process of identifying and assigning costs to the product or to the cost center for which the costs have been incurred. In the case of school food service, the products can be viewed as the meals served. The cost centers, on the other hand, may be defined as the individual school sites.

Before discussing methods of allocating costs to products and cost centers, it will be necessary to establish some fundamental guidelines for allocating costs. It is important to ask what principles will be used in allocating costs to food services. Of a variety of applicable alternatives, two principles will be discussed here: *direct costing* and *full absorption costing.* Both deal with alternatives for inclusion of overhead in production.

## Direct Costing

Expenses that are directly attributable to production, tending to increase and decrease in proportion to change in the operating rate, are included in direct costing. Fixed overhead is not; none of the recurring and continuing overhead expenses (such as depreciation and plant maintenance) are included. The reasoning is that these expenses were incurred as a consequence of decisions that had nothing to do with any particular units of production; that the expenses would have been incurred whether or not any specific units had been produced; and that corresponding expenses will be incurred in subsequent periods regardless of the quantity of current production (Hoffman 1970, pp. 14-16).

## Full Absorption Costing

All overhead expenses attributable to production are included under full absorption costing. The Food and Nutrition Service of the U.S. Department of Agriculture recommends the full absorption costing method of allocating costs, citing two rather compelling reasons. First, only by recording all costs chargeable to a fund or program can management properly control the school food service fund's total operation. For example, to make decisions, such as what prices are to be charged for meals, without full cost data could result in setting the price of meals too low or too high. Second, many indirect costs of a school food service fund, or of particular programs, are reimbursable by other funds and governmental agencies. Therefore, the accounting system must provide sufficient data to ensure the appropriate amount of reimbursement (U.S.D.A., Food and Nutrition Service 1973, p. 111.1).

Full costing in food service fund accounting involves two different types of allocations. The first type assigns costs to individual school locations. This type of allocation will be required for such services as centrally prepared meals, centralized delivery services, centralized inventory receiving and storage, and centralized administrative services; it may also be required for utility bills and general administrative costs that are allocated from the governmental unit to the school district. Such allocations may also be required from the food service fund to the school district where services are shared among all school funds.

The second type of allocation assigns costs that have been collected and recorded in total to individual programs (e.g., breakfast, Type A lunch, convenience foods) to achieve full program costing. Both types of allocations are discussed in detail for each of the various types of costs involved.

## General Allocation Procedures

Some costs are easily identifiable with the school location or program for which they are incurred; many are not. Some costs are incurred for all school locations and all programs simultaneously (e.g., accounting services). These are referred to as *joint* or *common costs*. Some costs may be readily identifiable with a particular location but not with specific programs at that location (e.g., the cost of equipment used to prepare food for all programs at a single school location). Other costs may be identifiable with specific programs but not with specific locations (e.g., printing and distributing weekly district-wide menus for a particular type of meal).

To provide school district and food service management with sufficient information to manage the total food service operation

**Figure 7.6: School Food Services Allocation Processes**

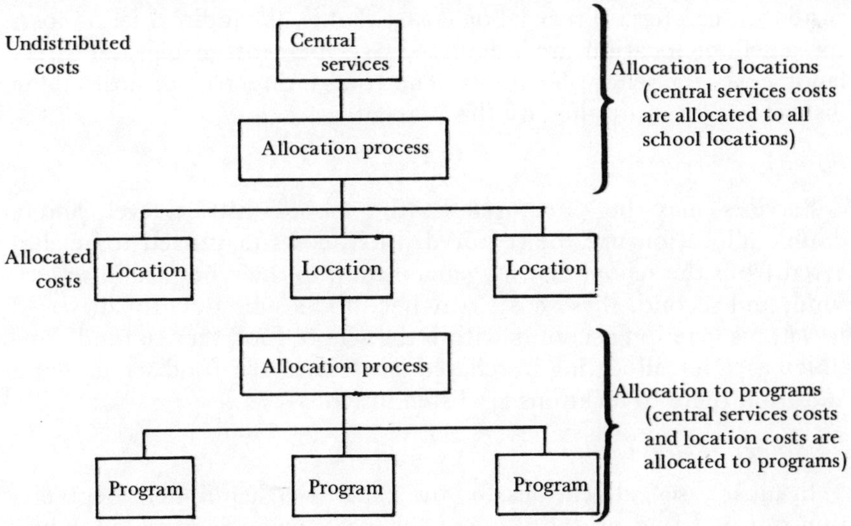

properly and to prepare claims for the maximum reimbursements to which the fund is entitled, all of the costs mentioned above must be allocated to the various school locations and programs for which they were incurred. The allocation process involves determining a reasonable distribution of costs to the program, location, and cost accounts for which the costs were incurred.

The overall flow of the allocation process is shown in figure 7.6. It illustrates the two allocation processes that are necessary to allocate fully all costs to programs and locations.

When allocating to programs, no journal entries or general ledger postings are required. The allocation takes place while reports are being prepared. To complete the reports, the general ledger account balance is divided among the various locations or programs.

## Allocation of Costs to Locations

### Labor

Most labor can be directly charged to a particular location because most employees work at a single school cafeteria. However, certain district-level employees in purchasing and administration will not be in a position to charge their salaries and benefits to the account of a particular school location. Their costs will have to be allocated to various locations.

Since this indirect labor cost of the district-level employees will be relatively small compared to total costs, the allocation process should be as simple as possible. A recommended method is to base this allocation on cafeteria direct labor costs; that is, the indirect labor costs for a school location are calculated as a percentage of total direct labor costs for school locations. The total indirect labor cost at the district level is multiplied by this percentage.

### Purchased Services

Services may be purchased at the school district level, and a double allocation may be required. First, costs may need to be allocated from the school district general fund to the school food service fund; and second, these costs may need to be subsequently allocated to various location accounts within the school food service fund. Possible bases for allocating purchased services to the food service fund and from there to locations are listed in table 7.7.

### Equipment Depreciation

In most cases, allocations for the expense of equipment depreciation can be based on the value of the assets being depreciated. When

## Table 7.7: Allocation Bases for Services Purchased by Food Service Operation

| Type of service | Basis of allocation from other school district funds to the school food service fund | Basis of allocation from school food service fund to school locations |
|---|---|---|
| Laundry and linen | Average daily participation calculated as a percentage of average daily attendance. | Number of personnel served. |
| Trash removal | Average daily participation calculated as a percentage of average daily attendance. | Cost of food sold at each location. |
| Extermination | Average daily participation calculated as a percentage of average daily attendance. | Number of hours spent at each school. |
| Accounting services | Number of transactions processed for the food service fund (if data are not available, use total dollar volume of the food service fund). | Number of transactions processed (if data are not available, use the total dollar volume). |
| Computer services | Total revenue of the food service fund. | The "size" of each location. (Computer services will normally be charged to the school food service fund for accounting services and payroll services. Thus, an allocation to each location should be made based on size.) |
| Transportation charges | Cost of food service (including leased or purchased vehicles calculated as a percentage of the total cost of school district vehicles). | The number of miles between the school location and the point from which delivery is made (for regular uses, such as delivery of food from a warehouse to preparation sites). (For all other service, use the actual miles or hours used by each location.) |
| Training | Training only allocated when personnel not assigned to a particular location are involved (in such cases, the total food service direct labor cost is calculated as a percentage of the total school district labor cost). | Only allocated when personnel not assigned to a particular location are involved (in such cases, the direct labor cost at each location should be used). |
| Utilities | Number of square feet of occupied floor space. | Number of square feet occupied floor space. |
| Repairs and maintenance | Number of hours actually used. | Number of hours actually used. |

**Table 7.7** *(continued)*

| Type of service | Basis of allocation from other school district funds to the school food service fund | Basis of allocation from school food service fund to school locations |
|---|---|---|
| Professional and technical services | Number of hours actually used, dependent upon the type of service purchased (total direct food service hours calculated as a percentage of total district labor hours is suggested). | Dependent upon the type of service purchased (direct hours at each location are the best basis, but other bases such as number of meals served at each location, if appropriate, will result in a reasonable allocation). |
| Rentals | Usually will not require allocation (when they do, the basis depends on the type of rental involved, e.g., hours of use, space required, number of transactions, and total food service fund revenue). | Usually will not require allocation (when they do, the basis depends on the type of rental involved, e.g., hours of use, space required, number of transactions, and total food service fund revenue). |
| Printing and binding | A percentage of total school district revenue when it is not a direct charge to a school food service fund. | Number of direct hours, job basis, or number of pages at each location may be used. |
| Miscellaneous | A percentage of total school district revenue when it is not a direct charge to a school food service fund. | Total revenue. |

Source: U.S. Department of Agriculture, Food and Nutrition Service, *School Food Service Financial Management Handbook for Uniform Accounting* (Washington, D.C.: U.S. Government Printing Office, 1973, document number FNS-104), pp. 111.7-111.9.

depreciating assets cannot be charged to individual location accounts, allocation of depreciation is based on utilization of assets (e.g., miles driven on vehicles).

## Allocation of Cost to Programs

To facilitate reporting to state agencies and to assist in managing various programs, it is necessary to allocate indirect costs to each of the programs. Since direct labor hours can be accumulated by program, no allocation process is required. In addition to direct labor, cost of food sold will need to be allocated to programs. All other costs will be allocated to programs only within the fund as a whole. Therefore, data will be available to management on these direct costs for each program at each location and for all costs for each program at the district level. The method of allocating cost of food sold and other costs are discussed below.

### Cost of Food Sold

Standard meal costs, discussed earlier, can be used to allocate the total cost of food sold for the school district and for each school location. The allocation computations are shown in exhibit 7.8. A

## Exhibit 7.8: Allocation of Cost of Food Sold to Program Accounts

1. 

| | Sales | School A | School B | School C | Total |
|---|---|---|---|---|---|
| | Breakfasts | 110 | 73 | 0 | 183 |
| | Type A lunches | 238 | 419 | 503 | 1,160 |
| | Total | 348 | 492 | 503 | 1,343 |

2. Standard meal costs: Breakfast, $.28; Type A lunch, $.54
3. Total actual cost of food sold: $703.81
4. Total standard cost of food sold:
$$(183 \times .28) + (1,160 \times .54) = \$677.64$$
5. Standard cost by school by program:
   School A - Breakfast    $(110 \times .28) = \$ 30.80$
   School A - Type A lunch  $(283 \times .54) = \$128.52$
   School B - Breakfast    $(73 \times .28) = \$ 20.44$
   School B - Type A lunch  $(419 \times .54) = \$226.26$
   School C - Type A lunch  $(503 \times .54) = \$271.62$
6. Percentages of standard cost by school by program:
   School A - Breakfast    $30.80 \div 677.64 = 4.5\%$
   School A - Type A lunch  $128.52 \div 677.64 = 19.0\%$
   School B - Breakfast    $20.44 \div 677.64 = 3.0\%$
   School B - Type A lunch  $226.26 \div 677.64 = 33.4\%$
   School C - Type A lunch  $271.62 \div 677.64 = 40.1\%$
7. Cost allocations by school by program:
   School A - Breakfast    $4.5\% \times 703.81 = \$ 31.67$
   School A - Type A lunch  $19.0\% \times 703.81 = \$133.72$
   School B - Breakfast    $3.0\% \times 703.81 = \$ 21.12$
   School B - Type A lunch  $33.4\% \times 703.81 = \$235.07$
   School C - Type A lunch  $40.1\% \times 703.81 = \$282.23$

standard unit of cost is estimated for each type of meal. This unit cost is multiplied by the actual number of meals served by program at each school location to calculate the total standard costs for all meals served. A percentage of program costs at each location is also calculated. This percentage is multiplied by total *actual* costs to arrive at the cost allocated to each program at each location. The cost for a given location is simply the sum of the costs allocated to the programs at that location.

### Indirect Costs

Indirect costs are allocated to the various programs of the school food service fund in a manner similar to that used to allocate such costs to locations. This allocation is performed after indirect costs have been allocated from the school district to the school food service fund, as described above. The various bases for allocations to programs are described in table 7.9.

## Table 7.9: Bases for Allocating Food Service Costs to Programs

| Element of cost | Basis for allocation |
|---|---|
| Labor | The total direct labor cost assigned to each program (all indirect labor will have to be allocated to programs). |
| Purchased services | Some purchased services may be chargeable directly to various programs, and some may be chargeable only to a limited number of programs. The various services are shown below. |
| Laundry and linen | Number of direct labor hours charged to each program. |
| Trash removal | Cost of food sold charged to each program. |
| Extermination | Cost of food sold charged to each program. |
| Accounting services | Total revenue accumulated for each program. |
| Transportation charges | Cost of food sold charged to each program for transportation charges in the delivery function (total revenue is accumulated for each program for all other transportation charges). |
| Training | Total number of meals served by each program. |
| Utilities | Total number of meals served by each program. |
| Repairs and maintenance | Total number of meals served by each program. |
| Professional and technical services | Allocation basis dependent on the nature of the service (if no other basis is logical, the number of meals served by each program should be used). |
| Rentals | For rentals of kitchen equipment, the actual or estimated number of hours used by each program (for vehicles, the same basis as transportation charges should be used; for other rentals, the total revenue accumulated for each program should be used). |
| Printing and binding | The number of meals served by each program. |
| Miscellaneous purchased services | The total revenue accumulated by each program. |
| Equipment depreciation | The total number of meals served by each program. |
| Other expenses | The total revenue accumulated by each program. |

Source: U.S. Department of Agriculture, Food and Nutrition Service, *School Food Service Financial Management Handbook for Uniform Accounting* (Washington, D.C.: U.S. Government Printing Office, 1973, document number FNS-104), pp. 111.11-111.13.

## Factors Affecting Food Service Operations

Like other logistical systems, food service is operated to achieve "constrained" objectives; that is, objectives are subject to restrictions or constraints imposed by other conditions. For example, three possible objectives of a school lunch program might be high lunch quality, variety of menu, and community participation. In its attempt to increase lunch quality, variety, and community participation, the district will be restricted by certain conditions, such as other management priorities and resources available for running the lunch program. In fact, the three objectives could conflict with each other. For example, community participants may desire less varied menus and more "local favorites." The very process of determining food service objectives deserves attention, because objectives are often assumed, and sometimes erroneously.

A still more basic issue underlies this problem, and that is the development of food service policies. In order to set about achieving constrained objectives, certain fundamental questions must already have been raised and answered. For example, should the food service program attempt to attract all types of students? Should breakfast be made available? Should pupils be required to leave campus at lunch time? Answers to fundamental questions like these are assumed. Attention in this section is focused instead on the process of evaluating management options in the light of interacting factors, given a set of objectives.

In attempting to attain its food service objectives, district management needs to understand how different strategies for providing food service are constrained by various factors, in order to determine the net benefit of each strategy. There are at least six general factors that interact so as to clearly affect the district's ability to pursue its food service objectives: (1) facilities, (2) menu planning, (3) food and supply procurement, (4) food preparation and service, (5) personnel management, and (6) financial administration. The first four factors may be termed operation activities; the last two are forms of staff support. The relative importance of staff support for each of the four operating activities varies. These six factors interact in different ways depending on the overall food service options that the district chooses to pursue (e.g., provide the service with district personnel or contract the service out). Indeed, it is difficult, if not impossible, to discuss the impact of these six factors on food service without, at the same time, recognizing that the specific impact will depend on the management option selected.

A wide range of conceivable options exists in managing food

service in schools. Two key variables affecting the management option are *system configurations* and *responsibilities*. Three major system configuration options are discussed here: (1) a central kitchen service, (2) independent cooking cafeteria service, and (3) a convenience food cafeteria service. Under the central kitchen service option food is prepared centrally and distributed immediately to sites for consumption. The independent cooking cafeteria service involves on-site preparation and service of the food. Convenience food involves delivery of prepackaged, usually frozen, food to sites for service (after minimal preparation).

The number of major options is increased greatly when the possibility is introduced of contracting out parts of food service. The general impact of contracting is shown in table 7.10. In order to show

### Table 7.10: Relative Impact of Six Factors on Two Major Food Service Options

| | Options | |
| --- | --- | --- |
| Factors affecting food service | Operations responsibility of district (centralized and decentralized) | Operations responsibility of contractor |
| Facilities | Modified as per district requirements | Modified as per contractor requirements |
| Menu planning | More direct control and responsibility on part of district | Less direct control and responsibility on part of district |
| Food and supply procurement | | |
| Food preparation and service | | |
| Personnel management | Greater economic uncertainty and administrative effort | Less economic risk and administrative effort |
| Financial management | Essential district responsibility in both cases | |

how management can efficiently assess many alternatives, six factors are discussed below, followed by a brief analysis of how the factors are affected by one another.

### Facilities

The facilities in which food is prepared and served are a major factor in achieving school lunch quality objectives because: (1) the type and cost of food that can be provided is dependent on the kitchen's equipment; and (2) the necessary kitchen facilities are usually difficult to obtain for both technical and budgetary reasons. Aspects that can constrain food service planning include facilities requirements, modernization plans in progress, building codes and sanitary regulations, and availability of supplementary financial assistance.

Numerous specific questions relate to these aspects of facilities. For example, what is the present mix of food service facilities in the district? How does the present mix differ from the theoretical physical requirements of different food preparation and service options (central kitchen, cafeteria, frozen food lunches, etc.)? How much money is in the present capital budget for kitchen modernization? What building codes and sanitary regulations exist that may limit the options? If the federal or state government offers subsidies for kitchen modernization, what percent does it reimburse and how available are the funds? Can kitchen equipment be leased from operating funds, and if so, is this financially advantageous to the district?

## Facility Requirements

To construct a detailed profile of facilities within a district, each school building must be assessed to determine present and future lunchroom purposes, kinds and amount of existing kitchen equipment, space available for new equipment, and existing gas, water, sewer, and electrical services. In addition, storage space must be checked for protection against theft, spoilage, and contamination from moisture, rodents, vermin, or heat, and for its relative efficiency for receipt and preparation of food. (See U.S.D.A., Agriculture Marketing Service 1956; U.S.D.A., Economic Research Service 1969.)

## Modernization Plans

To plan future facilities, the relationship between types of food service and facility requirements must be analyzed. One option, for example, is for a district to have a *central kitchen* that prepares soup and sandwiches or cold plate lunches for delivery to school sites. The schools in this case require only small three-burner stoves to heat soup and a small amount of storage space. Another option, *frozen or convenience-food cafeteria service,* requires both dry and refrigerated food storage and equipment, including ovens. A third, and more commonly encountered option, the *cooking cafeteria service,* requires a full complement of freezers, stoves, ovens, and utensils to refrigerate, prepare, cook, and warm the food.

### Building Codes

To plan facilities within legal stipulations and district objectives, a detailed plan should be developed and properly recorded integrating the facilities requirements of each school building, the modernization plans in process, construction regulations, and available funds. Whether this plan should be developed by existing staff or contracted out—by independent food service consultants, private food service contractors, or staff from the district business office with assistance from the state education agency—is a related and important question.

### Financial Assistance

In addition to the improvements that can be financed out of the district's capital budget, consideration should be given to the type and extent of supplementary financial assistance available. Such financial assistance is available through some state education agencies and under several federal programs, such as the Model Cities program.

## Menu Planning

Once facilities have been planned, the major factor affecting a district's school lunch program is menu planning. Determination of the content and variety of the lunches served must take into account the desired balance of lunch quality, cost, and student acceptance. At least four different variables can affect menu planning: nutritional requirements of the National School Lunch Program (termed Type A); cost savings that can be obtained through the use of donated commodities; the scope and type of program; and the nature of the specific planning system established.

### Nutritional Requirements

The National School Lunch Program provides one of the basic financial supports of the school lunch program. However, the program establishes nutritional requirements, Type A standards, that must be met to qualify for the subsidies. The Type A standards require that menus be planned to furnish at least one-third of the recommended daily dietary allowance of the National Research Council. For example, a Type A lunch "must contain, as a minimum, each of the following food components" in the amounts indicated (U.S.D.A., Food and Nutrition Service 1970):

One-half pint of fluid whole milk

Two ounces of meat, poultry, or fish; or two ounces of cheese or one egg; or one-half cup of cooked dry beans or dry peas; or four tablespoons of peanut butter; or an equivalent of a combination of the above list

Three-quarter-cup serving of vegetables or fruits, consisting of two or more vegetables or fruits or both

One slice of whole-grain or enriched bread or a serving of another type of bread, such as cornbread or muffins.

Obviously, these requirements place some limitation on what foods can be served. However, some experts have suggested that, with enough initiative, menus could be developed to provide far more variety than is presently available and still meet the requirements (Eindorff 1972).

## Donated Commodities

The donated commodity program of the U.S. Department of Agriculture provides another major opportunity to lower program costs. Under this program, the Department of Agriculture provides for the distribution of price-supported commodities—wheat (flour), rice, butter, cheese, dry milk, and corn (meal). It also provides for the distribution of other commodities through use of U.S. Customs receipts to purchase farm products, including meat, poultry, egg, fruits, and vegetables. A major tradeoff to be considered here is the fact that many of these donated commodities require further processing before they can be served.

## Scope and Type of Lunch Program

A third consideration is the scope and type of school lunch program (i.e., breakfast and lunch versus lunch only) and the basic type and variety of menus. Determining this requires balancing student tastes and nutritional requirements against projected costs. Since taste and eating habits usually vary with age and ethnic background, menu planners who wish to increase student participation or program popularity generally adopt an attitude of "consumer sovereignty" and serve the type and quality of food that students enjoy. The underlying philosophy will largely determine who should participate in menu planning. For example, districts that place greater emphasis on nutrition than on program popularity might well limit participation in menu planning to the operating personnel and professional staff; districts that want to increase student acceptance and build community responsiveness might find it worthwhile to allow students and parents to participate in menu planning, despite the additional administrative burdens.

## Specific Menu Planning System

A series of recipes must be developed for a two- to six-week menu cycle. The total quantity of food needed must be determined by planning the portion size for each item and then converting this quantity to the units of measure used in food purchasing. The overall cost of providing any menu can differ dramatically, depending on the quality of the planning. For example, the New Orleans public schools have developed computerized (linear programming) models in order to facilitate the administrative task of costing out menus and to develop more accurate control of food costs. That district claimed that the $2,000 per year that finances their semi-annual menu planning and production of monthly budget projections has substantially reduced food costs. In fact, the district claimed a savings of over $61,000 in one month alone. The system matches desired food items against current food costs, makes substitutions where appropriate, and develops alternative menu plans (Eindorff 1972, p. 12).

Menu planning will naturally vary greatly with the type of kitchen equipment available. The lead time required to plan, purchase, and store food items is normally quite long for both types of cafeteria service, frozen food and cooking. In frozen food operations, food is normally ordered from manufacturers in large quantities and shipped to refrigerated warehouses before distribution to the schools. In cooking operations, food is usually ordered from regional wholesalers. Therefore, in the case of the frozen food lunch, menu planning is limited to food stored in the warehouse; in the case of the cooked lunch, menu planning is limited to food previously included in the contract with the regional wholesalers. However, since cooking cafeterias have equipment to cook raw food and are not limited to heating frozen food, they do have the added flexibility of being able to order fresh meat, fish, and produce from local merchants.

Effectively planning school lunch menus requires that districts make the difficult tradeoffs between cost and quality as well as student tastes. There are a variety of methods to determine student tastes, including food preference surveys, analysis of consumption, and use of students to test new lunches. Once having determined what student tastes are, menu planners are faced with the difficult task of attempting to satisfy these tastes within federal nutritional requirements and budgetary limits.

Whatever the menus to be provided, the district must be able to carry out a number of complex technical tasks involved in planning the food service; five of these are particularly important.

## Food Research

To perform food research, the district must be able to find new ways to use donated commodities, test new food products and determine their acceptability, prepare or gather recipes, and provide necessary instructional materials for operating units.

## Quality Control

Controlling food quality requires the establishment of food specifications and preparation and service standards; in addition, federal, state, and local requirements must be met. Food to be purchased must be adequately described in type, quality, and quantity.

## Menu Planning System Development

A "menu planning system" allows for reviewing food items available from warehouses, master contracts, and local merchants; designing lunch menus for each day of the menu cycle; supporting the lunch menus with recipes or instruction wherever necessary; and providing the proper procedures for operating personnel to estimate their requirements and requisition food when needed. In addition, in order for food to be delivered on time, delivery must be properly scheduled in terms of warehouse capacity, distribution methods, and receiving procedures.

## Menu Evaluation and Costing

A system of menu evaluation and ordering should be developed to evaluate and balance the nutritional content of the lunches, their acceptability to students, the efficiency by which they can be prepared and served, and the cost at which they can be offered.

## Food Ordering

This system should provide a method to receive, record, and transmit orders from the various schools to the food suppliers.

All of these functions may be contracted out. The length of the menu cycle, the process of planning and approving the use of food preference surveys, the nutritional content, the use of donated commodities, and the type of lunch service would be specified in the contract's terms and conditions. A contractor will usually provide several illustrative menus from which the district can choose.

## Food and Supply Procurement

Procurement consists of converting the food requisitions prepared by the menu planners into purchase contracts with suppliers, as well as providing supporting facilities. Procurement capabilities include: preparing the request for proposal (verbal or written), receiving and analyzing bids, approving and letting contracts, receiving and inspecting food delivered, and verifying and paying vendor bills. The personnel required to perform this work include clerks, food buyers, inspectors, and accountants (all of whom may serve other programs in addition to food service).

The cost of procuring food is one of the greatest expenses to be considered in operating a school lunch program. The most economical means of procuring food will be constrained by the sources of supply with their respective cost and food inspection characteristics, the various ways of handling warehousing and food movement, and school board purchasing requirements that affect procurement activities.

## Source of Supply

If the district plans to do its own purchasing, it should review its requirements with a variety of suppliers to determine the best source and optimum ordering quantity for each type of food item. Food costs will vary widely depending on the source of supply and the quantity ordered. Further, suppliers differ in terms of the quantities they sell, the type of food they carry, and their costs. For example, a retail outlet sells food by item or case and lets the purchaser personally inspect for quality. Produce (fresh fruits and vegetables) and dairy items (largely, milk, eggs, and cheese) are purchased normally through retail outlets.

The wholesale dealer, on the other hand, usually sells food by the truckload and uses established food grading systems, which are stamped on the food containers. Meat and canned goods are normally purchased through these regional suppliers. Finally, the manufacturer normally sells food in carload lots that are inspected by federal food personnel on the manufacturer's premises. Frozen food items, as well as items processed from donated commodities (including bread and rolls in the bakery goods category, and butter in the dairy goods category), are purchased through these channels by the larger districts.

If food service is contracted for, procurement of both foods and related warehouse and distribution systems are normally provided by the contractor. The contractor's system of purchasing and inventory control, as well as his expertise in purchasing, will in large measure determine the food price that can be quoted to the districts.

Frequently, however, contracts specify that the school districts purchase certain items if they can get comparable prices or better utilize donated commodities. Such items include: milk, bread, and butter processed from donated commodities; desserts consisting of ice cream or fresh fruit purchased from local merchants; or canned items also available through donated commodities.

## Warehouse and Distribution

The purchase of food and supplies is only the first part of procurement; the other task is providing the necessary supporting facilities to warehouse and distribute the items purchased. These facilities can be provided in a variety of ways, including:

1. Requiring vendors to provide these facilities as part of their master contract and schedule daily or weekly shipments to the schools. This system is often used for meat, dairy products, bakery goods, and produce.

2. Renting dry or refrigerated space in public warehouses and using contract truckers to deliver items to schools. This system is often used for canned goods, frozen foods, and some utensils and tableware.

3. Using a central warehouse and distribution system. This system can be made part of an existing system for picking up and delivering office and custodial supplies, equipment, classroom supplies, and furniture, etc.

Storing and distributing food requires provision of warehouses and truck fleets either by the district, or by contracting with private warehouses and trucking firms. In any case, after a district has assessed its food storage facilities, it should then consider such constraints as the distance between schools, traffic congestion, and proximity to the source of supply.

## School Board Purchasing Policies

Food procurement options are constrained by the basic purchasing policies of the school district and the applicable laws of the city and state. Often these regulations require that food and related supplies be purchased at the lowest price quoted for the same quality items. This means that districts that do their own purchasing should establish procedures to: (1) write specifications on the exact quantity and quality of food wanted; (2) send bid requests to qualified suppliers; and (3) award contracts on the basis of the lowest cost offer that meets quality and quantity specifications. As an example, three applicable purchasing laws of the state and city of New York can be briefly summarized as follows:

1. For yearly orders of less than $1,000, a district need only seek three verbal quotations before assigning the order to a supplier;

2. For yearly orders of more than $1,000 but less than $5,000, no public advertisement is necessary, but sealed bids must be opened in public ceremony, and the contract awarded to the lowest bidder;

3. For yearly contracts over $5,000, the same rules apply but with the added requirements that a public advertisement be run for ten days, and that the contract awarding must be approved by the community district board and then registered with the controller (McKinsey 1971, p. 1-10).

## Food Preparation and Service

The final operations activity is the preparation and service of food. At this point the impact of preferred preparations options on preferred lunchroom management options must be analyzed. A large number of tradeoffs must be considered in determining the preferred method of preparing food. For example, central kitchen service can be limited to a few basic kinds of meals while a much wider selection of menus is usually available through contracted services (which could easily cost more). Completely equipped kitchens allow greater flexibility in food preparation, but costs are higher and trained cooks are scarce. While fresh food usually costs less than precooked items, labor costs are significantly higher since a full complement of cooks is required. Generally speaking, the more food that is processed and packaged by the supplier, the less labor is needed at the school to prepare and serve.

The specific requirements for carrying out food preparation and service will vary widely, depending on the kitchen facilities and the food preparation option selected. Food can be purchased and delivered with varying degrees of preassembly and prepackaging. Some schools have found it convenient to order food that can be immediately set on the service line, for example, milk cartons, slabs of butter, individually wrapped pieces of bread, and desserts. Further, some food suppliers prepare cold plates, sandwiches, or prepackaged dinners which can be served immediately or require limited processing. Also, maintaining facilities is a simple task if disposable utensils are used.

Each of the basic preparation options will have different people managing the lunchroom. District administration of food preparation gives the district responsibility for lunchroom management. Because contracting with a private food service firm reduces the number of necessary employees, school districts may consider the option of transferring control of employees to the contractor. Other factors, however, complicate the issue (e.g., management of students in the lunchroom, etc.), and it relates indirectly to general issues of personnel management.

## Personnel Management

District personnel policies vary depending on each district's evaluation of existing conditions and assessment of policy alternatives against their food service objectives. At least four constraining elements exist in determining personnel management policies for food service: union contracts, civil service regulations, evaluation of present school lunch employees, and general requirements for a personnel management system.

### Union Contracts

In situations where union contracts exist, a number of potentially constraining questions must be answered. Do the agreements guarantee employee tenure? What agreements and procedures are prescribed concerning fringe benefits, fair practices, salaries, vacations and holidays, hours of work and work week, and terminal leave? Further, what are the seniority policies, complaint and grievance procedures, discharge review procedures, reclassification methods, and general requirements that a district must discuss any major potential changes with the union?

### Civil Service Regulations

In instances where civil service regulations apply, they usually control such matters as working hours, annual and sick leave, overtime and meal allowance, probationary period of employment, conduct and discipline, salaries, leave regulations, etc. Civil service employees are appointed to positions on the basis of passing a civil service examination. Since civil service regulations only guarantee positions held by virtue of passing examinations, those employees appointed provisionally can be demoted in some cases.

### Present Employees' Capabilities

In evaluating current personnel in the lunchroom a number of possible criteria can be applied to compare "actual" to "desired." These include the productivity of the system and how it could be improved, the ethnic balance of employees, and the degree of local employment.

## Personnel System Requirements

The objective of the personnel system is that school lunch employees be effectively organized and competently supervised by an agency impowered by the school district. A food service personnel system includes procedures to recruit, hire, train, supervise, and terminate employees and maintain numerous personnel records required by governmental agencies. (Not all of these tasks can be relinquished if food services are contracted out to another agency.) Table 7.11 shows prototypical personnel specializations in school food service.

## Financial Administration

The task of financial administration can be divided into two major areas: the "internal" requirements of budgeting, accounting, cost control, and auditing; and the "external" requirements of procuring subsidy monies from city, state, and federal agencies. Financial administration cannot be contracted out, and its form differs radically under the different school lunch options; however, the necessary activities and skills are similar to those required for other district business. These activities are described below.

### Budgeting

An annual financial plan and subsequent modifications must be submitted. Districts managing their own lunch program prepare school lunch cost and revenue estimates as part of their normal budgeting procedures.

### Vouchering

District requisitions, delivery receipts, and vendors' invoices must be matched and compared, followed by the preparation of a voucher that is transmitted to the financial office for payment.

### Accounting

A general book of accounts must be maintained, to record vouchers paid, transfers between programs, funds reimbursement, payroll information, etc.

### Inventory Records

Monthly and year-to-date records of unit and dollar amounts for each class of food and supplies must be maintained at central warehouses (under district or contract control at individual schools).

# Table 7.11: Prototype Specializations in School Food Service

| Title | Relative salary | Duties/Responsibilities |
|---|---|---|
| Supervisor of School Lunches | $11,175-$13,276 | Plans and directs the overall operations of the school lunch, special milk, and commodity distribution programs in the junior high school division, or in the academic and vocational high schools in one or more boroughs; performs related work. |
| Chief School Lunch Manager | $10,175-$12,275 | Manages a very large size high school cafeteria or acts as principal technical and administrative assistant in the junior high school or the elementary school divisions, or supervises food production at the central kitchen; performs related work. |
| Head School Lunch Manager | $8,850-$10,750 | Manages a large high school cafeteria, or supervises the operation of a group of junior high school cafeterias or of a major unit of the central kitchen; performs related work. |
| School Lunch Manager | $7,500-$9,240 | Manages a junior high school cafeteria or a small high school cafeteria; supervises several elementary school cafeterias; or is assigned to appropriate responsibilities in other units of the school lunch program; performs related work. |
| School Lunch Loader and Handler | $7,000-$8,550 | Performs nonsupervisory work relating to the receipt, storage, and distribution of materials, equipment, supplies and foods in the Bureau of School Lunches; performs related work. |
| School Lunch Assistant (Cook) | $7,520-$8,635 | Performs quantity cooking duties in a very large junior high school cafeteria; performs related work. |
| Senior School Lunch Aide (Cook) | $7,000-$7,730 | Performs quantity cooking duties in an elementary or junior high school cafeteria; performs related work such as preparing requisitions for food supplies; keeping required records; setting up work schedules; inspecting all supplies as to quality, weight and/or count; following approved recipes and serving standardized portions. |
| School Lunch Assistant | $7,150-$8,265 | Performs supervisory work of a difficult and responsible nature in the preparation, distribution and service of school lunches; performs related work. |
| Senior School Lunch Aide | $6,700-$7,430 | Performs nonsupervisory work of moderate difficulty and responsibility in the preparation, distribution, and service of school lunches; performs related work. |
| School Lunch Aide | $6,150-$6,765 | Performs nonsupervisory work of moderate difficulty and responsibility, or supervisory work of ordinary difficulty and responsibility in the preparation, distribution, and service of school lunches; performs related work. |
| Senior School Lunch Helper | Annually: $5,050-$6,405 Hourly: $2.45-$2.77 | Performs nonsupervisory work of ordinary difficulty and responsibility, or routine supervisory work in the preparation, distribution, and service of school lunches; performs related work. |
| School Lunch Helper | Annually: $5,760-$6,130 Hourly: $2.30-$2.62 | Performs nonsupervisory work of ordinary difficulty and responsibility; performs related work. |

Source: McKinsey and Company, *Managing the School Lunch Program* (New York: Board of Education of the City of New York, 1971), p. 2-14.

## Cost Control

Menus must be costed out before approval; budgeted, actual, and standard cost information for labor, food, and overhead for each school on a monthly and year-to-date basis must be maintained. Constant surveillance of variance between budget and actual costs, against standards, and between schools will indicate areas for administrative cost reduction.

## Cash Control

Cash generated from sale of lunches and other sources must be received, recorded, and deposited.

## Reporting to District Superintendent and Board

Accounting records must be balanced and profit and loss statements must be prepared for the school lunch program for the district and each school.

## Auditing

Auditing is performed annually by an outside auditing agency and a report is made to the school board.

### Assessing the Interaction of Factors

The factors discussed above interact in complex ways. In analyzing food service (and other) operations, it is helpful to specify which variables impinge on other variables (e.g., C is largely determined by B, and B is largely determined by A). Figure 7.12 conveys a sense of this process. Twenty-one of the topics discussed in this chapter are arrayed in a matrix. The horizontal axis of the matrix is labeled "constraining variables," while the vertical axis is labeled "constrained variables." In filling in the matrix, management is specifying which variables have the greatest (and least) influence on the other variables. For example, the existence of financial aid for facilities and the amount of donated commodities affect many of the other variables under lunchroom management options (8), menu planning system (7), and warehouse and distribution system (7).

Some of the variables are not affected by other variables (e.g., civil service regulations, building codes and sanitary regulations, financial assistance for facilities, and nutritional requirements). These variables are determined outside the system being examined.

In addition to yielding a picture of constraining and constrained variables, the interaction map also provides a general measure of the

# Figure 7.12: Mapping the Interaction of Key Variables in Food Service

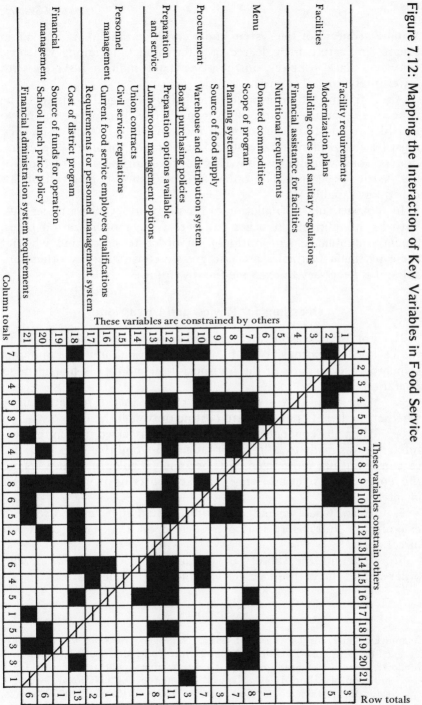

"connectedness" of the system under consideration. Many blacked-in squares indicate a high degree of interconnection among variables. Very few black-in boxes, on the other hand, indicate a system with fewer interconnecting parts.

Another kind of information yielded by the grid deals with the issue of sequential or simultaneous influence. It is possible for two variables to constrain each other at the same time; in such cases, they must be analyzed simultaneously. For example, variable 12 (preparation options available) is shown as constraining variable 18 (cost of the district program). The opposite is also shown, i.e., variable 18 constrains variable 12.

In this particular formulation of the problem several variables have virtually no impact on other variables (e.g., modernization plans, lunchroom management options). In order to determine whether these particular variables are also greatly constrained by other variables, it is necessary to examine the row totals.

## Questions for Review and Discussion

1.   For what reasons are standard costing techniques applied to food service operations? Would these same reasons argue for applying standard costs to parts of the transportation and supply management operations?

2.   What would be some general criteria to use in determining whether the benefits of standard costing outweigh the costs?

3.   When the concept of fixed costs was discussed in chapter two, reference was made to a "relevant range." Beyond that relevant range of consideration, most fixed costs become variable. In what ways has the concept of relevant range of fixed costs been ignored in this chapter?

4.   Under what general conditions would it be more useful to examine the full absorption costs of an operation as opposed to its direct costs?

5.   Assuming the validity of information in figure 7.12, in what order should the 21 food service variables be considered?

## References

Benninger, Lawrence J. "Standard Costs." *Handbook of Modern Accounting,* edited by Sidney Davidson, chap. 39. New York: McGraw-Hill, 1970.

Eindorff, Irene K. "A Study on Linear Programming Applications for the Optimization of School Lunch Menus." Washington, D.C.: National Center for Educational Research and Development, 1972. ERIC, no. ED067748.

Hoffman, Raymond A. "Inventories." *Handbook of Modern Accounting*, edited by Sidney Davidson, chap. 14. New York: McGraw-Hill, 1970.

McKinsey and Company. *Managing the School Lunch Program*. New York: Board of Education of the City of New York, 1971.

U.S. Department of Agriculture, Agriculture Marketing Service. *A Guide for Planning and Equipping School Lunch Rooms*. Washington, D.C.: U.S. Government Printing Office, 1956.

U.S. Department of Agriculture, Economic Research Service. *Establishing Central School Lunch Kitchens in Urban Areas: Problems and Cost*. Washington, D.C.: U.S. Government Printing Office, 1969. Agricultural Economic Report no. 72.

U.S. Department of Agriculture, Food and Nutrition Service. *A Menu Planning Guide for Type A School Lunches*. Washington, D.C.: U.S. Government Printing Office, 1956.

U.S. Department of Agriculture, Food and Nutrition Service. "National School Lunch Program." *Federal Register* (January 20, 1970). Washington, D.C.: U.S. Government Printing Office.

U.S. Department of Agriculture, Food and Nutrition Service. *School Food Service Financial Management Handbook for Uniform Accounting*. Washington, D.C.: U.S. Government Printing Office, 1973. Document no. FNS-104.

## Related Readings

Cozier, Amelia, and Batcher, Olive M. "Food Buying Guide for Child Care Centers." ERIC, no. ED101865, 1975. This guide provides information for estimating the amounts of food to buy to meet the required meal patterns for young children in child care centers under the Special Food Service Program for Children.

Florida State Department of Education. "Design Criteria: School Food Service Facilities." ERIC, no. ED082373, 1973. This guide is designed for personnel who plan food service facilities. It discusses the factors to be considered in food service planning, presents cost studies, and lists the responsibilities of those involved in the planning process. Other sections concern selection, procurement, and installation of equipment; food preparation and storage; and other special applications.

Payne, Norman E. "The Economics of Alternative School Feeding Systems." ERIC, no. ED082383, 1973. This study develops a uniform method for comparing costs of alternative school feeding systems. The study attempts to determine relative costs of providing meals under alternative production and distribution systems, establish standards relating to food costs and labor efficiency, and provide information that could be used in estimating cost changes associated with proposed modifications of an existing school lunch system or the selection of a system.

U.S. Department of Agriculture, Food and Nutrition Service. "School Food Service Financial Management Handbook for Uniform Accounting. Simplified System." ERIC, no. ED083741, 1974. This handbook is intended to assist those responsible for recording and reporting on the various financial activities of a school food service fund. It describes in a simplified form uniform accounting systems suitable for use by all school food authorities.

U.S. Department of Agriculture, Food and Nutrition Service. "Equipment Guide
for On-Site School Kitchens—Program Aid No. 1091." ERIC, no. ED
101419, 1975. This guide is designed to assist personnel concerned with
planning or equipping school food service facilities. The document indicates the minimum quantity of equipment needed to efficiently operate a
school food service, based on various sizes of operations ranging from 100
to 1,500 Type A lunches.

# 8

# Operations and Maintenance

Maintenance is one of the most pervasive logistical functions in education. In education parlance, *operations and maintenance* is used to connote the care and repair of capital goods, such as buildings, buses, computers, and heating systems. Although the applications are diverse, the underlying concepts of maintenance are surprisingly similar.

The first part of this chapter is devoted to a discussion of those underlying concepts, including availability, maintainability, and cost. The second part focuses attention on management and control of the maintenance functions, including maintenance budget planning and operating systems for unscheduled maintenance.

## Theoretical Foundations

The theoretical foundations of maintenance are found in the language of logistics and maintenance. This language reflects the concerns of the field: the terms used have meanings specific to the field. (Parts of this section are adapted from Blanchard 1974, pp. 23-52.)

### Availability

Availability, for example, has several distinct and useful meanings in reference to maintenance, all of which apply to the wide range of mechanical systems. Generally, availability is a measure of an item's readiness and accessibility at the start of a task at any unknown (random) point in time. There are several ways by which availability can be measured.

*Operational availability (OA)* is the probability that equipment (or a system) used under stated conditions in an actual operational environment will operate satisfactorily when called upon. Where *MTBM* equals mean time between maintenance and *MDT* equals mean maintenance downtime, then

$$OA = \frac{MTBM}{MTBM + MDT} .$$

The mean time between maintenance reflects the frequency of maintenance, which is a significant factor in determining support requirements.

*Achieved availability (AA)* is the probability that equipment used under stated conditions in an ideal support environment (i.e., where there are available tools, spares, manpower, etc.) will operate satisfactorily at any point in time. This definition excludes that supply time and administrative delay time needed for maintenance. It is expressed as

$$AA = \frac{MTBM}{MTBM + MAMT} ,$$

where *MAMT* equals mean active maintenance time. This includes corrective (unscheduled) and preventive (scheduled) maintenance times.

*Inherent availability (IA)* is similar to achieved availability, except that *IA* excludes preventive maintenance actions as well as supply time and administrative delay. It is expressed as

$$IA = \frac{MTBF}{MTBF + MCMT} ,$$

where *MTBF* equals mean time between failures and *MCMT* equals mean corrective maintenance time.

### Maintainability

The concept of availability is central to the management of maintenance functions because availability is a function of maintenance policies. The concept of *maintainability* is the characteristic of equipment design and installation that determines the ease, economy, safety, and accuracy with which equipment can be maintained. Maintainability can also be defined as a characteristic of design and installation that is expressed as the probability that an item will be retained in or restored to a specified condition within a given period of time, when maintenance is performed in accordance with prescribed procedures and resources.

Maintainability is a concept apart from maintenance. Maintainability is the ability of equipment to be maintained, whereas maintenance constitutes those actions taken to keep an item in an effective operational state or to restore it to that state. Maintainability is a design parameter, and maintenance is a result of design.

Maintainability can be specified, predicted, and assessed on both a qualitative and a quantitative basis. It is concerned with maintenance times, support requirements in design, and maintenance costs. Those measures most applicable to educational organizations (besides several discussed above) are as follows:

1. Mean corrective maintenance time (*MCMT*). Each time a system or equipment fails, a series of steps is required to repair the item and restore it to full operational status. Together these steps constitute a corrective maintenance cycle (see figure 8.1). The time required to complete a particular maintenance cycle is represented by *MCMTi*. When a number of maintenance cycles occur, the times for all events are combined to compute the mean corrective maintenance time, which is expressed as

$$MCMT = \frac{\sum\limits_{1}^{N} MCMTi}{N} = \frac{\Sigma(Fi)\ (MCMTi)}{\Sigma Fi} \ ,$$

where $N$ equals the number of events and $Fi$ equals the failure rate of the individual ($i$th) element of the time being measured, usually expressed in failures per equipment-operating hour. *MCMT* considers only active maintenance time, time spent working directly on the equipment. Logistics supply time and administrative delay time are not included. Although all elements of time are critical to the maintenance function, *MCMT* is primarily oriented to a measure of the "supportability" characteristic in the equipment design (i.e., what kinds of support are necessary to maintain the system).

2. Logistics supply time (*LST*) is that portion of nonactive maintenance time during which maintenance is delayed solely because a spare repair part, or essential tool, etc., is not immediately available.

3. Administrative delay, or waiting, time (*ADT*) is that portion of nonactive maintenance time during which maintenance is delayed for

# Figure 8.1: Corrective Maintenance Cycle

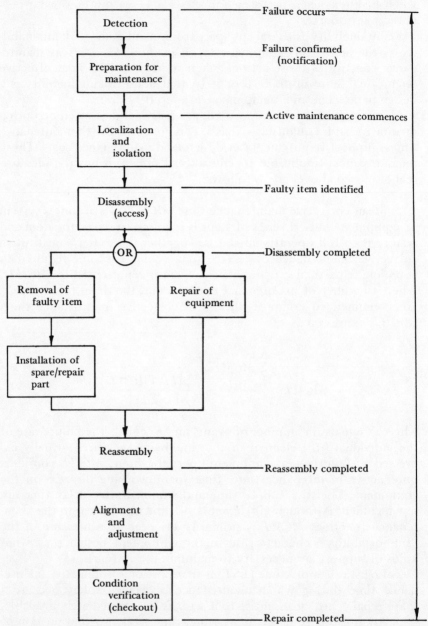

Source: Benjamin S. Blanchard, *Logistics Engineering and Management* (Englewood Cliffs, N.J.: Prentice-Hall, 1974), p. 39. Reprinted by permission.

administrative reasons (personnel assignment priority, inadequate staffing, and organizational constraints, for example).

4. Mean preventive maintenance time (*MPMT*). This is the mean elapsed time required to perform preventive, or scheduled, maintenance on an item. This may include calibration, servicing, inspection, overhaul, etc., and can either be accomplished while the system is in full operating condition or result in downtime. It is expressed as

$$MPMT = \frac{\Sigma (FPTi)\ (MPMTi)}{\Sigma (FPTi)}\ ,$$

where *FPTi* equals the frequency of the individual (*i*th) preventive maintenance action (in actions per equipment-operating hour), and *MPMTi* equals the mean elapsed time required for the *i*th preventive maintenance action. In this definition the concern is for preventive maintenance actions that result in system downtime. Again, *MPMT* includes only active maintenance time and not logistic supply or administrative delay time.

5. Mean active maintenance time (*MAMT*) is the average elapsed time required to perform preventive (scheduled) and corrective (unscheduled) maintenance. It excludes logistics supply and administrative delay time and is expressed as

$$MAMT = \frac{(F)\ (MCMT) + (FPT)\ (MPMT)}{F + FPT}\ ,$$

where *F* equals the corrective maintenance (or failure) rate, and *FPT* equals the preventive maintenance rate.

6. Maintenance downtime (*MDT*) constitutes the total elapsed time required to retain a system or equipment in, or restore it to, full operating status. *MDT* includes mean active maintenance time, logistic supply time, and administrative delay time. It is expressed as

$$MDT = \frac{\sum\limits_{1}^{N} (MAMTi) + LSTi + ADTi}{N}\ .$$

7. Mean time between maintenance (*MTBM*) is the average time between all maintenance actions (corrective and preventive) and is calculated as

$$MTBM = \frac{1}{1/MICM + 1/MIPM},$$

where *MICM* equals the mean interval of corrective maintenance and *MIPM* equals the mean interval of preventive maintenance.

The seven factors described above relate to elapsed time and do not provide a measure for manhours or costs, both of which are important factors to consider in maintenance management. Some of the additional measures that can be employed include maintenance manhours per equipment-operating hours (*MMH/OH*) and maintenance manhours per maintenance action (*MMH/MA*). These values can be predicted for various pieces of equipment and for individual maintenance acts. Also they can be aggregated to different organizational levels for purposes of planning; they are employed in determining specific support requirements and associated cost. Similarly, maintenance factors related to cost often provide valid indices for management—factors such as cost per maintenance action (*$/MA*) and cost per equipment-operating hours (*$/OH*). Cost considerations, however, involve the prior issue of life-cycle costs of equipment.

## Cost Factors

One of the fundamental cost concepts used in the analysis of systems and equipment is that of *life-cycle cost*. Life-cycle cost includes all costs associated with the system or equipment, including costs for research and development, investment, operation and maintenance, and phaseout. Costs are estimated by year for the major equipment and associated support. These estimates are derived from a combination of accounting records (historical data), bid prices, and predictions and are arrayed as a *cost stream,* or *cost profile,* such as the one in figure 8.2.

Estimates of life-cycle cost must be presented in terms of a given point in time, particularly in the evaluation of alternative proposals, where comparisons must be made on an equivalent basis. The given point in time is generally the present time (now); thus, the costs for each year in the life cycle are usually discounted to the present value.

*Discounting* is the application of a selected rate of interest to measure the differences in importance between dollars at the present time and anticipated dollars in the future. Discounting allows for the evaluation of cost streams for various alternative configurations as if they were occurring at one point in time, rather than spaced over the life of the item under consideration.

## Figure 8.2: Sample Cost Stream

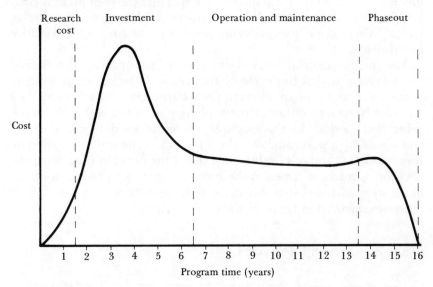

The fundamental assumption in consideration of present value is that receiving $100 today is preferable to the absolute assurance of receiving $100 one year from now. The question then is to determine how many dollars a year from now we would consider equal in worth to $100 now ($105? $110? $120?). The difference is attributable to the concept of interest. The concept of interest has been correctly labeled as "somewhat confusing" by some economists because it is a function of a number of factors, only one of which is the demand for and the supply of loanable money. (See Rogers and Ruchlin 1970, pp. 152-57 for a discussion of different kinds of interest.) The point remains, however, that future expenditures are preferable to present expenditures of the same amount. Likewise, future income is seen as less preferable to receiving present income in the same amount.

In determining the amount of difference, the interest (or discount) rate is useful because it aids in the analysis of total costs of alternative operating systems. "Without interest rates how can one choose, for example, between building a railroad that follows the natural contours of the land (thereby having a low capital cost but high current operating costs because of the hills and curves that must be traversed) and one using bridges, tunnels, and other devices which cut the operating costs but greatly increase the capital cost?" (Rogers and Ruchlin 1970, p. 157). The concept applies, on a smaller scale, when educational organizations invest in operating systems. The inclusion of interest charges makes comparable the high-present-cost/low-future-cost and the low-present-cost/high-future-cost alternatives. This is done by analyzing the life-cycle costs of alternative investments.

For the purposes of illustration, assume that costs are determined for a system with a life cycle of five years. Although costs actually occur continually or at discrete points throughout each year, they are usually treated either at the beginning or at the end of the applicable time period. In this example, the costs are determined at the end of each year throughout the life cycle. The object is to relate these costs in "today's" value since this is the point in time when the decision is made to invest in the system. Figure 8.3 presents a simple illustration of the system life cycle and the costs of each year, which must be conveyed in terms of the present value.

## Figure 8.3: System Life-Cycle Costs

For the first year, costs are estimated for each applicable item and are represented at point A. The question is, "What is the value of that total cost at point A in terms of the decision point?" This can be determined from the following single-payment present value expression:

$$P = F \left[ \frac{1}{(1 + i)^n} \right] ,$$

where $P$ equals present-value or present principal sum, $F$ equals future sum at some interest period hence, $i$ equals the annual interest rate, and $n$ equals the interest period. Assuming an interest rate of 10 percent, the present-value cost at point A is

$$P = \$1,000 \left[ \frac{1}{(1 + 0.1)} \right] = \$909.09. \tag{1}$$

For point B, this value becomes

$$P = \$3,500 \left[ \frac{1}{(1 + 0.1)^2} \right] = \$2,892.40. \tag{2}$$

Next, consider the present value of the costs at point A and point B combined. This is calculated from the expression

$$P = F_A \left[ \frac{1}{(1 + i)} \right] + F_B \left[ \frac{1}{(1 + i)^2} \right]. \tag{3}$$

Assuming the undiscounted estimates of \$1,000 and \$3,500 at points A and B respectively, the present value is

$$P = \$1,000 \left[ \frac{1}{(1 + 0.1)} \right] + \$3,500 \left[ \frac{1}{(1 + 0.1)^2} \right]$$

$$= \$3,801.49. \tag{4}$$

This continues until the costs for each year in the system life cycle are discounted to the present value and totaled. The total present-value cost for the system outlined in figure 8.3 is \$12,649.74. (The undiscounted total value is \$17,500.00.) When costs are different for each year in the life cycle, the present-value expression is a continuation of equations 1-4 or

$$P = FA \left[ \frac{1}{(1 + i)} \right] + FB \left[ \frac{1}{(1 + i)^2} \right] +$$

$$FC \left[ \frac{1}{(1 + i)^3} \right] + \quad \cdots \quad + FN \left[ \frac{1}{(1 + i)^n} \right].$$

(See chapter two for a discussion of cost-accounting concepts applicable to control of the maintenance function. Also, an extensive discussion of cost analysis data can be found in Blanchard 1974, Appendix A; and a thorough treatment of present-value concepts can be found in Thuesen, Fabrycky, and Thuesen 1971.)

## Maintenance Operating Policies

The theoretical dimensions discussed above provide means whereby maintenance policies can be established. *Maintenance policies* here refer to predetermined strategies for maintaining equipment. (These policies by no means constitute a comprehensive treatment of the logistics of maintenance. Other kinds of policy statements are required in the areas of personnel and school district program priorities, for example.) Maintenance policies take into account at least two fundamental considerations: the conditions under which various items or equipment are repaired and the conditions governing whether the various items will be repaired. The first of these can be designated *modes of maintenance,* and the second of these, *repair policies.*

### Modes of Maintenance

There are three general conditions, or modes, under which various items are maintained. *On-site maintenance* is performed at the operational site (school facility, vehicle, heating plant, for example). Generally it includes tasks performed by the using organization on its own equipment. On-site personnel are usually involved with the operation and use of equipment and have minimum time available for detailed system maintenance. In a school setting, for instance, custodians can usually make minor repairs on site but are constrained from more involved work in repairing heating and plumbing systems.

Maintenance at this level normally is limited to visual inspections, periodic checks of equipment performance, cleaning of equipment, some servicing, external adjustments, and the removal and replacement of some components. Personnel assigned to this level generally do not repair the removed components but forward them to the intermediate level. The least skilled personnel, from the maintenance standpoint, are assigned to this function. For example, because custodians usually have very limited responsibilities in the area of maintenance (as opposed to operations and housekeeping), they tend to be the least skilled among the maintenance staff. However, because they (and not maintenance personnel) are located on site in most school settings, they are in a better position to perform minor maintenance tasks.

*Intermediate maintenance* is performed by mobile, semimobile, and/or fixed specialized organizations and installations. This is perhaps the predominate mode of school maintenance. End items may be repaired by the removal and replacement of major modules, assemblies, or piece parts. Scheduled maintenance requiring equipment disassembly may also be accomplished in this mode. Maintenance personnel at this level are usually more specialized, more skilled, and better equipped than those at the on-site level, and they are responsible for performing more detailed maintenance.

Because school district operations tend to be highly decentralized, mobile and semimobile units often provide maintenance support to building-level custodians. In some instances these units are given virtually total on-site maintenance responsibility, although not assigned to any particular site. Mobile units may include vans or trucks containing test and support equipment (e.g., tools) and spares. The purpose of mobile maintenance units is to provide on-site maintenance that on-site personnel cannot provide in order to return the system to full operational status as soon as possible.

*Centralized (depot) maintenance* supports the accomplishment of tasks above and beyond the capabilities available at the intermediate level. The centralized facility or depot may be a specialized repair facility for the manufacturer's plant, where complex and bulky equipment, large quantities of spares, environment control provisions, etc., can be provided if required. The high-volume potential in centralized facilities fosters the use of assembly-line techniques. This in turn permits the use of relatively unskilled labor for a large portion of the work load, with highly skilled specialists concentrated in key areas, such as fault diagnosis and quality control.

Often some pieces of equipment will receive scheduled maintenance at a central facility and unscheduled maintenance on-site or via mobile units (for example, audio-visual equipment and electronic monitoring devices). The three modes of maintenance discussed above are summarized in table 8.4.

Determining the modes of maintenance for the hundreds of maintainable items is not simple. Fortunately, a number of factors in combination will often dictate the most appropriate mode for a given item. These include the portability of the system, many of the availability and maintainability factors discussed earlier, and the priorities established regarding scheduled and unscheduled repair.

### Repair Policies

Within the general structure outlined in table 8.4, there are a number of possible repair policies. A repair policy specifies to what

## Table 8.4: Major Modes of Maintenance

| Criteria | On-site maintenance | Intermediate maintenance | Depot maintenance |
|---|---|---|---|
| Done where? | At that place where the equipment or system is in operation | Mobile or semimobile units or on-site | Depot facility or manufacturer's plant |
| Done by whom? | On-site personnel with relatively low maintenance skills (e.g., school custodians) | Mobile-unit personnel, usually with intermediate and somewhat specialized skills | Depot facility personnel or manufacturer's production personnel (mix of intermediate fabrication skills and high maintenance skills) |
| Type of work accomplished | Visual inspection<br>Operational checkout<br>Minor servicing<br>External adjustments<br>Removal and replacement of some components | Detailed inspection and system checkout<br>Major servicing<br>Major equipment repair and modifications<br>Relatively more complicated adjustments<br>Limited calibration<br>Overload from on-site maintenance | Complicated factory adjustments<br>Complex equipment repairs and modifications<br>Overhaul and rebuild<br>Detailed calibration<br>Supply support<br>Overload from intermediate level of maintenance |

extent an equipment item will be repaired (if at all). One or more policies may be stated as part of the initial maintenance concept regarding a specific piece of equipment. The repair policy may dictate that an item should be designed to be nonrepairable, partially repairable, or fully repairable.

A *nonrepairable* item is one that is discarded when a failure occurs; it is generally modular in construction and relatively inexpensive to replace. Remaining parts are either recycled or disposed of. If this policy is selected for an item, design criteria should call for a built-in self-test capability to verify a failure in the system.

Items with the nonrepairable designation are usually easily removable (e.g., a plug-in appliance) and not internally accessible, with few or no test points, plug-in assemblies, etc. Logistic support requirements for these items are minimal. Spare units must be stocked at each intermediate-level facility or stored on site; no lower-level spares are required. Test and support equipment are necessary only initially to check out units as they enter the inventory; no maintenance test equipment is required. The objective here is to weigh the cost of spares and unit disposal against the cost of repairs.

A *partially repairable* system may assume various forms, and selection of this repair policy is dependent on system operational requirements as well as on modes of maintenance. The operational availability (*OA*) of the system may, for example, dictate a mean downtime requirement of such short duration that it can be met only by providing for quick repair capability at the on-site level. Since the personnel skills and equipment available at the on-site level are limited, the need exists to select and install equipment for easy failure identification.

In the intermediate mode, which is designed to support on-site maintenance, a different requirement exists. Service-level policies may dictate that certain units be designated nonrepairable when unscheduled maintenance is required (i.e., the unit is replaced) and repairable when scheduled maintenance is required. The repair policy will stipulate which items are repairable under each of the modes of maintenance, considering all applicable modes of maintenance, since a decision for one mode will affect the other modes.

A *fully repairable* system entails the greatest amount of logistic support in terms of test and support equipment, spare and repair parts, personnel and training, technical data coverage, and facilities. As an aid in establishing and evaluating the various possible repair policies, the following questions may be employed as a guide:

1. Are the anticipated scheduled and unscheduled maintenance functions defined for each maintenance level?

2. Are the applicable availability and maintainability factors identified for each maintenance level (e.g., operational availability, mean preventive maintenance time, maintenance manhours per maintenance action)?

3. Are the applicable factors consonant with school district operational requirements? Are they compatible from one maintenance level to the next?

4. What are the estimated personnel types and skill levels for each maintenance level?

5. What facility requirements are anticipated?

6. What are the anticipated maintenance environmental requirements associated with each level (e.g., transportation, storage, working conditions)?

A complete and comprehensive answer to these questions may not be possible at the initial stage of the life cycle of a particular piece of equipment or system. However, these requirements must be identified on a preliminary basis in order to arrive at a preferred repair policy approach.

## Budget Planning

Generally, budget planning for maintenance is not unlike budget planning of other functions in education. Strategies are used for determining current levels of "service," for assessing future needs, and for "costing out" both. The attempt is made here to treat those aspects of maintenance budgeting that are unique to it, including the peculiar indices used for assessing current service levels and planning future service levels. These activities generally involve three steps:

1. Determining (historically) what a specialist can "normally" accomplish during a specified period of time (usually a day or a year);

2. Utilizing identifiable indices (such as the maintainability factors discussed above) to predict aggregate work loads; and

3. Using 1 and 2 to derive manpower and material requirements.

Although custodial (housekeeping) functions are often discussed apart from maintenance (or repair) functions, it is more useful here to lump them together. The two most widely used budgeting strategies that have been applied to both housekeeping and repair may be termed the *formula approach* and the *standards-for-workloading approach.*

The formula approach is rather similar to the approach used to allocate such diverse items as state aid to school districts and secretaries to school sites within districts. Factors deemed relevant are combined into a functional relationship so that when values are assigned to the appropriate variables, estimates of manpower or material requirements result. For example, many educational organizations at one time built their maintenance budgets on the gross square footage of all buildings coupled with an "experience" factor and some guessing as to the percentage increase to apply each year. As it became apparent that operations and maintenance (*O* and *M*) needs were significantly influenced by other variables (such as the number of people usually occupying the building), these were incorporated into the formula. Additional variables found in custodial personnel requirements included age of building, number of teachers, students, rooms, and size of site.

The formula often used for determining custodial personnel allocations to school sites on the basis of a particular variable is

$$Aij = \frac{Nij}{Fi} ,$$

where $Aij$ equals the number of custodial positions allocated on the basis of variable $i$ to school $j$; $Nij$ equals the number (or amount) of variable $i$ in school $j$; $Fi$ equals the $i$ factor or number (or amount) of variable $i$ used in determining all allocations. If more than one factor is used, then the total allocation of custodial personnel to a school site is (assuming all factors are weighted equally)

$$Tj = \frac{\Sigma Aij}{n} ,$$

where $Tj$ equals the total allocation of custodial personnel to school $j$; and $n$ equals the number of factors.

Exhibit 8.5 shows how custodial personnel requirements are estimated. In calculating the custodial entitlement for the Ellwanger-Barry School on the basis of the teacher factor, the number of teachers in the school is divided by the predetermined amount of that factor that is used for allocation purposes. Allocations are determined for each of the other four factors in the same way. These are then averaged to determine the number of custodial personnel

## Exhibit 8.5: Worksheet for Estimating Custodial Personnel Requirement

School: Ellwanger-Barry

1. Teacher factor = $\dfrac{\text{number of teachers}}{8}$ = $\dfrac{}{8}$ =

2. Pupil factor = $\dfrac{\text{number of pupils}}{225}$ = $\dfrac{}{225}$ =

3. Room factor = $\dfrac{\text{number of rooms}}{11}$ = $\dfrac{}{11}$ =

4. Area factor = $\dfrac{\text{total area of building}}{15,000}$ = $\dfrac{}{15,000}$ =

5. Site factor = $\dfrac{\text{number of acres}}{2}$ = $\dfrac{}{2}$ =

TOTAL =

$\dfrac{\text{Total}}{5}$ = number of custodians needed for daily cleaning

*Notes:* 1. The room factor includes offices, toilets, classrooms, gym, lunchroom, etc. Break large areas, such as gym and library, into classroom equivalents by dividing by 1,000 square feet.
2. Site factor considers only that portion of the site that is normally the responsibility of the custodian.
3. In computation, carry figures to two decimal places.

needed for daily cleaning. Note that extended accuracy is to be carried out throughout the computations. Whether the resulting figure is rounded up or down will be a function of negotiation and available resources.

While the formula approach for maintenance (repair) can take the same general form, the implied relationship between factors and manpower requirements is usually not as specifically stated. For example, building maintenance cost determinations have been built around the classifications of building construction (i.e., what type of building is the variable):

1. Wood-frame construction
2. Masonry-wood (wood floors and wood-frame partitions)
3. Masonry-concrete or masonry-steel frame, fireproof and with concrete floors

(These factors were in use at Texas A. & M. University when cited in Smith 1966.)

The amount of money to be allocated for building maintenance can be determined by applying a *maintenance cost factor* to the total replacement cost for each construction classification. This maintenance cost factor is a percentage of the replacement cost and will vary for the three building classifications. Replacement cost can be determined by using a current appraisal chart. (This is usually done by multiplying the original building cost by the factor given in the table for the type of construction and year built.)

The corresponding maintenance cost factors for buildings in one educational institution (Smith 1966) are

1. Wood-frame construction                1.75 percent
2. Masonry-wood construction           1.30 percent
3. Masonry-concrete or masonry-steel   1.10 percent
   with concrete floors

In this particular case the cost factors were increased .15 percent for buildings with air conditioning, and supervisory costs (other than the salary of the work foreman) were not included. It was also assumed that buildings were in good repair: deferred maintenance and major rehabilitation were budgeted separately. Note that both the maintenance cost factors and the custodial allocation factors discussed earlier must be determined historically.

The standards-for-workloading approach to maintenance budgeting is similar to the formula approach in that factors are applied against variables to determine requirements. The difference is that the variables are tasks and the factors are the number of units of time it takes for the tasks to be accomplished.

In the custodial area, workloading is determined by assessing an individual's capability for performing a daily routine of housekeeping specific areas, such as offices, classrooms, laboratories, and lavatories. Time studies for the routines must be undertaken, and time standards established for typical rooms in the same or similar categories. These work standards or rates are then used in determining personnel requirements. See exhibit 8.6.

Implicit in exhibit 8.6 is the assumption that the custodial functions listed will be performed every day. Many custodial tasks can probably be performed less often for adequate maintenance, while others should be done more frequently. The frequency of custodial functions is often a function of available funds, and alternative standards of custodial care can be developed for different levels of funding. See exhibit 8.7.

## Exhibit 8.6: Custodial Daily Work Load

School: _____

| Area | Rate | No. | Total minutes |
|---|---|---|---|
| Regular classroom | 20 min. each | | |
| Special classroom (science, band) | 25 min. each | | |
| Shops | __ min. each | | |
| Auditorium | __ min./1000 sq. ft. | | |
| Library | 14 min./1000 sq. ft. | | |
| Gymnasium | 5 min./1000 sq. ft. | | |
| Shower and locker room (combination) | 30 min. each | | |
| Toilet (multiple) | 30 min. each | | |
| Toilet (single) | 5 min. each | | |
| Corridor | __ min./1000 sq. ft. | | |
| Administrative offices | __ min. each | | |
| Custodial storerooms | 15 min. each | | |
| Cafeteria | __ min./1000 sq. ft. | | |
| Heating plant | 30 min. | | |
| Grounds | 30 min./acre | | |

Total minutes: _____

Equivalent manhours: _____

*Notes:* Emergencies, periodic cleaning and maintenance, lunch or dinner time, "breaks," etc., are not included in the above.

The times listed for specific areas are averages based on work performed by a trained custodian and will vary under specific conditions. Some examples of such variations are:
1. Shops: Checking lights and doors, emptying trash barrel, 3 min.
   Full cleaning, 2 min./100 sq. ft.
2. Corridors: Smooth, 5 min./1,000 sq. ft.
   Rough, 16 min./1,000 sq. ft.
   Oiled wood, 10 min./1,000 sq. ft.
3. Offices: Small, 5 min.
   Large, 15 min.
4. Cafeteria: Sweeping, 7 min./1,000 sq. ft.
   Sweeping and damp mopping, 23 min./1,000 sq. ft.
   Sweeping, wet mopping, and rinse, 42 min./1,000 sq. ft.
5. Auditorium: If fixed seats, 16 min./1,000 sq. ft.
   If movable seats, figure chair-moving time and gym-sweeping rate
6. Heating plant: Time based on automatic controls; plant needs only periodic inspection

In summary, there are six general steps involved in developing workload procedures for budgeting purposes:

1. Catalog spaces as follows: office, classroom, laboratory, etc.
2. Study the times it takes several different janitors to perform duties at a normal rate, and observe the different methods employed by each janitor.
3. Average all times in like areas. (This procedure for developing

## Exhibit 8.7: Variable Standards of Maintenance Reflecting Funding Levels

*Minimum Standard*
(does not include window washing, floor maintenance, or evening-school work)
   1. Offices, lounges, libraries, conference rooms, classrooms, and laboratories
      *Daily:* Unlock door and turn on lights
           Dust rooms
           Clean out ashtrays on desks, tables, etc.
           Empty trash cans
           Sweep floor
           Turn out lights, lock door
           Clean chalkboards, chalk trays, and erasers
      *Weekly:* Vacuum rugs
   2. Bathrooms
      *Daily:* Clean and disinfect all urinals, commodes, and lavoratories
           Wet mop floor
           Clean and wash all mirrors
      *Weekly:* Thoroughly clean bathrooms (including scrubbing all tile)
   3. Halls and stairways
      *Daily:* Sweep and dust
      *Weekly:* Damp mop at least once per week
*Median Standard*
(with window washing and floor maintenance included)
To Minimum Standard, add the following:
      *Daily:* Buff floors
           Spot-clean walls
           Vacuum rugs
      *Weekly:* Dust venetian blinds and special furniture
      *Semiannually:* Wash windows
      *Floor maintenance:* Special crew on scheduled cycle for stripping, waxing, and refinishing floors
*Ideal Standard*
To Median Standard, add the following:
      *Daily:* Polish brass
      *Twice daily:* Clean heavily loaded classrooms, blackboards, and erasers
      *Weekly:* Clean light fixtures
      *Annually:* Wash venetian blinds
           Shampoo rugs
      *Special services:* Includes moving furniture and equipment within a building and more frequent dusting of high areas
      *Evening-school service*

Source: Adapted from J. McCree Smith, *Maintenance Budgeting* (Richmond, Ind.: National Association of Physical Plant Administrators of Universities and Colleges, 1966), pp. 99-101. ERIC, no. ED026799.

"standard times" is much like the procedure for developing "standard costs" discussed in chapter seven, "Food Service.")

    4. Divide buildings into floors, and calculate each floor workload by multiplying the number of areas by their respective average times

for cleaning (e.g., six offices at ten minutes per office equals sixty minutes of time required).

5. Add all times together and divide by the number of minutes janitors work each day. (The result is the number of men required to perform the duties at the level of housekeeping desired.)

6. To establish cost estimates for budgeting purposes, group positions and multiply the number in each group of positions by the proposed wage range for that group.

Manpower requirements for each of the standards can be calculated this way and compared to the number currently employed. This method of budgeting shows what work can be expected for each of the different levels of maintenance, how many people it will take (at what cost) at each level of maintenance, and how the manpower requirements at each level compare with the current staffing.

Workloads for maintenance functions are determined in much the same way as for custodial functions. Budgeting planning activities would include defining the responsibilities of each shop (e.g., auto, hardware, paint, pipe, carpentry) and using statistical analysis to determine unit workloads with annual output possible for one workman. Output would be based on a productive year of a predetermined number of hours. For example, an 1,800-hour year would result from subtracting three weeks of vacation, two weeks of holidays, and two weeks of sick leave from fifty-two 40-hour weeks in a year (45 weeks times 40 hours per week equals 1,800 hours).

The units of work vary significantly among the trades. In a paint shop, for example, the annual output for one workman can be determined by the amount of painting done (e.g., 90,000 square feet of paintable surface such as walls, ceilings, and trim, both interior and exterior). This results in an average production of 50 square feet per hour (including time spent in preparation and painting trim). In the pipe shop the unit workload could be calculated as a function of the number of plumbing fixtures one workman can repair annually.

Unit workloads need not be related to specific functions of work. For example, in the areas of plastering, sheet metal, brick masonry, roofing, carpentry, and general electrical maintenance, unit workloads can be derived as a function of gross square footage of buildings.

In all cases of budget planning for custodial and maintenance functions, it is necessary to develop some concept of productivity. The usual procedure for accomplishing this is historical observation. However, recording and evaluating the performance of many relatively small tasks is not a trivial undertaking. The decision to undertake such recordkeeping must be predicated on the assumption that it will ultimately improve planning and control of the operations and maintenance function. This will not necessarily be the case in every situation.

## Unscheduled Maintenance Operations

Although unscheduled maintenance, by definition, implies "emergency," steps can be taken to make it operate with a minimum of confusion. There are several reasons for monitoring and controlling unscheduled maintenance operations in educational organizations. First, unscheduled maintenance can threaten the operation of the organization. Second, it is relatively costly. A cost comparison in the Memphis city schools, for example, revealed that emergency service was costing two and one-half to three times as much as the same repair on a regular basis (Oswalt 1964, p. 10). Third, determining the pattern of unscheduled maintenance can be extremely useful in modifying preventive maintenance programs (which would reduce the need for unscheduled maintenance).

If emergencies qualify as candidates for unscheduled maintenance, what then constitutes an emergency (in terms of repairs to physical plants)? Standards will vary among organizations, but an organization needs to have a relatively unambiguous definition of what its standard is. For example: "An emergency endangers the health or safety of people; presents a hazard to the building and contents or other physical property; breaches building security or disrupts the school program" (Oswalt 1964).

Virtually all emergencies so defined involve three variables:

1. A physical item (door, toilet, thermostat)
2. A malfunction of some kind (will not lock, leaking, not operating)
3. A particular service required (locksmith, plumber, electrician)

Knowing the first two pieces of information makes it possible to prescribe the third. However, before the precise specifications and the schedule of service can be determined, additional information is required, such as the location of the emergency and the degree of seriousness.

Although these data about reported emergencies will enable the maintenance department to function on a day-to-day basis, additional information is required for management decisions of a higher order. For example, periodic summaries of emergencies by location and by equipment type can provide much of the basis for modifying replacement policies and revising plans for scheduled maintenance. The relationship between information and decision is summarized in figure 8.8.

In one instance where the general form of this system has been computerized (Memphis), virtually all emergency repairs were coded under one of forty-seven item headings, with up to eight repairs under a single heading. Further, it was determined that twenty-one different types of service were required for emergency repairs. As an example, "Item 28, problem 1, service 15" constitutes a code to indicate a leaking gas pipe requiring plumbing service. In addition to merely recording the emergency in this way, a checklist was appended to each problem definition to assure that every reasonable effort to correct the situation was made at the school and that proper and adequate information was transmitted to the person who was to dispatch the service (Oswalt 1966). The potential utility of upper-level management information in the maintenance area is best conveyed via two examples from the operation in Memphis.

*Example 1: Impact of unscheduled maintenance information on operations and preventive maintenance.* The statistical report on the first six months of one school year showed a 70 percent increase in sewer stoppages as compared to the same six months of the previous year. As a result of this unusually high increase in emergencies, an all-out study was undertaken to determine the cause and to develop methods of reducing the problem. The type and quality of paper goods that were supplied for restrooms were studied. Although the toilet tissue was breaking up satisfactorily when introduced into the sewer system, an unusual amount of hand towels were being flushed into the sewer and were not breaking up. This prompted action designed to prevent towels from being introduced into the sewer line and an effort to find a reasonably priced paper towel that would be serviceable and also break up in water. Many of the problems were occurring in cafeteria kitchens were food waste disposals were in use. In order to minimize these problems, kitchen sewers were flushed by running additional water through the disposal and adjoining sinks for a few minutes after the disposal operation had been shut down for the day. Chemical solvents were used in some of the lines on a periodic treatment basis. Problem sewers were identified, and in some cases replacements were made. Even with continued growth in the system, the sewer stoppages were reduced by 19 percent the following year.

# Figure 8.8: Information from Unscheduled Maintenance Operation Needed by Middle and Upper Management

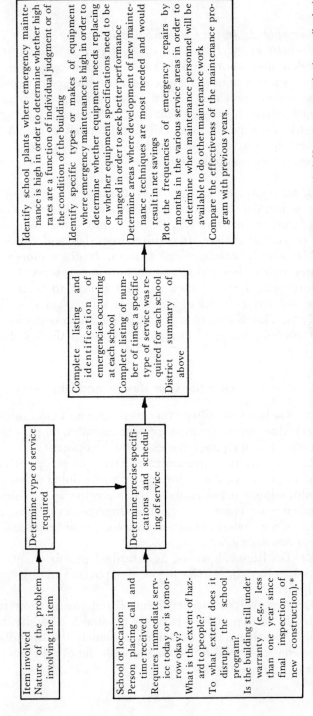

Needed by middle management relative to each emergency

Decisions to be made by middle management

Information needed periodically by upper management

Decisions to be made periodically by upper management

**Item involved**
Nature of the problem involving the item

**Determine type of service required**

**School or location**
Person placing call and time received
Requires immediate service today or is tomorrow okay?
What is the extent of hazard to people?
To what extent does it disrupt the school program?
Is the building still under warranty (e.g., less than one year since final inspection of new construction).*

**Determine precise specifications and scheduling of service**

Complete listing and identification of emergencies occurring at each school
Complete listing of number of times a specific type of service was required for each school
District summary of above

Identify school plants where emergency maintenance is high in order to determine whether high rates are a function of individual judgment or of the condition of the building
Identify specific types or makes of equipment where emergency maintenance is high in order to determine whether equipment needs replacing or whether equipment specifications need to be changed in order to seek better performance
Determine areas where development of new maintenance techniques are most needed and would result in net savings
Plot the frequencies of emergency repairs by months in the various service areas in order to determine when maintenance personnel will be available to do other maintenance work
Compare the effectiveness of the maintenance program with previous years.

*Often the architect is the one to be informed of any problems arising in new buildings during the warranty period. He or someone else is usually designated as the one to have corrections made on any problems that result from defects in materials or workmanship.

*Example 2: Impact of unscheduled maintenance information on performance specifications of material and equipment.* Statistics revealed that door problems were second only in number to sewer stoppages as a major classification of emergency repairs. A study of these repairs revealed a need to provide special reinforcing for frequently used doors and frames. Such reinforcing is now being provided in both new construction and replacements. Although growth makes the statistics meaningless in the area, major problems have shown a very marked reduction.

In summary, we can say that maintenance is an operating system that is intimately related to many other systems. For example, unscheduled maintenance involves people and consequently relates to the personnel system. It requires materials and consequently relates to the supply management system. It costs money and therefore relates to the budgeting and accounting systems. In discussing "the maintenance system" then, it is important to keep in mind that we have isolated a cluster of highly interrelated activities for purposes of analysis. This is not to say that other systems could not be isolated that include some of the maintenance activities discussed in this chapter.

## Questions for Review and Discussion

1.  Is the availability of a certain piece of equipment (e.g., a computer) due more to management maintenance policies or to the inherent design characteristics of the equipment?

2.  List twenty mechanical systems or pieces of equipment that must be made available (on either a scheduled or unscheduled basis) in educational organizations. What are the approximate mean times between maintenance for each of these pieces of equipment?

3.  Under what conditions is a long maintenance downtime tolerable, even desirable?

4.  Do life-cycle costs, as described in this chapter, cover all the costs involved in purchasing or not purchasing a system or piece of equipment?

5.  Among the twenty items listed in question two, which are probably nonrepairable? Partially repairable? Totally repairable?

6.  Are there any situations in which the formula approach for maintenance would not coincide with the overall maintenance objectives of an organization?

7. How does the program of the unscheduled maintenance affect the program of scheduled maintenance? How does the program of scheduled maintenance affect the program of unscheduled maintenance?

## References

Blanchard, Benjamin S. *Logistics Engineering and Management.* Englewood Cliffs, N.J.: Prentice-Hall, 1974.
Oswalt, Felix E. "Computerized Maintenance of Memphis Schools." ERIC, no. ED074612, 1964.
Rogers, Daniel C., and Ruchlin, Hirsch S. *Economics and Education.* New York: The Free Press, 1970.
Smith, J. McCree. "Maintenance Budgeting." ERIC, no. ED026799.
Thuesen, H. G.; Fabrycky, W. J.; and Thuesen, G. J. *Engineering Economy.* Englewood Cliffs, N.J.: Prentice-Hall, 1971.

## Related Readings

Association of Physical Plant Administrators (Corvellis, Oreg.). "Comparative Unit Cost and Wage Rate Report on Maintenance and Operation of Physical Plants of Universities and Colleges." ERIC, no. ED077434, 1971. This report provides unit cost and wage rate information for 1969-1970 on the maintenance and operation of physical plants of universities and colleges. Data are divided into unit costs per gross feet and wage rate survey. Each section is grouped by region, by enrollment, and by top level of academic program. The appendix includes questionnaire forms and adopted standards.
George, Norvil L. *Effective School Maintenance.* West Nyack, N.Y.: Parker Publishing, 1969. This book stresses the practical aspects of school maintenance, describing the principles and effective maintenance practices that serve as guides for superintendents of schools and heads of maintenance departments. Part I deals with the administrative practices of an efficient maintenance program, and Part II discusses the daily maintenance problems, attempting to disclose the magnitude of the maintenance problems that may appear in a school district.
Gland, J. R., and Wilday, C. A. *Custodial Management Practices in the Public Schools.* Chicago, Ill.: Research Corporation of Association of School Business Officials, 1975. The report of a study of the management practices in public school custodial programs of selected Indiana public schools. It reviews the seven management functions (planning, organizing, controlling, coordinating, directing, staffing, and evaluating) as they pertain to custodial management.
Hill, Frederick W., and Colmey, James W. *School Custodial Services.* Minneapolis, Minn.: T. S. Denison, 1968. Concerned with the organization of the custodial services of a school district, employment and training procedures, and other services related to the custodial and maintenance functions of a school district.

Association of School Business Officials (Chicago, Ill.) and Council of Educational Facility Planners (Columbus, Ohio). "Educational Facility Abstract Journal." ERIC, no. ED027702, 1968. Combining eight separate publications of the Council of Educational Facility Planners Abstract Service, this compendium provides resumes of school plant research and planning information of national relevance. Document resumes are organized in the following categories: (1) determining school plant requirements, (2) architectural services, (3) legal aspects, (4) finance, (5) the building, and (6) operation and maintenance. A cross reference is included.

Florida State Department of Education. "A Survey Report of School Plant Management for Escambia County, Florida." ERIC, no. ED036069, 1965. Analyzes data collected by survey teams concerned with maintenance and operation of school plants in relation to organization, administration, budgeting, expenditures, purchasing, staffing, warehousing and distribution, maintenance shops, administrative practices, performance standards and efficiency. The basic purposes of a maintenance and operations program for a school are stated, recommendations made, and worksheets for estimating custodial personnel requirements and daily workloads included.

# PART III

# ALLOCATION SYSTEMS

# 9

# Budget Planning Using PERT

Much of what educational managers do relates directly to allocating scarce resources to achieve organizational objectives. Allocation activities include school district budgeting, classroom scheduling, setting attendance boundaries, and distributing aid to school districts from state and federal sources. In each of these instances, allocation decisions are made within the contexts of desired objectives, limited resources, and political constraints.

In part three several management tools are applied to various allocation processes. Management tools include project mapping, responsibility charting, sorting, decision rules, and mathematical models.

In this chapter school district budgeting is viewed as a logical network of discrete activities, the accomplishment of which is constrained by time and other activities. Our purpose here is not to outline "the" way school district budgets are (or ought to be) developed. (A number of current sources are available that describe model budgeting practices for school districts. See Curtis 1971; Haggart 1972; and Hartley 1968.) Rather, our purpose is to choose one of the many ways that budgets are developed and show how mapping can be used to make the process more coherent and understandable.

Chapter ten, "Organizing Personnel for Budgeting," also focuses on school district budgeting. However, we shift attention from developing the network of activities to determining how people relate to the network of activities and to each other. Specifically, responsibility charting is used to organize the efforts of personnel in the budgeting process.

To attempt to describe the budgeting process in school districts is like trying to describe the way a building is built. A very general description would cover most cases but probably omit many instructive details and variations. On the other hand, a very specific description would probably include details that would apply precisely in only a few cases. The description below includes a moderate amount of detail as applied to an "average" district.

The chief budget officer must list the important budget-related activities in order to plan his or her time and to coordinate the activities of other participants in the process. The level of detail that the administrator uses in drafting the budget calendar will depend on the degree to which exhaustive detail will improve the overall quality of the budgeting process.

*General* budget calendars serve a useful purpose in indicating roughly when types of activities usually take place. They can also briefly portray how the business manager will interact with various groups, and what those groups will be doing, and when.

Exhibit 9.1 is an example of a very general budgeting calendar; it indicates some of the things that the business manager should do when meeting with various groups during the budget year, such as receiving reports from some groups, initiating conferences with others, and reporting to still others. Other important tasks that the

## Exhibit 9.1: General Calendar of Budgeting Activities

| | |
|---|---|
| September | Formation of committees for planning, supplies, salary scheduling, etc. Report to board of education on budget accounts. |
| October | Receive preliminary reports of some committees (others continue study). Begin study of school plant needs. Regular meetings of board of education. |
| November | Plan community group discussions with committees acting as panels. Inform public about what is going on. Regular and special reports to board of education. |
| December | Estimate needs for next year, such as custodial supplies and fuel. Report to board of education. |
| January | Receive requisitions from teachers for classroom supplies. Hold conferences with teaching and nonteaching staff about requests for ensuing year. Receive reports from citizens' groups working with teachers. Make reports to board of education. |
| February | Board meets with salary schedule committee to receive reports and suggestions. Continue citizens' group meetings on specific aspects. Draw up tentative schedule of receipts expected. |
| March | Receive final reports of various committees that are prepared to report. Report tentative budget. Develop plans for presentation at annual meeting. Make reports to board of education. |
| April | Board presents tentative budget. Hold meetings of citizens to discuss items in budget. Adoption of budget by board. |
| May | Annual meeting of school district administration to approve budget. Distribution of annual report to voters. |
| June | Order supplies for summer delivery. Make annual reports to state education department. Close current accounts. |
| July | Open new accounts for new year. |

business manager must initiate are included here, such as ordering supplies in June for summer delivery.

Although general budget calendars, such as this one, show the approximate timing of general activities, they do not do justice to the complexity of the budgeting process or to the coordinative effort required to manage budget development. The practicing budget officer may need a more comprehensive description of the budgeting process in order, for instance, to describe to other individuals or groups how and where they fit in the budgeting process. For example, it may be useful to show the social studies department in the high school that its recommendations about new and different curriculum materials need to be submitted to the principal by November 10 if those recommendations are to affect the principal's request for instructional supplies money, which, in turn, has to be submitted by November 15.

In order to indicate how the coordination of various activities actually occurs in the budgeting process, the budget officer will probably have to resort to some managerial tools. This is especially true if he or she also wants to show efficiently the changing responsibilities of each of the participants.

One of the best known and most widely used techniques for the planning, scheduling, and control of such projects is the PERT chart. A PERT chart gives the budget officer a disciplined and logical base for handling a project. It provides a clear picture of the scope of the total project, which helps to earmark essential jobs and eliminate unnecessary ones, and it aids in identifying who has responsibility for performing specific tasks.

The steps usually required in building and using a PERT chart are:

1. List activities to be included in the project.
2. Chart the list of activities.
3. Develop a time estimate for each activity and calculate the duration of the entire project and the critical path(s) as well as the amount of slack in the other paths.
4. Schedule activities in a calendar.
5. Modify each of the above, as necessary.

Although in reality the steps of this sequence are overlapping, they are discussed separately here. The "project," in our example, is building a budget for a school district, and the "project manager" is the chief business official of the school district.

## Listing Activities in the Budgeting Process

The budget officer compiles a list of all the activities, jobs, or work phases that he or she feels should be included in the budgeting process. This list of activities identifies and describes the work that will be necessary to accomplish the project objectives. Activities require *people* to perform them, *time,* and *other resources.* The list of activities should cover three major phases of the budgeting process: (1) the overall planning phase; (2) the actual budget-development phase; and (3) the approval phase, in which the results of the development process are demonstrated.

More specifically, the planning phase includes an evaluation of the district's educational offerings (and any program revisions), an evaluation of its support systems, an updating of the census data, and an estimate of revenues from nontax sources. Debt service schedules are reviewed, the need for additional capital outlay is explored, and the physical facilities are surveyed. Equally important is the establishment or updating of the district's educational objectives as guides for the superintendent and the staff as they develop financial requests.

Once the background data have been gathered, the budget-development process goes into full swing. This phase involves preparation of the various requests in light of district parameters; negotiations; translation of the requests into appropriate categories and codes; discussions with the citizens' advisory committee; development of the financial plan for underwriting the anticipated expenses; incorporation of anticipated revenues from all sources; and approval of any borrowing programs needed to balance the income schedule and the expenditure schedule.

The approval phase, when approval is by public referendum, is set in motion by the school board's acceptance of the developed budget. It involves publishing notices, holding a public meeting, developing and implementing voter registration plans, printing the budget, and holding the referendum on the proposed budget.

Table 9.2 is a list of seventy-five activities and the person or group primarily responsible for the completion of each. This list may serve as an example of the level of detail that might be useful in planning the budgeting process. Clearly, many of the listed activities have to be undertaken simultaneously in order to develop the budget in time. On the other hand, some activities cannot be started until others have been completed. For example, the school business official cannot very well revise estimates of cafeteria expenses until the cafeteria manager has made the estimates. The need to structure the sequence

## Table 9.2: Activities in the Budgeting Process

| Activity | Who performs | Start-Finish (PERT events) |
|---|---|---|
| Evaluate last year's program | Superintendent | 1—3 |
| Conduct (update) district census | Administrative assistant | 1—2 |
| Review debt service schedule | School business official Bank official | 1—4 |
| Conduct individual school plant surveys | Principals | 1—5 |
| Revise education and recreation programs | Principals, coordinators, directors | 3—6 |
| Estimate anticipated state and federal revenue | School business official | 2—7 |
| Estimate anticipated local nontax revenue | Cafeteria manager, principals, directors of special areas | 2—8 |
| Estimate total revenue and expense for budget period | School business official | 8—9 |
| Revise education and recreation programs | Assistant superintendent of instruction | 6—9 |
| Determine educational objectives and policy | Superintendent and school board | 9—10 |
| Prepare estimates of school board and central administration expense requests for supplies, equipment, and personnel | District clerk | 10—13 |
| Distribute budget preparation information | School business official | 9—11 |
| Revise school board and central administration expense requests | Assistant superintendent and business official | 13—22 |
| Revise school board and central administration expense requests | Superintendent | 22—62 |
| Review school board and central administration expense requests | Citizens' advisory committee | 62—23 |
| Tentatively approve board of education and central administration expense requests | School board | 23—24 |
| Prepare building-level administration and instruction expense requests for supplies, equipment, and capital improvement | Principals, coordinators, directors | 10—14 |
| Prepare building-level conference expense requests | Coordinators | 10—15 |
| Prepare building-level personnel expense requests for both classified and certificated personnel | District-level administrators, principals, coordinators, directors | 10—16 |
| Revise building-level certificated personnel requests | Assistant superintendent of instruction | 16—25 |
| Revise building-level budget requests for certificated personnel, supplies, and equipment | Assistant superintendent of instruction and school business official | 25—27 |
| Revise building-level classified personnel requests | School business official | 16—27 |

## Table 9.2 *(continued)*

| Activity | Who performs | Start-finish (PERT events) |
|---|---|---|
| Revise instruction expense requests for regular and special schools and community services | School business official | 27–30 |
| Prepare building-level expense requests for supplies, equipment, and maintenance | Principals | 11–17 |
| Prepare building-level expense requests for supplies, equipment, and maintenance | Administrative assistant for buildings and grounds | 17–26 |
| Revise building-level expense requests for plant personnel | Administrative assistant for buildings and grounds | 26–27 |
| Prepare estimates for fuel, utilities, contracted services, and miscellaneous plant expenses | Administrative assistant for buildings and grounds | 26–29 |
| Revise plant operation and maintenance expense requests | School business official | 29–31 |
| Revise plant operation and maintenance expense requests | Superintendent | 31–32 |
| Revise instruction expense requests for regular and special schools and community services | Superintendent | 30–33 |
| Revise instruction expense requests for regular and special schools and community services | School board | 33–42 |
| Revise plant operation and maintenance expense requests | School board | 32–43 |
| Prepare and exchange professional staff/school board negotiation proposals | Instruction staff and school board | 42–44 |
| Conduct professional staff/school board negotiations | Instruction staff and school board | 44–46 |
| Review instruction expense requests for regular and special schools and community services | Citizens' budget advisory committee | 42–46 |
| Tentatively approve instruction expense requests for regular and special schools and community services | School board | 46–49 |
| Adjust central administration personnel salary expense requests | School business official | 46–24 |
| Develop and exchange secretarial staff/school board negotiation proposals | Secretarial personnel and school board | 42–45 |
| Conduct secretarial staff/school board negotiations | Secretarial personnel and school board | 45–46 |
| Develop and exchange custodial staff/school board negotiation proposals | Custodial personnel and school board | 43–47 |
| Conduct custodial staff/school board negotiations | Custodial personnel and school board | 47–48 |
| Review plant expense operation and maintenance requests | Citizens' budget advisory committee | 43–48 |

## Table 9.2 *(continued)*

| Activity | Who performs | Start-finish (PERT events) |
|---|---|---|
| Tentatively approve plant operation and maintenance expense requests | School board | 48—49 |
| Prepare regular transportation expense requests | Public and parochial principals and directors of special areas | 11—18 |
| Prepare special transportation expense requests | District clerk, principals | 11—19 |
| Revise transportation expense requests | School business official | 19—34 |
| Prepare expense requests for oil, gas, insurance, and maintenance of vehicles | School business official | 34—35 |
| Revise all transportation expense requests | Superintendent | 35—36 |
| Revise all transportation expense requests | School board | 36—50 |
| Review transportation expense requests | Citizens' budget advisory committee | 50—51 |
| Tentatively approve transportation expense requests | School board | 51—52 |
| Prepare expense requests for cafeteria personnel, supplies, and equipment | Cafeteria manager | 11—20 |
| Revise expense requests for cafeteria personnel, supplies, and equipment | School business official | 20—37 |
| Revise expense requests for cafeteria personnel, supplies, and equipment | Superintendent | 37—38 |
| Revise expense requests for cafeteria personnel, supplies, and equipment | School board | 38—40 |
| Prepare and exchange cafeteria staff/school board negotiation proposals | Cafeteria staff and school board | 40—28 |
| Conduct cafeteria staff/school board negotiations | Cafeteria staff and school board | 28—63 |
| Prepare capital improvement expense requests | Administrative assistant for buildings and grounds | 5—12 |
| Revise capital improvement expense requests | School business official | 12—21 |
| Revise capital improvement expense requests | Superintendent | 21—39 |
| Revise capital improvement expense requests | School board | 39—40 |
| Review capital improvement and cafeteria expense requests | Citizens' budget advisory committee | 40—41 |
| Tentatively approve interfund transfer expense requests | School board | 54—49 |
| Calculate retirement, social security, health insurance, and other undistributed expense requests | School business official | 49—52 |
| Revise debt service expense requests | School business official | 52—53 |
| Approve financing plan for approved tentative budget | School board | 53—54 |
| Approve budget for presentation to public | School board | 54—55 |

**Table 9.2** *(continued)*

| Activity | Who performs | Start-finish (PERT events) |
|---|---|---|
| Publish required legal notices | District clerk | 54–56 |
| Develop plans for registration and voting on school budget | School board | 55–57 |
| Print detailed tentative budget | Administrative assistant | 57–59 |
| Distribute detailed tentative budget to public | Administrative assistant | 59–58 |
| Present completed tentative budget to public | Citizens' budget advisory committee and school board | 55–58 |
| Conduct public hearing on budget | School board, superintendent, school business official | 58–56 |
| Hold annual meeting on budget | Superintendent | 56–60 |
| Conduct vote on school budget | District clerk | 60–61 |

Source: Guilbert C. Hentschke and John Shaughnessy, "The Budgeting Process," *Research Bulletin* 13, no. 3 (April 1973): 1, 3-13, and 14, no. 1 (November 1973): 1, 4-15. Reprinted by permission.

of these activities gives rise to the second step in the building of a PERT chart.

## Charting the List of Activities

The PERT chart provides an efficient way to "lay out" a list of activities so that their relationships can be clearly seen. Although whole volumes have been written about the principles and finer points of PERT charting (see, for example, Schoderbek and Digman 1967), we need concern ourselves here with only those aspects that will aid in structuring the relationships among activities.

In PERT charting, *activities* are symbolized by arrows. There are seventy-five activities in the budgeting example, and thus there will be seventy-five arrows in that PERT chart. These activities will be connected to each other by *events*. An event indicates the end of an activity and the beginning of another activity. In PERT charting, events are symbolized by circled numbers. Any activity can be described by reference to two numbers: the number of the event that starts the activity and the number of the event that ends the activity. For example, in figure 9.3 the activity "estimating next year's revenue" can be identified simply as 1–6. Unlike activities, events require no time, people, or other resources.

In constructing a PERT chart, only a few rules need to be kept in mind:

1. Only one activity can connect any pair of events; that is, each activity has a unique pair of starting and ending events.

2. Any number of activities may feed into, or out of, any event.

3. No activity can begin until all the activities connecting to its starting event have been completed.

4. The length of the arrow representing each activity has no significance, but its direction is significant.

### Figure 9.3: Portraying a PERT Activity

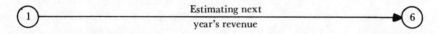

An example might be helpful at this point. Suppose the entire project consisted solely of estimating next year's revenue and required only the following activities:

1. Conduct census.
2. Estimate local tax revenue.
3. Estimate local nontax revenue.
4. Estimate state and federal revenue.
5. Estimate total revenue available.

The PERT chart would probably look like figure 9.4.

This little PERT chart is instructive for several reasons. First, referring to conventional PERT symbols and rules and working backward,

### Figure 9.4: PERT Chart—Estimating Next Year's Revenue

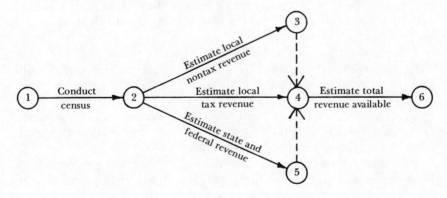

we see that total revenue cannot be estimated until estimates of local tax and nontax revenue and/or state and federal revenue have been completed. But these estimates cannot be made until a census of the district has been conducted. (The census would be necessary in order to calculate such things as probable enrollment next year, probable total property valuation, probable number of children who would qualify as recipients under Title I of the Elementary and Secondary Educational Act, etc.)

Figure 9.4 is also useful because it introduced the concept of the *dummy activity,* which is indicated by a broken arrow. Activities 3–4 and 5–6 are called dummy activities because they take no time or resources to accomplish. Dummy activities are used to indicate simultaneous activities, all of which need to be completed before other activities can begin. In the example, the three simultaneous, or parallel, activities are 2–3, 2–4, and 2–5. The activity of estimating total revenue cannot start until these three activities have been completed. In a word, dummy activities are used to feed parallel activities into a single event (in this case, event 4).

With these few rules in mind, it is possible to assemble the list of seventy-five budgeting activities (table 9.2) into a PERT chart (figure 9.5). Any activity in table 9.2 can be located on this chart by finding its unique pair of starting and ending events, which are listed next to each activity in the table. The first activity, for example, is "evaluate last year's program." It is bounded on this chart by events 1 and 3.

Keep in mind that both the activities and the resulting chart serve only as examples. Local conditions, traditions, and laws will likely dictate major modifications. The network of activities in figure 9.5 is really a beginning, not a final product. The logic of the network is not necessarily fixed even though at this time it might be logical. Unforeseen activities may need to be included in the network, and others may need to be reordered or deleted. In this, as in all planning activities, the amount and timing of updating should depend in part on benefits anticipated from it.

An examination of the budgeting activities (table 9.2) and how they are organized (figure 9.5) makes it apparent that objects and functions are the focus of the budgeting process. That is, the categories of things budgeted include expenses of certificated personnel (e.g., teachers), classified personnel (e.g., custodians), equipment, fuel, maintenance, secretarial staff, etc., which are objects of expenditure or functional groups of expenditures.

Budgeting strategies other than the object/function approach have been proposed for educational organizations. For example, in

# Figure 9.5: PERT Chart—District Budgeting Process (with time estimates)

Key

2.4  duration of that activity (in weeks)

(34.8)  cumulative duration of that activity, including all activities preceding it on that path (in weeks)

—— critical path

– – – dummy activity

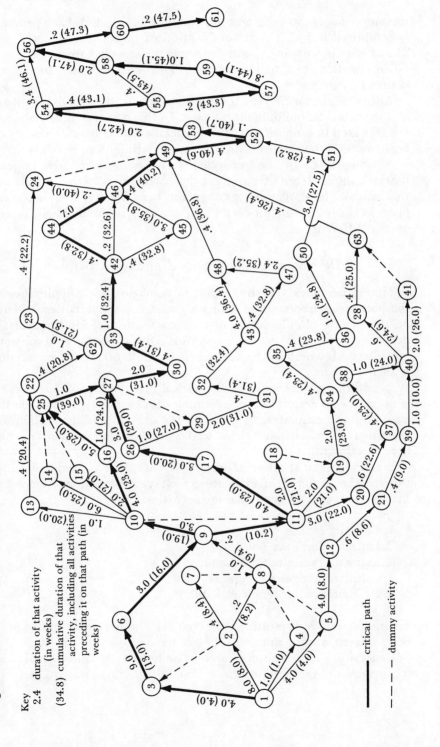

*program budgeting,* programs are the things budgeted. Each program is comprised of a different combination of objects (certificated personnel, equipment, etc.), and programs are usually targeted at a specified clientele (e.g., tenth-grade U.S. History is designed for all students in tenth grade).

Another, not entirely distinct, budgeting strategy focuses primary attention on the building unit, or *site*. In this case, pools of resources are allocated to building sites (using specified formulas). Decisions on how to spend the resources are then made within each building.

Although each of the budgeting strategies discussed here appears dramatically different from the other two, the relevant issue is not the name of the budgeting strategy but, behaviorally, what is to take place in the budgeting process. PERT charting helps shed light on the precise differences.

## Developing a Time Estimate for Each Activity

Timing becomes very important in managing the complexities of the budgeting process. The ability to start certain activities depends on the successful completion of earlier activities. In addition, certain deadlines have to be met (e.g., specified dates for budget submission) regardless of whether the necessary groundwork has been accomplished.

In addition to determining the logical relationship of activities, it is necessary to determine time estimates for each activity and, on the basis of these estimates, to calculate the duration of the entire project and the critical path(s), as well as the amount of slack in each noncritical path.

Perhaps the most efficient way to discuss these concepts is to return to the example of estimating next year's revenue. Remember that the process consisted of these activities:

1. Conduct census.
2. Estimate local tax revenue.
3. Estimate local nontax revenue.
4. Estimate state and federal revenue.
5. Estimate total revenue available.

Figure 9.4 was the resulting PERT chart. The next task in this project is to estimate the duration of each activity.

Generally, the person in charge of an activity is able to make the most realistic estimate of how long it will take to complete it.

Assume that an administrative assistant is in charge of 1—2 and the business administrator is in charge of 2—3, 2—4, 2—5, and 4—6. (Recall that it is not necessary to consider 3—4 and 5—4 because, by definition, dummy activities take no time.) These two people would be responsible for developing an initial estimate of the duration of each of the activities for which they are responsible. (The usual procedure when using PERT in cases where the activity duration is uncertain is to secure three different time estimates and, from these, to determine statistically a probable time for the activity. This procedure is discussed in more detail in the appendix to this chapter. Because of the relatively stable nature of the structure of the budgeting process, resorting to probability estimates will not likely yield significant improvement in the management of the budgeting process.)

In this example, a week has been judged the most useful *unit of time* for budget process analysis. One week is defined as five working days. Thus, .2 represents two-tenths of a workweek, or one workday; .1 represents one-half workday; and 3.0 represents three workweeks. Assume that the time estimates that the administrative assistant and the business administrator arrived at for each of the activities in the chart are those listed in table 9.6.

### Table 9.6: Time Estimates of the Revenue-Estimating Project

| Activity | Duration (in weeks) |
|---|---|
| ①—② | 3.2 |
| ②—③ | .8 |
| ②—④ | 1.8 |
| ②—⑤ | 2.6 |
| ②—⑥ | .6 |

It is now possible to predict how long the whole project will take (assuming that the estimates are reasonably accurate). Total project duration is estimated by first calculating the time it takes to complete *each* path in the network. A path is a sequence of activities defined (explicitly or implicitly) by beginning and ending events. The path that takes the most time (has the longest duration) is the *critical path,* and the duration of the critical path is the duration of the whole project. In the case of the revenue-estimating project, there are three distinct paths, each with a different duration (exhibit 9.7). The time estimates for the activities along each path are summed in order to determine the duration of the critical path and therefore the entire project. In this case, the critical path is estimated to take 6.4 weeks. Additionally, it can be inferred that if any activity on the

## Exhibit 9.7: Calculating the Duration of the Revenue-Estimating Project

The possible paths of the project are:

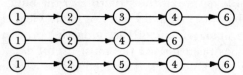

The duration of each path is calculated as follows:

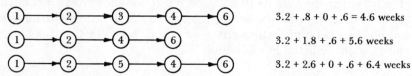

3.2 + .8 + 0 + .6 = 4.6 weeks

3.2 + 1.8 + .6 + 5.6 weeks

3.2 + 2.6 + 0 + .6 + 6.4 weeks

Therefore, the path with the longest duration is:

critical path is not completed on time, the whole project will not be completed on time. On the other hand, if activities not on the critical path are late, it will not necessarily delay the whole project. For example, if activity 2—4 were a half-week (.5) late, it would consume 2.2 weeks instead of 1.8 weeks. As a result, the path of 1—2—4 would be 3.2 weeks plus 2.2 weeks (5.4 weeks) instead of 3.2 weeks plus 1.8 weeks (5.0) weeks. Would this cause the whole project to be late by half a week? No. In fact, if activity 2—4 started on time, it could be as much as .8 week late and not affect the completion date of the project. See figure 9.8. In this case activity 2—4 has .8 week of *slack,* the time that it can be late without affecting the duration of the entire project. Since activity 4—6 cannot begin until all activities feeding into it have been completed, both 2—4 and 2—3 have some slack because the *cumulative duration* of each is less than that of activity 2—5.

The concepts of critical path and slack time can be very useful when managing the diverse efforts of different people in the budget-

## Figure 9.8: Cumulative Duration and Slack of Activities in Revenue-Estimating Project

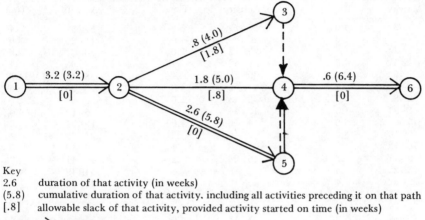

Key
2.6 duration of that activity (in weeks)
(5.8) cumulative duration of that activity. including all activities preceding it on that path
[.8] allowable slack of that activity, provided activity started on time (in weeks)
⟹ critical path

– – – – – dummy activity

ing process. They can aid in pinpointing which are the most important deadlines to monitor as well as in assessing the probable impact of not meeting particular deadlines. In addition, these concepts are useful when revising estimates of time and resources necessary for completing the task, and even in modifying the logic (structure) of the network itself.

As unforeseen circumstances arise during the course of the project, it may be necessary to accommodate them by updating and consequently modifying the chart. In general, the PERT chart is updated whenever it appears that doing so will clarify the status and future of the project. Duration estimates of the activities in the PERT chart of the district budgeting process are listed in table 9.9 and are shown on the chart (figure 9.5).

Simply because estimates were made about the duration of each of the activities, there is little way of actually knowing beforehand which activities will take more time and which will take less. For this reason it is useful to know which activities are on the critical path (i.e., have no slack time) and how much slack is available for each of the other activities. If an activity on the critical path takes more time than estimated, the whole project will be late (if nothing else has changed to counteract this). An activity not on the critical path can

## Table 9.9: Duration of Activities in the Budgeting Process
(in tenths of a week)

| Activity | Time | Activity | Time | Activity | Time |
|----------|------|----------|------|----------|------|
| 1−3 | 4.0 | 26−27 | 3.0 | 51−52 | .4 |
| 1−2 | 8.0 | 26−29 | 1.0 | 11−20 | 3.0 |
| 1−4 | 1.0 | 29−31 | 2.0 | 20−37 | .6 |
| 1−5 | 4.0 | 31−32 | .4 | 37−38 | .4 |
| 3−6 | 9.0 | 30−33 | .4 | 38−40 | 1.0 |
| 2−7 | .4 | 33−42 | 1.0 | 40−28 | .6 |
| 2−8 | .2 | 32−43 | 1.0 | 28−63 | 2.0 |
| 8−9 | 1.0 | 42−44 | .4 | 5−12 | 4.0 |
| 6−9 | 3.0 | 44−46 | 7.0 | 12−21 | .6 |
| 9−10 | 3.0 | 42−46 | .2 | 21−39 | .4 |
| 10−13 | 1.0 | 46−49 | .4 | 39−40 | 1.0 |
| 9−11 | .2 | 46−24 | .2 | 40−41 | 2.0 |
| 13−22 | .4 | 42−45 | .4 | 54−49 | .4 |
| 22−62 | .4 | 45−46 | 3.0 | 49−52 | .4 |
| 62−23 | 1.0 | 43−47 | .4 | 52−53 | .1 |
| 23−24 | .4 | 47−48 | 2.4 | 53−54 | .4 |
| 10−14 | 6.0 | 43−48 | 4.0 | 54−55 | .4 |
| 10−15 | 2.0 | 48−49 | .4 | 54−56 | 3.4 |
| 10−16 | 4.0 | 11−18 | 2.0 | 55−57 | .2 |
| 16−25 | 5.0 | 11−19 | 2.0 | 57−59 | .8 |
| 25−27 | 1.0 | 19−34 | 2.0 | 59−58 | 1.0 |
| 16−27 | 1.0 | 34−35 | .4 | 55−58 | .4 |
| 27−30 | 2.0 | 35−36 | .4 | 58−56 | 2.0 |
| 11−17 | 4.0 | 36−50 | 1.0 | 56−60 | .2 |
| 17−26 | 3.0 | 50−51 | 3.0 | 60−61 | .2 |

overrun its time estimate by as much as its amount of slack without making the whole project late (if nothing else has changed).

In calculating the duration of each of the paths in a network, we generally work "forward," that is, from the beginning to the end of the project. In calculating the critical path(s) of the project and slack in the project, it is easier to work "backward," from the end of the project to its beginning. The path durations can be used to advantage here. Referring to figure 9.5, we work backward from event 61, to event 60, to event 56. So far we are on the critical path because there are no parallel paths. Now the path splits in two, 58−56 and 54−56. The path with the longer duration, 58−56 (47.1 weeks is greater than 46.1 weeks), is the critical path. And the amount of slack inherent in the other activity is the difference of the two durations (47.1 minus 46.1 equals 1.0 week of slack for activity 54−56).

We then proceed backward along the critical path, repeating the same comparisons. As we progress backward in this particular case, notice that the critical path splits into two critical paths at event 27 and flows back together at event 9. (There can be numerous critical paths, since the term is merely a designation of those activities that have zero slack.) We work our way back to the beginning of the project, and (in this particular case) we neglect activities that are not part of the critical path. We can then go back to those paths we neglected and repeat the same process. All we have to remember is that *slack* is the amount of time it would take to place a given activity on a critical path.

## Scheduling Activities on a Calendar

Once the cumulative duration and the slack of each activity are known, we are in a position to calculate at least two important *calendar dates* for each activity: when an activity is scheduled to start and the latest date an activity can start without making the whole project late.

Actually, we need two additional pieces of information: an overall starting date and a schedule of holidays. We need the starting date to provide the fixed, or 0.0, point from which to count. We need a schedule of nonworking days because our estimates are based on working days. In scheduling dates we skip those Monday-through-Friday dates that are not working days.

For the sake of our example we have fixed the starting date as Monday, April 4. In addition, we have excluded certain dates from consideration because they are nonworking dates. (See table 9.10.)

## Analyzing the Structure, Sequence, and Timing of Activities

PERT charting is just like any other tool: the quality of the product is a function more of the hands in which the tool is placed than of the tool itself. Whether PERT charting clarifies and aids in the budgeting process or further confuses it will depend in large part on how well those responsible for budgeting understand the process themselves and on the degree to which they desire to involve others in the process.

Even after the activities, the network, and the related times have been established, reasoned judgment continues to play a large role. The project at this point needs to be critically analyzed and reviewed. If the school business official in charge of the budgeting process constructs a PERT network, he would do well to write an accompanying review and analysis when the plan is submitted to the superintendent and/or school board for approval. This budgeting

## Table 9.10: Schedule of Activities

| Activity | | Duration activity | Expected duration before activity starts | Starting | | Slack | Latest allowable duration before activity starts | Latest allowable starting | |
|---|---|---|---|---|---|---|---|---|---|
| Start event | End event | | | Day | Date | | | Day | Date |
| 1 | 3 | 4.0 | 0.0 | Mon. | 4/3 | 0.0 | 0.0 | Mon. | 4/3 |
| 1 | 2 | 8.0 | 0.0 | Mon. | 4/3 | 6.6 | 6.6 | Wed. | 5/10 |
| 1 | 4 | 1.0 | 0.0 | Mon. | 4/3 | 7.4 | 7.4 | Tues. | 5/16 |
| 3 | 5 | 4.0 | 0.0 | Mon. | 4/3 | 27.8 | 27.8 | Thurs. | 10/12 |
| 3 | 6 | 9.0 | 4.0 | Mon. | 5/1 | 0.0 | 4.0 | Mon. | 5/1 |
| 2 | 7 | .4 | 8.0 | Mon. | 5/29 | 6.6 | 14.6 | Wed. | 7/12 |
| 2 | 8 | .2 | 8.0 | Mon. | 5/29 | 6.6 | 14.6 | Wed. | 7/12 |
| 8 | 9 | 1.0 | 8.4 | Tues. | 5/30 | 6.6 | 15.0 | Mon. | 7/17 |
| 6 | 9 | 3.0 | 13.0 | Mon. | 7/3 | 0.0 | 13.0 | Mon. | 7/3 |
| 9 | 10 | 3.0 | 16.0 | Mon. | 7/24 | 0.0 | 16.0 | Mon. | 7/24 |
| 10 | 13 | 1.0 | 19.0 | Mon. | 8/14 | 20.2 | 39.2 | Mon. | 1/15 |
| 9 | 11 | .4 | 16.0 | Mon. | 7/24 | 0.0 | 16.0 | Mon. | 7/24 |
| 13 | 22 | .4 | 20.0 | Mon. | 8/21 | 19.8 | 39.8 | Thurs. | 1/18 |
| 22 | 62 | 1.0 | 20.4 | Tues. | 8/22 | 19.4 | 39.8 | Thurs. | 1/18 |
| 62 | 23 | 1.0 | 20.8 | Thurs. | 8/24 | 18.4 | 39.2 | Mon. | 1/16 |
| 23 | 24 | .4 | 21.8 | Thurs. | 9/27 | 18.0 | 39.8 | Thurs. | 1/18 |
| 10 | 14 | 6.0 | 19.0 | Mon. | 8/14 | 3.0 | 22.0 | Mon. | 9/4 |
| 10 | 15 | 2.0 | 19.0 | Mon. | 8/14 | 7.0 | 26.0 | Mon. | 10/2 |
| 10 | 16 | 4.0 | 19.0 | Mon. | 8/14 | 0.0 | 19.0 | Mon. | 8/14 |
| 16 | 25 | 5.0 | 23.0 | Mon. | 9/11 | 0.0 | 23.0 | Mon. | 9/11 |
| 25 | 27 | 1.0 | 28.0 | Mon. | 10/16 | 0.0 | 28.0 | Mon. | 10/16 |
| 16 | 27 | 1.0 | 23.0 | Mon. | 9/11 | 5.0 | 28.0 | Mon. | 10/16 |
| 27 | 30 | 2.0 | 29.0 | Mon. | 10/23 | 0.0 | 29.0 | Mon. | 10/23 |
| 11 | 17 | 4.0 | 19.0 | Mon. | 8/14 | 0.0 | 19.0 | Mon. | 8/14 |
| 17 | 26 | 3.0 | 23.0 | Mon. | 9/11 | 0.0 | 23.0 | Mon. | 9/11 |
| 26 | 27 | 3.0 | 26.0 | Mon. | 10/2 | 0.0 | 26.0 | Mon. | 10/2 |
| 26 | 29 | 1.0 | 26.0 | Mon. | 10/2 | 3.4 | 29.4 | Tues. | 10/24 |
| 29 | 31 | 2.0 | 29.0 | Mon. | 10/23 | 3.4 | 32.4 | Tues. | 11/14 |
| 31 | 32 | .4 | 31.0 | Mon. | 11/6 | 3.4 | 34.6 | Wed. | 12/6 |
| 30 | 33 | .4 | 31.0 | Mon. | 11/6 | 0.0 | 31.0 | Mon. | 11/6 |

| | | | | | | | | | |
|---|---|---|---|---|---|---|---|---|---|
| 33 | 42 | 1.0 | 31.4 | Tues. | 11/7 | 0.0 | 31.4 | Tues. | 11/7 |
| 32 | 43 | 1.0 | 31.4 | Tues. | 11/7 | 3.4 | 34.8 | Thurs. | 12/7 |
| 42 | 44 | .4 | 32.4 | Tues. | 11/7 | 0.0 | 32.4 | Tues. | 11/14 |
| 44 | 46 | 7.0 | 32.8 | Thurs. | 11/16 | 0.0 | 32.8 | Thurs. | 11/16 |
| 42 | 46 | .2 | 32.4 | Tues. | 11/14 | 7.2 | 39.6 | Wed. | 1/17 |
| 46 | 49 | .4 | 39.8 | Thurs. | 1/18 | 0.0 | 39.8 | Thurs. | 1/18 |
| 46 | 24 | .2 | 39.8 | Thurs. | 11/14 | 0.2 | 40.0 | Mon. | 1/22 |
| 42 | 45 | .4 | 32.4 | Tues. | 11/16 | 4.0 | 36.4 | Tues. | 12/19 |
| 45 | 46 | 3.0 | 32.8 | Thurs. | 11/14 | 4.0 | 36.8 | Thurs. | 12/21 |
| 43 | 47 | .4 | 32.4 | Tues. | 11/16 | 3.8 | 36.2 | Mon. | 12/18 |
| 47 | 48 | 2.4 | 32.8 | Thurs. | 11/14 | 3.8 | 36.6 | Wed. | 12/20 |
| 43 | 48 | 4.0 | 32.4 | Tues. | 12/19 | 3.4 | 35.8 | Thurs. | 12/14 |
| 48 | 49 | .4 | 36.4 | Tues. | 8/14 | 3.4 | 39.8 | Thurs. | 1/18 |
| 11 | 18 | 2.0 | 19.0 | Mon. | 8/14 | 12.4 | 31.4 | Tues. | 11/7 |
| 11 | 19 | 2.0 | 19.0 | Mon. | 8/28 | 12.4 | 31.4 | Tues. | 11/7 |
| 19 | 34 | 2.0 | 21.0 | Mon. | 9/11 | 12.4 | 33.4 | Tues. | 11/21 |
| 34 | 35 | .4 | 23.0 | Tues. | 9/12 | 12.4 | 35.4 | Tues. | 12/12 |
| 35 | 36 | .4 | 23.4 | Fri. | 9/15 | 12.4 | 35.8 | Thurs. | 12/21 |
| 36 | 50 | 1.0 | 23.8 | Fri. | 9/22 | 12.4 | 36.2 | Tues. | 12/18 |
| 50 | 51 | 3.0 | 24.8 | Fri. | 10/13 | 12.4 | 37.2 | Mon. | 1/8 |
| 51 | 52 | .4 | 27.8 | Mon. | 8/14 | 12.4 | 40.2 | Mon. | 1/22 |
| 52 | 20 | 3.0 | 19.0 | Mon. | 9/4 | 13.8 | 32.8 | Thurs. | 11/16 |
| 20 | 37 | .6 | 22.0 | Wed. | 9/6 | 13.8 | 35.8 | Thurs. | 12/14 |
| 37 | 38 | .4 | 22.6 | Mon. | 9/11 | 13.8 | 36.4 | Tues. | 12/19 |
| 38 | 40 | 1.0 | 23.0 | Mon. | 9/18 | 13.8 | 36.8 | Thurs. | 12/21 |
| 40 | 28 | .6 | 24.0 | Wed. | 9/20 | 14.8 | 38.8 | Thurs. | 1/11 |
| 28 | 63 | 2.0 | 24.6 | Mon. | 5/1 | 14.8 | 39.4 | Tues. | 1/16 |
| 5 | 12 | 4.0 | 4.0 | Mon. | 5/29 | 27.8 | 31.8 | Thurs. | 11/9 |
| 12 | 21 | .6 | 8.0 | Wed. | 5/31 | 27.8 | 35.8 | Thurs. | 12/14 |
| 21 | 39 | .4 | 8.6 | Mon. | 6/5 | 27.8 | 36.4 | Tues. | 12/19 |
| 39 | 40 | 1.0 | 9.0 | Mon. | 9/18 | 27.8 | 36.8 | Thurs. | 12/21 |
| 40 | 41 | 2.0 | 24.0 | Mon. | 10/2 | 13.8 | 37.8 | Thurs. | 1/4 |
| 41 | 59 | .4 | 26.0 | Mon. | 1/22 | 13.8 | 39.8 | Thurs. | 1/18 |
| 54 | 52 | .4 | 40.2 | Wed. | 1/24 | 0.0 | 40.2 | Mon. | 1/22 |
| 49 | 53 | .1 | 40.6 | Thurs. | 1/25 | 0.0 | 40.6 | Wed. | 1/24 |
| 52 | 54 | .4 | 40.7 | | | 0.0 | 40.7 | Thurs. | 1/25 |

**Table 9.10** (continued)

| Activity | | Duration activity | Expected duration before activity starts | Starting | | Slack | Latest allowable duration before activity starts | Latest allowable starting | |
| --- | --- | --- | --- | --- | --- | --- | --- | --- | --- |
| Start event | End event | | | Day | Date | | | Day | Date |
| 54 | 55 | .4 | 42.7 | Thurs. | 2/8 | 0.0 | 42.7 | Thurs. | 2/8 |
| 54 | 56 | 3.4 | 42.7 | Thurs. | 2/8 | 1.0 | 43.7 | Thurs. | 2/15 |
| 55 | 57 | .2 | 43.1 | Mon. | 2/12 | 0.0 | 43.1 | Mon. | 2/12 |
| 57 | 59 | .8 | 43.3 | Tues. | 2/13 | 0.0 | 43.3 | Tues. | 2/13 |
| 59 | 58 | 1.0 | 44.1 | Mon. | 2/19 | 0.0 | 44.1 | Mon. | 2/19 |
| 55 | 58 | .4 | 43.1 | Mon. | 2/12 | 1.6 | 44.7 | Thurs. | 2/22 |
| 58 | 56 | 2.0 | 43.5 | Wed. | 2/14 | 0.0 | 43.5 | Wed. | 2/14 |
| 56 | 60 | .2 | 47.1 | Mon. | 1/12 | 0.0 | 47.1 | Mon. | 1/12 |
| 60 | 61 | .2 | 47.3 | Tues. | 1/13 | 0.0 | 47.3 | Tues. | 1/13 |

example is used again in the next chapter, and such an analysis is included there.

## Questions for Review and Discussion

1.  In what general ways would the budgeting process of a private educational organization differ from that of a public one?
2.  Can the network of activities actually be developed without considering, at the same time, the time required for each activity?
3.  Under what conditions might it be desirable to alter the network of activities halfway through the completion of the project?
4.  If the budgeting project described in this chapter were not finished on time, what would the apparent consequences be? What would be the probable consequences of not finishing a building project on time? A curriculum project? Compare the consequences.
5.  How would a PERT chart be constructed if it were to be used to *evaluate* a budgeting process that had been operating in the same manner year after year?

## Appendix A: Estimating Durations of Project Activities

In this chapter we used a single "best" estimate of the duration of each activity. It is often useful (but more complicated) to develop several different estimates for the duration of an activity. An *optimistic* time estimate, for example, would be the time required to complete the activity under ideal conditions, where no unforeseen problems arise. Ideal conditions are assumed to occur only once in a hundred times. The *most likely* time estimate is that which allows for an average number of good and bad breaks. The *pessimistic* time is the time required for the activity under the most adverse conditions imagined; the chances of it occurring are arbitrarily assumed to be one in one hundred.

A weighted average of these three types of estimates is the *expected* time that the activity will take. The expected time estimate has a 50-50 chance of being achieved. The two extremes, $To$ and $Tp$, are given an equal weight, and $Tm$ is given a weight of 4, since it is the most likely time to occur. The expected time can be formally represented by the following relationship:

$$Te = \frac{To + 4Tm + Tp}{6}.$$

## Figure 9A.1: Three Time Estimates for Each Activity (in weeks)

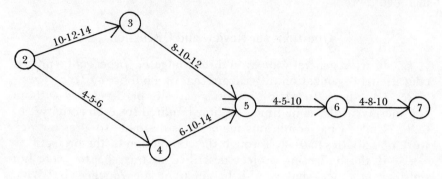

## Table 9A.2: Calculations of *Te* for Figure 9A.1

| Activity | *To* | *Tm* | *Tp* | *4Tm* | *To + 4Tm + Tp* | *Te = To + 4Tm + Tp/6* |
|----------|------|------|------|-------|-----------------|------------------------|
| 2–3 | 10 | 12 | 14 | 48 | 72 | 12 |
| 2–4 | 4 | 5 | 6 | 20 | 30 | 5 |
| 3–5 | 8 | 10 | 12 | 40 | 60 | 10 |
| 4–5 | 6 | 10 | 14 | 40 | 60 | 10 |
| 5–6 | 4 | 5 | 10 | 20 | 34 | 5.7 (approx.) |
| 6–7 | 4 | 8 | 10 | 32 | 46 | 7.7 (approx.) |

## Figure 9A.3: Showing Expected Times for Each Activity

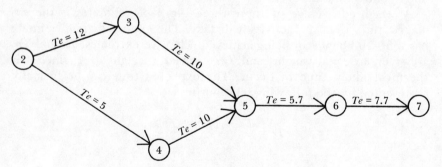

See figure 9A.1 for a small PERT chart using three time estimates. In table 9A.2, *Te* is calculated for each activity in the project. The results are portrayed in figure 9A.3.

Expected times may be treated like single estimates for purposes of calculating total project duration, the critical path, slack, etc. However, when using this probabilistic concept, it becomes equally important to also develop measures of the amount of deviation from the expected values. Consider, for example, activities 3–5 and 4–5 in figure 9A.1. Both have the same estimate of most likely time (10) and the same estimate of expected time (also 10). However, *To* and *Tp* are 8 and 12 for activity 3–5, and 6 and 14 for activity 4–5. The "spread" of activity 4–5 is larger. This means that the *actual* completion time of activity 4–5 could be "off" (different from the expected time) more than the actual completion time of activity 3–5. Essentially, there is more uncertainty associated with the expected duration of activity 4–5. Even though the expected times are the same for the two activities, the spread of possible times for each is different. The same concept applies to groups of activities as well as entire projects.

This spread can be measured in terms of standard deviation (s.d.), which is a statistical statement of variability. As calculated below, it is an amount of positive or negative deviation from the expected time. This deviation spans about 68 percent of the possible actual times. The standard deviation of an activity is calculated as follows:

$$\frac{Tp - To}{6}.$$

The standard deviations of the activities in the example are calculated in table 9A.4. The standard deviation of activity 3–5 is only

**Table 9A.4: Computations of Standard Deviation of Activities**

| Activity | $Tp$ | $To$ | $Tp - To$ | s.d. of activity $(Tp - To)/6$ |
|---|---|---|---|---|
| 2–3 | 10 | 14 | 4 | .66 |
| 2–4 | 4 | 6 | 2 | .33 |
| 3–5 | 8 | 12 | 4 | .66 |
| 4–5 | 6 | 14 | 8 | 1.33 |
| 5–6 | 4 | 10 | 4 | .66 |
| 6–7 | 4 | 10 | 4 | .66 |

half that of activity 4—5 (.66 vs. 1.33). This means that 68 percent of the time activity 3—5 will take between 9.34 weeks (10 — .66) and 10.66 weeks (10 + .66), while activity 4—5 will take between 8.67 weeks (10 — 1.33) and 11.67 weeks (10 + 1.33) 68 percent of the time.

The standard deviation of a network of a series of events can be calculated, with the s.d. of an event being the square root of the sum of the square of the standard deviations of the activities leading up to the event. For example, the standard deviation for event 5 in path 2—3—5 is calculated as follows:

$$
\begin{aligned}
\text{s.d.} &= \sqrt{(\text{s.d. of activity } 2{-}3)^2 + (\text{s.d. of activity } 3{-}5)^2} \\
&= \sqrt{(0.66)^2 + (0.66)^2} \\
&= 0.933 \text{ or about 1 week.}
\end{aligned}
$$

This means that event 5 is *expected* to occur at the end of 22 weeks. Further, there is about 68 percent probability that the event will occur within a week of when it is expected. (An extended version of this discussion is found in Handy and Hussain 1969, pp. 45-60.)

## References

Brown, Henry A. *A Time Network Analysis of Procedures Used in Selected Districts to Develop the School Budget.* Ed.D. dissertation, Teachers College, Columbia University, 1970.

Cook, Desmond L. *Program Evaluation and Review Technique.* Washington, D.C.: U.S. Office of Education, 1966.

Curtis, William H. *Educational Resources Management System.* Chicago: Research Corporation of the Association of School Business Officials, 1971.

Foley, W. J., and Han, G. G. *Planning an Educational Budget by Program through Financial Resource Allocation.* Iowa City, Iowa: Management Information System, Iowa Educational Information Center, University of Iowa, 1971.

Haggart, Sue, ed. *Program Budgeting for School District Planning.* Englewood Cliffs, N.J.: Educational Technology Publications, 1972.

Handy, H., and Hussain, R. M. *Network Analysis for Educational Management.* Englewood Cliffs, N.J.: Prentice-Hall, 1969.

Hartley, Harry J. *Educational Planning Programming Budgeting.* Englewood Cliffs, N.J.: Prentice-Hall, 1968.

Wildavsky, Aaron B. "Budget as a Political Process." *International Encyclopedia of the Social Sciences,* vol. 2. New York: Crowell Collier Educational Corporation, 1968.

## Related Readings

Abt, Clark C. "An Education System Planning Game." ERIC, no. ED025843, 1965. Discusses objectives and procedures for playing a game designed to aid learning about the intricacies of school planning.

Cook, Desmond. "An Overview of Management Science in Educational Research." ERIC, no. ED025002, 1968. Defines management science and discusses four trends in the field of educational research: (1) use of scientific problem-solving methods, (2) use of MIS, (3) emphasis on long-range planning, and (4) use of systems concepts.

Katzenbach, Edward L. "Planning, Programming and Budgeting Systems: PPBS and Education." Cambridge, Mass.: New England School Development Council. ERIC, no. ED025856, 1969. Evaluates both PPBS and program budgeting, highlighting pros and cons as they apply to education.

Piele, Phillip. "Planning Systems in Education." ERIC, no. ED025855, 1969. A literature review that examines sixteen selected documents processed by ERIC that deal with the application of several kinds of planning systems to educational programs. Particular attention is given to PPBS, PERT, and other types of planning models.

Schoderbek, Peter P., and Digman, Lester A. "Third Generation, PERT/LOB." *Harvard Business Review* 45, (September-October 1967), pp. 100-10. This article describes a new technique (PERT/LOB) which combines the potential of the program evaluation and review technique (PERT) with line of balance (LOB). Between the two techniques, the three stages of management (development, transition, and production) are controlled.

# 10
# Organizing Personnel for Budgeting

The previous chapter focused largely on the relationships among activities; in this chapter, we will deal with the relationships between people and activities. Most formal attempts to do this in organizations result in what we commonly call job descriptions and/or organization charts. The uses of these devices are discussed here, as well as their limits. However, many management operations, including budgeting, cut across traditional lines of authority and require different methods of relating people and activities. Linear responsibility charting is used in this chapter to show how a variety of people from different parts of an organization are coordinated for the budgeting process. The chapter concludes with a brief evaluation of the budgeting example that has been used in this and the preceding chapter, pointing out how the organization of the budgeting processes affects the way resources are allocated, and how PERT and linear responsibility charting can be used to clarify the process.

## Traditional Methods of Relating People to Tasks

Role descriptions attempt to convey (1) what an individual in that role is to do and (2) how the individual in that role is to relate to other individuals in other roles. Job descriptions emphasize the former, while organizational charts emphasize the latter.

### Job Descriptions

Generally, job descriptions are most useful in describing in some detail the nature of the tasks involved in an individual job and least useful in portraying relationships among jobs or tasks. The job description of the assistant superintendent for business affairs (A.S.B.A.), shown in exhibit 10.1, comprises fourteen task areas,

## Exhibit 10.1: Job Description: Assistant Superintendent for Business Affairs

I.   Budgeting and Financial Planning
Assists in coordinating the views of administrators, teachers and citizens in translating the educational needs and aspirations of the community into a composite financial plan. Understands the effect of the educational program on the financial structure of the community and exercises sound judgment in maintaining a proper balance between the two. Conducts long-term fiscal planning in terms of community resources and needs. Is sensitive to the changing community, particularly in regard to the economy, and is alert to all sources of new revenue and outside events which affect the community. Should be well versed on taxation at all levels. Recognizes that he is constantly dealing with scarce resources and endeavors to employ systems analysis and the concept of planning-programming-budgeting-evaluating systems to all aspects of financial planning in order to provide his district with the best educational experience for each dollar spent or resource used.

II.   Purchasing and Supply Management
Is responsible for all purchases, including equipment and supplies for new buildings as well as for existing buildings. Considers the educational implications associated with each purchasing decision, prepares suitable specifications and standards and utilizes good purchasing principles and procedures. Is also responsible for warehousing, storing, trucking and inventory control.

III.   Plant Planning and Construction
Works with administrators, teachers and lay personnel in determining and planning for school plant needs and in acquiring school sites and managing school property after the educational standards have been determined. Works with architects to see that needs are properly translated into final plans, with attorneys and financial advisors to effect suitable financing, with bidders to secure economical contracts and with contractors to provide satisfactory building facilities.

IV.   School-Community Relations
Helps interpret the educational program to the public by preparing materials for distribution, addressing and working with service clubs, the PTA and citizens' committees, and through contacts with press, radio and television services. Provides the superintendent and other staff members, as well as the board, with facts that help them in their relations with the public. Interprets the business area of educational programs to the public and to the educational staff.

V.   Personnel Management
Recruits or helps to secure personnel for all positions in the area of school business management. Handles individual and group problems related to working conditions, benefits, policy and procedure, and provides guidance and information in connection with severance from service for all personnel.

VI.   In-Service Training
Organizes and directs a program of in-service training aimed at increasing the skills of school business management personnel and at developing proper attitudes toward the educational objectives of the school district.

VII.   Operation and Maintenance of Plant
Has the responsibility for providing, operating and maintaining facilities which will assure maximum educational utility as well as a healthful, comfortable, safe environment for pupils, teachers and the public.

VIII.   Transportation
Supervises the operation and maintenance of the school bus fleet to insure safe, economical and comfortable transportation for children.

## Exhibit 10.1 *(continued)*

IX.   Food Services
      Has general responsibility for the operation of the school food services by providing
      economical and satisfactory facilities, and efficient management in the operation of
      the school lunch program, in close cooperation with those staff members charged with
      the educational aspects of such service.

X.    Accounting and Reporting
      Establishes and supervises the accounting system necessary to provide school officials
      and administrators with accurate financial facts as the basis for formulating policies
      and decisions. Provides the proper safeguards for the custody of public funds and
      makes possible complete and revealing reporting both locally and statewide.

XI.   Data Processing
      When desirable, introduces data processing to provide better and more complete
      accounting records. May establish or assist in establishing appropriate data banks, elec-
      tronic files, and data processing procedures to provide management information for
      appropriate decision making, forecasting and evaluation.

XII.  Grantsmanship
      Assists in obtaining special educational funds from private foundations, from state or
      provincial departments of education, from state or provincial legislatures and from fed-
      eral sources such as the U.S. Office of Education. Makes certain that proposals are
      administratively sound from the business point of view. Insures that records are main-
      tained and financial reports published.

XIII. Office Management
      Supervises clerical personnel in the business office(s) and, upon occasion, in other
      school offices. Reviews form design and updates form requirements as needed. Estab-
      lishes procedures for record keeping, maintaining all records that prudence and legal
      requirements demand.

XIV.  Educational Resources Management
      Recognizes that he is constantly dealing with scarce resources and endeavors to em-
      ploy systems analysis and the concept of planning-programming-budgeting-evaluating
      systems to all aspects of financial planning in order to provide his district with the best
      educational experience for each dollar spent or resource used. Consider the multi-year
      or long term impact of all aspects of the educational program.

Source: Frederick W. Hill, *The School Business Administrator* (Chicago: Research Corporation of the Association of School Business Officials, 1970), pp. 18-21. Reprinted by permission.

including school-community relations, in-service training, budgeting,
and accounting. The distinctions between the tasks are rather clearly
delineated, but the manner in which the school business administrator relates to other positions is not clear.

### Organization Charts

Organization charts are often seen as complementing job descriptions. They are more useful than job descriptions in describing how
the positions relate to each other and less useful in describing the

tasks of individual positions. In figure 10.2, for example, we see that the A.S.B.A. directly supervises the director of buildings and grounds, the business manager, the director of cafeteria, and the director of transportation, and is one of four individuals who are in a "line" position directly under the superintendent.

While the organization chart says nothing about the tasks involved in the job of the assistant superintendent for business, it does tell us with whom he or she must work in order to accomplish those tasks. However, the chart usually does not convey the complexity of these relationships because they are not described in terms of the tasks to be accomplished. Job descriptions of the individuals involved usually shed little additional light.

In the case of operation and maintenance, for example, the job description states that the A.S.B.A. has "responsibility for . . . operating and maintaining facilities." Yet in the organizational chart it appears that the A.S.B.A. does not have total authority for this. The building principals, who are the immediate supervisors of the building custodians, share this responsibility. The A.S.B.A., through the director of buildings and grounds and the systemwide maintenance men, has only a line of cooperation with the building custodians.

Although there is no direct linkage of any kind between the building principals and the A.S.B.A. on the organization chart or in the job description, it is highly probable that they work directly with each other on such tasks as developing priorities for building maintenance and operation. There are many other cases where job descriptions and organization charts do not convey an adequate description of tasks and relationships. In budgeting, financial planning, and school-community relations, for example, the A.S.B.A. comes in working contact with the board, the lay advisory committee, other assistant superintendents, the professional advisory committee, and his immediate superior and subordinates as well. The nature of these relationships varies with the individual or group and with the task in question. This fact is not acknowledged in the organization chart and can be stated only in the most general language in the job description.

## Linear Responsibility Charting

Linear responsibility charting, like job descriptions and organization charts, is a management device for formally documenting and communicating how people are organized to accomplish tasks. It attempts to combine specific task descriptions of individual positions

# Figure 10.2: Organization Chart of Medium-size School District

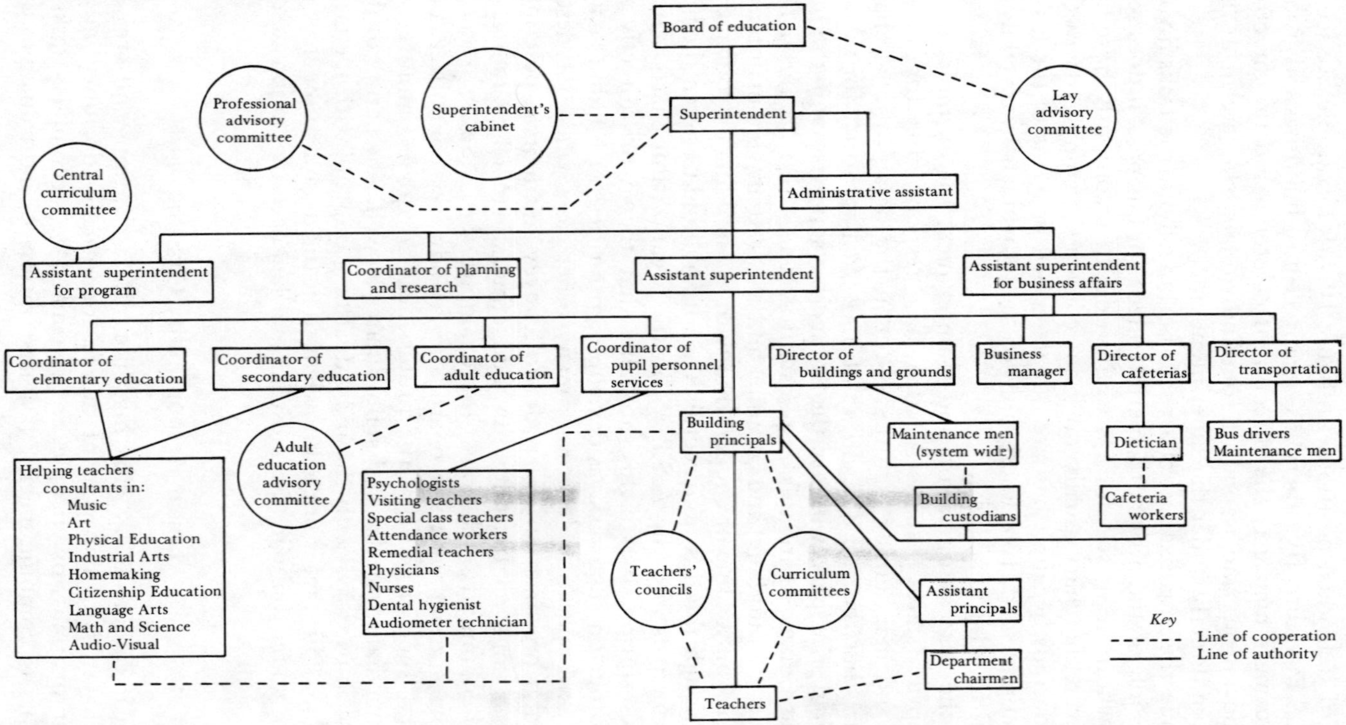

Source: D. E. Griffiths; D. L. Clark; D. R. Wynn; and L. Iannacone, *Organizing Schools for Effective Education* (Danville, Ill: The Interstate Printers and Publishers, 1964), p. 129. Reprinted by permission.

with explicit descriptions of the ways in which the individual positions relate to each other. What it is and how it works are best explained by using the budgeting example of the previous chapter.

In the budgeting process network, the person responsible for carrying out each activity was identified. For example, the school business official was identified as being responsible for the successful completion of activity 9—11, "distribute budget preparation information." And in activity 13—22, "revise school board central administration budget request," the school business official shared responsibility with the assistant superintendent of education.

A basic organizing question remains, however: when we specify who is responsible for the successful completion of an activity, have we adequately described their roles? For some people in some situations this may be adequate; but usually it will not be, and it is useful here to discuss why and what we can do that will be adequate.

Several interrelated inadequacies might be stated. First, the person *responsible* for completion of the activity is only one of a number of people who will be involved in the activity. There will be people who have *general supervision* over the project, those who *do the actual work*, those who *must be consulted*, those who *must be notified*, etc. In short, there are a number of ways that people in different positions relate to the accomplishment of an activity and, consequently, to each other. A person in a given position (e.g., the business manager) may be involved in *some* way in many activities but have actual responsibility for only a fraction of them. (This concept is markedly different from the assumption implicit in the traditional pyramid organization charts, which are merely a simple portrayal of overall functional authority models. As described earlier such organization charts are usually combined with detailed position descriptions and organizational manuals, which in turn are developed around organizational roles and not project themes such as the budgeting process.)

In short, it is useful to show the extent of the authority exercised by each person involved in an activity when two or more people have overlapping authority and responsibility. What is needed is a method for showing how people relate to other people as a function of the activities that they need to accomplish. One such device is a *linear responsibility chart* (LRC). There are only three ingredients in the linear responsibility chart: *activities, organizational titles,* (e.g., superintendent), and *transformation functions* (how people relate to the task; e.g., must be notified, has actual responsibility, provides general supervision). The general form of the linear responsibility chart is shown in table 10.3.

## Table 10.3: General Form of Linear Responsibility Chart

| Tasks or activities | Position titles | | | | | |
|---|---|---|---|---|---|---|
| | 1 | 2 | 3 | 4 | . . . . . . | n |
| 1 | 11 | 12 | 13 | 14 | | 1n |
| 2 | 21 | 22 | 23 | 24 | | 2n |
| 3 | 31 | 32 | 33 | 34 | | 3n |
| 4 | 41 | 42 | 43 | 44 | | 4n |
| n | n1 | n2 | n3 | n4 | | nn |

11, 12, 13, . . . . , nn = transformation functions

*Note:* Transformation function 23 describes the role played by the person occupying position 3 in accomplishing task 2.

The relationships among the three ingredients can best be described by referring to the revenue-estimating example discussed in the previous chapter and summarized in figure 9.4, which is repeated

## Figure 10.4: PERT Chart—Estimating Next Year's Revenue

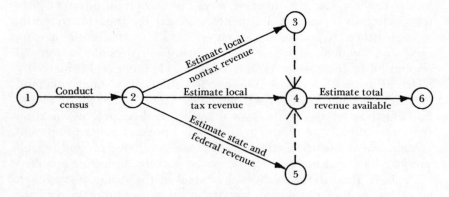

here (figure 10.4). In constructing a linear responsibility chart of this project, the first step is to determine the most useful transformation functions. For this example, assume that the following information is desired for each activity:

A. Who is responsible for the successful completion of the activity?
B. Who does the actual work (if different from A)?
C. Who must be consulted during the performance of the activity?

  D. Who must receive a report resulting from the completion of the activity?
  E. Who must be notified about the completion of the activity (other than D)?

These five questions translate into the following transformation functions:

  A. Actual responsibility
  B. Actual work
  C. Must be consulted
  D. Receive report
  E. Must be notified

The next step involves developing a list of activities in the project. Recall that the revenue-estimating activities were

  1. Conduct census.
  2. Estimate local tax revenue.
  3. Estimate local nontax revenue.
  4. Estimate state and federal revenue.
  5. Estimate total revenue available.

Next, list those people, bodies, or agencies who might be involved in the project. In the revenue-estimating project this could include the following:

  1. School board
  2. Superintendent
  3. Assistant superintendent of education
  4. School business official
  5. Administrative assistant education
  6. Administrative assistant business

Having created the parts of the linear responsibility chart, the final task is linking people to activities with transformation functions. The responsibility chart for estimating next year's revenue could appear much like table 10.5.

In this example, even though the school business official is ultimately responsible for all the activities, it is apparent that (1) many other organizational units are involved, in different ways, in the successful completion of the activities, and, consequently, (2) the school

Table 10.5: Linear Responsibility Chart—Estimating Next Year's Revenue

| | | | | Organizational units | | | | | |
|---|---|---|---|---|---|---|---|---|---|
| Activities | Board | Superin-tendent | Assistant superintendent of education | School business official | Administrative assistant/ education | Administrative assistant/ business | Building principals | Directors | Cafeteria manager |
| 1–2 Conduct census | E | D | | A | | B | | | |
| 2–4 Estimate local tax revenue | | | | A | | | | | |
| 2–3 Estimate local nontax revenue | | | C | A | | | C | C | C |
| 2–5 Estimate state and federal revenue | | | | A | | | | | |
| 4–6 Estimate total revenue | E | D | | A | | | | | |

A Has actual responsibility
B Does the work
C Must be consulted
D Must receive report
E Must be notified

business official relates differently to each of the organizational units *depending on the activity.*

Specifically, the school business official will need to file copies of the census and the total revenue estimate with the superintendent and notify the board of its completion. The business official must also consult people who are indirectly responsible for most income-producing activities in the school: in this case, the building principals, assistant superintendent, directors, and the cafeteria manager. Finally, we see that the administrative assistant for business will actually be doing the administrative work of conducting the census under the guidance of the business official.

## Using the Linear Responsibility Chart To Organize Personnel

Just as it was necessary to determine how much detail is desired in a PERT chart, it is necessary to determine how much detail is useful when developing linear responsibility charts. In the revenue-forecasting example cited in this chapter, the list of activities could have been expanded, as well as the number of organizational units involved and the kinds of transformation functions. What could be gained in increased insight and/or coordination of the project might be offset by undue complexity and the increased probability of misrepresentation. Again, the appropriate level of detail should be determined by its anticipated usefulness. In the linear responsibility chart of the budgeting process (table 10.6), a particular level of detail was chosen. Someone using that chart as a model would have to determine the possible benefits of more or less detail in his or her own situation.

Both PERT and LRC are useful partly because of the questions they raise as well as the answers they provide. Consider, in our example, the role of the citizens' budget advisory committee vis-à-vis the school board. By inspecting both the PERT design and the LRC of the budgeting process, it becomes readily apparent that the school board is active in the budget development process. Also, at first glance, the citizens' budget advisory committee seems relatively active. It reviews the budget elements before the tentative budget is assembled and presented to the public; in other districts, the budget is presented to the citizens' committee only after it has been prepared by the superintendent and staff. However, more information is necessary to ascertain whether or not this is a significant difference. After all, it really depends on what the committee review means and, indeed, if the committee does more than inspect and ask questions.

## Table 10.6: Linear Responsibility Chart of the Budget Development Process

| Activity | Description | School board | Superintendent | Assistant superintendent of education | Administrative assistant for buildings and grounds | Administrative assistant | School business official | Building principal | Coordinators | Directors | Cafeteria manager | Clerk | Citizens' budget advisory committee | Instructional staff | Secretarial staff | Custodial staff | Cafeteria staff | Voters | Private school administrator |
|---|---|---|---|---|---|---|---|---|---|---|---|---|---|---|---|---|---|---|---|
| | | | | | | | Organizational units | | | | | | | | | | | | |
| 1–3 | Evaluate last year's program | C | A | B | | | C | D | D | D | B | | D | | | | | | |
| 1–2 | Conduct (update) district census | | | | A | | A | B | B | B | B | | | | | | | | |
| 1–4 | Review debt service schedule | | | | | | A | | | | | | | | | | | | |
| 1–5 | Conduct individual school plant surveys | | | | C | D | | A | | | | | | | | | | | |
| 3–6 | Revise education and recreation programs | | | C | C | | | B | B | B | | | | | | | | | |
| 2–7 | Estimate anticipated state and federal revenue | | | B | | | A | B | B | B | | | | | | | | | |
| 2–8 | Estimate anticipated local nontax revenue | | | | | | A | B | B | B | | | | | | | | | |
| 8–9 | Estimate total revenue and expense for budget period | D | D | D | | | A | | | | | D | | | | | | | |
| 6–9 | Revise education and recreation programs | C | C | A | | | C | | | | | | | | | | | | |
| 9–10 | Determine educational objectives and policy | A | B | D | D | D | D | D | D | D | | D | D | D | | | | | |
| 10–13 | Prepare estimates of board and administration expense requests | | B | D | D | | D | | | | | | | | | | | | |
| 9–11 | Distribute budget preparation information | | D | | | | D | | | | | A | | | | | | | |
| 13–22 | Revise board and administration expense requests | | A | | | | A | | | | | | | | | | | | |
| 22–62 | Revise board and administration expense requests | | A | | | | | | | | | | D | | | | | | |
| 62–63 | Revise board and administration expense requests | D | D | | | | | | | | | | A | | | | | | |

| Range | Task | | | | | | | |
|---|---|---|---|---|---|---|---|---|
| 23–24 | Tentatively approve board and administration expense requests | A | | | | | | |
| 10–14 | Prepare building-level administration and instruction expense requests | | C | | A | B | | C |
| 10–15 | Prepare building-level conference expense requests | | C | A | C | A | | C |
| 10–16 | Prepare building-level personnel expense requests | | | D | | | | |
| 16–25 | Revise building-level certificated personnel requests | C | C | B | C | A | | B |
| 25–27 | Revise building-level budget requests for certificated personnel, supplies, and equipment | A | A | D | D | B | | |
| 16–27 | Revise building-level classified personnel requests | D | D | A | A | | | |
| 27–30 | Revise instruction expense requests | C | | A | C | | | |
| 11–17 | Prepare building-level requests for supplies, equipment, and maintenance | B | B | A | C | | | |
| 17–26 | Revise building-level requests for supplies, equipment, and maintenance | | | A | A | C | D | |
| 26–27 | Revise building-level requests for plant personnel | | | A | A | C | D | D |
| 26–29 | Prepare estimates for fuel, utilities, etc. | | | | A | D | | |
| 29–31 | Revise plant operation and maintenance requests | | D | | A | | | |
| 31–32 | Revise plant operation and maintenance requests | D | A | A | | | | B |
| 30–33 | Revise instruction expense requests | A | A | C | C | | | |
| 33–42 | Revise instruction expense requests | A | B | B | D | | | |
| 32–43 | Revise plant operation and maintenance requests | A | | | | | | |
| 42–44 | Prepare and exchange professional staff/school board proposals | A | | | | | | D |
| 44–46 | Conduct professional staff/school board negotiations | A | B | B | B | | | A |
| 42–46 | Review instruction expense requests | D | A | E | B | | A | A |
| 46–49 | Tentatively approve instruction expense requests | A | D | E | E | | | |

# Table 10.6 (continued)

| Activity | Description | School board | Superintendent | Assistant superintendent of education | Administrative assistant for buildings and grounds | Administrative assistant | School business official | Building principal | Coordinators | Directors | Cafeteria manager | Clerk | Citizens' budget advisory committee | Instructional staff | Secretarial staff | Custodial staff | Cafeteria staff | Voters | Private school administrator |
|---|---|---|---|---|---|---|---|---|---|---|---|---|---|---|---|---|---|---|---|
| 46–24 | Adjust administration personnel salary expense requests | | | C | | | A | | | | | C | | | | | | | |
| 42–45 | Develop and exchange secretarial staff/school board negotiation proposals | A | B | | | | B | | | | | | | | | | | | |
| 45–46 | Conduct secretarial staff/school board negotiation proposals | | A | | | | B | | | | | | | | A | | | | |
| 43–47 | Develop and exchange custodial staff/school board negotiation proposals | A | B | | | | B | | | | | | | | A | | | | |
| 47–48 | Conduct custodial/school board negotiations | | A | | | | B | | | | | | | | | | | | |
| 43–48 | Review plant operation and maintenance expense requests | D | | | | | | | | | | | | | | | | | |
| 48–49 | Tentatively approve plant operation and maintenance requests | A | E | | | | D | | | | | | A | | | | | | |
| 11–18 | Prepare regular transportation expense requests | | | | | | D | A | B | B | | | | | | | | | |
| 11–19 | Prepare special transportation expense requests | | | | | | D | A | B | A | | | | | | | | | |
| 19–34 | Revise transportation expense requests | | | | | | D | A | | A | | | | | | | | | |
| 34–35 | Prepare requests for oil, gas, insurance, and maintenance of vehicles | D | | | | | A | | | | | | | | | | | | C |
| 35–36 | Revise all transportation expense requests | D | A | | | | A | | | | | | | | | | | | C |

Organizational units

| Activity no. | Activity | | | | | | |
|---|---|---|---|---|---|---|---|
| 36–50 | Revise all transportation expense requests | A | D | | | D | A |
| 50–51 | Review transportation expense requests | D | | E | | A | |
| 51–52 | Tentatively approve transportation expense requests | A | | | | | C |
| 11–20 | Prepare cafeteria expense requests | D | D | | A | | |
| 20–37 | Revise cafeteria expense requests | D | A | A | | | |
| 37–38 | Revise cafeteria expense requests | A | | | | | |
| 38–40 | Revise cafeteria expense requests | A | D | D | | | |
| 40–28 | Prepare and exchange cafeteria staff/school board negotiations | A | B | B | A | | |
| 28–63 | Conduct cafeteria staff/school board negotiations | A | A | B | A | | B |
| 5–12 | Prepare capital improvement expense requests | | A | C | | | |
| 12–21 | Revise capital improvement expense requests | D | | A | | | |
| 21–39 | Revise capital improvement expense requests | D | A | | | | |
| 39–40 | Revise capital improvement expense requests | A | | | | D | |
| 40–41 | Review capital improvement and cafeteria expense requests | A | D | | A | | |
| 54–49 | Tentatively approve interfund transfer requests | A | | D | | D | |
| 49–52 | Calculate retirement, social security, and other undistributed expense requests | A | | A | | | |
| 52–53 | Revise debt service expense requests | A | | A | | | |
| 53–54 | Approve financing plan for approved tentative budget | A | B | B | | | |
| 54–55 | Approve budget for presentation to public | A | E | E | | D | |
| 54–56 | Publish required legal notices | | | | | A | |
| 55–57 | Develop plans for registration and voting on budget | A | B | | | B | |
| 57–59 | Print detailed tentative budget | D | D | D | A | D | |
| 59–58 | Distribute detailed tentative budget to public | | | | A | | |

# Table 10.6 (continued)

| Activity | Description | School board | Superintendent | Assistant superintendent of education | Administrative assistant for buildings and grounds | Administrative assistant | School business official | Building principal | Coordinators | Directors | Cafeteria manager | Clerk | Citizens' budget advisory committee | Instructional staff | Secretarial staff | Custodial staff | Cafeteria staff | Voters | Private school administrator |
|---|---|---|---|---|---|---|---|---|---|---|---|---|---|---|---|---|---|---|---|
| | | | | | | | | | | | | | Organizational units | | | | | | |
| 55–58 | Present completed tentative budget to public | A | | | | | | | | | | | A | | | | | | |
| 58–56 | Conduct public hearing on budget | A | B | B | | | B | | | | | | D | | | | | D | |
| 56–60 | Hold annual meeting on budget | | A | B | | | B | | | | | | D | | | | | D | |
| 60–61 | Conduct vote on school budget | D | D | | | | | | | | | A | D | | | | | D | |

A Has actual responsibility for completion of activity
B Does the work (other than A)
C Must be consulted and receive final report
D Must receive copy of report
E Must be notified of activity completion (other than D)

If it were a deliberate body with directives to recommend revisions, it would make quite a difference whether it saw the budget in its formative stages or saw the whole tentative statement at once.

This last point would provoke a closer look at the data to clarify the role of the citizens' committee. Some of the board members may assume that the committee plays a significant role in the budget development process because it is involved relatively early. The data reveal that this is not necessarily the case. As can be seen from a thorough reading of the LRC, the committee is really a reactive review panel. It enters the picture after goals and policy have been established, after expenditure requests have been submitted by the professional and nonprofessional staff, after deletions and revisions have been made by district officials, and even after the school board itself has reviewed and revised the document data. Clearly, if the committee is to play a significant role, its activities would need to be more direct and placed at critical points in the network. With the apparent slack time available throughout the network, it would be relatively easy to incorporate them more actively.

In this example, PERT and LRC also point up the general lack of involvement of teachers and the relatively heavy involvement of the school board in the administrative detail in budget building.

## General Uses of PERT and LRC

The overall quality of allocation operations is improved the degree that the roles and relationships of the individuals involved are clearly delineated. While the relationship of PERT and LRC to communications has not been explicitly covered here, it is evident that these network tools can be well used to enhance communication. They provide a frame of reference for activities, and if they are clearly intelligible without complex analysis, one should be able to see at a glance who are involved in a set of activities and the nature of their responsibility vis-à-vis each activity.

Further consideration suggests that the PERT chart is very valuable when more than just routine activity is involved. For example, the PERT design could be used in managing contract negotiations, an ambiguous area where problems could emerge and demand the redistribution of manpower to keep the total process on schedule. Problem spots could be anticipated along the design well in advance of their occurence. While such a thing as illness cannot always be anticipated, heavy involvements of district leaders in other school activities (e.g., court cases, new curriculum demands, proposals for federal funding) might be dovetailed with network events.

PERT and LRC could serve as tools for clarifying tasks, needs, responsibilities, and interrelationships. Several smaller PERT/LRCs could be devised to detail the subsystems, with top management coordinating the subsystems. Thus, PERT/LRC could dissolve some of the mystery that often fogs a really straightforward operation. It could also provide an excellent tool for clarifying expectations and time commitments for doing the necessary work. Motivation is likely to be influenced positively when people are aware of how much someone else depends on their work. In short, PERT/LRC provides the big picture often missing in day-to-day activities.

The PERT chart shows estimated time *necessary* for task completion. It would be perhaps more valuable to present a chart with a rationale and calendar for the *ideal* beginnings of activity sets. Given expertise in school district management, a superintendent could develop a strategy for incorporating not just earliest and latest allowable starting times but also a set of ideal starting dates to create a more effective budgeting system. For example, it may be feasible to distribute budget forms on November 7, but not necessarily ideal. It is advisable to consider what teachers and others have been doing just prior to, or will be doing just after, their budget activities. It might be very unappealing to present teachers with budget forms one or two days after the grading period or a few days before a holiday. Ideal dates certainly present potential for a new dimension of PERT.

Finally, professional staff might be justifiably challenged to apply PERT/LRC to other aspects of school life in order to take some of the randomness out of procedures for which streamlining would be a boon. Facilities planning, curriculum development, textbook studies, task force projects, inservice meetings represent a few areas for fruitful investigation. (For some specific examples see Handy and Hussain 1969, chap. 7.)

## Questions for Review and Discussion

1.   Under what circumstances would job descriptions and organizational charts be more useful than linear responsibility charts?

2.   List five transformation functions not mentioned in the chapter that could apply to projects undertaken in educational organizations.

3.   What conditions should exist to justify the cost of developing a linear responsibility chart for a project?

4.   Would linear responsibility charts be useful in evaluating job performance? If so, how?

5.   What specific changes could be made in the linear responsibility chart of the budgeting process to more fully involve the community? What changes in the network of activities could be made to improve their involvement?

6.   Would the changes discussed in question 5 be likely to have any effect on the way resources were allocated in the district? How?

## References

Griffiths, D. E.; Clark, D. L.; Wynn, D. R.; and Iannacone, L. *Organizing Schools for Effective Education.* Danville, Ill.: Interstate Printers & Publishers, 1964.

Handy, H., and Hussain, R. M. *Network Analysis for Educational Management.* Englewood Cliffs, N.J.: Prentice-Hall, 1969.

Hill, Frederick W. *The School Business Administrator.* Chicago: Research Corporation of the Association of School Business Officials, 1970.

## Related Readings

Cleland, D. I., and King, W. R. *Systems Analysis and Project Management.* New York: McGraw-Hill, 1968. A modern view of systems analysis and project management presented in a form that demonstrates their essential unity and their applicability in a wide variety of industrial and governmental management environments, this book discusses the foundation for both the planning and the execution phases of modern management (the systems approach). It also deals with the strategic decisions involved in planning and with the execution of decisions as a major part of the manager's responsibility.

Candoli, I. C.; Hoch, W. G.; Ray, J. R.; and Stallar, D. H. *School Business Administration: A Planning Approach.* Boston: Allyn & Bacon, 1973. Explores the role and setting of school business administration from an historical as well as a modern perspective. The tools and tasks of the administrator are discussed in detail.

Knezevich, Steven J. "The Systems Approach to School Administration: Some Perceptions on the State of the Art." ERIC, no. ED025853, 1967. Why the systems approach has not permeated school administration: the problems it causes, and possible solutions to those problems.

Hinds, Richard H. "Educational Program Planning and Related Techniques." ERIC, no. ED029375, 1969. An annotated bibliography containing ninety-seven entries to aid those interested in the problems and techniques of comprehensive program planning.

# 11
# Classroom Scheduling

This chapter is a continuation of the discussion of allocation systems. Whereas the previous two chapters dealt with allocating resources to programs (budgeting), this chapter deals with allocating clients to services (classroom scheduling). The long-standing problem of classroom scheduling has emerged anew as a topic of interest in management operations for at least two reasons. One reason is that the scheduling process is increasingly seen as the crucial intersection of curricular implementation and resource-allocation strategies. The second reason can be traced to the growing technical requirements of scheduling. These developments imply the possibility of "contracting out" school scheduling.

School scheduling is representative of a class of allocation problems called *roster-scheduling problems*—which most people encounter every day. These problems frequently occur in transportation, when people use buses, taxis, elevators, etc., on a first-come, first-served basis. Hotels, motels, restaurants, and hospitals are usually run the same way. Schools, according to systems analysts, are like other roster-scheduling settings, where demands are "patched" with "services" at "locations." Although true to a point, the complexity inherent in some school-scheduling operations indicates that school scheduling is in many ways different.

When school scheduling is conceived as a roster-scheduling problem, all subjects, rooms, and instructors are individually listed, and these lists are then compared with student course requests. Most students are then placed into courses. Conflicts are often displayed in matrices designed to simplify their resolution. For example, in exhibit 11.1 the diagonal display indicates the number of students who have indicated preferences for each of two conflicting courses (i.e.,

276

## Exhibit 11.1: Student Course Election Matrix List

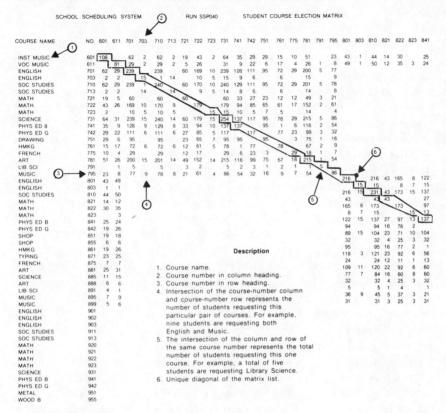

Source: *School Scheduling Manual* (Detroit: Burroughs Corporation, 1972), pp. 3-10. Reprinted by permission.

courses scheduled to meet at the same time). These conflicts can be resolved in a variety of ways, such as changing student choices or course offerings.

To overcome technical scheduling problems and create more educationally useful schedules, school administrators have called on computer technicians. In order to benefit from their expertise, administrators have had to learn to communicate with these technicians, comprehend their frame of reference, and understand the limitations of the computer. Many schools have used keypunching and automatic card-sorting devices to assist in matching student requests with available classes, and in determining when extra sections of classes should be added or dropped.

The use of electronic data-processing devices may create the impression that a single "best" school schedule is achievable. There are only four or five variables to take into account, including teacher preferences (about what should be offered and what they want to teach and when), student preferences, and whether the requisite space is available and reasonably close to other classes. These variables have the advantage of being precisely measurable. For example, teacher A can request precisely how many sections of United States history she wishes to teach, and student B is able to specify a desired set of courses (including those he knows are required for graduation).

An optimum schedule, however, is one that is better than *any* other schedule; and *all* alternative schedules simply are not worth examining. The primary reason is that most of the variables cited above conflict with themselves and other variables. For example, it is extremely unlikely that all teachers' preferences for course assignments and schedules will coincide with students' preferences, availability of space, and state curriculum requirements. For a middle or high school of even moderate size, there is a very large number of possible combinations of course offerings and scheduled times, each resulting in a complex set of conflicts. It is impossible to develop the optimum school schedule because it is impossible to know precisely the conflicts of any one schedule ahead of time, and because there are so many alternative scheduling options.

What, then, is the most that the administrator can hope to accomplish when scheduling a school? He or she can attempt to develop a satisfactory (as opposed to optimum) school schedule. A satisfactory schedule reduces conflicts to an acceptable (not necessarily minimum) level, and packages the curriculum in such a way that it is administratively simple, but also "good enough" instructionally. The most difficult question to resolve is also the most basic: what packaging of courses (e.g., duration, frequency, and size) is most likely to achieve instructional goals? The three sections of this chapter deal with different aspects of this question. The first section discusses the impact of curriculum on school scheduling; the second section assesses the impact of school scheduling on building utilization; and the third section discusses the aspects of classroom scheduling that are amenable to computerization.

## Impact of Changing Curricula on School Scheduling

The kinds of schedules used by schools, especially in the advanced grades, are proliferating. They reflect the growing trend toward flexible curricula that are designed for the learning needs of individual students. Consequently, the simple roster-scheduling discussed above requires modifications and more detailed structuring in order to provide curricular flexibility.

A sampling of the kinds of departures from traditional, fixed scheduling is found in exhibits 11.2-11.8. These master schedules, compiled by the Educational Research Council of America in Columbus, Ohio, illustrate the almost limitless forms of a flexible school schedule, with classes varying in size, duration, and frequency. The apparent strengths of each type of schedule are discussed briefly here.

The simple-block schedule (exhibit 11.2) represents one of the most basic instructional designs. Although it is easy to set up, it allows for varying group size for different learning activities. It could be called a traditional schedule. The back-to-back schedule (exhibit

**Exhibit 11.2: Simple Block Schedule**

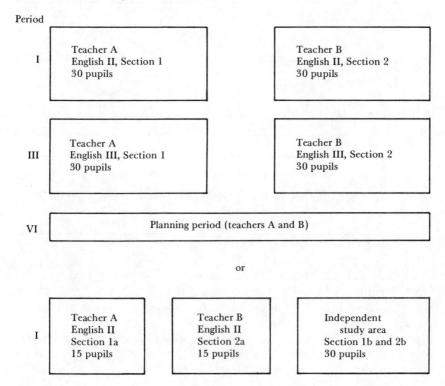

11.3) is much like the simple-block except that the number of time blocks is increased and teachers are teaching the same subject "back to back."

## Exhibit 11.3: Back-to-Back Schedule

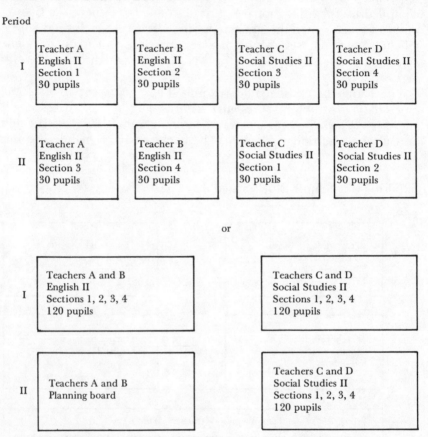

The interdisciplinary schedule (exhibit 11.4) is designed to allow team teaching of two or more disciplines. The school-wide block schedule (exhibit 11.5) represents an extension of the interdisciplinary schedule. In this schedule cross-discipline teams work in large blocks of time. This type of schedule is often used when a relatively high degree of curricular decision-making has been granted to instructional teams.

## Exhibit 11.4: Interdisciplinary Schedule

Period

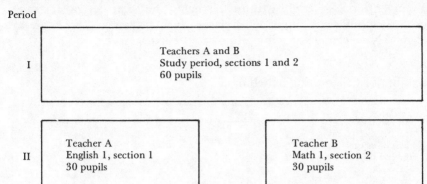

| | | |
|---|---|---|
| I | Teachers A and B<br>Study period, sections 1 and 2<br>60 pupils | |
| II | Teacher A<br>English 1, section 1<br>30 pupils | Teacher B<br>Math 1, section 2<br>30 pupils |
| III | Teacher A<br>English 1, section 2<br>30 pupils | Teacher B<br>Math 1, section 1<br>30 pupils |

## Exhibit 11.5: School-Wide Block Schedule

| | Grade 7 | Grade 8 | Grade 9 |
|---|---|---|---|
| 1<br>2 | Fine Arts<br>Team F | United Studies<br>Team 8 | United Studies<br>Team 9 |
| 3<br>4 | Physical Education<br>Team P | (English, Social<br>Studies, Math,<br>and Science) | |
| 5<br>6 | | | |
| 7<br>8 | United Studies<br>Team 7 | Physical Education<br>Team P | |
| 9<br>10 | | Lunch | Lunch |
| 11<br>12 | Lunch | Fine Arts<br>Team F | United Studies<br>Team 9 |
| 13<br>14 | United Studies<br>Team 7 | United Studies<br>Team 8 | |
| 15<br>16 | | | Physical Education<br>Team P |
| 17<br>18 | | | Fine Arts<br>Team F |

The rotating schedule (exhibit 11.6) is actually a rearrangement of a conventional schedule without changing the basic design. It can be used to modify the duration of classes during the week (Example 3), or merely to change the time of day that classes meet.

## Exhibit 11.6: Rotating Schedule

Example 1:
All six courses meet at a different period for each of the five days in the week.

| Period | M | T | W | Th | F |
|---|---|---|---|---|---|
| I | 1 | 2 | 3 | 5 | 6 |
| II | 2* | 3 | 5 | 6 | 1 |
| III | 3 | 5 | 6 | 1 | 2 |
| IV | 4 | 4 | 4 | 4 | 4 |
| V | 5 | 6 | 1 | 2 | 3 |
| VI | 6 | 1 | 2 | 3 | 5 |

Example 2:
Similar to Example 1 except that the seven courses meet only four times per week.

| Period | M | T | W | Th | F |
|---|---|---|---|---|---|
| I | 1 | 7 | 6 | 5 | 4 |
| II | 2 | X | 7 | 6 | 5 |
| III | 3 | 2 | 1 | 7 | 6 |
| IV | 4 | 3 | 2 | 1 | 7 |
| V | 5 | 4 | 3 | 7 | 1 |
| VI | 6 | 5 | 1 | 3 | 2 |

Example 3:
Similar to Example 1 except that the six courses meet between three and five times per week and weekly contact minutes range from 45 to 90 minutes.

| Minutes per period | M | T | W | Th | F |
|---|---|---|---|---|---|
| 45 | 1 | 6 | 5 | 4 | 1 |
| 45 | 2 | 1 | 5 | 5 | 3 |
| 60 | 3 | 2 | 1 | 6 | 4 |
| 60 | 4 | 3 | 2 | 1 | 5 |
| 90 | 5 | 4 | 3 | 2 | 6 |

*Numbers in the matrices represent different course offerings taken by a group of students.

The block-modular and the flexible-modular schedules are more complex. The block-modular schedule (exhibit 11.7) is like the simple-block schedule in that students are scheduled into sections as blocks. It is more complex in that all students do not move between classes at the same time. This makes possible the offering of courses with different durations (from two to four modules), although each meeting of a particular course is of the same duration. For example, in exhibit 11.7 Health is always scheduled in two-module time intervals. The flexible-modular schedule (exhibit 11.8) is much like the block-modular schedule with the additional complicating factor that the duration of meeting time of a particular course can vary for different days of the week. For example, in the single student's

Exhibit 11.7: Block Modular Schedule

A block modular schedule grid. The left column is labeled "13-minute modules" numbered 1 through 29. The chart is divided into three grades, each with four Sections (I, II, III, IV).

**Grade 7 — Section I, II, III, IV**

- Section I: Language; Health; English / Social Studies; Math / Science; Clubs / Orchestra / Band; Physical Education / Geography; Humanities
- Section II: Health; English / Social Studies; Language; Math / Science; Clubs / Orchestra / Band; Physical Education / Geography; Humanities
- Section III: Math / Science; Language; English / Social Studies; Typing; Choir / Individual study / Lunch; Humanities
- Section IV: Math / Science; Typing; English / Social Studies; Language; Choir / Individual study / Lunch; Humanities

**Grade 8 — Section I, II, III, IV**

- Section I: Physical Education; Humanities; Social Studies; Language / English; Clubs / Orchestra / Band; Health / Language; Math / Science
- Section II: Physical Education / Geography; Humanities; English / Social Studies; Language / Social Studies / Health; Clubs / Orchestra / Band; Language; Math / Science
- Section III: Humanities; Physical Education / Geography; Typing; Math / Social Studies; Choir / Individual study / Lunch; English / Social Studies; Language
- Section IV: Humanities; Geography; Math / Science; Language; Typing; English / Social Studies

**Grade 9 — Section I, II, III, IV**

- Section I: Math / Science; Language / Health; Physical Education / Geography; Humanities; Clubs / Orchestra / Band; English / Social Studies; Health / English / Social Studies
- Section II: Math / Science; Health; Geography / Math / Science; Humanities; Clubs / Orchestra / Band; English / Social Studies; Language
- Section III: English / Social Studies; Language; Humanities; Physical Education / Geography; Choir / Individual study / Lunch; Math and Science; Typing / Language; Math / Science
- Section IV: English / Social Studies; Typing; Humanities; Geography; Individual study; Language; Math / Science

# Exhibit 11.8: Flexible Modular Schedule

Individual student's schedule

| 16-minute modules | Monday | Tuesday | Wednesday | Thursday | Friday |
|---|---|---|---|---|---|
| 1 | World Geography (small group, Room 110) | World Geography (Room 110) | Biology 2 (small group or lab, Room 126) | World Geography (small group, Room 110) | English 5 (small group, Room 111) |
| 2 | | | | | |
| 3 | Individual Study (open lab, instructional materials center, lounge, art, etc.) | Individual Study | | Individual Study | Individual Study |
| 4 | | | | | |
| 5 | | Art I (Room 118) | | | Physical Science (small group or lab, Room 206) |
| 6 | | | Individual study | | |
| 7 | | | Physical Science (small group, Room 203) | Art I (Room 118) | |
| 8 | | | | | |
| 9 | | | Individual Study | Individual study | |
| 10 | | Individual Study | | | |
| 11 | Lunch | Lunch | Lunch | Lunch | Lunch |
| 12 | Individual Study | | Individual Study | Language lab | Individual Study |
| 13 | | | | | |
| 14 | Math 2 (large group, Room 119) | Individual Study | Math 2 (Room 119) | English 3 (small group, Room 111) | Math 2 (Room 201) |
| 15 | | | | | |
| 16 | Individual Study | | | | |
| 17 | | English 2 (small group or lab, Room 126) | Individual Study | Individual Study | World Geography (Room 126) |
| 18 | Physical Science (small group or lab, Room 106) | | | Biology 2 (large group, Room 126) | |
| 19 | | | | | |
| 20 | | Biology 2 (small group or lab, Room 126) | | | |
| 21 | Individual Study | | | Math 2 (small group, Room 201) | Individual Study |
| 22 | | Math (small group, Room 201) | | | |
| 23 | French 1 (Room 109) | | French 1 (Room 109) | | French I (Room 109) |
| 24 | | | | | |

schedule, World Geography is scheduled for three modules of time on Monday, Tuesday, and Thursday, and for two modules of time on Friday. The flexible-modular schedule permits variations of activities and grouping patterns, facilitates organization of course structures, and allows for the use of different instructional modes and staffing ratios. It is also relatively costly to develop. For extended discussions of problems involving flexible modular scheduling see Swaab (1974) and Congreve (1972).

Decisions about curricular packaging require a balance between learning benefits that accrue from more flexible and complex schedules and the increased costs that necessarily accompany these schedules. More flexible curricula usually require increased planning, preparation, and coordination among teachers. Also, modifications in scheduling can be constrained by, or significantly alter, utilization rates of buildings.

## Impact of School Schedules on Building Utilization

Determining utilization rates in the elementary school is a rather straightforward process. If the school has $X$ students and $Y$ rooms, the student-classroom ratio is $X/Y = Z$. The $Y$ figure can be considered in terms of either academic classrooms or total student capacity, but it must be used consistently.

In junior and senior high schools there is more potential for flexible use of special rooms to increase the capacity of the school. The number of students per classroom ($Z$) will vary depending on overall school loading and instructional plans. If rated school capacity (set by the school board or the state) is represented by $C$, then $C/Y$ is designated as the *rated* average room loading, as distinct from $X/Y$ which is the *actual* average room loading. Also, $X/C$ is one form of a school-utilization factor.

The form of a school's schedule, which is a function of curricular policies, can clearly affect the utilization rate of that school. The best possible school-utilization factor is not necessarily representative of the best educational facilities. The relationship between schedules, facilities, and utilization is most effectively illustrated by an example.

Exhibit 11.9 shows five different elementary school buildings; each has a different configuration of classrooms, but all have the following common schedule and loading:

Number of students | 480
Number of classes (groups of students) | 12

## Exhibit 11.9: Comparing School Utilization Among Schools

School

**(1)** | Academic classrooms (12) | Art room (1) | Music room (1) | Gym (2) | Cafeteria (4)

Total classroom equivalents = 12 + 1 + 1 + 2 + 4 + 4 = 24

Auditorium (4)

**(2)** | Academic classrooms (12) | Art room (1) | Music room (1) | Gym (2) | Cafetorium (4)

Total classroom equivalents = 12 + 1 + 1 + 2 + 4 = 20

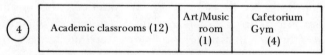

**(3)** | Academic classrooms (12) | Art room (1) | Music room (1) | Cafetorium Gym (4)

Total classroom equivalents = 12 + 11 + 1 + 4 = 18

**(4)** | Academic classrooms (12) | Art/Music room (1) | Cafetorium Gym (4)

Total classroom equivalent = 12 + 1 + 4 = 17

**(5)** | Academic classrooms (12) including art/music | Cafetorium Gym (4)

Total classroom equivalent = 16

Source: J. J. O'Brien, ed., *Scheduling Handbook* (New York: McGraw-Hill, 1969), pp. 310-11. Reprinted by permission.

| | |
|---|---|
| Periods per week | 40 |
| Academic program | 31 periods per week |
| Art program | 1 period per week per class |
| Assemblies | as required |
| Physical Education | 2 periods per week per class |
| Lunch program | 5 periods per week per class |

School 1 has the equivalent of 24 classrooms (i.e., the school can accommodate up to 24 class-size groups of children, if all the facilities are used). Schools 2 through 5 have combined some special-purpose rooms into multi-use spaces. The number of classroom equivalents for Schools 2 through 5 ranges from 16 to 20.

What impact do the special-purpose spaces have on the utilization of rooms in the school? The room utilization rate is calculated as:

$$U_i = \frac{O_i \times N}{E_i \times S} \ .$$

In this equation, $U_i$ is the utilization of room type i (i = 1, 6); $O_i$ is the occupancy of room type i (in periods per class week); $N$ is the number of groups of children who will use room type i (12 in all cases); $E_i$ is the classroom equivalency of the gym (4); and $S$ is the possible number of sessions that can be held in room type i (40 per week in all cases).

The utilization rate of academic classrooms in School 1 is calculated as follows:

$$\frac{(40 - 9) \times 12}{1 \times 40 \times 12} = 77.9\%.$$

The occupancy rate of the academic classrooms in School 1 is only 31 (40 − 9) periods per class per week because children in School 1 will be spending at least nine hours out of their academic classrooms in specialized spaces (all of the other programs are conducted in specialized spaces). Room utilization rates for each of the five schools are presented in table 11.10. For example, the utilization of academic classrooms in School 5 is 82.5 percent because the art and music programs are conducted in the academic classrooms.

The impact of specialized spaces on overall school utilization is more dramatic. School utilization is calculated as a function of the utilization rates of the individual room types:

$$T_k = \frac{\Sigma\ (Ui \times Ri)}{C_k} \ .$$

In this equation $T_k$ is the utilization rate of school K (K = 1, 5); $Ui$ is the utilization rate of room type i (i = 1, 6); $Ri$ is the number of classroom equivalents in room type i in school K; and $C_k$ is the total number of classroom equivalents in school K. For example, the utilization rate of School 1 is calculated from the information in table 11.11 as follows:

$$\frac{77.5\ (12) + 30\ (1) + 30\ (1) + 30\ (2) + 37.5\ (4) + 0\ (4)}{24} = 50\%.$$

Calculations of the utilization rates of the five elementary schools are shown in table 11.11. It is clear that schools with fewer specialized spaces will have, other things being equal, significantly higher utilization rates (75 percent as opposed to 50 percent). This example points up the problematic interaction of facilities planning and curriculum planning. Less directly, it shows that in enrollment-growth situations, scheduling for high space utilization can reduce the rate at which additional facilities must be constructed (a rationale behind many year-round education plans).

### Table 11.10: Comparing Room Utilization Among Elementary Schools

| School | Classrooms | Art | Music | Gym | Cafeteria | Auditorium |
|---|---|---|---|---|---|---|
| 1 | $\dfrac{(40-9)\times12}{1\times40\times12}$ | $\dfrac{1\times12}{1\times40}$ | $\dfrac{1\times12}{1\times40}$ | $\dfrac{2\times12}{2\times40}$ | $\dfrac{5\times12}{4\times40}$ | Varies |
|  | 77.5% | 30% | 30% | 30% | 37.5% | 0 |
| 2 | 77.5% | 30% | 30% | 30% | 37.5% | Combined |
| 3 | 77.5% | 30% | 30% | 52.5% | Combined | Combined |
| 4 | 77.5% | 60% | Combined | 52.5% | Combined | Combined |
| 5 | $\dfrac{40-7\times12}{1\times40\times12}$ |  |  | 52.5% | Combined | Combined |
|  | 82.5% |  |  |  |  |  |

Source: Adapted from J. J. O'Brien, ed., *Scheduling Handbook* (New York: McGraw-Hill, 1969), pp. 310-11. Reprinted by permission.

### Computer Assistance in Scheduling

Computers have had an impact on scheduling in three general areas: collecting and preparing data, scheduling "runs" (initial attempts to develop a satisfactory schedule), and generating reports. In general, reporting and scheduling have been simplified at the expense of greater complexity in data preparation and software debugging (getting the computer program to operate correctly).

The information required for computer scheduling is the same as that required for scheduling by hand. The format, however, is different. Almost all data that must enter a computer scheduling program

## Table 11.11: Comparing Overall Utilization Among Elementary Schools

| School | Classroom equivalents | Percentage of classroom equivalents in School 1 | Utilization factor | | | | |
|---|---|---|---|---|---|---|---|
| | | | Class | Art/Music | Gym | Cafeteria | Auditorium |
| 1 | 24 | 100% | $\dfrac{77.5(12) + 30(1) + 30(2) + 37.5 + 0(4)}{24} = 50\%$ | | | | |
| 2 | 20 | 83.3% | $\dfrac{77.5(12) + 30(1) + 30(1) + 30(2) + 37.5(4)}{20} = 60\%$ | | | | |
| 3 | 18 | 75% | $\dfrac{77.5(12) + 30(1) + 30(1) + 52.5(4)}{18} = 66.7\%$ | | | | |
| 4 | 17 | 70.8% | $\dfrac{77.5(12) + 60(1) + 52.5(4)}{17} = 70.6\%$ | | | | |
| 5 | 16 | 66.7% | $\dfrac{82.5(12) + 52.5(4)}{16} = 75\%$ | | | | |

Source: Adapted from J. J. O'Brien, ed., *Scheduling Handbook* (New York: McGraw-Hill, 1969), pp. 310-11. Reprinted by permission.

are read by a machine from cards, which have either been hole-punched or marked by pencil. (If the cards are punched, a *card reader* interprets the presence or absence of light through the holes. If the cards are marked with a pencil, an optical scanner interprets the presence or absence of lead.) At the moment, hole-punched cards can be read faster (300 cards per minute) and more reliably than cards marked with a pencil, but hole-punching is usually more expensive and time consuming. (Obviously, if scheduling is contracted for, it should be determined whether data preparation is included in the price.)

Normally, four kinds of data are fed into the machine: student course requirements, anticipated course offerings, anticipated master schedule, and alternate course offerings. The most recent computer scheduling programs have eliminated the necessity of creating a tentative master schedule. Such programs require additional data, however, such as the total school resources (rooms, staff, etc.), and then proceed to develop a master schedule.

There is little advantage in utilizing a computer for creating tentative schedules. In this area card sorting machinery is sufficient. When the stage of report generation is reached, however, computers can handle and cross-reference data with unchallenged efficiency. A typical computer-based scheduling system develops a variety of reports for different uses.

One type of output is an alphabetical listing of students by grade. This list can be used to confirm that no student's course requests were omitted from the run. The second most valuable output is the conflict matrix. Prior to developing a preliminary master schedule the administrator uses the matrix to see what course offerings were or were not chosen by sufficient numbers of students, how many students chose each course (i.e., how many sections are needed), and how many students chose particular pairs of courses. The computer also produces error reports. Almost all programs contain an editing operation designed to stop the machine when an excessive number of errors are encountered or when the errors are extremely significant. Error reports indicate flaws in the input data that prevent students from being scheduled. Possible examples are two courses with the same title or number or a course with zero seat capacity.

Once a master schedule which meets curriculum, staff, and contractual requirements has been created, the task remains of determining how many students will be accommodated by the schedule without irresolvable conflict. There are five possible outcomes for students during a scheduling run:

1. They can be successfully scheduled in their requested courses or alternates;

2. They can get listed on "overload conflict" if there are no remaining seats in the requested course;

3. They can get listed on "early-release conflict" if desired courses meet after they are scheduled to be off for a work-study program, etc.;

4. They can get listed on "resolvable conflict" if they have requested two courses which meet simultaneously;

5. They can get listed on "course dropped—study-hall conflict" if there is an unresolvable conflict and an unrequested ("study hall") course replaces the course desired.

The procedures for computer scheduling are similar to those for scheduling without a computer. The program counts the number of sections of a course and ranks the courses on that basis. The most difficult to schedule are those courses that offer only one section. These "singletons" are given top priority, with students who request these courses usually scheduled first. Second priority is given to singleton courses that list alternatives. The computer then considers courses with multiple sections. The general rule is to schedule first those courses most likely to produce conflicts. After sorting student requests into classrooms the computer attempts to equalize class size.

In the final phase of computer scheduling the following lists are produced:

1. Seat availability. As of the most recent scheduling run, how many vacant seats are there in each class?

2. Room utilization. How much is each available room being used?

3. Teacher loading. How many students are being taught by each teacher during each period?

4. Successfully scheduled students. Which students were successfully scheduled into their first or alternate choices?

5. Student conflicts. Which students have a course conflict? Which courses were they successfully scheduled into and which courses are in conflict?

6. Homeroom. Which students have been assigned to which homerooms?

7. Students by class. Which students have been scheduled into which classes?

8. Number of students scheduled by period, by day, and by semester. How many students are in each class at any time throughout the year?

9. Study hall. Which students have been assigned to which study halls?

10. Student schedule. What is each student's schedule?

11. Student class year. Which students are in each grade in school?

Computer technicians bring to school scheduling a certain expertise with the machine and a certain naiveté regarding the operation of schools. School administrators accordingly play a fundamental role in informing technicians about scheduling needs. Administrators are concerned not to "lose control" over a schedule they are responsible for and must live with, and, indeed, there is no reason to abdicate direction simply because computer technicians have come on the scene. Certain simple precautions can be taken:

1. Prior to contractual agreement with a computer firm, the administrator should find out which schools it has scheduled, and with what results.

2. The administrator should allow additional lead time for the problems that may be encountered by the technicians. Computer turn-around times as estimated by the firm are extremely optimistic for the first-time use of computer schedules.

3. The administrator should demand an operation manual and a complete explanation of any delays. The manual is especially valuable in determining whether the particular program proposed is appropriate. Systems requiring program modifications are assessed additional costs. Manuals contain glossaries and fairly complete descriptions of the computer operation, and can be understood by an educated layman.

4. The administrator should not harbor the common belief in the immutability of computer results and the necessity of complete reliance on the computer. If the master schedule drawn from the computer is unsatisfactory, it can be redrawn. It is possible that resolving conflicts "by hand" will be more efficient than successive computer runs.

5. The administrator should be aware of the flexibility of the computer in terms of handling data. Should there be some pressing reason, additional output in a form other than the packaged reports developed by the vendor can be produced at the client's insistence (and usually at the client's expense).

## Questions for Review and Discussion

1. In what ways (if any) would classroom scheduling at a college or university be different from classroom scheduling at a junior high school?

2. Do the master schedule options described in the chapter reflect different educational philosophies? If so, what are they?

3. What kinds of errors are more likely to occur when undertaking a relatively complex school schedule?

4. In what ways do facilities constrain scheduling options?

5. How (if at all) do computers alter the way that students get scheduled into programs?

## References

Burroughs Corporation. *School Scheduling Manual.* Detroit: Burroughs Corporation, 1972.

Congreve, Willard J. *Flexibility in School Programs.* Worthington, Ohio: C. A. Jones Publishing Company, 1972. LB 2806 C568.

O'Brien, J. J., ed. *Scheduling Handbook.* New York: McGraw-Hill, 1969.

Swaab, Alexander M. *School Administrator's Guide to Flexible Modular Scheduling.* West Nyack, N.Y.: Parker Publishing Company, 1974. LB 1038 S88.

## Related Readings

Carter, J. "A New Approach to Class Scheduling." ERIC, no. ED010598, 1967. This report used a computer to produce alternative schedules for graduate students and faculty to use in designing a college semester schedule.

Filene, R. "A Student Report on Student and Teacher Reactions to Modular Scheduling." ERIC, no. ED021313, 1969. This report deals with student and teacher reactions to a recently instituted program of flexible scheduling and independent study time.

Harding, Robert E. *Problem of Generating Class Schedules for Schools.* Ann Arbor, Mich.: University Microfilms, 1969. A mathematical approach to generating class schedules. It deals primarily with linear programming models as the vehicle for solving scheduling problems. The problems of linear programming relate to scheduling as a result of three basic characteristics: (1) the size of the computational load, (2) the unavailability of efficient integer programming algorithms, and (3) lack of knowledge concerning methods for transforming the general problem so that integer solutions are found without the use of integer programming algorithms. This book explores each of these problems in detail, attempting to alleviate their detrimental effect on scheduling.

Knudarig, Everett C. "Responsibilities of a Member UMSSP School." ERIC, no. ED010972, 1967. This article discusses the use of flexible scheduling and the use of correspondence courses to maximize opportunities in a limited curriculum.

Swaab, A. M. *School Administrators' Guide to Flexible Modular Scheduling.* West Nyack, N.Y.: Parker Publishing Company, 1974. This book progresses from an overall view of traditional schedules, to the concept of flexible modular scheduling, to the mechanics of creating flexible modular scheduling, to problems of institutional change and, finally, to evaluation and research.

Wiley, W. D., and Bishop, L. K. *The Flexible Scheduled High School.* West Nyack, N.Y.: Parker Publishing Company, 1968. This book deals in detail with computerized flexible scheduling. It ranges from definition of terms, to a discussion of concepts, to the implementation of computer programs that are used for flexible scheduling.

# 12
# Formulas for Resource Allocation

There are often many possible ways that a given bundle of resources can be allocated, with no single way being "best." The number is so large, in fact, that it would be impractical and costly to attempt to consider all the alternatives. On the other hand, it could be equally costly to allocate resources on the basis of criteria which have no relationship to the goals of the organization. In attempting to walk the middle ground between these two extremes, educational managers often develop mathematical formulas which incorporate *some* of the allocation criteria of the organization and rely on these formulas to allocate a large portion of their resources.

An example of this kind of formula was implied in exhibit 8.5. Using the information in that exhibit, it is possible to write a formula which will determine the number of custodians to be allocated to each school building in a district. Of the possible factors that could be considered in arriving at this allocation decision, only five are actually considered: the number of teachers in the school, the number of pupils in the school, the number of rooms in the school, the total area of the school building, and the number of acres of the school site. The formula is:

$$Ci = (Ti/8 + Pi/225 + Ri/11 + Ai/15{,}000 + Si/2)/5,$$

where $Ci$ is the number of custodians to be allocated to School i, $Ti$ is the number of teachers at School i, $Pi$ is the number of pupils at School i, $Ri$ is the number of rooms in School i, $Ai$ is the area of School i's building in square feet, and $Si$ is the size of School i's site in acres.

*295*

Using this formula, if a school employs eight teachers for 225 students in an eleven-room building of 15,000 square feet on two acres, it would be allocated one custodian. While fractional results of the computations (e.g., 1 1/2 custodians), have to be evaluated on an individual basis, the formula efficiently deals with a large part of this allocation problem.

Two kinds of commonly used allocation formulas are discussed here: those dealing with distribution of state financial assistance to local school districts; and those dealing with distributions of financial and other resources to individual schools within a school district. In both cases attention is directed toward allocation objectives, specific allocation formulas or decision rules, and problems of analyzing allocation operations (including assessing the impact of allocation formulas).

## Allocating State Financial Assistance to School Districts

Although the financing of elementary-secondary public education is both complex and constantly changing, a simplified model is presented in figure 12.1 to provide a basis for introducing state aid allocation formulas. As shown in table 1.9, school districts receive

### Figure 12.1: Financing Elementary-Secondary Public Education

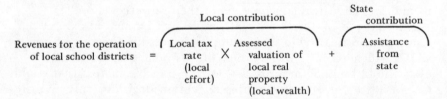

revenue from a wide variety of sources. However, local taxes and state assistance constitute by far the largest revenue sources. The local dollar contribution to education is raised by taxing property at a specified rate. State contributions to local school districts are often a function of the local contribution. The allocation formulas discussed here represent several of the major methods for determining the state contribution that have evolved over the last three-quarters of a century. Simplified versions of the formulas are given for purposes of comparison.

## The Flat Grant Approach

In its most basic form, the *flat grant* form of state assistance amounts to a fixed sum of money:

school           local                 state contribution
district   =   contribution   +   as a fixed amount of
revenue                            money per unit.

The state pays a fixed amount to the district based on some unit of measure in the district (e.g., average daily attendance of pupils or number of teachers employed). The unit of measure used is important in determining the impact of the flat grant formula (e.g., a flat grant based on average daily attendance vs. a flat grant based on number of teachers employed). The differences are shown in figures 12.2 and 12.3. In figure 12.2, the distribution has been uniformly shifted upward. That is, in terms of dollar amounts the difference

**Figure 12.2: State Aid Distribution from a Flat Grant Formula Based on Average Daily Attendance**

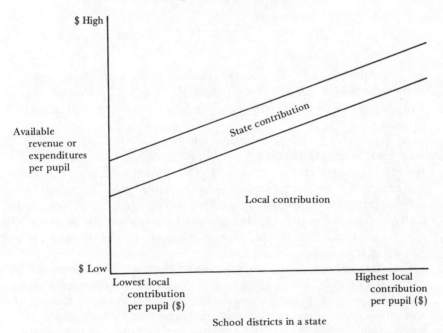

**Figure 12.3: State Aid Distribution from a Flat Grant Formula Based on Teacher Revenue Units**

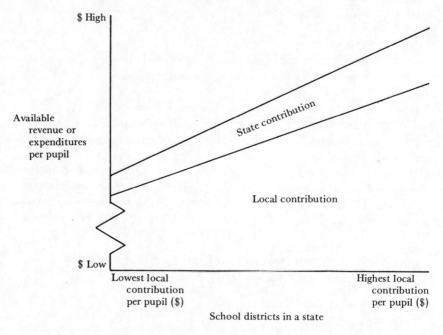

between the richest and poorest districts is the same (although the percentage difference has been reduced). This is because the average daily attendance in a district is not a function of either local wealth or local effort.

In figure 12.3, the distribution has been shifted in favor of the wealthier districts. In terms of dollar amounts, the difference between the richest and poorest districts has increased. This is because the number of teachers (the unit of payment of the flat grant) that a district purchases is clearly a function of the financial ability of the district. As a consequence, the rich get richer when the state agrees, in effect, to pay part of the cost of a service. How this works is described below.

The flat grant was developed around the turn of the century by Ellwood P. Cubberley (1906). One of the main objectives of Cubberley's plan was to expand educational offerings in communities. He was anxious for secondary school instruction to become more widespread, and he also sought the institution of kindergartens, manual and physical training classes, evening schools, special classes, and vocational schools. He believed that the efforts of school districts to expand their offerings should be rewarded on a "teacher-employed" basis. That is, for every teacher employed by a district, the state paid a portion of that teacher's cost, and there was no limitation on the use of teachers. Thus, districts could hire new teachers and have the costs shared by the state. Such a financial incentive usually stimulates local expenditures. However, in Cubberley's program, the stimulation of expenditures in any district is limited by the wealth of that district. (For an extended discussion of the effects of the flat grant and other formulas, see Benson 1968, pp. 154-90.)

Another of Cubberley's objectives was to promote local property tax relief. However, in the early twentieth century the property tax was the major source of state, as well as local, revenue; and the property tax is regressive, i.e., it has a disproportionately heavy impact on the poor (because the poor spend a high proportion of their income on housing). Thus, poorer districts had already paid a disproportionate share of state revenue, and Cubberley's state aid program did not promote local tax relief. Today, however, when many states rely on nonproperty taxes, a flat grant promotes some local tax relief.

## The Foundation Program Approach

The *foundation program* is a mechanism designed to guarantee a minimum fixed amount of revenue per student in a school district. It is determined in three steps. First, a minimum (or foundation) level of revenue per pupil necessary for an "adequate" educational program is determined by the state. Second, a local district, by taxing itself at a specified level, determines if its local contribution is more or less than this foundation amount. Third, if the local contribution is less than the foundation, the state makes up the difference. The general formula for this is:

If the local contribution per student (based on a uniform tax rate) is greater than the foundation, then
    local revenue per student = local contribution per student.
If the local contribution per student (based on a uniform tax rate) is less than the foundation, then

local revenue     the local contribution     (foundation minus the
per student    = per student           + local contribution
                                               per student).

The impact of this formula is shown in figure 12.4. The level of

## Figure 12.4: State Aid Distribution from a Foundation Plan
(key district is district with average local contribution)

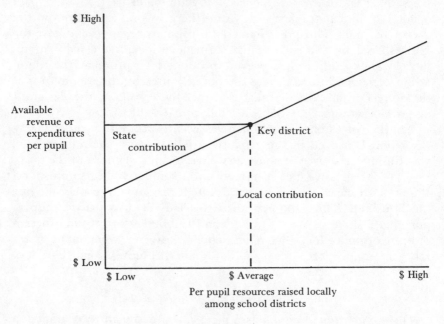

the foundation is very important in determining the degree to which the program succeeds in equalizing per pupil revenues among school districts. The foundation is determined by picking a *key district*, one whose local contribution at the fixed tax rate equals the amount of the foundation. If the key district is the richest district in the state, revenues are equalized throughout the state, as shown in figure 12.5. If the key district is a district of average expenditure, as shown in figure 12.4, then per pupil revenues are equalized only up to the point of the foundation.

Since in practice the level of the foundation is invariably below the real cost of schooling, the district must raise additional funds to cover the costs not provided by the foundation funds. Because of the varying degrees of district wealth, poor communities must exert a proportionately greater tax effort than rich communities in order to obtain the same amount of local funds. In inflationary periods, poor districts are further disadvantaged. State legislatures are often reluctant to raise the level of the foundation, permitting inflation to take away the buying power of the educational dollar.

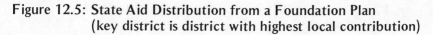

## Figure 12.5: State Aid Distribution from a Foundation Plan
### (key district is district with highest local contribution)

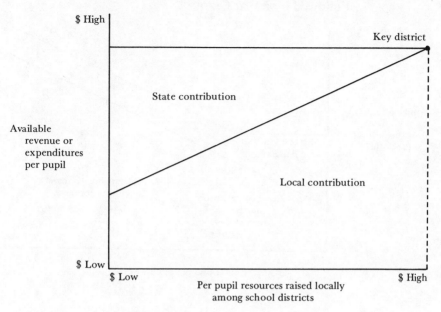

It has been argued that all communities should contribute to the foundation program at the rate that the wealthiest district would pay without state aid. However, in practice, the key district is frequently one with average educational expenditures. This results in a higher tax rate among districts in the state.

### The Combination Flat Grant and Foundation Approach

These two allocation methods can be used in combination. The impact of the combined methods depends on which formula is considered first (for the same foundation level and the same amount of flat grant). If the foundation level is applied to district revenues first, the general revenue pattern among school districts is both more equal and, in total, higher than if the formulas were applied in reverse order. This is shown in figure 12.6. If the flat grant is administered first the opposite occurs, as shown in figure 12.7.

Depending on the level of the foundation and the amount of the flat grant, the impact of one can more than offset the impact of the other. Figure 12.8 shows the expenditure patterns of California elementary school districts during 1969-1970. Every district, regardless

## Figure 12.6: State Aid Distribution from Administering a Foundation Plan (key = average district) Followed by a Flat Grant

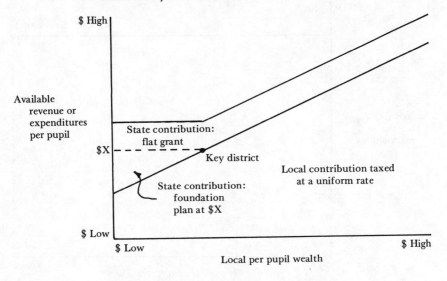

## Figure 12.7: State Aid Distribution from Administering a Flat Grant Followed by a Foundation Plan (key = average district)

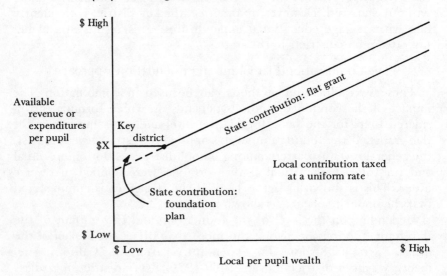

## Figure 12.8: Expenditure Ability of California Elementary School Districts (assuming uniform local tax of $1.50)

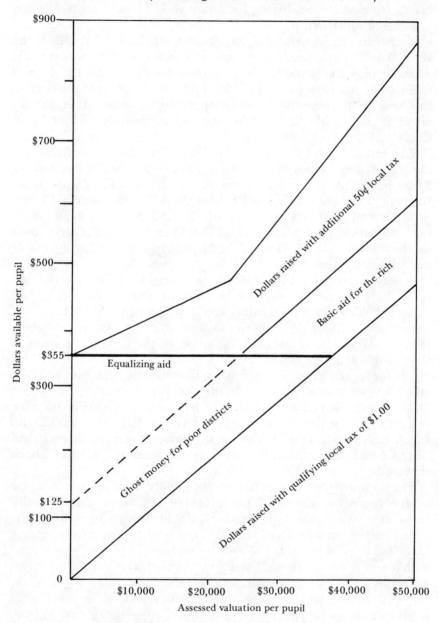

of wealth, received flat-grant aid in the amount of $125.00 per pupil. This amount was added to the amount generated in each district by taxing itself at the qualifying local rate of $1.00 per hundred dollars of assessed valuation.

If the district is willing to tax its property at this rate, then the state would pay the district the difference, if any, between (1) $125.00 plus the amount per pupil raised locally, and (2) a fixed foundation amount per pupil ($355.00 for elementary districts in this case). With these two formulas operating in combination, the net effect is to provide $125.00 in state aid to wealthy districts! (See figure 12.8.)

The actual impact of these formulas on two particular districts is illustrated here. When West Covina taxes at the qualifying rate of $1.00 per hundred for elementary schools, it raises $76.88 per pupil. In theory, the state then adds to this the $125.00 "basic aid" (flat grant) per pupil, yielding a total of $201.88. Since the state under the foundation plan guarantees $355.00 per pupil, the district then receives an additional $153.12 in "equalizing" funds for a total of $278.12 in state money.

However, assuming the $355.00 guarantee, West Covina would receive the same amount of state aid with or without the $125.00 in basic aid. That is, the district would still receive $278.13—all in "equalizing" funds. For West Covina, the flat grant is "ghost money." (For a more detailed discussion of the legal implication of this finance plan, see Sugarman 1972.)

On the other hand, for a district like Beverly Hills the $125.00 takes on substance. With a $1.00 tax rate, Beverly Hills raises $870.00 per elementary pupil, which is too much to qualify for equalizing aid. Nevertheless, it still receives the flat grant of $125.00, which has the effect of widening the resource gap between it and West Covina. The general intent of equalization has, in effect, been thwarted.

The foundation formula has another, more basic, effect. Because of the regressive nature of the property tax, funds raised locally above the foundation level impose a tax burden on households. As stated earlier, this impact varies from district to district, depending on differences in per pupil assessed valuation. The impact also varies within each school district. Within communities, there are income differences among households, and therefore the ability to pay taxes varies. Lower- and average-income families will strain more than wealthy families to pay taxes. Again, the result is the opposite of tax relief.

Strayer and Haig (1923), the developers of the foundation program approach, believed that incentive payments were inconsistent with the equalization objective. Therefore, the foundation program does not provide for the stimulation of local expenditures. The initiative for expanding educational offerings resides with the state. If the state decides a new offering is necessary, funds will be included in the foundation program. If a local district wants to initiate a new offering of its own, it must tax itself beyond the level required for the foundation program. Therefore, districts are often unwilling to experiment with innovative programs.

## The Weighted-Pupil Measures Approach

The formulas discussed so far are calculated on the basis of equality of revenue among students. The concept discussed here deals with providing for groups of students (e.g., physically handicapped) who require extra revenue.

Paul Mort (1960) advanced a number of refinements to the basic Strayer-Haig plan, which might be termed *weighted-pupil measures* (see Benson 1968, pp. 157-67). Determining the unit cost (cost per student) of the minimum educational program caused problems for both Cubberley and Strayer and Haig. Different schools had different unit costs. Mort refined the task unit of average daily attendance used in the Strayer-Haig formula. He developed the weighted-pupil measure, which took into account any unusual costs (i.e., transportation, small school districts, or schools with a large number of secondary pupils). The weighted-pupil measure assumes that it costs more to educate certain types of children. For example, it may cost 1.3 times as much to educate a secondary school child as it does to educate an elementary school child, because of such added expenses as special purpose facilities for vocational and science subjects and smaller class sizes in these subjects.

In recently adopting the weighted-pupil measures for its finance formula, Utah educational policymakers found a number of compelling advantages:

1. The costs of education are more directly related to number of students than to any other factor. The previous system used in the state (distribution units) was difficult to implement, since it was not always related to the number of students. It is relatively easy to convert weighted-pupil measures into distribution units if necessary.

2. Recent court cases were concerned with the inequality of cost per pupil. The weighted-pupil system tends to build equity into a finance formula, because all classifications of pupils receive their

proportionate share of revenue increases and all share proportionately if there are revenue decreases.

3. This approach reduces the number of categorical grants required in the financing of educational programs.

4. A number of other states are moving in this direction, because it usually results in a formula that is relatively easy to understand and apply.

Some of the actual weightings used in the Utah finance plan are shown in exhibit 12.9. This exhibit lists the weightings for programs

## Exhibit 12.9: Weightings for Programs for Handicapped Children (Utah's School Finance Formula)

Handicapped-children units shall be computed in accordance with the following schedules:

| (a) For each pupil in average daily attendance in programs for: | Multiply the number of handicapped children in | |
| --- | --- | --- |
| | regular class by: | self-contained class by: |
| Educable mentally retarded | .70 | 2.28 |
| Trainable mentally retarded | 1.00 | 2.53 |
| Learning disabilities | .73 | .00 |
| Emotionally disturbed | 1.10 | 3.09 |
| Deaf and hard of hearing | 1.60 | 2.50 |
| Speech and hearing disabilities | .30 | .00 |
| Motor handicapped | 1.20 | 2.88 |
| Visually impaired | 1.60 | .00 |
| Homebound and hospitalized | .00 | 1.80 |
| Training center multiple handicapped | .00 | 2.78 |

(b) Multiply the number of weighted-pupil units in the district in regular programs computed elsewhere (kindergarten, elementary, secondary, and small schools) by 9 percent.

(c) Add (a) and (b) and divide by two to obtain the number of weighted-pupil units in these programs.

for handicapped children, and describes the procedure whereby the number of weighted pupils is calculated. (For a more detailed description of Utah's finance system for public education, see Talbot 1973.)

In Utah, weighted-pupil measures are incorporated in a foundation plan. Mort's influence is clearly present in the Utah finance plan: he established the *largest* wealthy district as the key district on which the foundation program is based. This alteration eliminated the small, idiosyncratic district that was extremely wealthy. Such "freak" districts necessitated large amounts of state aid to support the foundation programs, assuming the richest district was chosen as the key district. Mort also adjusted the rate of local contribution downward so that almost all districts received some state aid.

By refining the task unit, Mort more accurately depicted the costs of educating a pupil. A higher degree of equalization is attained by this refinement, because the more accurate the description of the costs, the more appropriate the tax rate that produces the revenue.

Mort also provided local tax leeway which resulted in some stimulation of local expenditure. Larger amounts of state aid may serve to increase local expenditure, because localities do not entirely reduce spending as the state contribution increases.

In summary, Mort's refinements of the Strayer-Haig plan further the equalization objective by more accurately describing the costs of educating a pupil. They also promise a degree of local tax relief, but do not offset the overall tax burden of the Strayer-Haig plan when the key district is not the largest and wealthiest district. And they provide for the stimulation of local expenditures for education.

## The Percentage-Equalizing Approach

The *percentage-equalizing* grant is a device by which the state government shares in supplying funds to meet a locally determined volume of school expenditure. It is like a *matching grant* except that this term often is interpreted to mean dollar-for-dollar matching; under the percentage-equalizing grant, the state's share varies from one district to the next, being small in rich districts and large in poor districts.

In theory, the percentage-equalizing grant promises to attain equalization, local tax relief, and the stimulation of local expenditures. Equalization of tax burden is accomplished because all districts taxing themselves at a certain rate receive the same amount of state financial support (assuming the key district is the wealthiest district in the state). Each district determines its tax rate, and for each rate levied the state supplies a specific amount of aid, determined by the following formula:

$$Ai = (1 - C \cdot Yi \div Y)\, Ei,$$

where $Ai$ is the state grant to district i, $C$ is an arbitrary constant normally having a value of between 0 and 1, $1 - C$ is the percentage of the cost of local education services that the state is willing to pay,

$Yi$ is the assessed valuation per pupil in district i, and $Y$ is the assessed valuation per pupil of the key district. $Y$ is often calculated as the state average,

$$\frac{\Sigma Yi}{n}, i = 1, n.$$

$Ei$ is the school expenditure in district i.

The following example is adapted from Benson (1968, pp. 177-81):

Assume that a state is willing to pay 60 percent of the cost of local educational services $(1 - C = .60)$, that the key district is defined as the average per pupil assessed valuation in the state ($13,000), and that the expected per pupil revenue level is $500. The percentage of state aid to a poor district with $5,000 in per pupil wealth is calculated as follows:

$$1 - .40 \times \frac{5,000}{13,000},$$
$$1 - .40 \times .384,$$
$$1 - .154,$$
$$.846 \text{ or } 84.6\%.$$

At a uniform local tax rate of 1.54 percent, this relatively poor district can raise $77 per pupil of the $500. The state's share is 84.6 percent of $500, or $423.

Consider a relatively rich district ($30,000 in per pupil wealth) under the same circumstances. The state share in that district's budget is determined as follows:

$$1 - .40 \times \frac{30,000}{13,000},$$
$$1 - .40 \times 2.31,$$
$$1 - .924,$$
$$.076 \text{ or } 7.6\%.$$

At a uniform local tax rate of 1.54 percent, this relatively rich district can raise $462 per pupil of the $500. The state's share is 7.6 percent of $500, or $38.

Thus, a poor district, in levying a certain tax rate, receives the same amount of total funds as the key district would if it taxed itself at the same rate. Local tax relief is attained, for the level of expenditure in a district is directly related to the effort a community wishes to exert rather than to its tax base. In addition, a community can decide to increase its educational expenditure without undue economic hardship.

Where the percentage-equalizing grant has actually been implemented, however, the results leave much to be desired. First, the key district is the district with an average level of educational expenditure in the state. Thus, equalization of the tax burden cannot occur unless the rich districts pay into a state fund in order to adjust their wealth downward. No state using the percentage-equalizing grant has used this approach to equalization. Thus, every district taxing at a certain rate will receive in local and/or state funds only the amount of funds the key district can raise at the same rate. When more funds are needed, which is usually the case, districts richer than the key district can raise more revenue at a lower tax rate than poor districts. Generally then, the percentage-equalization approach has much the same effect as the foundation approach: when the key district is the average district, revenues are equalized only up to that point.

Another factor inhibiting total equalization is the provision in many percentage-equalizing plans (e.g., Rhode Island) for a minimum-aid ratio for every district in the state. Thus, both rich and poor districts are guaranteed state aid. This obviously benefits rich districts, since poor districts receive support under the equalizing program anyway.

Because the key district represents the average level of expenditure, and rich districts do not pay to the state excess funds, and a ceiling is usually imposed on state aid, equal expenditures among districts are assured only to the point where the costs of education are equalized by the formula. Expenditures beyond this point must be raised by the local property tax, and the advantages of rich districts in obtaining funds are obvious when it is known, for example, that in New York State in 1972-73 (which had a percentage-equalizing formula at the time) most districts expended more funds per student than the maximum level at which the state would provide reimbursement.

## The Power-Equalizing Approach

In recent years several alternative school finance plans have been developed that could serve as guides for a new system for financing public education. One such plan is district *power equalizing* (Coons, Clune, and Sugarman 1970). In the power-equalizing plan, instead of the educational offering being a function of effort alone, the legislature specifies a given revenue yield for a certain tax a district chooses to impose on itself. That is, whatever the amount of local collection, the district is permitted to spend per pupil only that amount fixed by statute for the tax rate locally chosen. The formula describing this plan amounts to a schedule of operating revenues guaranteed for different tax rates. For example,

| if a district taxes itself at: | it receives from the state: |
|---|---|
| less than 5 mills | no aid |
| between 5 and 14 mills | $700 plus $50 for each mill over 5 |
| between 15 and 25 mills | $1200 plus $25 for each mill over 15 |

Power equalizing promotes interdistrict equalization of tax burdens because each effort produces a specific amount of revenue for education. Power equalizing also promotes the stimulation of local expenditures because a community does not suffer economic hardship if it wants to increase its support of education. The effect of power equalizing on tax relief depends on the source of state revenue. If the state relies on the property tax, poor households bear a heavier burden than wealthy households because of the regressivity of the property tax.

A number of state legislatures have found the power-equalizing approach appealing in recent years, for several reasons. In addition to offering potential for great equalization of revenue, it does not place a rigid constraint on local effort, as do plans with uniform tax rates. Further, while not forcing districts to spend at a particular level, it can encourage them to do so. The sample formula presented above, for example, encourages all districts to spend at the level of $1,200 per pupil (by taxing themselves at 15 mills). For every mill added to the tax rate below 15 the district receives an extra $50 per pupil. But for every mill added to the tax rate above 15 the district receives only an extra $25 per pupil.

## The Philosophical Bases of State Aid Formulas

The philosophical bases of state assistance can be obscured by the objectives, mechanisms, and impact of the different approaches. Implicit in each of the finance plans is a set of objectives. In most plans the main objective is to reduce financial inequalities in per-pupil operating expenditures within school districts. In addition, the plans of Cubberley and Mort include the objective of promoting the expansion of educational offerings. A third objective implicit in several plans is local tax relief. It is apparent that some of these objectives can conflict with each other.

Clear-cut distinctions among the methodologies can best be expressed in terms of mechanisms. Certain plans provide for supplementation of local resources after the district taxes itself at a maximum level. In other plans, the dispensation of aid is tied to the kinds of expenditures incurred (e.g., number of teachers hired) or students served ("weighting" various classifications of pupils).

The impact of each of the formulas varies greatly in terms of the stated objectives. Failure to completely accomplish objectives usually can be traced to the particular administration of the formula rather than to the formula's abstract design. For example, the concept of leveling up to the key district could, in theory, accomplish the objective of equalizing expenditures. Making the key district an average district instead of the wealthiest district, however, precludes this.

There is an assumption which underlies the formulas discussed above: the benefits of public education do not accrue only to the individual who is educated. All the formulas imply that some of the benefits of education accrue to society. These social benefits may be described in terms of a more productive labor market, a citizenry more active in governmental affairs and less prone to criminal acts, etc. It is because of the perceived benefits to society that the state assumes some of the responsibility for funding education. The argument is that if the individual were solely responsible for purchasing his own education, without any state assistance, he would only consume enough to benefit himself, given the resources at his disposal. The state must subsidize education, thereby making it possible for the individual to receive enough to benefit society.

Acknowledging that society benefits in some ways by an individual's education, there are, nevertheless, different conceptions of the role of the state in contributing to public education. One is that the state is responsible for providing a minimum amount of education (defined in terms of course offerings, expenditure levels, or some other measure). That minimum amount is required of all students. Above that minimum amount, localities may purchase whatever additional educational resources they want. (Elements of this idea are found in the flat grant and the foundation plan approaches.)

Alternatively, the state may feel that a large proportion of the benefits of education accrue to society. Therefore, from the state's perspective education is very important, and all individuals should have equal access to all levels of education. This idea implies that the state is fully responsible for funding school operations rather than for developing funding plans which permit variations in revenue among localities.

Finally, the state may feel that the social benefits of education are large but that local control is also important. The state's position in this conflict is to guarantee each locality which taxes itself at a particular rate the same amount of revenue for education (the power-equalizing and percentage-equalizing approaches).

## Allocating Resources to Schools Within a District

Use of previously determined allocation formulas is not necessarily synonymous with "lack of sensitivity to individual needs," "centralized management," or "absence of involvement in decision making." Allocation formulas can be tailored to suit different school management styles. In fact, most school districts with more than a few school sites have developed their own inventory of formulas for allocating resources. Moreover, these formulas vary depending on who has responsibility for which decision. Consider three hypothetical school districts, each with a different strategy for determining how resources are allocated. For our discussion, the three strategies are called *site-budget approval, line allocation formulas,* and *total resource allocation formulas.*

### Site-Budget Approval

This method involves the development by the building staff of a budget for virtually all its projected needs for the coming year. This budget is submitted to the central office and then modified on the basis of negotiation between site and central office staff. The budget (and subsequent operation) of each site is unique because it is negotiated without reference to the other sites. This model has the advantage of being particularly sensitive to the needs and objectives of each school.

Site-budget approval requires the development of site plans and programs. Also, it consumes a lot of administrative time in negotiations. Further, the ability of a school to secure resources often depends on the building principal's ability to negotiate a favorable budget, which can result in great variation among schools in terms of ratios such as dollars per pupil. School principals compete for scarce resources, and the "winners" may not be those with the greatest need but those with the greatest persuasive ability.

## Line Allocation Formulas

This method is much more prevalent in school districts. A different formula is used for each of the major budgetary items found in a school building. Examples of the items and allocation formulas are listed in table 12.10. Each formula refers to a major "line" in a school budget. Some items are allocated on a one-per-school basis (e.g., librarians). Others are based on the number of children enrolled in each school (e.g., other expenses of instruction). In some cases the formula is not apparent because only the results of the formula are indicated (e.g., custodians).

Although the buildings principals and staff of each of the schools in this district may have ultimate responsibility for program development, the central office is clearly responsible for determining the mix of resource inputs in the schools. If the formulas are adhered to, each school will have its share of each type of resource.

If instructional programs can be described as components in budget lines, then a school plans and operates programs within a given distribution of such components. A chief argument for allocating resources this way is equal treatment; another is ease of administration. Personnel projections are more easily made; there is less negotiation in staffing schools; and at the school level, less planning is necessary because much of the budget request each year is predetermined.

The primary arguments against the use of these formulas are the reverse of the arguments for them. Equal treatment, for example, is a double-edged sword; there are possible circumstances that argue the benefits of unequal treatment. Consider how variation of the following among schools in a district would affect education:

1. Age and condition of the building
2. Utilization rates
3. Student turnover rate
4. School location
5. Community expectations
6. Staff performance
7. Instructional program

There are many variables that could make the operating circumstances of a particular school unique. How, then, can the need to consider the unique requirements of individual schools be reconciled with the equally worthy goals of avoiding favoritism in allocation and reducing administrative work as much as possible?

## Table 12.10: Line Allocation Formulas for Selected School Accounts

| Account code | Account description | Formula |
|---|---|---|
| 210 | Instructional salaries | |
| 211 | Principals' salaries | One principal and three vice-principals in each school, except as designated in article VI, section 11-C, page 62, of the Board Policy Manual. |
| 212 | Supervisors' salaries | One curriculum assistant for two periods each day in school. District personnel as determined by Board of Trustees. |
| 213 | Teachers' salaries | |
| 213.1 | Regular certificated staff | A ratio of one certificated staff member for every 22 students except as follows: School A, 21.5; School B, 19.5. The following assignments are exempt from the above ratio and are in addition to basic staff allowance: special education, driver training, curriculum assistant, and teachers given out-of-class assignments by the superintendent of schools. Students enrolled in classes exempt from ratio formula should be deducted from total enrollment figures. Non-teaching activities are deducted from above figure and budgeted under 214. |
| 214 | Other certificated salaries of instruction | |
| 214.1 | Librarians' salaries | A certificated librarian for each school on basis of actual placement on salary schedule. |
| 214.2 | Counselors' salaries | One hour of counseling time for every 75 students. Total counseling salaries are part of basic ratio in 213.1. |
| 220 | Classified salaries of instruction | |
| 221 | Regular clerical salaries | The following are maximum allowances: Five secretaries and clerks (including mimeo clerk) are allowed as basic staff for each school up to 1,000 enrollment. One of above clerks to be assigned as school treasurer. Add one-fifth time of clerical person for each 100 students in excess of 1,000. Library staff is assigned on basis of formula allowing for two classified persons for each school as basic staff and one-fifth time of clerical person for each additional 200 students in excess of 1,000 up to total enrollment of 2,000. Maximum clerical staff for school of 1,000 is 9. Maximum clerical staff for school of 2,000 is 13. |
| 222 | Student clerical salaries | Maximum allowance for student clerks for all services should not exceed 80 cents for each student enrolled. Maximum allowance for school of 2,000 enrollment is $1,600. |
| 230 | Textbooks | Maximum allowance of $4.00 per student plus $250.00 for book replacement, plus $6.50 per unit of growth over previous year for new schools that have not previously reached capacity. This allowance may be adjusted by borrowing from or adding to the 240 account. The combined total for the two accounts should not exceed the combined allowance for each account. |

| 290 | Other expenses of instruction | Total maximum allowance for each school based on the following allowance for each student enrolled: School A, $22.50; School B, $22.50; School C, $22.50; School D, $22.50; School E, $25.50; School F, $28.50; plus additional allowance of $5.00 per unit of growth over previous year in new schools that have not previously reached capacity. Include in the above allowances for attendance office. Additional allowance for conventions as established by administrative policy, article VI, section 1-D. Allow $300 additional for EMR classes and allow for blind students on basis of previous experience. |
| 400 | Health service | A full-time nurse in each school. |
| 410 | Certificated salaries of health personnel | Allow 15 cents per unit of enrollment. |
| 490 | Other expense of health service | |
| 600 | Operation of school plant | |
| 610-620 | Classified salaries of operation Gardening salaries | Two gardeners assigned to each school. District staff to consist of a gardener, foreman, three equipment operators, a gardener leadman, and five gardeners, for a total of ten. |
| 730 | Replacement of equipment | Not to exceed five percent of total assessed value of school equipment as reflected on inventory of previous fiscal year. Limitations are placed on school total and not on departmental figures. If total inventory values are not available, limitation of $4.00 per unit of enrollment. Individual items to be listed. |
| 791 | Repairs of buildings | Based on survey of needs as shown on work requests but limited to a total cost of $15.00 per unit of enrollment. |
| 793 | Repair of equipment | Based on survey of actual need as reflected on work request and experience of previous years but not to exceed a total cost of $3.50 per unit of enrollment. |

One somewhat questionable alternative is to build more complex formulas. Consider school secretaries and clerks. In table 12.10 they are allocated as a function of enrollment (five per 1,000 enrollment plus one-fifth per 100 over 1,000 enrollment). By looking at what they do, however, we can see that the need for secretaries and clerks is a function of many things: the number of calls received per day; the curriculum development activities of the faculty; whether the mimeograph machine in the school is fast or slow; whether the principal's secretary "covers" for the principal because he or she is heavily involved in activities that require absence from school; whether the secretaries have to help the attendance and book clerks because the school has a high turnover rate. To make them more sensitive to the idiosyncratic needs of each school, formulas must take more things into consideration.

Although more complex formulas would, by definition, be sensitive to more variables, this approach may not be practical for several reasons. First, more complex formulas are more difficult to administer. Specifically, more data is required to determine the status of each school site. Second, more complex formulas are more sensitive to structural changes in the district and therefore require more frequent modification and updating. Third, more complex formulas involve more "exceptions" that must be negotiated between the central office and the building staff, which leads back to the first model of pure negotiation (site-budget approval).

## Total Resource Allocation Formulas

This approach represents an attempt to combine the advantages of the other two models while minimizing their disadvantages. In its general form, the total resource allocation formula is composed of units of expenditures which are allocated to school sites. After setting an expenditure level for each school, the school building-level staff determines the proportion of the appropriated sum that is to be spent for each line item in the budget. The following example may clarify how this approach works. For the sake of brevity the example is limited to personnel allocation to high schools in a district.

All personnel allocations to the high schools in XYZ School District are made in units, a unit being equivalent to the average annual salary of a high school teacher. A single allotment of units provides for all personnel services, instructional and support, for each school.

The formula for the distribution of units in specific high schools is in four parts: support services; basic instruction and supervision; additional support services for pupils reading at least two years below grade level; and a discrete allotment for optional programs and special needs.

1. *Support services.* A constant twenty units is allocated to each school for minimum services common to all schools regardless of size. This is to provide the basic organizational structure, such as a principal and a minimum number of supportive positions. In addition, each school will be allocated eight units per 1,000 pupils for registers in excess of 1,000, with a maximum of thirty-five units. This provides additional support services for larger high schools. From this formula, School A is allocated 44 units. (See sample computation in exhibit 12.11.)

## Exhibit 12.11: Computing Personnel Units for Support Services

Two schools of 2,000 and 4,000 pupils respectively would receive 20 units each, plus 8 for the 2,000-pupil school and 24 for the 4,000-pupil school.

$$\text{School of 2,000 pupils:} \quad \frac{8\,(2,000 - 1,000)}{1,000} \quad = \quad 8 \text{ units additional}$$

$$\text{Total:} \quad 8 + 20 \quad = 28 \text{ units for support services}$$

$$\text{School of 4,000 pupils:} \quad \frac{8\,(4,000 - 1,000)}{1,000} \quad = 24 \text{ units additional}$$

$$\text{Total:} \quad 24 + 20 \quad = 44 \text{ units for support services}$$

2. *Basic instruction and supervision.* The formula to calculate the number of units for this area is:

$$\frac{1.05 \times \text{weighted estimated register} \times \text{weighted daily pupil load}}{\text{average class size} \times \text{number of academic or basic instruction periods per day}}.$$

Based on experience in the district, a constant of 1.05 is written into the formulas to provide for relief periods for the assistant principals in charge of supervision. The weighted estimated register is the total number of pupils estimated to be in the school, some of whom have been given special weightings because of their characteristics. In one example there are only two types of students: regular students, whose weight is 1.0, and students reading more than 0 but less than 2 years below grade level, whose weight is 1.07. Of the 3,000 pupils who will be at the high school next year 1,000 will be reading at least two years below grade level.

The weighted daily pupil load is the principal's estimate of the daily average number of periods per pupil required for next year's programming. The subjects are weighted for varying contractual class size maximums:

| | |
|---|---|
| Academic | 1.00 |
| Physical education and music | 0.68 |
| Industrial arts and home economics | 1.22 |

See table 12.12 for computation of the weighted pupil daily load, and exhibit 12.13 for computation of units for basic instruction and supervision.

### Table 12.12: Calculating Weighted Pupil Daily Load

| Subject | Factor | Proportion of daily load | Weighted number |
|---|---|---|---|
| Academic | 1.00 | 4 | 4.00 |
| Physical education and music | 0.68 | 1 | 0.68 |
| Industrial arts and home economics | 1.22 | 1 | 1.32 |
| Weighted daily load | | 6 | 6.10 |

### Exhibit 12.13: Computation of Units for Basic Instruction and Supervision

Given:

School register: 3,000 pupils (2,000 regular + 1,000 with between 0 and 2 years of reading retardation)

Average daily pupil load: 6 periods (1 physical education or music, plus 1 industrial arts or home economics, plus 4 academic subjects)

Weighted register: $2,000 + (1,000 \times 1.07) = 3,070$

Computation:

$$\text{Units} = \frac{\text{relief factor} \times \text{weighted register} \times \text{weighted daily pupil load}}{\text{average class size} \times \text{number of academic or basic instruction periods per day}}$$

$$= \frac{1.05 \times 3070 \times 6.10}{32 \times 4}$$

$$= 153.6 \text{ or } 154$$

3. *Additional support services for pupils reading at least two years below grade level.* This part of the formula is based on perceived needs for services such as guidance and remedial reading. For every 100 severely retarded readers in the school an additional 1.64 are

allocated. For example, 200 severely retarded readers would qualify a school for an additional 3.28 or, rounded off, 3 units.

4. *Discrete allotment for optional programs and special needs.* This part of the formula is initiated at the request of the school and the discretion of the superintendent. A certain amount of the total allotment of units (say, 3 percent) is set into this category for distribution to specific schools on an application basis.

The number of units available to School A would be determined by totaling the units to which it is entitled under each of the four formulas above. In the example we have been using, assume the school qualified for no units under the fourth formula; it would be credited with 44 + 154 + 3 = 201 personnel units.

Once building administrators know the number of personnel units that are allocated to them, they can plan, cooperatively or otherwise, the staffing patterns best suited to the individual needs of their schools. This model allows the superintendent broad discretion.

A sampling of titles and conversion factors of people who might be employed in a large high school is shown in exhibit 12.14. If

## Exhibit 12.14: School Personnel Conversion Factors (Weighted Unit Value of Sample Titles)

Pedagogic titles

| | |
|---|---|
| Principal | 2.1 |
| Assistant principal | 1.4 |
| Guidance counselor | 1.1 |
| Teacher (basic unit) | 1.0 |
| Laboratory specialist | 0.8 |
| School secretary | 0.7 |
| Sub. school secretary interns | 0.4 |
| Industrial arts technician | 0.5 |

Administrative titles

| | |
|---|---|
| Account clerk | 0.4 |
| Accountant | 0.7 |
| Accountant (assistant) | 0.6 |
| Accountant (senior) | 0.8 |
| Administrative assistant | 0.8 |
| Assistant stockman | 0.4 |
| Budget examiner | 1.0 |
| Business officer | 0.9 |
| Clerk | 0.4 |
| District business officer (fiscal and accounting) | 1.0 |
| Machinist helper | 0.8 |
| Nurse's aide | 0.5 |
| Senior audio-visual technician | 0.7 |
| Senior human resources specialist | 0.8 |
| Senior intergroup relations officer | 0.7 |
| Special officer | 0.6 |
| Stockman | 0.6 |

**Exhibit 12.14** *(continued)*

| | |
|---|---|
| Paraprofessional hourly employees | |
| Educational assistant | 0.2 |
| Family assistant | 0.2 |
| Family worker | 0.2 |
| Health service aide | 0.2 |
| Junior neighborhood worker | 0.4 |
| School aide | 0.2 |
| School neighborhood worker | 0.3 |
| Senior school neighborhood worker | 0.7 |
| Teacher aide | 0.2 |
| Per-session personnel | |
| Major non-athletic extracurricular (per 2 hour session) | .0015 |
| School secretary (per day) | |
| Summer service | .003 |
| Peak load | .003 |

School A was allocated 201 personnel units, for example, the program would be staffed with a number of different job types, the total "value" of which would be 201 units.

Although subject to constraints of unions and the "politics of planning," principals and faculty have greater staffing flexibility under site budgeting than when each personnel type is allocated individually to schools. This leads to a final observation on the use of formulas and negotiation in budgeting: although formulas are developed primarily for ease of administration, the presence of complex allocation formulas is not necessarily synonymous with centralized planning and decision making.

## Questions for Review and Discussion

1. Are the philosophical assumptions behind a district power equalizing state aid plan different from those behind a foundation state aid plan?

2. Is it possible for the distributional effects of the state aid finance plans discussed in this chapter to be identical for a given state? If so, choose two alternative state aid formulas and cite the conditions necessary for making the distributional effects the same.

3. In what ways could state assistance based on weighted pupil measures affect the operation and expenditure patterns of school districts?

4. What assumptions about building principals underlie each of the three allocation strategies discussed in this chapter: site-budget approval, line allocation formulas, and total resource allocation formulas?

5. In what ways, if any, does the allocation of resources to colleges and departments within a university differ from allocating resources to buildings within a school district?

## References

Benson, Charles S. *The Economics of Public Education.* Boston: Houghton Mifflin, 1968.

Coons, John; Clune, William; and Sugarman, Stephen. *Private Wealth and Public Education.* Cambridge, Mass.: Harvard University Press, 1970.

Cubberley, Ellwood P. *School Funds and Their Apportionment.* New York: Teachers College, Columbia University, 1906.

Mort, Paul R.; Reusser, Walter C.; and Polley, John W. *Public School Finance.* Third edition. New York: McGraw-Hill, 1960.

New York State Commission on the Quality, Cost, and Financing of Elementary and Secondary Education. *Report.* Vol. 1. New York: The Commission, 1972.

President's Commission on School Finance. *Schools, People, and Money.* Washington, D.C.: The Commission, 1972.

Stabu, Frederick W. "Court Decisions and the Financing of Education." *Theory into Practice* II, no. 2 (April 1972): pp. 27-38.

Strayer, George, and Haig, Robert. *Financing of Education in the State of New York.* New York: MacMillan, 1923.

Sugarman, Stephen D. "The Current System of Financing Public Education in California." *Equality of Educational Opportunities,* edited by Guilbert C. Hentschke, pp. 17-45. Denver: Department of Education, 1972.

Talbot, Walter. "Utah's School Finance Program." *Financing Educational Opportunity,* edited by Guilbert C. Hentschke, pp. 57-82. Denver: Department of Education, 1973.

Updegraff, Harlan, and King, Leroy A. *Survey of the Fiscal Policies of the State of Pennsylvania in the Field of Education.* Philadelphia: University of Pennsylvania, 1922.

## Related Readings

Barkin, E., and Hettich, W. "The Elementary and Secondary Education Act: A Distributional Analysis." ERIC, no. ED022244, 1969. This study analyzes interstate redistribution of federal tax money under Title One ESEA of 1965.

Harris, Marshall A. "Description and Analysis of the Process and Methodology of a School Finance Study in Florida." ERIC, no. ED084698, 1974. This document examines the study team organization, their methods of data collection and analysis, and their recommendations for school finance reform. Included are recommendations that might be useful in setting up state school finance studies.

Keyserling, Leon H. "Achieving Nationwide Educational Excellence. A Ten Year Plan to Save the Schools." ERIC, no. ED033879, 1970. This document reports the results of a study that examined the needs of the public schools during the decade ahead, and proposed a plan by which federal, state, and local resources can be marshalled to meet these needs.

Swanson, Austin D. "Full State Funding vs. Power Equalizing." ERIC, no. ED082360, 1974. This paper examines the merits of a district power equalizing formula when it is compared to full state funding of a uniform expenditure level.

Washington State Legislature. "Remote and Necessary." ERIC, no. ED053839, 1971. This report reviews Washington's 1965 apportionment formula, which used weighting factors that provided additional state funds resulting from the operations of small districts.

# 13
# Linear Programming

*Linear programming* (LP) is a general mathematical model that can be used to allocate scarce resources among competing activities, within given constraints, in order to attain certain objectives. Possible objectives are (1) to maximize the number of students taught within a given budget constraint; (2) to minimize instructional expenses given the costs of various factors and a minimum number of students; or (3) to minimize the distance students have to travel, given the distances between homes and schools, the capacities of schools, and racial balance constraints. (Linear programming was used to solve this problem in chapter six.) These examples show how it is possible to include and vary a number of constraints.

Educators have been slow in making use of linear programming for several reasons. It is a relatively new tool, and there has not been much time for educational applications to be developed. Very few educators have become acquainted with this tool during their professional training programs. The mathematicians or computer programmers needed to provide solutions to linear programming problems have not been generally available to educators.

Probably the most important reason for the limited use of linear programming, and the improbability of a change in the future, is the inability or reluctance of educators to express the goals of educational programs in terms that can be measured objectively and to relate these goals to contributing factors. This is a prerequisite for linear programming techniques. However, expressing goals in terms that can be measured objectively is not easy, and even when the goals can be appropriately expressed, it is difficult to establish relationships between them and the decision variables that contribute to their fulfillment.

The function of this chapter, then, is to acquaint the reader with the general form of linear programming and the areas where it has proven useful, so that problems amenable to such treatment can be recognized. The mathematics of linear programming are not stressed here, because linear programming problems are not usually solved by educational managers in isolation. Rather, they work with staff analysts who are responsible for solving such problems. Moreover, a number of previously written, or "canned," computer programs exist at many computer installations to alleviate the somewhat tedious work of solving mathematical programming problems.

Linear programming is applicable when a program is directed toward some measurable goal. The program must also conform to certain criteria, or constraints. What are some educational goals that are amenable to linear programming? Exhibit 13.1 lists some examples.

## Exhibit 13.1: Education Goals Amenable to Linear Programming Model

Maximize:
   1. Student achievement
   2. Teacher experience
   3. Teacher training
   4. Time for instruction
   5. Availability of instructional materials
   6. Utilization of facilities
   7. Opportunity for extracurricular activities
   8. Subject offerings
   9. Nutritional value of school lunches
Minimize:
   1. Cost of
      a. total education
      b. school lunches
      c. facilities
      d. transportation
      e. interest on bonds
      f. equipment and supplies
   2. Pupil-teacher ratio
   3. Transportation time
   4. Dropouts
   5. Distance students must travel to school
   6. Distance students must travel between classes
   7. Class size
   8. Underachievers

Source: Ralph A. Van Dusseldorp, Duane E. Richardson, and Walter J. Foley, *Educational Decision-Making through Operations Research* (Boston: Allyn & Bacon, 1971), p. 64. Reprinted by permission.

Clearly, some of the goals listed in this exhibit are more easily related to contributing factors than others. For example, minimizing transportation time is more amenable to LP modeling than maximizing student achievement simply because the "causes" of transportation time are much more clearly understood than the "causes" of student achievement. Unless a rather precise statement can be made about factors contributing to a goal, linear programming is probably not the appropriate tool. Whether it is appropriate or not will usually become apparent during the attempt to formulate a linear programming model of the problems.

Smythe and Johnson list the following steps in formulating linear programming models:

A. Recognition of the problem
B. Formulation of the mathematical model
  1. Identification of the decision variables
  2. Choice of a measure of effectiveness
  3. Symbolic representation of the objective function
  4. Identification of the constraints
  5. Algebraic representation of the constraints
C. Estimation of the parameters of the model (Smythe and Johnson 1966, p. 187)

Once these steps have been accomplished, the problem is relatively easily solved with linear programming. (Either a solution is provided or it is determined that the problem as stated does not have a feasible solution.) The major difficulty in linear programming lies in the formulation of the problem, not in the solution. Perhaps one of the best ways to see how linear programming works is to take one very simple problem and walk through graphic and algebraic solutions. Though a problem of the type outlined below would usually be solved using high school level algebra, it is useful here for describing the steps involved in setting up and solving a more complex linear programming problem.

### Example 1: Mathematics Instruction in the Midville School District

Midville School District has at least 6,000 students who must be taught new math next school year. The local teachers' union has come up with a team teaching program in math that will handle a class of sixty students at a cost of $24,000 a year. The teams will provide individualized, continuous progress instruction to all competency levels of students.

It has come to the attention of a school board member that Behavioral Research Services has also developed a program for instruction in mathematics. The BRS team is composed of a teacher, a teacher's aide, and a computer-based student information system. This instructional system is advertised as being able to teach a class of fifty students the same material as the union teacher team at a cost of $18,000. (It is also "individualized," etc.)

The board member got unanimous consent from the other board members to try some BRS teams. The union, however, after some hard bargaining, got the board to agree to two stipulations: first, the number of union teacher teams must be at least equal to the number of BRS teams; second, no matter what, at least seventy union teacher teams must be hired.

The superintendent must recommend how many teams of each type should be hired. In addition to the above constraints, the recommendation should be for as inexpensive a program as possible. What should be the recommendation?

## Formulation of the Problem

A. *Recognition of the problem.* Having read the problem the superintendent has a strong hunch that it can be formulated as a linear programming problem. Why? The problem has "competing activities" (two instructional teams in math) among which we "optimize the allocation of scarce resources" (money), subject to certain "constraints" (e.g., at least 6,000 students, at least 70 union teacher teams).

B. *Formulation of the mathematical model.*

1. Decision variables. What must be decided is how many of each kind of team to hire. Therefore, let $X_1$ equal the number of BRS teams and $X_2$ equal the number of union teams.

2. Measure of effectiveness. The optimum decision will be the least costly one. Therefore, the measure of effectiveness will be in terms of dollars.

3. Objective function. Given 2, the objective function will be to minimize cost $(Z)$. The cost will be the unit price of $X_1$ times $X_1$ plus the unit price of $X_2$ times $X_2$. The unit price of the BRS team is $18,000 ($A_1$ equals $18,000$), and the unit price of the union team is $24,000 ($A_2$ equals $24,000$). Therefore, the objective function is

$$Z = A_1 X_1 + A_2 X_2 \text{ (dollars).}$$

4. Identify constraints. Three constraints can be identified. First, mathematics instruction must be provided for at least 6,000

students. Second, it was stipulated that the number of BRS teams be less than or equal to the number of union teams. Third, it was stipulated that at least seventy union teams be hired. There is a fourth, implicit, constraint that says that $X_1$ and $X_2$ cannot be less than zero. (The superintendent cannot hire, for example, minus three BRS teams.)

5. Algebraic representation of constraints. These constraints can be written as follows:

$$C_1 X_1 + C_2 X_2 = 6{,}000 \text{ students,}$$

where $C_1$ equals students taught by one BRS team (50) and $C_2$ equals students taught by one union team (60);

$$X_1 \leqslant X_2 \text{ (instructional teams);}$$
$$X_2 \geqslant 70 \text{ (instructional teams); and}$$
$$X_1 \geqslant \text{zero, } X_2 \geqslant \text{zero.}$$

C. *Estimation of the parameters of the model.* This brings the superintendent to the last (and in many LP applications, the most difficult) step in formulating the problem, estimating the parameters of the model. This involves assigning numeric values to the parameters $a_1$, $a_2$ ... $a_n$, i.e., determining just how much effect a unit of each of the decision variables will have on the object variable. In this particular example, the values of the parameters are known ($A_1$ equals \$18,000 and $A_2$ equals \$24,000). However, if the problem were one of maximizing achievement (instead of minimizing costs), the objective function would be stated in terms of achievement, and it would have to be determined how much a unit of each type of team would contribute to achievement (rather than how much a unit of each type of team would cost). In some cases, the effect can be judged by past experience and research. In other cases, objective evidence will not be available and the subjective judgment of educators will have to be used to estimate the effect.

## Solution of the Problem

Once the educational administrator has gone through the preceding steps of formulating the problem, it is ready to be solved. Most linear programming problems are solved using computer assistance. The computer program will probably solve the problem by an algebraic method called the simplex technique. (An explanation of how the simplex technique works can be found in most textbooks that deal with linear programming explicitly or with operations research generally. See, for example, Dantzig 1963, pp. 95-119; Thierauf and Grose 1970, pp. 239-58.)

Although we will not go through the mathematics of the simplex technique here, it is important for the educational manager to have a general idea about how LP problems are solved. This can be better communicated by solving a simple problem graphically. Although limiting the analyst to problems that can be graphed (two decision variables), graphing is one of the better ways to communicate generally, if somewhat abstractly, how LP problems are solved.

Four steps are usually involved in graphic solutions.

1. Set up a grid with $X_1$ values on one axis and $X_2$ values on the other. Figure 13.2 shows the range of possible numbers of BRS teams on the $Y$ axis (i.e., the possible values of $X_1$). On the $X$ axis is the range of possible numbers of union teams (i.e., possible values of $X_2$).

2. Graph the constraints and determine the area of feasible solutions. The constraints of the problem can be represented as lines on the grid (see figure 13.2). Graphing *inequalities* or boundaries is not precisely like graphing *equations*. In linear programming a feasible solution must be on a line or to one side of it *but not the other*. Small arrows are drawn for each of the constraints indicating which side of each line represents a feasible solution, given only that one constraint. Once all of the constraints are drawn it is possible to determine if there is a feasible solution to the problem, i.e., if there is any area remaining on the graph that has not been ruled out with constraints. In this problem there is a feasible solution. It is an area on the feasible side of each constraint line. In fact, the area of the feasible solutions in this problem is unbounded. A bounded solution is constrained on all sides. (Unless otherwise noted, constraints will be referred to as equations even though some may technically be termed inequalities.)

What the educational manager has at this point is many possible solutions from which to choose. (Without an area of feasible solutions the problem would be unsolvable. If, for example, we changed the constraints $X_2 \geqslant 70$ to $X_2 \leqslant 40$, we would have an unsolvable problem, because no point on the graph would satisfy all the constraints.) The next step represents a way to select an optimum solution from among the feasible solutions.

3. Graph a cost relationship between the two decision variables (instructional strategies) at an arbitrarily determined dollar amount. In other words, draw an equal-cost curve between the two variables.

**Figure 13.2: Constraints and Feasible-Solution Area**

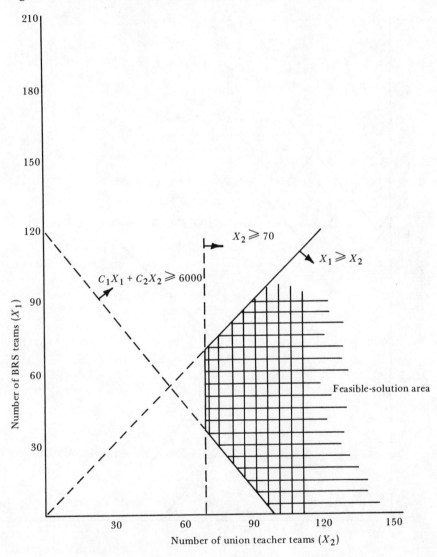

In figure 13.3, several equal-cost curves have been superimposed on the feasible-solution area. One of these, representing an expenditure of $3.6 million, is a line through those points on the graph that represent different combinations of the two instructional strategies that would cost that much. A second line on the graph represents the

## Figure 13.3: Equal-Cost Curves

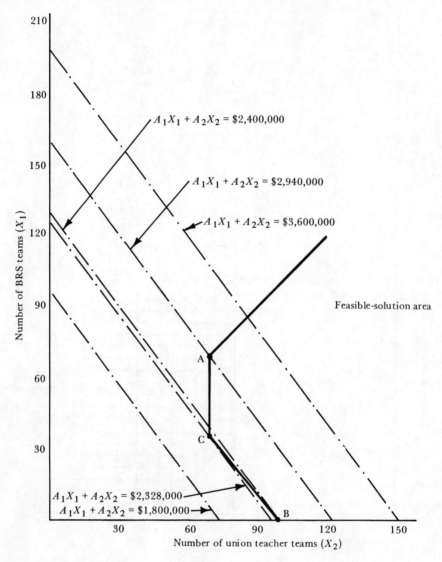

product combinations at an equal cost of $1.8 million. This line does not pass through the feasible-solution area and is therefore not a solution to this problem. Notice that the smaller the dollar amount of the equal-cost line, the closer it is to the origin of the graph (0, 0) and that all of the equal-cost lines have the same slope.

4. Move the cost relationship line toward the origin as far as it can go and still stay within the feasible-solution area. Remembering that the optimum solution is one that costs the least, the problem is solved graphically by drawing equal-cost lines closer and closer to the origin while staying within the feasible-solution area.

As equal-cost curves are drawn that represent increasingly smaller amounts of money, it is not necessary to examine all possibilities. In fact, as shown in figure 13.3, it is necessary to consider only those points of intersection of the graphed constraints (A, B, C). The optimum solution will be at one of these points (in which case there is a *unique optimum* solution), or there will be an infinite number of optimum solutions, which will lie along one of the lines passing through one or more of these points.

Because of this, the third equal-cost line is constructed to pass through point A ($2.9 million). However, it is possible to draw a "less cost" equal-cost curve through point B ($2.4 million) and still be in the feasible-solution area. Finally, the "least cost" equal-cost curve that still lies within the feasible-solution area ($2,328,000) is isolated at point C. At this point the educational manager finds that by hiring seventy union teams and thirty-six BRS teams, the least-cost solution that satisfies the constraints is found (the combination will be able to service at least 6,000 students; there are at least as many union teams as BRS teams; and there are at least seventy union teams).

Even with the optimum solution to the problem, the superintendent may well wish to analyze it further. One way is to perform sensitivity analysis on the problem. This can be done by systematically varying the constraints (for example, changing $X_2 \geqslant 70$ to $X_2 \geqslant 60$, 55, 50, 45 . . .) and seeing how the changes affect the final decision.

Although the steps of formulating a problem have been described earlier, only one, relatively simple, problem has been examined here. To understand the possibilities of linear programming it is necessary to look at a range of LP applications. Two examples of linear programming applied to transportation are presented in chapter six. Two other applications are described below. One deals with minimizing the costs of a salary schedule which is composed of several compensation factors. The second involves minimizing deviations between goals in a higher education organization and what can actually be achieved within a given set of constraints. Other applications are mentioned in the section on Related Readings.

## Example 2: Salary Schedules in Elementary-Secondary Education
## (adapted from Bruno 1969)

In this application, linear programming is used to develop an alternative to the "step and column" method of determining salaries of certificated personnel in elementary-secondary education, a method which rewards only two characteristics of the individual: years of experience and number of units of graduate credit. The model described permits a number of other relevant factors to be incorporated in the salary schedule in a manner which is internally consistent. The objective function in this case is to minimize the cost of rewarding personnel on the basis of these factors, subject to a variety of constraints.

To set this problem up, five steps are required: (1) identifying salary hierarchy by job classifications; (2) defining important compensation factors for each function; (3) determining values and weights for each factor; (4) specifying constraints; and (5) specifying the objective function.

### Salary Hierarchy

One basis (of many) for determining which job should be compensated at a higher rate than another is to look at the scope of an individual's responsibility (e.g., a district, a school, a department, a class, or a student). Approximately corresponding jobs would be superintendents, principals, department heads, teachers, and teacher aides. This hierarchy of responsibility is also the general hierarchy for compensation (e.g., principals usually make more than teachers).

### Compensation Factors

This step could constitute a major departure from current compensation practices. As stated earlier, most elementary-secondary salary schedules consider only years of experience and number of graduate credit hours. Other school districts supplement this with a list of "extra assignments," each of which is compensated at a specific dollar amount. This step, essentially, requires an administrative answer to the following question: "What characteristics of individuals or their job make them worth more to the school district?" There is obviously not a universally acceptable answer to this question.

Nine factors affecting an individual's compensation are suggested in the example described here:

1. The type of area in which the school is located $(X_1)$;
2. The subject matter being taught $(X_2)$;

3. Supervisory responsibilities $(X_3)$;

4. The highest academic degree earned $(X_4)$;

5. Years of work experience $(X_5)$;

6. Special distinctions or awards $(X_6)$;

7. Number of college units completed beyond the highest degree earned $(X_7)$;

8. Number of in-service hours earned $(X_8)$; and

9. The additional workload (relative to others in the same job classification) $(X_9)$.

These represent several of the unknowns that will be solved once the entire problem is set up. The values of $X_1$ through $X_9$ will be the dollar worth of one unit of each factor. This is explained below.

## Values and Weights of Factors

In addition to specifying each factor, it is necessary to determine the values over which that factor can range. Consider for example, $X_4$, highest degree attained. The values over which that factor could range are: Ph.D. or Ed.D., M.A., M.Ed., B.A. or B.S., or A.A. In this case the lowest value is A.A. and the highest is Ph.D. or Ed.D.

It still must be determined how much more one degree is worth than another. Is an M.Ed. worth twice as much as a B.A.?, as an A.A.?, and so on. In the example the relative weights assigned to the values of this factor are as follows:

| Weight | Degree |
|--------|--------|
| 5 | Ph.D. or Ed.D. |
| 4 | M.A. |
| 3 | M.Ed. |
| 2 | B.A. or B.S. |
| 1 | A.A. |

This weighting implies that a doctorate is worth five times as much as an A.A. degree, but only one and one-fourth as much as an M.A. degree. The values and weights for the nine variables used in this example are shown in table 13.4.

In this table, the number of employees possessing each value for each factor are multiplied by each weight for the value to get a weight for that value and a weighted total for each factor. For example, for factor $X_6$, special awards, there are thirty-six employees with such awards and 1,350 without them. The number with awards is multipled by its appropriate weight ($36 \times 1 = 72$) and the number without awards is multiplied by its appropriate weight($1,350 \times 1 =$

## Table 13.4: Factors Included in the Model*

| Factor | Variables | Relative weight and characteristics | | Number of employees possessing this characteristic | Weighted total for each characteristic |
|---|---|---|---|---|---|
| Learning environment | $X_1$ | 3 | Difficult | 220 | 660 |
| | | 2 | Medium | 1166 | 2332 |
| | | 1 | Easy | 0 | 0 |
| | | | | | 2992 |
| Subject matter or special skills | $X_2$ | 3 | High priority | 236 | 708 |
| | | 2 | Medium | 1015 | 2030 |
| | | 1 | Low priority | 135 | 135 |
| | | | | | 2873 |
| Supervisory responsibility | $X_3$ | 7 | Single district wide | 2 | 7 |
| | | 6 | District wide | 5 | 30 |
| | | 5 | Simple school wide | 5 | 25 |
| | | 4 | School wide | 25 | 100 |
| | | 3 | Department wide | 90 | 270 |
| | | 2 | Class wide | 1200 | 2400 |
| | | 1 | Student | 60 | 60 |
| | | | | | 2892 |
| Highest academic degree attained | $X_4$ | 5 | Ph.D. or Ed.d. | 20 | 100 |
| | | 4 | M.A. | 120 | 480 |
| | | 3 | M.Ed. | 1100 | 3300 |
| | | 2 | B.A. | 1100 | 2200 |
| | | 1 | A.A. | 46 | 46 |
| | | | | | 6126 |
| Work experience | $X_5$ | 7 | 12-  years | 16 | 112 |
| | | 6 | 10-12 years | 100 | 600 |
| | | 5 | 8-10 years | 300 | 1500 |
| | | 4 | 4- 8 years | 400 | 1600 |
| | | 3 | 4- 6 years | 500 | 1500 |
| | | 2 | 2- 4 years | 50 | 100 |
| | | 1 | 0- 2 years | 20 | 20 |
| | | | | | 5432 |
| Special awards and distinctions | $X_6$ | 2 | with | 36 | 72 |
| | | 1 | without | 1350 | 1350 |
| | | | | | 1422 |
| College credits completed in addition to degree | $X_7$ | 5 | 28-  units | 600 | 3000 |
| | | 4 | 22-28 units | 500 | 2000 |
| | | 3 | 15-21 units | 200 | 600 |
| | | 2 | 8-14 units | 50 | 100 |
| | | 1 | 0- 7 units | 36 | 36 |
| | | | | | 5736 |
| In service units completed | $X_8$ | 5 | 41- | 600 | 3000 |
| | | 4 | 31-40 | 600 | 2400 |
| | | 3 | 21-30 | 100 | 300 |
| | | 2 | 11-20 | 56 | 112 |
| | | 1 | 0-10 | 30 | 30 |
| | | | | | 5842 |

**Table 13.4** *(continued)*

| Factor | Vari-ables | Relative weight and characteristics | Number of employees possessing this characteristic | Weighted total for each characteristic |
|---|---|---|---|---|
| Relative additional work-load in the hierarchy | $X_9$ | 5 District wide | 6 | 30 |
| | | 4 School wide | 30 | 120 |
| | | 3 Department wide | 90 | 270 |
| | | 2 Class wide | 1200 | 2400 |
| | | 1 Student | 60 | 60 |
| | | | | 2880 |

*Notice that each characteristic within each factor can be weighted. For example a year of experience for an administrator might be weighted twice that for a teacher. This example, however, will assume equal weights for each characteristic in each factor for all job functions in a school district.

Source: James E. Bruno, "Using Linear Programming Salary Evaluation Models in Collective Bargaining Negotiations with Teacher Unions." *Socio-Economic Planning Sciences* 5, no. 3 (March 1969), p. 110. Reprinted by permission.

1,350). These are then summed to yield the weighted total of importance points for the special awards and distinctions factor.

## Constraints

It is now possible to state, in terms of the factors, constraints of the highest and lowest salaries within each job classification. For example, in job classification 1 (districtwide responsibility such as superintendent), the highest salary $(h_1)$ will be less than or equal to:

$$3X_1 + 3X_2 + 7X_3 + 5X_4 + 7X_5 + 2X_6 + 5X_2 + 5X_8 + 5X_9,$$

i.e., the sum of the products of the highest values for each factor and the dollar amount of that factor. The lowest salary for job classification 1 $(l_1)$ is, on the other hand, greater than or equal to:

$$X_1 + X_2 + 6X_3 + 3X_4 + X_5 + X_6 + X_7 + X_8 + X_9.$$

All of the lowest coefficients are not necessarily 1. In factor $X_3$ (supervisory responsibility), for example, the least supervisory responsibility that someone with job classification 1 can have is districtwide (6). The upper and lower salary constraints for each job classification are presented in exhibit 13.5.

# Exhibit 13.5: Highest and Lowest Salaries for Each Job Classification

Districtwide (e.g., superintendent)

$$3X_1 + 3X_2 + 7X_3 + 5X_4 + 7X_5 + 2X_6 + 5X_7 + 5X_8 + 5X_9 \leq l_1 \quad (1)$$
$$X_1 + X_2 + 6X_3 + 3X_4 + X_5 + X_6 + X_7 + X_8 + 5X_9 \geq h_1 \quad (2)$$

Buildingwide (e.g., principal)

$$3X_1 + 3X_2 + 5X_3 + 5X_4 + 7X_5 + 2X_6 + 5X_7 + 5X_8 + 4X_9 \leq l_2 \quad (3)$$
$$X_1 + X_2 + 4X_3 + 3X_4 + X_5 + X_6 + X_7 + X_8 + 4X_9 \geq h_2 \quad (4)$$

Departmentwide (e.g., department head)

$$3X_1 + 3X_2 + 3X_3 + 5X_4 + 7X_5 + 2X_6 + 5X_7 + 5X_8 + 3X_9 \leq l_3 \quad (5)$$
$$X_1 + X_2 + 3X_3 + 2X_4 + X_5 + X_6 + X_7 + X_8 + 3X_9 \geq h_3 \quad (6)$$

Classroomwide (e.g., teacher)

$$3X_1 + 3X_2 + 2X_3 + 5X_4 + 7X_5 + 2X_6 + 5X_7 + 5X_7 + 2X_9 \leq l_4 \quad (7)$$
$$X_1 + X_2 + 2X_3 + 2X_4 + X_5 + X_6 + X_7 + X_8 + 2X_9 \geq h_4 \quad (8)$$

Individual (e.g., teacher aide)

$$3X_1 + 3X_2 + X_3 + 2X_4 + 7X_5 + 2X_6 + 5X_7 + 5X_8 + X_9 \leq l_5 \quad (9)$$
$$X_1 + X_2 + X_3 + X_4 + X_5 + X_6 + X_7 + X_8 + X_9 \geq h_5 \quad (10)$$

Having defined the highest and lowest salaries for each job classification, it is necessary to define the relationships of salaries within and among job classifications. For example, it is necessary to answer the question: "Within a job classification, how much less than the highest salary can the lowest salary be?" In the problem described here, the lowest salary in job classification 1 $(l_1)$ is defined as being greater than or equal to 80 percent of the highest salary $(h_1)$. The "percentage spread" constraint for each job classification is

$$l_1 \geqslant 0.80 \, h_1,$$
$$l_2 \geqslant 0.75 \, h_2,$$
$$l_3 \geqslant 0.60 \, h_3,$$
$$l_4 \geqslant 0.55 \, h_4,$$
$$l_5 \geqslant 0.50 \, h_5,$$
$$h_2 \geqslant 0.95 \, l_1,$$
$$h_3 \geqslant 0.90 \, l_2,$$
$$h_4 \geqslant 0.85 \, l_3,$$
$$h_5 \geqslant 0.80 \, l_4.$$

For example, the top salary in job classification 2 $(h_2)$ must be greater than or equal to 95 percent of the lowest salary in job classification 1 $(l_1)$ or $h_2 \geqslant 0.95 \, l_1$.

It is also necessary to specify the minimum acceptable dollar difference between the highest salaries on each job classification, such as:

$$h_1 - h_2 \geqslant \$3{,}000,$$
$$h_2 - h_3 \geqslant \$3{,}000,$$
$$h_3 - h_4 \geqslant \$1{,}500,$$
$$h_4 - h_5 \geqslant \$1{,}500.$$

It may be desirable to ensure that no single factor account for more than a certain part of an individual's salary. This can be accommodated by placing upper and lower bounds on the dollar values that the factors $(X_1$ through $X_9)$ can assume. Examples of these constraints are as follows:

$$\$250 \leqslant X_1 \leqslant \$1{,}000,$$
$$\$200 \leqslant X_2 \leqslant \$1{,}000,$$
$$\$100 \leqslant X_3 \leqslant \$2{,}500,$$
$$\$100 \leqslant X_4 \leqslant \$2{,}000,$$
$$\$\,50 \leqslant X_5 \leqslant \$\,\,\,500,$$

$$\$250 \leqslant X_6 \leqslant \$1,000,$$
$$\$\ 50 \leqslant X_7 \leqslant \$\ \ 300,$$
$$\$\ 20 \leqslant X_8 \leqslant \$\ \ 100,$$
$$\$100 \leqslant X_9 \leqslant \$2,500.$$

## Objective Function

The objective function of this problem is to minimize total expenditure on salaries subject to the thirty-two constraints mentioned above. Specifically it is

$$\text{Minimize } Z = 2992X_1 + 2873X_2 + 2892X_3 + 6126X_4 + 5432X_5$$
$$+ 1422X_6 + 5736X_7 + 5842X_8 + 2880X_9.$$

## Solution of the Problem

The values of each of the factors determined by solving the problem are shown in table 13.6. With these values we can solve the objective function to determine the total salary cost ($11,916,248).

**Table 13.6: Value for Each Factor in the Salary Evaluation Scheme**

| Factor | Description | Value |
|--------|-------------|-------|
| $X_1$ | Difficulty of learning environment | $250.00 |
| $X_2$ | Subject matter priority | $527.37 |
| $X_3$ | Supervisory level | $100.00 |
| $X_4$ | Highest academic degree | $100.00 |
| $X_5$ | Work experience | $50.00 |
| $X_6$ | Special awards or distinctions | $1000.00 |
| $X_7$ | College credits | $50.00 |
| $X_8$ | In-service units | $20.00 |
| $X_9$ | Additional workload | $2402.63 |

Source: James E. Bruno, "Using Linear Programming Salary Evaluation Models in Collective Bargaining Negotiations with Teacher Unions." *Socio-Economic Planning Sciences* 5, no. 3 (March 1969). Reprinted by permission.

Also with these $X$'s, or factor values, we can determine the theoretically highest and lowest salaries for each job classification. This involves going back to equations (1) through (10) in exhibit 13.5 and plugging in the actual values of $X_1$ through $X_9$. The results of this process are shown in table 13.7.

To determine his or her salary under this model an individual needs to specify for a given job classification the values of his or her own factors. For example, consider a teacher ($3X_3$) with an M.A. ($4X_4$), a classwide workload ($2X_9$) in a difficult learning environ-

## Table 13.7: Optimal Salary Schedule

| | | | |
|---|---|---|---|
| Function 1 | Superintendents | (highest) | $18,575 |
| | Assistants | (lowest) | $14,860 |
| Function 2 | Principals | (highest) | $15,642 |
| | Assistants | (lowest) | $12,207 |
| Function 3 | Department head | (highest) | $13,564 |
| | Department head | (lowest) | $8,429 |
| Function 4 | Teacher | (highest) | $10,537 |
| | Teacher | (lowest) | $7,102 |
| Function 5 | Teacher aide | (highest) | $7,434 |
| | Teacher aide | (lowest) | $4,500 |
| Objective function | | Total district cost | $11,916,248 |

Source: James E. Bruno, "Using Linear Programming Salary Evaluation Models in Collective Bargaining Negotiations with Teacher Unions." *Socio-Economic Planning Sciences* 5, no. 3 (March 1969). Reprinted by permission.

ment $(3X_1)$, two years experience $(1X_5)$, seven additional college credits $(1X_8)$, five in-service credits $(1X_8)$ with no distinction $(1X_6)$, and no particular skill area $(2X_2)$. That individual's salary would be calculated as follows:

$$3X_1 + 2X_2 + 3X_3 + 4X_4 + 1X_5 + 1X_6 + 1X_7 + 1X_8 + 2X_9 =$$
$$3(\$250) + 2(\$527.37) + 3(\$100) + 4(\$100) + \$50 +$$
$$\$1,000 + \$50 + \$20 + 2(\$2,402.63) = \$8,431.$$

### Changing the Constraints

If this linear programming approach to salary determination was attempted, a number of alternative forms of the problem would need to be examined before one acceptable to all parties could be chosen. One method of exploring alternative forms requires assessing the effects of different constraints on the solution.

In the problem just examined, for instance, the value of factor $X_1$ was calculated at its minimum permissible level. That is, the unit amount of compensation based on the degree of difficulty of the learning environment was solved at $250. The solution would be affected if that constraint were changed, say, from $250 \leqslant X_1 \leqslant$ $1,000 to $X = \$450$ or $X = \$650$. The effects of these two changes on the solution are shown in table 13.8. This process of modifying the constraints can be used as a way of arriving at a model which is acceptable to all parties concerned. The next example shows, among other things, how mathematical models might be modified after early solutions to the problem are analyzed.

## Table 13.8: Alternate Optimal Salary Schedules with Factor $X_1$ (Learning Environment) Increased in Increments of $200

| Factors | | | |
|---|---|---|---|
| $X_1$ (parameterized) | 250 | 450 | 650 |
| $X_2$ | 527 | 327* | 200 |
| $X_3$ | 100 | 100 | 505 |
| $X_4$ | 100 | 100 | 100 |
| $X_5$ | 50 | 50 | 50 |
| $X_6$ | 1000 | 1000 | 904 |
| $X_7$ | 50 | 50 | 50 |
| $X_8$ | 20 | 20 | 20 |
| $X_9$ | 2402 | 2402 | 2020 |
| District cost (objective function) | $11,916,248 | $11,940,048 | $12,107,913 |
| Function 1 (highest) | $18,575 | $18,575 | $19,198 |
| (lowest) | $14,860 | $14,860 | $15,358 |
| 2 | $15,642 | $15,642 | $16,167 |
| | $12,207 | $12,207 | $12,277 |
| 3 | $13,564 | $13,564 | $13,641 |
| | $8,429 | $8,429 | $8,488 |
| 4 | $10,537 | $10,537 | $10,610 |
| | $7,102 | $7,102 | $7,125 |
| 5 | $7,434 | $7,434 | $7,484 |
| | $4,500 | $4,500 | $4,500 |

Source: James E. Bruno, "Using Linear Programming Salary Evaluation Models in Collective Bargaining Negotiations with Teacher Unions." *Socio-Economic Planning Sciences* 5, no. 3 (March 1969). Reprinted by permission.

## Example 3: Higher Education Planning
## (adapted from Lee and Clayton 1972)

This example utilizes a variation of linear programming (called *goal programming*) to maximize the degree of accomplishment of multiple goals in a higher education institution. Again, the purpose here is to describe the general form of the problem so that the reader may gain an appreciation of the wide variety of linear programming applications.

### Background

Operating policies of universities are based on the combined philosophy of many conflicting factions of the university community, including funders, administrators, faculty, students, and staff. As a consequence, these operating policies are often based on multiple goals which are competitive and even conflicting. With limited available resources for pursuing university goals, administrators have to eliminate some goals, postpone some, and reduce others in scale, in order to fit desirable goals into practical and feasible objectives. The problem described here represents a method for allocating scarce resources among competing goals in such a way that resources are used most effectively.

Goal programming (GP) is a special extension of linear programming. In the conventional linear programming method, the objective function is unidimensional, e.g., either maximize profits or minimize costs. The GP model handles multiple goals in multiple dimensions. This is particularly useful because goals set by an educational manager are often achievable only at the expense of other goals.

Because GP is a more sophisticated form of linear programming, it imposes additional requirements on the model-builder. In GP there is a need to establish a hierarchy of importance among incompatible goals so that the low order goals are considered only after the higher order goals are satisfied or have reached the point beyond which no further improvements are desirable. If the educational manager can rank goals in terms of their contributions or importance to the organization, the problem can be solved by GP. The problem described here uses data from a college of business within a university. Seven goals of this college and their respective rankings are presented in exhibit 13.9.

## Exhibit 13.9: Example of Ranked Goals of a College of Business

$M_7$ = Maintain the necessary requirements for accreditation by the American Association of Colleges and Schools of Business
$M_6$ = Assure adequate salary increases for the academic staff, graduate assistants, and general staff
$M_5$ = Assure adequate number of faculty by meeting desired faculty/student ratios and by having instruction available for the needed student credit hours
$M_4$ = Attain a desirable distribution of the academic staff with respect to rank
$M_3$ = Maintain desired faculty/staff ratio
$M_2$ = Maintain desired faculty/graduate research assistant ratio
$M_1$ = Minimize cost

## Objective Function

GP goes about goal maximization, ironically, by minimization. Instead of trying to maximize the objective criterion directly, the deviations between goals and what can be achieved within the given set of constraints are minimized. The deviational variable is represented in two dimensions, positive and negative deviations from each goal. Then, the objective function becomes the minimization of these deviations, based on the relative importance or "preemptive priority" weights assigned to them. (The objective function may include real variables in addition to the deviational variables.) In this example, the general form of the objective function can be expressed as:

$$\text{Minimize } Z = \sum_{i=1}^{7} (d_i^+ + d_i^-),$$
$$d^+, d^- \geqslant 0.$$

Or, minimize the sum of the positive and negative deviations of the seven goals shown in exhibit 13.9. Incidentally, if overachievement of a goal is acceptable, $d_i^+$ can be eliminated from the objective function. On the other hand, if underachievement is acceptable, $d_i^-$ can be eliminated. If the exact achievement of the goal is desired, both $d_i^+$ and $d_i^-$ must be included.

The deviational variables $d_i^+$ and $d_i^-$ must then be ranked from the most important to least important. By doing this the lower order goals are considered only after the higher order goals are achieved as desired. Ranking takes several forms. First the goals themselves are ranked as in exhibit 13.9. Then for each goal, "coefficients of regret" must be assigned to each possible amount of deviation from the desired achievement level of the goal.

## Constraints

In the GP model, each goal is defined as one or more constraints. Because there are seven goals in this problem, there will also be at least seven constraints. The data required to construct the constraints in this problem are presented in exhibit 13.10. Each of these seven constraints (goals) is discussed in some detail below.

## Exhibit 13.10: Data Requirements of the Goal Programming Model

Variables

$x_1$ = number of graduate research assistants
$x_2$ = number of graduate teaching assistants
$x_3$ = number of instructors
$x_4$ = number of assistant professors without terminal degree
$x_5$ = number of associate professors without terminal degree
$x_6$ = number of full professors without terminal degree
$x_7$ = number of part-time faculty without terminal degree
$x_8$ = number of special professors without terminal degree
$x_9$ = number of staff
$y_1$ = number of assistant professors with terminal degree
$y_2$ = number of associate professors with terminal degree
$y_3$ = number of full professors with terminal degree
$y_4$ = number of part-time faculty with terminal degree
$y_5$ = number of special faculty with terminal degree
$w$ = total payroll increase from prior year, comprised of faculty, staff, and graduate assistant salary increases

## Exhibit 13.10 *(continued)*

Constants

$a_1$ = percentage of academic staff classified as full-time faculty
$a_2$ = percentage of academic staff at the undergraduate level with terminal degree
$a_3$ = percentage of academic staff at the graduate level with terminal degree
$a_4$ = estimated number of undergraduate student credit hours required per session
$a_5$ = estimated number of graduate student credit hours required per session
$a_6$ = desired undergraduate faculty/student ratio
$a_7$ = desired graduate faculty/student ratio
$a_8$ = desired faculty/staff ratio
$a_9$ = desired faculty/graduate research assistant ratio
$b_{14}$ = projected undergraduate student enrollment for the coming academic year
$b_{15}$ = projected graduate student enrollment for the coming academic year
$b_{16}$ = desired percentage increase in salary for graduate assistants
$b_{17}$ = desired percentage increase in salary for faculty
$b_{18}$ = desired percentage increase in salary for staff

Maximum teaching loads, desired proportion of each faculty type, and average annual salary defined as:

| | Desired | Teaching loads | | |
| Variable | proportion | Undergraduate | Graduate | Salary |
| --- | --- | --- | --- | --- |
| $x_1$ | $c_1$ | $b_1$ | $b'_1$ | $s_1$ |
| $x_2$ | $c_2$ | $b_2$ | $b'_2$ | $s_1$ |
| $x_3$ | $c_3$ | $b_3$ | $b'_3$ | $s_2$ |
| $x_4$ | $c_4$ | $b_4$ | $b'_4$ | $s_3$ |
| $x_5$ | $c_5$ | $b_5$ | $b'_5$ | $s_4$ |
| $x_6$ | $c_6$ | $b_6$ | $b'_6$ | $s_5$ |
| $x_7$ | $c_7$ | $b_7$ | $b'_7$ | $s_6$ |
| $x_8$ | $c_8$ | $b_8$ | $b'_8$ | $s_7$ |
| $x_9$ | — | — | | $s_8$ |
| $y_1$ | $c_9$ | $b_9$ | $b'_9$ | $s_3$ |
| $y_2$ | $c_{10}$ | $b_{10}$ | $b'_{10}$ | $s_4$ |
| $y_3$ | $c_{11}$ | $b_{11}$ | $b'_{11}$ | $s_5$ |
| $y_4$ | $c_{12}$ | $b_{12}$ | $b'_{12}$ | $s_6$ |
| $y_5$ | $c_{13}$ | $b_{13}$ | $b'_{13}$ | $s_7$ |

Source: Sang M. Lee and Edward R. Clayton, "A Goal Programming Model for Academic Resource Allocation." *Management Science* 18, no. 8 (April 1972), pp. B-398–B-399. Reprinted by permission.

## Accreditation

The first accreditation constraint states that a certain percentage of the academic staff must be full-time faculty. This constraint may be stated generally as:

$$\frac{\text{the number of full-time academic staff}}{\text{the total number of academic staff}} \geq \text{some percentage.} \quad (1)$$

This constraint can be stated more specifically using the information contained in exhibit 13.10:

Add all of the numbers represented by variables $X_3$ through $X_6$, $X_8$, $Y_1$ through $Y_3$, and $Y_5$. Divide this by the sum of the numbers represented by the following variables: $X_2$ through $X_8$ and $Y_1$ through $Y_5$. The resulting quotient must be greater than or equal to the required percentage of academic staff that is classified as full-time faculty.                                                          (2)

While more specific, "equation" (2) is more cumbersome to write and to follow. This constraint could be stated just as specifically and more clearly by using only the symbols which represent the variables (as used earlier in this chapter and in chapter six). This equivalent of equations (1) and (2) is given in equation (3):

$$\frac{X_3 + X_4 + X_5 + X_6 + X_8 + Y_1 + Y_2 + Y_3 + Y_5}{\begin{array}{c} X_2 + X_3 + X_4 + X_5 + X_6 + X_7 + X_8 + Y_1 + Y_2 \\ + Y_3 + Y_4 + Y_5 \end{array}} \geqslant A_1. \qquad (3)$$

Equation (3) is more specific than equation (1) and shorter than (2), but still quite lengthy. It can be rewritten in a more concise manner without losing its clarity, as follows:

$$\frac{\sum_{i=3}^{6} X_i + X_8 + \sum_{i=1}^{3} Y_i + Y_5}{\sum_{i=2}^{8} X_i + \sum_{i=1}^{5} Y_i} \geqslant A_1. \qquad (4)$$

Equation (4) uses the Greek letter sigma which, in mathematical notation, means "sum up the following numbers." For example, $\sum_{i=3}^{6} X_i$ is equivalent to saying, add together $X_3$, $X_4$, $X_5$, and $X_6$. Literally, it says sum the values of $X_i$ where $i$ varies from $X_3$ through $X_6$. Equations (1), (2), (3), and (4) are equivalent, except that equation (1) is a little less specific than the other three.

A second factor in accreditation has to do with the percentage of faculty required to possess the terminal degree (e.g., Ph.D., D.B.A., J.D., Ed.D., and LL.D.). It is assumed in this problem that $X_2$ through $X_7$ and $Y_1$ through $Y_5$ are available for graduate teaching responsibilities. These constraints can be written as follows:

$$\frac{\sum_{i=1}^{3} Y_i}{\sum_{i=2}^{7} X_i + \sum_{i=1}^{3} Y_i} \geqslant A_2 \tag{5}$$

and

$$\frac{\sum_{i=1}^{5} Y_i}{X_8 + \sum_{i=1}^{5} Y_i} \geqslant A_3. \tag{6}$$

The denominator of the fraction in equation (5) contains the sum of all faculty who are available for undergraduate teaching assignments ($X_2$ through $X_7$ and $Y_1$ through $Y_3$), while the numerator contains only those available for undergraduate teaching assignments who also have terminal degrees ($Y_1$ through $Y_3$). This fraction must be greater than or equal to a certain desired percentage in order to meet accreditation standards.

Similarly, the denominator of the fraction in equation (6) contains the sum of all faculty who are available for graduate teaching assignments ($X_8$ plus $Y_1$ through $Y_5$), while the numerator contains only those available for graduate teaching who also have terminal degrees ($Y_1$ through $Y_5$).

A third factor in accreditation deals with a maximum number of student credit hours per session (for both graduate and undergraduate) that a faculty member may teach. It is not necessary to formulate a separate constraint for this requirement, since it is easily incorporated into later constraints by selecting appropriate desired class sizes and teaching loads.

### Number of Academic Staff

One of the most important determinants of the number of academic staff requirements is the estimated number of student credit hours (both graduate and undergraduate) needed per session. With this information plus the maximum desired teaching loads of faculty members, the requirement of academic staff can be determined. The constraints for this requirement are listed below in equations (7) (undergraduate) and (8) (graduate):

$$\sum_{i=2}^{7} B_i X_i + \sum_{i=1}^{5} B_{i+8} Y_i \geqslant A_4 \tag{7}$$

and

$$\sum_{i=2}^{7} B_i' X_i + \sum_{i=1}^{5} B_{i+8}' \, Y_i \geqslant A_5 . \tag{8}$$

In equations (7) and (8) the products of staff numbers and teaching loads are being summed. The results are stated in terms of estimated number of student credit hours required per session. In equation (7), for example, the products of $B_2 X_2$ through $B_7 X_7$ and $B_9 Y_1$ through $B_{13} Y_8$ are summed, and this sum must be greater than or equal to a specified number of undergraduate student credit hours required per session.

Equation (8) is identical to equation (7) with the exceptions that graduate teaching load figures are substituted for the undergraduate teaching load figures (all of the B's are replaced by B''s), and that $A_5$ represents graduate student credit hours.

Another aspect to be considered in the determination of academic staff requirements is the desired faculty/student ratio. Equation (9) describes this constraint at the undergraduate level, while equation (10) describes it at the graduate level:

$$\frac{\sum_{i=2}^{7} X_i + \sum_{i=1}^{3} Y_i}{B_{14}} \geqslant A_6 \tag{9}$$

and

$$\frac{X_8 + \sum_{i=1}^{5} Y_i}{B_{15}} \geqslant A_7 . \tag{10}$$

In equations (9) and (10) appropriate staff numbers are divided by appropriate student enrollment figures. Before introducing somewhat more abstract mathematical notation in the next constraint, it might be useful to provide one more literal translation of the summation notation we have been using. Equation (10) states that we first add the following numbers of staff: special professors without terminal degree, assistant professors with terminal degree, associate professors with terminal degree, full professors with terminal degree, part-time faculty with terminal degree, and number of special faculty with terminal degree. This sum is then divided by the projected under-graduate student enrollment for the coming academic year. The equation states that the resulting quotient must be greater than or equal to the desired graduate faculty/student ratio.

## Distribution of Academic Staff

It is necessary to impose some constraints on the distribution of academic faculty. If there were no constraints, the model would call for the most productive type of faculty in terms of teaching load, salary, and accreditation, i.e., instructors and the assistant professors with terminal degrees. In the model discussed here it is assumed that the college wants to minimize the number of faculty without terminal degrees and to maximize those with terminal degrees. This means, first, that the desired proportions of academic staff without terminal degrees must be less than or equal to the actual number of academic staff without terminal degrees. Second, the desired proportions of academic staff with terminal degrees must be greater than or equal to the number of academic staff with terminal degrees.

These constraints can be written as follows:

$$\prod_{i=2}^{8} C_i \cdot T \leqslant \prod_{i=2}^{8} X_i, \tag{11}$$

$$C_{12} \cdot T \leqslant Y_4, \tag{12}$$

$$\prod_{i=1}^{3} C_{i+8} \cdot T \geqslant \prod_{i=1}^{3} Y_i, \tag{13}$$

$$C_{13} \cdot T \geqslant Y_5. \tag{14}$$

In these equations, $\prod$ represents the "product" of the indicated terms and T represents $\sum_{i=2}^{8} X_i + \sum_{i=1}^{5} Y_i$. This constraint sets a "floor" below which the number of academic staff without terminal degrees is not permitted to fall. Each staff type is constrained individually, much like what is done for $Y_4$ and $Y_5$ in equations (12) and (14).

## Number of Nonacademic Staff

Due to the ever-increasing amount of stenographic services required by the academic staff, it is necessary to provide adequate staff support. This objective may be incorporated into the model by designing a constraint which reflects a desired faculty/staff ratio:

$$\frac{\sum_{i=2}^{8} X_i + \sum_{i=1}^{5} Y_i}{X_9} \geqslant A_8. \tag{15}$$

## Number of Graduate Research Assistants

To provide adequate research support for the academic staff, it is necessary to assign graduate research assistants to faculty members. This can be considered by introducing a constraint for desired faculty/graduate research assistant ratio:

$$\frac{\sum_{i=3}^{8} X_i + \sum_{i=1}^{5} Y_i}{X_1} \geqslant A_9. \tag{16}$$

## Salary Increases

To attract and maintain adequate staff, it is necessary to provide periodic salary increases. Although market conditions vary greatly, there exists some competition for faculty members. To meet this competition, salary increases are offered according to the policy of the institution. The payroll increase constraint may be stated as:

$$B_{16}\left(S_1 \sum_{i=1}^{2} X_i\right) + B_{17}\left(S_2 X_3 + \sum_{i=3}^{7} S_i X_{i+1} + \sum_{i=3}^{7} S_i Y_{i-2}\right)$$
$$+ B_{18}(S_8 X_9) \leqslant W. \tag{17}$$

While this constraint may appear difficult to interpret at first glance, closer inspection reveals that all of the terms are merely the products of three types of variables: desired percentage increases in salary X salary X number of people occupying a position. For example, in the first term of the constraint, the desired percentage increase in salary for graduate assistants ($B_{16}$) is multiplied by the salary of graduate assistants ($S_1$) which, in turn, is multiplied by the number of graduate research and teaching assistants. The sum of these salary terms in the constraint must be less than or equal to the desired total payroll increase (comprising faculty, staff, and graduate assistant salary increases).

## Total Payroll Budget

The increase in the salaries of faculty, staff, and graduate assistants represents only one facet of the entire budget. The total payroll budget is obviously a major concern. The total payroll constraint can be expressed as:

$$S_1 \sum_{i=1}^{2} X_i + S_2 X_3 + \sum_{i=3}^{7} S_i X_{i+1} + \sum_{i=3}^{7} S_i Y_{i-2} +$$
$$S_8 Y_9 + W = P, \tag{18}$$

where $P$ represents the total payroll budget. The first five terms of the constraint are products of unit salaries and numbers of personnel. The last term represents the total increase over these salaries.

To review briefly, then, the objective function is to minimize the sum of the positive and negative deviations of the seven goals shown in exhibit 13.10. Equations (4) through (18) portray the constraints of the problem. A numerical example follows.

## Numerical Example of Goal Programming

The priority structure used in the numerical example is the same as that shown in exhibit 13.9. Data for the example are presented in table 13.11. The process of substituting actual data into the con-

## Table 13.11: Data for Numerical Example of Goal Programming

| Variable | Teaching load | | Desired proportion | | Salary |
| | Undergraduate | Graduate | Maximum | Minimum | |
|---|---|---|---|---|---|
| $x_1$ | 0 | 0 | — | — | \$ 3,000 |
| $x_2$ | 6 | 0 | 7% | — | 3,000 |
| $x_3$ | 12 | 0 | 7 | — | 8,000 |
| $x_4$ | 9 | 0 | 15 | — | 13,000 |
| $x_5$ | 9 | 0 | 5 | — | 15,000 |
| $x_6$ | 6 | 0 | 2 | — | 17,000 |
| $x_7$ | 3 | 0 | 1 | — | 2,000 |
| $x_8$ | 0 | 3 | — | 1% | 30,000 |
| $x_9$ | — | — | — | — | 4,000 |
| $y_1$ | 6 | 3 | — | 21 | 13,000 |
| $y_2$ | 6 | 3 | — | 14 | 15,000 |
| $y_3$ | 3 | 3 | — | 23 | 17,000 |
| $y_4$ | 0 | 3 | 2 | — | 2,000 |
| $y_5$ | 0 | 3 | — | 2 | 30,000 |

Source: Sang M. Lee and Edward R. Clayton, "A Goal Programming Model for Academic Resource Allocation." *Management Science* 18, no. 8 (April 1972), p. B401. Reprinted by permission.

straints and the objective function is not discussed here, but is included in the appendix to this chapter. The results of the problem are discussed here, as well as how initial results may point to the need to reformulate the problem.

The GP model provides three types of solutions: (1) identification of the input (resource) requirements to attain all the desired goals; (2) the degree of goal attainments with the given inputs; and (3) the degree of goal attainments under various combinations of inputs and goal structures.

In the first run, the problem is solved to determine the input requirements necessary to achieve all the goals presented by the dean
of the college of business. The results of the first run are presented in
exhibit 13.12. The solution of the first run indicates that all goals are

## Exhibit 13.12: Results of First Run of GP Model

| Goal attainment | |
|---|---|
| Accreditation | Achieved |
| Salary increase | Achieved |
| Faculty/student ratios | Achieved |
| Faculty/staff ratio | Achieved |
| Faculty distribution | Achieved |
| Faculty/graduate assistant ratio | Achieved |
| Minimize cost | $2,471,000 |

Variables

| | |
|---|---|
| $x_1 = 32$ | $x_8 = 1$ |
| $x_2 = 10$ | $x_9 = 38$ |
| $x_3 = 10$ | $y_1 = 42$ |
| $x_4 = 22$ | $y_2 = 20$ |
| $x_5 = 7$ | $y_3 = 34$ |
| $x_6 = 0$ | $y_4 = 0$ |
| $x_7 = 1$ | $y_5 = 3$ |
| $w = \$176,000$ | |

achieved at a total cost of $2,471,000. Since the minimization of
cost is treated as the goal with the lowest priority factor, the solution
identifies the input requirements necessary to attain all the goals.

Several factors need to be considered in evaluating the results of
the first run. First, the desired faculty distribution may be impossible
to obtain in reality. Second, the total cost derived by the first solution may far exceed the amount of funds the dean is able to obtain.

Suppose, for example, that 1 percent of the academic staff are
professors without terminal degrees. The optimum solution called for
zero. There is nothing that can be done about this situation, so the
constraint for this type of academic staff should be changed to read:
$0.01T - X_6 - D_{12} + D_{12} = 0$, instead of $0.02T - X_6 - D_{12} + D_{12} =
0$, as is shown in the appendix. Further, suppose the dean believes his
maximum allocation of funds will be $1,850,000. This fact will force
a change in the total salary constraint. As shown in the appendix, the
right-hand side of the total salary constraint was set at 0, since we
were considering cost minimization as the lowest priority. Now, it
will be set at $1,850,000.

In the second run, the dean treats the avoidance of deficit operations as the second priority goal, after meeting accreditation require-

ments. Also, he adjusts the constraint concerning faculty distribution of full professors with no terminal degrees. The objective function is presented in the appendix. The solution to the second run is presented in exhibit 13.13. The result of the second run indicates that

## Exhibit 13.13: Results of Second Run of GP Model

Goal attainment

| | |
|---|---|
| Accreditation | Achieved |
| Avoid deficit | Achieved |
| Salary increase | Achieved |
| Faculty/student ratio | Achieved |
| Faculty distribution | Not achieved—several ranks were not represented in this solution |
| Faculty/staff ratio | Not achieved—no staff |
| Faculty/graduate research assistant ratio | Not achieved |

Variables

$x_1 = 0$      $x_8 = 0$

$x_2 = 9$      $x_9 = 0$

$x_3 = 20$      $y_1 = 28$

$x_4 = 20$      $y_2 = 18$

$x_5 = 7$      $y_3 = 30$

$x_6 = 1$      $y_4 = 0$

$x_7 = 1$      $y_5 = 0$

$w = 135,000$

$\text{cost} = \$1,850,000$

with \$1,850,000 appropriated to the college, the dean is unable to achieve all the desired goals. In fact, due to the priority structure of the goals, there is no money available to hire any clerical staff after achieving the higher priority goals. Also, the desired faculty/graduate research assistant ratio was not attained.

Now, suppose that the dean presented the result of the second run to the president of the university and that he was successful in obtaining an additional \$120,000. Based on the result of the second computer run, the dean knows that he should assign higher priorities to the faculty/staff and the faculty/graduate research assistant ratios.

In the third run, the dean again assigned the highest priority to the accreditation requirements and the second priority factor on the cost minimization to \$1,970,000. To ensure an adequate level of staff support he assigned the third priority to the faculty/staff ratio and the fourth priority to the faculty/graduate research assistant ratio. The faculty/student ratio was assigned the sixth priority, followed by the faculty distribution ratios. The objective function for the third run is presented in the appendix. The results are presented in exhibit 13.14. As shown there, the most important academic goals of the

## Exhibit 13.14: Results of Third Run of GP Model

Goal attainment
    Accreditation                       Achieved
    Salary increase                    Achieved
    Faculty/staff ratio             Achieved
    Faculty/graduate research assistant  Achieved
       ratio
    Faculty/student ratios         Achieved
    Faculty distribution          Not achieved—again several ranks were not presented
                                     in this solution
Variables

| | |
|---|---|
| $x_1 = 26$ | $x_9 = 32$ |
| $x_2 = 9$ | $y_1 = 27$ |
| $x_3 = 22$ | $y_2 = 18$ |
| $x_4 = 19$ | $y_3 = 26$ |
| $x_5 = 6$ | $y_4 = 9$ |
| $x_6 = 1$ | $y_5 = 0$ |
| $x_7 = 0$ | $w = 144,000$ |
| $x_8 = 0$ | cost = \$1,970,000 |

college are met by restructuring the priority levels and by acquiring an additional \$120,000.

This application of linear programming to education is instructive for several reasons. First, the solution provides added insight into the problem. This insight helps the user to reexamine and modify the form of the problem. Problems of this type often must be formulated in several different ways. Second, it points out that linear programming can be of assistance in dealing with large, "messy" problems as well as small-scale, obviously quantitative problems.

Linear programming is a rather sophisticated technique, and one in which very few educational managers will be personally competent. However, it is important for managers to know enough about the technique and its application so that specialists can be brought in when the need arises.

## Questions for Review and Discussion

1.   In exhibit 13.1 there is a list of twenty-two different types of goals which may be amenable to linear programming. Which of these goals could be modeled most easily? Which would be the most difficult? Why?

2.   What assumptions (implicit and explicit) are made about the effectiveness of the two math program options in Example 1? Are there other instructional programs in elementary/secondary or higher education institutions about which these assumptions could not be made?

3. What conceivable response would teachers' unions have to linear programming application to salary schedules? In what ways would politics affect the form of problems solvable by linear programs?

4. Some would argue that the assignment of relative weights to variables in Example 2 is too arbitrary and, therefore, invalid. Others would argue that relative weights are already assigned to these kinds of variables, and that the linear programming model merely forces the user to be explicit. What is your opinion?

5. What kinds of goals would be appropriate for a goal programming model of an elementary-secondary educational institution? What would the constraints specify?

### Appendix A: Constraints and Objective Functions for Numerical Example of GP Model (adapted from Lee and Clayton 1972, pp. B-401–B-407)

### First Run

Objective Function

$$\text{Minimize } Z = M_7 \sum_{i=1}^{3} d_i^- + M_6 d_{22}^- + 2M_5 d_5^- + 2M_5 d_7^-$$
$$+ M_5 d_4^- + M_5 d_6^- + M_4 \sum_{i=8}^{13} d_i^- + M_4 d_{18}^-$$
$$+ M_4 \sum_{i=14}^{17} d_i^+ + M_4 d_{19}^+ + M_3 d_{20}^+ + M_2 d_{21}^+$$
$$+ M_1 d_{23}^+.$$

Constraints for Accreditation

It is required that 75 percent of the academic staff be full-time faculty according to the American Association of Colleges and Schools of Business. Since in our model $x_3$ to $x_6$, $x_8$, $y_1$ to $y_3$, and $y_5$ are considered full-time, we may write:

$$\sum_{i=3}^{6} x_i + x_8 + \sum_{i=1}^{3} y_i + y_5 - 0.75 \left( \sum_{i=1}^{8} x_i + \sum_{i=1}^{5} y_i \right)$$
$$+ d_1^- - d_1^+ = 0.$$

It is also required that at least 40 percent of the academic teaching staff at the undergraduate level possess terminal coverage. This is expressed as:

$$\sum_{i=1}^{3} y_i - 0.40[\sum_{i=2}^{7} x_i + \sum_{i=1}^{3} y_i] + d_2^- - d_2^+ = 0.$$

At least 75 percent of the academic staff teaching graduate studies are required to possess terminal coverage. This is expressed as:

$$\sum_{i=1}^{5} y_i - 0.75[x_8 + \sum_{i=1}^{6} y_i] + d_3^- - d_3^+ = 0.$$

### Constraints for Number of Academic Staff

To determine the faculty requirement, it is necessary to forecast the total number of student credit hours of instruction needed. In this example, the projected student enrollment is 1,820, the average number of credit hours/student taken at the college is 10, and the desired class size is set at 20. Therefore, 910 total student credit hours can be calculated by means of the following formula:

(Projected enrollment) · (Number of credit hours/student)/
(Desired class size)

$$6x_2 + 12x_3 + 9x_4 + 9x_5 + 6x_6 + 3x_7 + 6y_1 +$$
$$6y_2 + 3y_3 + d_4^- - d_4^+ = 910.$$

For the graduate student credit hours of instruction, we forecast 100 hours per session. The procedure is similar to the undergraduate forecast and the constraint becomes:

$$3x_8 + 3y_1 + 3y_2 + 3y_3 + 3y_4 + 3y_5 + d_5^- - d_5^+ = 100.$$

The next aspect to be considered in the determination of the required academic staff is the desired faculty/student ratio at both the graduate and undergraduate level. The forecasted enrollments in the next year at undergraduate and graduate levels are 1,820 and 100, respectively. The desired undergraduate faculty/student ratio is about 1/20 and the desired graduate faculty/student ratio is about 1/10. (The desired faculty/student ratio is based on the AACSB accreditation regulations and the dean's academic policy.) These constraints then become, for the undergraduate requirement:

$$\sum_{i=2}^{7} x_i + \sum_{i=1}^{3} y_i + d_6^- - d_6^+ = (0.05)(1,820) = 91$$

and for the graduate faculty:

$$x_8 + \sum_{i=1}^{5} y_i + d_7^- - d_7^+ = (0.10)(100) = 10.$$

Constraints for the Distribution of Academic Staff

It is necessary to impose some constraints on the distribution of the academic faculty according to the desired proportion of the total faculty for each type of staff.

$$0.07T - x_2 + d_8^- - d_3^+ = 0,$$
$$0.07T - x_3 + d_9^- - d_9^+ = 0,$$
$$0.15T - x_4 + d_{10}^- - d_{10}^+ = 0,$$
$$0.05T - x_5 + d_{11}^- - d_{11}^+ = 0,$$
$$0.02T - x_6 + d_{12}^- - d_{12}^+ = 0,$$
$$0.01T - x_7 + d_{13}^- - d_{13}^+ = 0,$$
$$0.01T - x_8 + d_{14}^- - d_{14}^+ = 0,$$
$$0.21T - y_1 + d_{15}^- - d_{15}^+ = 0,$$
$$0.14T - y_2 + d_{16}^- - d_{16}^+ = 0,$$
$$0.23T - y_3 + d_{17}^- - d_{17}^+ = 0,$$
$$0.02T - y_4 + d_{18}^- - d_{18}^+ = 0,$$
$$0.02T - y_5 + d_{19}^- - d_{19}^+ = 0,$$

where $T = \sum_{i=2}^{8} x_i + \sum_{i=1}^{5} y_i$.

*Number of staff.* In order to insure adequate staff for clerical and administrative work, the desired faculty/staff ratio is set at 4 to 1 by the dean. The constraint is then:

$$T - 4x_9 + d_{20}^- - d_{20}^+ = 0.$$

*Number of graduate research assistants.* We set the desired faculty/graduate research assistant ratio at 5 to 1. Hence, the constraint is:

$$\sum_{i=3}^{8} x_i + \sum_{i=1}^{5} y_i - 5x_1 + d_{21}^- - d_{21}^+ = 0.$$

Cost of Academic Staff, Graduate Assistants, and Staff

The total salary increase constraint can be expressed as:

$$0.06[3{,}000 \sum_{i=1}^{2} x_i] + 0.08(8{,}000x_3 + 13{,}000x_4 + 15{,}000x_5$$

$$+\ 17{,}000x_6 + 2{,}000x_7 + 30{,}000x_8 + 13{,}000y_1 + 15{,}000y_2$$

$$+17{,}000y_3 + 2{,}000y_4 + 30{,}000y_5) + 0.06(4{,}000x_9)$$

$$-\ w + d_{22}^{-} - d_{22}^{+} = 0,$$

where there is a 6 percent increase for graduate students and staff and an 8 percent increase for faculty.

The total payroll constraint for the entire college will be:

$$3{,}000x_1 + 3{,}000x_2 + 8{,}000x_3 + 13{,}000x_4 + 5{,}000x_5 + 17{,}000x_6$$

$$+\ 2{,}000x_7 + 30{,}000x_8 + 13{,}000y_1 + 15{,}000y_2 + 17{,}000y_3$$

$$+\ 2{,}000y_4 + 30{,}000y_5 + 4{,}000x_9 + w + d_{23}^{-} - d_{23}^{+} = 0.$$

## Second Run

Objective Function

$$\text{Minimize } Z = M_7 \sum_{i=1}^{3} d_i^{-} + M_6 d_{23}^{+} + M_5 d_{22}^{-} + 2M_4 d_5^{-}$$

$$+\ 2M_4 d_7^{-} + M_4 d_4^{-} + M_4 d_6^{-} + M_3 \sum_{i=8}^{11} d_i^{-}$$

$$+\ M_3 d_{13}^{-} + M_3 d_{18}^{-} + M_3 d_{12}^{+} + M_3 \sum_{i=14}^{17} d_i^{+}$$

$$+\ M_3 d_{19}^{+} + M_2 d_{20}^{+} + M_1 d_{21}^{+}.$$

## Third Run

Objective Function

$$\text{Minimize } Z = M_7 \sum_{i=1}^{3} d_i^{-} + M_6 d_{23}^{+} + M_5 d_{22}^{-} + M_4 d_{20}^{+}$$

$$+\ M_3 d_{21}^{+} + 2M_2 d_5^{-} + 2M_2 d_7^{-} + M_2 d_4^{-}$$

$$+\ M_2 d_6^{-} + M_1 \sum_{i=8}^{11} d_i^{-} + M_1 d_{13}^{-} + M_1 d_{18}^{-}$$

$$+\ M_1 d_{12}^{+} + M_1 \sum_{i=14}^{17} d_i^{+} + M_1 d_{19}^{+}.$$

## References

Bruno, James E. "Using Linear Programming Salary Evaluation Models in Collective Bargaining Negotiations with Teacher Unions." *Socio-Economic Planning Sciences* 5, no. 3 (March 1969): 103-118.

Dantzig, George B. *Linear Programming and Extensions.* Princeton, N.J.: Princeton University Press, 1963.

Lee, Sang M., and Clayton, Edward R. "A Goal Programming Model for Academic Resource Allocation." *Management Science* 18, no. 8 (April 1972): B-395—B-408.

Smythe, William R., Jr., and Johnson, Lynwood A. *Introduction to Linear Programming, with Applications.* Englewood Cliffs, N.J.: Prentice Hall, Inc., 1966.

Thierauf, Robert J., and Grose, Richard A. *Decision Making through Operations Research.* New York: John Wiley & Sons, 1970.

Van Dusseldorp, Ralph A.; Richardson, Duane E.; and Foley, Walter J. *Educational Decision-Making through Operations Research.* Boston: Allyn & Bacon, 1971.

## Related Readings

Alkin, Marvin C. "The Use of Quantitative Methods as an Aid to Decision Making in Educational Administration." ERIC, no. ED028525, 1969. This article briefly discusses three quantitative tools which may be used in education administration: (1) the Leontief input-output analysis, mainly applicable to budget analysis and planning; (2) linear programming, which maximizes effective resource allocation within given constraints; and (3) queuing theory, which is used to relate facilities to services within given time periods.

Carman, Robert A. "Linear Programming with Application to Educational Planning." ERIC, no. ED051563, 1971. This document discusses the value of linear programming in finding minimum and maximum solutions to problems of resource allocations. Three models using this technique are given for the areas of educational finance, school district personnel compensation, and instructional program evaluation.

Findorff, Irene K. "A Study of Linear Programming Applications for the Optimization of School Lunch Menus." ERIC, no. ED067748, 1972. This document summarizes the results of a project that was designed to adapt, test, and evaluate a computerized information and menu planning system utilizing linear programming for use in school lunch programs.

Monteverda, G. L. "Some Psycholinguistic Aspects of Programmed Instruction in the Language Laboratory." ERIC, no. ED061800, 1972. This paper proposes the use of linear programming in language instruction.

Pogany, P. P. "Application of Linear Programming Models to Determine Optimum School Attendance Areas and Busing Schedules, Subject to Varying Racial Composition." ERIC, no. ED074637, 1973. This study applied the conventional linear transportation program to the student assignment problem and investigated methods of measuring the achieved level of desegregation.

# PART IV

# PLANNING SYSTEMS

# 14

# Enrollment Forecasting

Why plan? What steps are involved in planning? Who is involved in the planning process? What is the relationship between planning and budgeting? These are a few of the important questions in educational planning. This chapter focuses primarily on the technical aspects of planning and, secondarily, on the integration of technical and comprehensive aspects.

Planning is the continuous, systematic, step-by-step process of changing present organizational environments and goals to fit new situations. The process requires specific objectives supported by the study and analysis of various alternatives.

One of the essential planning tools is forecasting. The distinction between planning and forecasting is that the forecaster makes no attempt to influence the future, and the planner does. (There is no consensus on this point. Fox (1953), for example, defines forecasting as a form of planning because it requires the identification of probable future conditions and a selection among those conditions.)

As organizational operations and management problems grow increasingly complex, resources more limited, and competing demands more strident, a distinction between strategic (long-range) and operational (short-range) planning becomes important. According to Ansoff (1965), strategic planning deals with issues that affect the organization's livelihood and direction; operational planning deals with short-range, day-to-day problems. Thus, planning activities vary in range, magnitude, and consequences.

*Forecasting* is generally defined as the projection of specified future events within a certain time frame, usually on the basis of incomplete information. (There are a number of books devoted entirely to the techniques of forecasting. See, for example, Wolfe 1966.)

*361*

Essentially an art, forecasting can be effectively used in combination with other techniques to reduce the elements of risk and uncertainty in traditional management decisions, such as policy formulation and program planning.

The accuracy of a forecast depends on the intellectual and material resources available and the validity of the methods used. The amount of effort that goes into a forecast should be a function of the "stakes," i.e., how much error one can afford. In theory, the marginal investment in the forecasting effort should equal the marginal value of any improved accuracy in the forecast.

There are many possible levels of effort that can go into a forecast. In general, a forecast improves to the extent that the following steps are carried out: (1) obtaining accurate and reliable data, (2) preparing the data properly, (3) stating the basic assumptions of the model, (4) using a consistent calculus or mechanical means, (5) applying more than one kind of forecasting method with independent bases, and (6) applying sound judgment and intuition.

In short, the forecaster should follow the principle of scientific prediction, systematically correlating past conditions and variables to future events. To an increasing extent, the forecaster in education calls upon skills in research design and mathematical modeling. In this chapter we will examine those models which have been most widely used in predicting student enrollments in public elementary-secondary education. Specifically, we will examine two mathematical methods which rely primarily on past enrollment data and one relatively straightforward demographic model which uses housing information. Chapter fifteen is devoted to more complex modeling techniques which require the use of computers.

## The Use of Assumptions in Forecasting

There is no one best way to project populations. Many techniques have been developed, ranging from primitive "eyeballing the data" to highly sophisticated, computerized methods. Probably the most widely used practice is to recall the rate of population change in the past year and, based on that, to make some guess about next year. In this case, the population is usually small and the arithmetic required is simple. At the other end of the spectrum, we find computer-simulation models of entire nations, analyzing simultaneously the effects of hundreds of variables on demographic change several decades in the future. The staff employed for this type of analysis could easily equal the entire administrative staff of an average school district.

(Applications of such computer models in educational planning are discussed in chapter fifteen.)

Although these two examples are extreme in terms of sophistication, magnitude, attention to detail, and cost, they have at least one basic procedure in common—certain assumptions are made about the past. The person using the "eyeballing" approach may assume, for example, that since ten people moved to town last year, ten more will move to town this year. It may also be assumed that although twenty people were lost in a flood last year, it is unlikely that twenty people will be lost this year, because a dam was built. Since the town lost ten people last year (ten moved in and twenty were washed out), one could project that next year the town will either lose ten or twenty people or gain zero, ten, twenty, or thirty people. Whatever projection is arrived at will depend on the assumptions made. Computer-simulation model builders make this type of assumption, although their assumptions may be greater in number and much more complex.

In general, the kinds and numbers of assumptions made in projecting populations depend on three factors:

1. *The level of detail desired.* If the goal is simply to project an aggregate number of people at some future time, then assumptions about change in the aggregate population need to be made. If, on the other hand, it is necessary to project not only changes in number but also changes in composition of the population (e.g., percentage of population over the age of sixty-five, or number of children in the "average" family), extensive sets of further assumptions must be made. These might include assumptions such as longer life expectancy, fewer marriages, or declining birth rate.

2. *The span of time between the present and the last projection.* If the projection is over a relatively short period of time, many important variables can be held constant. For example, if a three-year projection is being made, and it is known that the birthrate has been declining slightly over the last fifteen years, it might reasonably be assumed that the trend will not change drastically over the next three years. If, on the other hand, population changes for a twenty-five year period are being projected, then whatever is happening to the birthrate is very important and certain additional assumptions must be made.

3. *The degree of accuracy desired.* Projections should, of course, be as accurate as possible, but that leaves a lot of room to determine what is feasible given the resources available. With almost unlimited

resources, a computer-simulation team can be hired. The team will examine the variables related to population change and make assumptions about those variables. Although there is no guarantee of accuracy, chances are that the team's projection will be closer to what actually develops than the projection of one person who thinks for two minutes and predicts. The benefits of increased accuracy in forecasting must always be weighed against the increased costs incurred.

The decision as to how much effort to put into a projection rests with the person who needs the projection. The probability of greater reliability is increased as additional relevant variables are considered. But the more variables considered, the more assumptions need to be made about them. Where should the line be drawn?

To project populations for a five-year period, it is necessary to assume that some things will remain in the future as they were in the immediate past, and that if they change, they will do so in a predictable manner.

Six general assumptions need to be made (that is, considered and tested in the light of available data) when projecting populations of schoolchildren for a five-year period:

1. *Mortality.* There will be no major change in the death rate for any group in the population. Or, the rate of change will be $X$ percent.

2. *Fertility.* Over the last ten to fifteen years, the fertility rate of American women has declined and then leveled off. It is assumed that over the next five years no dramatic change in the birthrate will take place. Or, for a particular demographic position, the rate of change will be $X$ percent.

3. *Local economic conditions.* During the next five years, trends in land use, such as industrial and residential development, will continue as in the immediate past or change at a predictable rate.

4. *Boundaries.* There will be no changes in local political boundaries, especially school district boundaries. Or, if anticipated, the particular change will be incorporated into the analysis (e.g., annexation of additional land).

5. *Administrative policy.* The school district policy on attendance, promotion, and pupil retention and acceleration will not change significantly over the next five years, or it will change at a predictable rate.

6. *Act of God.* No major natural catastrophe will occur.

Given these assumptions, the characteristics of future district student populations can be seen as predictable. However, enrollment-based and census-based populations projections (discussed below), require secondary assumptions.

## Forecasting Using Enrollment-Based Data

If demographic indicators are relatively stable (unchanging or changing at a steady rate), enrollment histories can be used as a basis for predicting enrollments in the near future (about three years). There are many techniques for computing these data. In this section, two of the most widely used will be examined, *cohort survival* and *curve fitting.*

### Cohort Survival

Changes in population, and therefore in school enrollment, are influenced by many factors, such as migration of families to and from a community, birthrate, and building development. On a short-term enrollment projection, a major assumption is that the trends in all these variables will remain fairly constant during the next several years. The necessity of this assumption should become apparent as the method is described.

The cohort-survival projection technique was first used in the late 1920s. Since then, many planners have incorporated its principles in their work. The essential procedures are:

1. Identify the *cohort,* the group of subjects to be studied. An example of the cohort would be students in each grade in a given school or district.

2. Determine the *survival rate* (or percentage change) of the cohort in the immediate past. To do this in the case of grade enrollments, record the number in each grade for the past five years and determine the percentage of the class that moved on to the next grade. Estimate an average survival rate for all grades for each year.

3. Project the enrollment for each grade in the next year (the first year of the planning period) by multiplying the average survival rate by the latest enrollment in the preceding grade.

4. Estimate the beginning class for the planning period from the best sources available (for example, preschool figures in the census data).

5. Project enrollment for each grade of the planning period by

multiplying average rates by enrollments previously computed, moving the cohort ahead to the next grade.

6. Total the projected enrollment for the entire planning period.

For example, given the district enrollment history shown in table 14.1, the number of students in each grade level in the district can be

**Table 14.1: Enrollment History of a K-8 School District**

| Grade | Four years ago | Three years ago | Two years ago | One year ago | Present year |
|-------|------|------|------|------|------|
| Kindergarten | 270 | 394 | 481 | 601 | 786 |
| Grade 1 | 285 | 345 | 526 | 600 | 787 |
| Grade 2 | 247 | 345 | 403 | 541 | 686 |
| Grade 3 | 222 | 299 | 404 | 466 | 610 |
| Grade 4 | 199 | 233 | 326 | 441 | 552 |
| Grade 5 | 219 | 232 | 304 | 355 | 529 |
| Grade 6 | 164 | 223 | 264 | 342 | 425 |
| Grade 7 | 149 | 198 | 262 | 316 | 431 |
| Grade 8 | 127 | 168 | 212 | 279 | 361 |
| Totals | 1,882 | 2,437 | 3,182 | 3,941 | 5,167 |

projected. First, compute the survival rates by dividing the number of children in grade $X + 1$ during the year $Y + 1$ by the number of children in grade $X$ during the year $Y$. For example, as indicated in table 14.2, divide the number of third graders three years ago by the number of second graders four years ago and find the percentage change, or survival rate, of that group of children: 299 divided by 247 is 121.1 percent or an increase of 21.1 percent. These calculations are completed for each grade and year to get an average survival for each grade.

Next, project the number of students in grade $Y + 1$ during year $X + 1$ by multiplying the number of children in grade $Y$ during year $X$ by the average survival rate. For example, there are 786 children in kindergarten in the current year and, on the average, enrollment in kindergarten increases by 29.2 percent. Therefore, it can be predicted that the number of children in the first grade in planning year 1 will be about 1,106 (129.2 percent multiplied by 786 children).

The number of children in the district who are one, two, and three years old can be determined using the census data. From this information, an estimate can be made of the number of children entering kindergarten in the future. For example, from the data on the number of four-year-olds in the district, it is estimated that 870

Table 14.2: Determining Cohort-Survival Rate

| Year | Four years ago | Three years ago | Two years ago | One year ago | Present | Average survival rate | Projected enrollment | | |
|---|---|---|---|---|---|---|---|---|---|
| | | | Enrollment/Survival rate | | | | Planning year 1 | Planning year 2 | Planning year 3 |
| Kintergarten | 270 | 394 | 481 | 601 | 786 | | 870* | 788* | 760* |
| Grade 1 | 285 | 345 (127.8%) | 526 (133.5%) | 600 (124.8%) | 787 (131.0%) | 29.2% | 1,016 | 1,124 | 1,018 |
| Grade 2 | 247 | 345 (121.1%) | 403 (116.8%) | 541 (102.8%) | 686 (114.3%) | 13.7% | 894 | 1,155 | 1,278 |
| Grade 3 | 222 | 299 (121.1%) | 404 (117.1%) | 466 (108.2%) | 610 (112.8%) | 14.8% | 788 | 1,026 | 1,326 |
| Grade 4 | 199 | 233 (104.9%) | 326 (109.0%) | 441 (109.2%) | 552 (118.5%) | 10.4% | 673 | 870 | 1,133 |
| Grade 5 | 219 | 232 (116.7%) | 304 (130.5%) | 355 (108.5%) | 529 (119.9%) | 19.0% | 657 | 801 | 1,035 |
| Grade 6 | 164 | 223 (102.0%) | 264 (113.8%) | 342 (112.5%) | 425 (119.7%) | 12.0% | 592 | 736 | 897 |
| Grade 7 | 149 | 198 (120.7%) | 262 (117.5%) | 316 (119.7%) | 431 (126.0%) | 20.9% | 514 | 716 | 890 |
| Grade 8 | 127 | 168 (112.7%) | 212 (107.0%) | 279 (106.5%) | 361 (114.2%) | 10.1% | 474 | 566 | 788 |
| Totals | 1,882 | 2,437 | 3,182 | 3,941 | 5,167 | | 6,478 | 7,782 | 9,125 |

From survey data: children presently living in district

children will enter kindergarten in planning year 1. (If census data are not readily available, estimates of future kindergarten enrollments can be made by using least squares with kindergarten data. Least squares are discussed in the next section, "Curve Fitting.")

Having estimated kindergarten enrollments, it is possible to continue making projections using the average survival rate. For example, the first-grade enrollment in planning year 2 can be projected by multiplying the kindergarten enrollment estimate for planning year 1 by first-grade average rate of survival:

$$870 \text{ children} \times 129.2\% = 1{,}124 \text{ children.}$$

Add the numbers to obtain estimates of total enrollment in the future. This type of procedure can be used to project percentage changes of minority populations or any other cohort.

## Curve Fitting

Another method used to forecast enrollments is *curve fitting*. Using the freehand method, the first step is to construct a graph with years on the $X$ axis and numbers of students enrolled on the $Y$ axis. Then plot the enrollment for each of the years for which past data are available. From this *scatter diagram,* it is often possible to visualize a smooth curve that approximately "fits" the data. Such a curve is called an *approximating curve.* In figure 14.3, for example, the data appear to be well approximated by a straight line, and the curve is approximately linear. In figure 14.4, however, although a definite trend exists, it is nonlinear.

In figures 14.3 and 14.4 a smooth curve is drawn through the data and then extended beyond the plotted points in an attempt to estimate enrollment at a particular time in the future. In any curve-fitting exercise, whether freehand or mathematically derived, the accuracy of the estimates is entirely dependent on the assumption that relevant past trends will continue.

Another way to fit curves to data is by using equations consisting of various relationships between $X$ and $Y$. There are many such equations, but this discussion will be limited to the equation for a straight line (the most widely used):

$$Y = a_0 + a_1 X,$$

where $a_0$ and $a_1$ are constants. (For a description of how to mathematically derive this and other curves, see a standard textbook on statistics, such as Dixon and Massey 1969, pp. 193-215.)

## Figure 14.3: Fitting a Straight Line Through Data Points

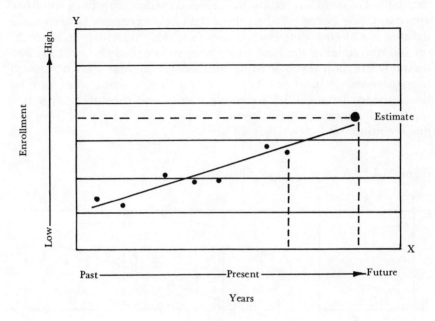

## Figure 14.4: Fitting a Curved Line Through Data Points

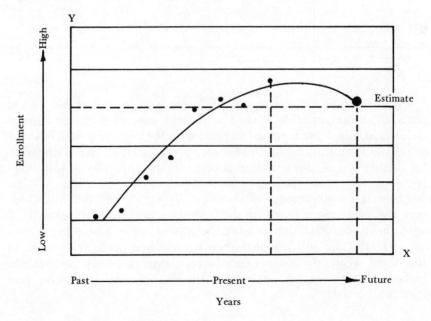

The goal is to fit a straight line (represented by that equation) to the data. To avoid subjective judgment on structuring lines (or other approximating curves) to fit sets of data, it is necessary to agree on a definition of *best-fitting line* (or other curve). One widely used method for determining the best fit of a curve is called the *least-squares* method. (Technically a least-squares line is the line drawn through the scatter diagram of points on a graph that minimizes the sum of the squared distances between the points and the line.) With this method the squares of the vertical distances of the points from the line are minimized. See figure 14.5.

## Figure 14.5: A Line of Least Squares

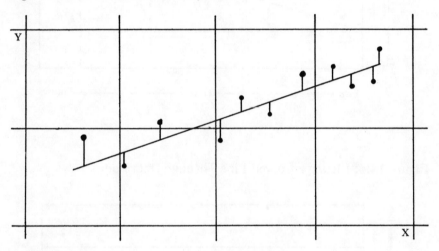

Figure 14.6 shows the results of fitting a least-squares line to the enrollment data in table 14.1. The present enrollment in the district is 5,167. Using least squares, the estimate for next year is 5,744; the year after that, 6,552; and the following year, 7,359. The mathematical calculation of this example is given in the appendix to this chapter.

There is no single best method for projecting enrollments. Compare the projections based on the least-squares method in figure 14.6 with those based on the cohort-survival technique. The cohort-survival estimates are much higher than those based on least squares. In the third year, the cohort-survival estimate is nearly 24 percent higher. Clearly, further analysis of the assumptions and techniques used is required.

## Figure 14.6: Comparing Projections Based on Cohort-Survival and Least-Squares Methods

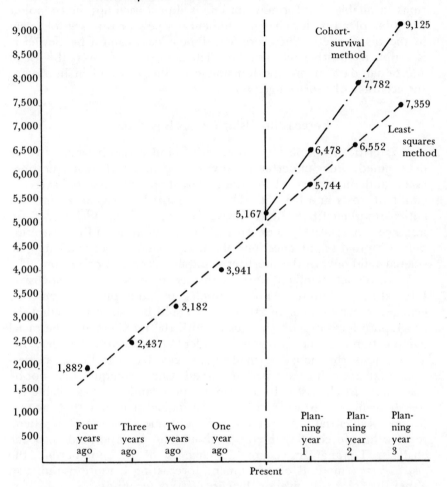

On closer examination, it might be argued that one technique "fits" the data better than another. Of all the curves that could have been mathematically fitted to the data we chose the straight line. Possibly some other curve would fit better. The data for four years ago and for the present are above the least-squares line, while the data between these years are below. That could suggest a curve that increases at an increasing rate (rather than the line, which increases at a constant rate). Therefore, in this particular case, it is possible that the cohort-survival method fits the data better.

As stated earlier, predictions are only as valid as the assumptions on which they are based. Many factors might modify the assumptions: available land for new housing is almost used up; the economic situation of a district changes suddenly; a new private school opens in the district, etc. Therefore, enrollment data cannot be viewed in isolation from other relevant data. The next section covers the use of additional data in making long-range predictions and in improving the accuracy of short-range predictions.

## Forecasting Using Census-Based Data

It is critically important to keep in mind precisely what is to be determined when undertaking any analytical effort. The questions asked and the degree of accuracy sought in the answers have concomitant costs and benefits. The costs must be weighed against the anticipated benefits. Cohort-survival and curve-fitting techniques, for instance, are relatively inexpensive, but they are useful in answering only a limited set of questions about future enrollment and are considered valid only in the short term and under certain conditions.

Various factors might warrant the use of other, more expensive, forecasting techniques. For example, in addition to predicting changes in the number of students, it could be useful to predict the geographic locations of changes in both the numbers and the racial composition of the projected student population. Further, the assumptions that must be made with regard to enrollment projections that use cohort-survival or curve-fitting techniques may not be reasonable in all cases. In a district where land is still available for new housing, for instance, it is not reasonable to assume that the rate of new residential construction will continue as in the past. Therefore, other forecasting methods should be incorporated into the analysis. To analyze geographic changes of the population, the *census-based* method of enrollment forecasting is more useful than either the cohort-survival or the curve-fitting technique.

The census-based approach to school demography is not unlike the method used to project population changes for states and nations. This method (1) relies on a detailed picture of the population at one time, (2) predicts changes in such key variables as housing development and the job market, and (3) projects the population at a designated future time.

At the risk of oversimplification, we can say that the procedure assumes a relationship between knowns and unknowns. For example:

present population (known) + factor → future population (estimated),
present job market (known) + factor → future job market (estimated).

Although the concept of deriving the prediction factor appears simple, deriving and validating the factors can be a very complex process.

Census data are gathered from each household and organized according to geographical area. The basic information needed from each household might include:

1. Age of each child
2. Race
3. Length of residence
4. Type of dwelling unit
5. Age of dwelling unit
6. Occupation of household head

These data can be manipulated so that the following factors can be developed for each geographical area:

1. A *yield factor* for each age group per type of dwelling unit. (For example, for a particular area the average single-family residence might yield 1.8 children in the age group of five to nine years.)
2. The racial composition of each age group.
3. A list of the numbers of each age group in the district, including median ages and the percentage of each age group in the total population.
4. Comparisons between:
    a. length of residence and type of dwelling unit;
    b. length of residence and age of dwelling unit;
    c. length of residence and occupation of household head;
    d. length of residence and race.

Other ingredients necessary to make the projections will come from an enrollment-based method (such as curve fitting or cohort survival). In most cases, both census data and enrollment data are necessary to obtain the desired projections. Whereas survival rates are fundamental building blocks in projections based on enrollment, *yield factors* provide a means for making projections based on housing types, employment opportunities, etc. As an example, projections based on the yield factors of dwelling units are discussed here.

The dwelling-unit yield factor will be used to project the growth or decline of total population and student population in the district. In order to project population in this manner, information on planned future development is necessary. Approximately how many more residential dwelling units are planned in the next five years? How great will be the decrease in the number of dwelling units, because of condemnation, right of eminent domain, etc. over the next five years? Although no one has a crystal ball, there are several ways to get approximate answers to these questions. City or county planning offices have information on such things as zoning of vacant land, rezoning plans, number and types of building permits issued, and site-plan approvals. Area developers also have fairly specific plans, usually dependent on certain economic factors. An estimate of the numbers and types of future dwelling units can thus be derived.

To make a population projection, each of the planned developments within a district can be analyzed in terms of its characteristics and matched with one or more census areas within the district with similar characteristics. The dotted line in figure 14.7 encloses one of the planned developments in a district. The type of dwelling unit planned for that development is very similar to the type of dwelling unit already existing in Tract 5 Area 3 and Tract 4 Area 2.

Tract 4 Area 2 currently yields 157 children in the 0-4 age group from its 287 single-family residences. Tract 5 Area 3 yields 257 children in the same age group from its 371 single-family residences. A composite yield of children for the two areas would be 414 per 658 housing units or .63 children per household. Therefore, .63 children between ages 0-4 per single-family residence can be expected from the new housing development. Over a period of five years, with the expected increase of at least 300 similar housing units, it can be predicted that the corresponding increase of children in the 0-4 age group in that area would be about 190 (.63 multiplied by 300).

The projected yields of any age group for any tract can be predicted in this way. Also, the same procedure can be used to project populations of a particular racial or ethnic heritage. By making appropriate assumptions about the relationships between age groups and grades in schools, it is possible to derive estimates of future student populations.

When student population projections are based on census data, it is possible to locate where, within the district, changes are likely to take place. This information is as crucial in growing suburban areas as in inner cities, since zoning changes and housing developments have effects similar to those of urban renewal and intracity migration.

## Figure 14.7: Example of Matching Census Areas to Planned Development

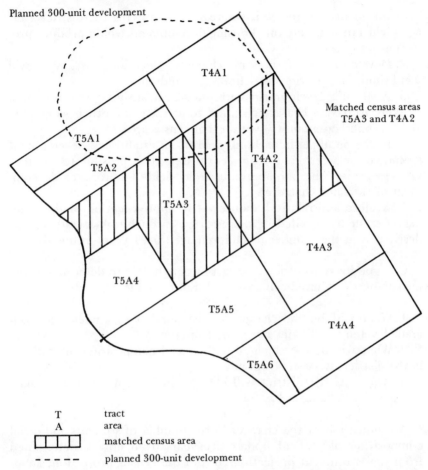

Planned 300-unit development

T4A1

Matched census areas
T5A3 and T4A2

T5A1

T5A2

T4A2

T5A3

T4A3

T5A4

T5A5

T4A4

T5A6

| T | tract |
| A | area |
| ⬚⬚⬚⬚ | matched census area |
| − − − − | planned 300-unit development |

*Note:* In this particular case, two matched census areas are immediately adjacent to their matched developments. However, matching is not necessarily done on the basis of geographical proximity. Rather, it is done on the basis of (1) type (owned/rented); (2) size (number of bedrooms); and (3) cost of housing units. Therefore, geographic proximity is a nonrelated factor, i.e., developments may or may not be adjacent to their matched census areas.

Source: Guilbert C. Hentschke and David K. Wiley, *Analysis of Demographic Change, a Report to the Board of Education* (San Jose, Calif.: Franklin-McKinley School District, 1969), p. 23.

This description of the census method has been based on the following assumptions (in addition to those discussed earlier):

1. Intradistrict variance is so great that applying the district average yield ratios to any one housing development would produce projections of questionable validity.

2. Developments of the same character (location, cost, type) will yield similar proportions of school-age children.

3. A specific development within a significantly larger census area is likely to have a character similar to at least one other geographic area (or microcommunity) within that census area.

4. If the pupil-per-household yield of an established development is known, or ascertained from census data, it is possible to use that ratio to project the pupil-per-household yield of a proposed development of the same character.

5. A close and relatively conservative approximation of the number of students enrolled in kindergarten through eighth grade can be derived from the number of children aged 5-13 years in the district.

One good way to review forecasting activities is to determine if the initial questions have been answered. For example:

1. What will be the changes in the number of students at each grade level in the district five years from now?

2. What will be the changes in the racial composition of students in the district five years from now?

3. Where in the district will changes in both number and racial composition take place?

An indication of the changes in the number of students and racial composition of student bodies five years from now is determined from the enrollment projections. From the census projection, an indication is obtained as to where population changes will take place. See figure 14.8. With this information, it is possible to improve the quality of planning decisions particularly in the areas of: (1) new construction, (2) curriculum development, and (3) budgeting.

Updating of projections on a yearly basis will also aid in planning decisions. Such an updating will require a reexamination and possible alteration of the general assumptions made when first projecting the population for a school district.

**Figure 14.8: Demographic Change Based on Five-Year Projection of Census Data**

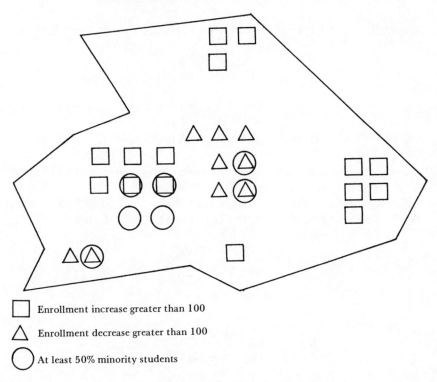

☐ Enrollment increase greater than 100

△ Enrollment decrease greater than 100

◯ At least 50% minority students

## Questions for Review and Discussion

1.   Would any of the methods discussed in this chapter be useful in forecasting future enrollments of children with specific learning disabilities, such as physical handicaps? If not, what activities might conceivably be undertaken to forecast these figures?

2.   How would least-squares curve fitting be used in forecasting the assessed valuation in a school district?

3.   All other factors being equal, is population forecasting more important in large school districts than in small ones? Why or why not?

4.   Does the census-based approach forecast enrollments as accurately in districts with declining enrollment as in districts with increasing enrollment? Why?

5.   In what ways is the problem of forecasting enrollments in a college for the next five years different from forecasting enrollment

in a school district? What specific kinds of assumptions 'would have to be examined when forecasting higher education enrollments?

## Appendix A: Using Least Squares To Estimate Future Enrollments

$$Y = aX + b$$

where

$$a = \frac{\Delta Y}{\Delta X} = \frac{Y_2 - Y_1}{X_2 - X_1}.$$

In this equation, $a$ is the slope of the least-squares line, and $b$ is called the $Y$ intercept. It is a constant which is the value of $Y$ when $X = 0$.

The least-square line approximating the set of points $(X_1, Y_1)$, $(X_2, Y_2) \ldots, (Y\sim, Y\sim)$ has the equation $Y = aX + b$, where

$$a = \frac{N\Sigma XY - (\Sigma X)(\Sigma Y)}{N\Sigma X^2 - (\Sigma X)^2}$$

and

$$b = \frac{(\Sigma Y)(\Sigma X^2) - (\Sigma X)(\Sigma XY)}{N\Sigma X^2 - (\Sigma X)^2}.$$

In our example, the set of given points that represent five years of enrollment data are as follows (see figure 14.6):

$$(X_1 Y_1) = (1, 1882),$$
$$(X_2 Y_2) = (2, 2437),$$
$$(X_3 Y_3) = (3, 3182),$$
$$(X_4 Y_4) = (4, 3941),\text{ and}$$
$$(X_5 Y_5) = (5, 5167).$$

To solve the above equations for $a$ and $b$ the following data must be calculated:

$N, \Sigma X, \Sigma Y, \Sigma XY, \Sigma X^2$,
$N$ = the number of points = 5,
$\Sigma X = X_1 + X_2 + X_3 + X_4 + X_5 = 15$,
$\Sigma Y = Y_1 + Y_2 + Y_3 + Y_4 + Y_5 = 16609$,

$\Sigma XY = X_1 Y_1 + X_2 Y_2 + X_3 Y_3 + X_4 Y_4 + X_5 Y_5 = 57901$, and
$\Sigma X^2 = X_1{}^2 + X_2{}^2 + X_3{}^2 + X_4{}^2 + X_5{}^2 = 55$.

Solving for $a = \dfrac{N(\Sigma XY) - (\Sigma X)(\Sigma Y)}{N\Sigma X^2 - (\Sigma X)^2}$

$$= \frac{5(57901) - (15)(16609)}{5(55) - (15)^2}$$

$$= \frac{289505 - 249135}{275 - 225}$$

$$= \frac{40370}{50}$$

$$= 807.4$$

Solving for $b = \dfrac{(\Sigma Y)(\Sigma X^2) - (\Sigma X)(\Sigma XY)}{N\Sigma X^2 - (\Sigma X)^2}$

$$= \frac{(16609)(55) - (15)(57901)}{5(55) - (15)^2}$$

$$= \frac{913495 - 868515}{275 - 225}$$

$$= \frac{44980}{50}$$

$$= 899.6.$$

Using $a$ and $b$ to forecast the enrollment for planning years 1, 2, and 3:

planning year 1 = point $X_6$, $Y_6$ where $X = 6$;
planning year 2 = point $X_7$, $Y_7$ where $X = 7$; and
planning year 3 = point $X_8$, $Y_8$ where $X = 8$.

Solving the equation $Y = aX + b$ for each planning year:

planning year 1:
$$\begin{aligned}
Y_6 &= aX_6 + b, \\
&= 807.4(6) + 899.6, \\
&= 4844.4 + 899.6, \\
&= 5744.
\end{aligned}$$

planning year 2:

$$Y_7 = aX_7 + b,$$
$$= (807.4)7 + 899.6,$$
$$= 5651.8 + 899.6,$$
$$= 6551.4.$$

planning year 3:

$$Y_8 = aX_8 + b,$$
$$= (807.4)8 + 899.6,$$
$$= 6459.2 + 899.6,$$
$$= 7358.8.$$

These estimates are plotted in figure 14.6.

## References

Ansoff, H. Igor. *Corporate Strategy*. New York: McGraw-Hill, 1965.

Dixon, W. J., and Massey, Frank J., Jr. *Introduction to Statistical Analysis*. New York: McGraw-Hill, 1969.

Fox, William M. *The Management Process: An Integrated Functional Approach*. Homewood, Ill.: Richard D. Irwin, 1963.

Hentschke, Guilbert C., and Wiley, David K. *Analysis of Demographic Change, a Report to the Board of Education*. San Jose, Calif.: Franklin-McKinley School District, 1969.

Wolfe, Harry D. *Business Forecasting Methods*. New York: Holt, Rinehart and Winston, 1966.

## Related Readings

Engelhardt, N. L. "Here's a Five Year Plan for Forecasting." *Nation's Schools* 73, no. 5 (May 1974): pp. 51-54. This article presents a four-step procedure for projecting district enrollments for the next five years.

Liu, B. A. "Estimating Future School Enrollments in Developing Countries." ERIC, no. ED078545, 1973. This manual is designed to provide some help to the educational statistician or equivalent technician who is faced with the task of providing estimates of future school enrollment in a developing country. The author considers some of the factors determining the growth of enrollment, the need for estimating future enrollment, and the characteristics of short-term, medium-term, and long-term estimates. Some of the terms used in connection with estimates of future enrollment are defined, the types of basic data needed are specified, and the kinds of methods generally used are explained briefly.

Midwest Research Institute. "Techniques of Institutional Research and Long Range Planning for Colleges and Universities." ERIC, no. ED085823, 1974. The material in this volume was developed for use in a series of workshops on institutional research and planning for colleges and universities. The workshop sessions made extensive use of computers. This was made possible through Plantran II, a computer simulation system designed to make the power of the computer available to the higher education executive without special computer knowledge. Although the material in this manual exploits the capabilities of the Plantran system, computer processing is not required for use of the models. Eight basic techniques of projecting enrollments are reviewed. These generalized techniques can be applied to any type of institution and to any type of enrollment. The crucial task is the matching of projection methods with the objective of the projection effort, which requires the judgment of a knowledgeable administrator.

Oliver, R. M. "Models for Predicting Gross Enrollment at the University of California." ERIC, no. ED080085, 1973. The purpose of this report is to discuss and compare two mathematical models for predicting student enrollments at the University of California. One has been proposed in the scientific literature and the second has been used by the state of California since 1963 to forecast student enrollments. The specific problems addressed in this report are the prediction of gross enrollments (i.e., freshmen, sophomores) for a particular campus of the University as a whole. Although the experimental data is restricted to undergraduates, the discussion and conclusions are probably appropriate to graduate levels as well.

Wing, P. "Higher Education Enrollment Forecasting: A Manual for State-Level Agencies." ERIC, no. ED101647, 1975. The primary objectives of this manual are to provide enrollment forecasting practitioners with guidance about the use of specific forecasting techniques and procedures and to foster greater understanding of these important planning tools. In additions to general discussion of such topics as accuracy, uses, assumptions, and data requirements, the manual provides illustrations of the application of several of the most widely used techniques. A review of the literature is provided in an appendix.

# 15
# Personnel and Resource Forecasting

One of the basic decisions a planner must make is what degree of accuracy and validity to demand of projections. Every planner wants the greatest possible accuracy, but increased accuracy usually costs more. The question is: will the increased costs be more than offset by the increased benefits?

The methods for projecting future school enrollments that were outlined in the previous chapter can be done easily by hand. Those discussed here are largely computer-based, because of their complexity and magnitude; they are relatively more costly and presumably yield more accurate and detailed information.

These more complex models require an understanding of computer simulation, including the general steps involved in creating one. This is discussed first, along with a computer simulation of demographic change in a community. That simulation is used to project student enrollments, just as the methods discussed in the previous chapter. The relative sophistication and complexity of the simulation, however, is much greater. The final section of the chapter is devoted to the description of a computer simulation which forecasts the demands for personnel and nonpersonnel resources.

## Computer Simulation

Taken together, this chapter and chapter fourteen point out two general ways that forecasting can be undertaken: simple extrapolation and modeling/simulation. Simple extrapolation refers here to forecasting by projecting the values of a single variable into the future. Curve fitting (discussed in chapter fourteen) is one of the primary extrapolation techniques. Modeling/simulation refers to the process of attempting to mirror relationships among different variables.

*Simulation* is defined as the act of performing experiments on a model of a given system (Schmidt and Taylor 1970, p. 4). *System* can be defined as a collection of entities that act together toward the accomplishment of some logical end. (For example, in this section two systems are isolated for examination: one is composed of those major factors that influence future enrollments; the other, of those factors that influence future demands on resources.)

A *model* is a representation of a system. Mathematical models are designed to capture the logical interactions and relations of the entities of the system being studied. The importance of the mathematical, or quantitative, approach to systems analysis has been well established over the past twenty-five years, as its wide use—in industry, the military, all levels of government, and, more recently, in education—demonstrates. In many cases, systems can be adequately represented by a mathematical model, which will involve an equation or a series of equations that vary in complexity according to the complexity of the system being analyzed. Many systems, however, are very complex, and a computer is essential to manipulate the large number of components involved. Computer-simulation models, therefore, are often used to describe interactions that exist in the real-world system but are too difficult to express adequately in a purely mathematical model.

Generally, in attempting to develop a mathematical model of a given system, one of the following situations can arise:

1. The system proves amenable to both description and analysis by a mathematical model. (See chapter thirteen, for example, for the application of linear programming to several education problems.)

2. No standard model fits, and the analyst chooses to create a simulation model of the system. (Examples would include the demographic and resource-demand models discussed in this chapter.)

3. The analyst decides not to use a simulation model, and what remains is the direct experimental approach. Here, alternative courses of action are identified and the best is selected by direct experimentation.

Within this context let us look at some of the major advantages and disadvantages of computer simulation. Among the advantages:

1. The model of a system, once constructed, may be employed as

often as desired to analyze different conditions or situations (as we shall see later).

2. In many cases it is far cheaper to gather information from a simulation of the real world than from the real world itself.

3. Simulations are useful in analyzing proposed systems for which information is at best sketchy.

4. Computer modeling can be employed to analyze conditions that might prove injurious or detrimental to people or things of value.

The greatest disadvantage of simulation has little to do with the technique itself; the disadvantage arises because people often use simulation even when it is not the most appropriate method. Until people become more familiar with this method, they will continue to employ it in situations where other analytical techniques are more suitable.

Although there has been a wide range both in the subject matter to which simulation has been applied and in the approach to using simulation, there are several basic steps common to many simulations:

1. Definition of the problem to be studied
2. Planning of the overall project
3. Formulation of a mathematical model of the object
4. Construction of a computer program for the model
5. Validation of the model
6. Design of experimental "runs" of the simulation
7. Execution of the simulation and analysis of the results

The first two steps are common to almost all analytic endeavors. While these two steps may seem obvious, they are nonetheless important. No study should proceed until a clear statement of the problem and the objectives are established. Estimates can then be made of the work to be done and the time required. (See the discussion of PERT and linear responsibility charting in chapters nine and ten for techniques of estimating the amount of work in a project.) Nor is the usefulness of the plan finished when the study has started; the plan can control the progress of the work and prevent the study from becoming unbalanced through concentration on one aspect of the problem at the expense of another. (In simulation studies a common failing is to become so engrossed in simulating that more detail is extracted than is needed or can be supported by the data available.)

The third step, constructing a model, really has two parts: (1) the structure of the model is determined by deciding what aspects of the system are significant for the problem at hand, and (2) correct data must be gathered. Analysis of the data requirements is expedited by recognizing the kinds of variables encountered in building models. A *relevant variable* is a characteristic or attribute of the system that is observed to take on a range of values and that in some way affects the measure of performance of the system. A *parameter* is a characteristic or attribute of the system that has only one value over all foreseeable ranges of operation (but may change as different alternatives are studied). A parameter or variable having a value that affects but is itself unaffected by the system is an *exogenous factor*. It represents a factor in the environment of the system under study. A parameter or variable having a value determined by other variables in the system is an *endogenous factor*. These distinctions will become clearer as specific models are examined.

The fourth step, construction of a computer program for the model, is a relatively well-defined task, given a mathematical model. It is not necessarily easy and can be very time-consuming, but the model establishes the specifications of what must be programmed. Actually, the question of how difficult it is to program a model often influences how the model is constructed. The tasks of producing a model and a computer program are likely to be carried out simultaneously rather than sequentially.

The fifth step, validation of the model, is a process requiring a good deal of judgment. To a large extent, this problem is the complement of the formulation of the model. Inferences made in establishing the model are checked by observing if the model behaves as expected. Errors can, of course, occur when programming a model. Ideally, however, the errors of the model and the errors of programming should be separated by validating the mathematical model before embarking on the programming. This is not easy to do, however, because the reason for simulating in the first place is usually that the implications of the mathematical model are unclear.

The sixth step is designing a set of experiments to meet the study objectives. Factors to be considered include the cost of running a computer model and, of course, answering the basic questions for which the simulation was designed.

The seventh step, execution of the simulation and analysis of the results is, in a sense, the purpose of the exercise. Once the results are analyzed, however, more questions are usually raised which require modifications in the simulation.

## Modeling Demographics

Building on two topics, forecasting (of enrollment and resources) and computer simulation, this section describes the development, appreciation, and digital-computer simulation of a demographic model suitable for long-term planning. The simulation model is based on the cohort-survival methodology (a more complex version of what was discussed in chapter fourteen) and projects population character-istics (e.g., population numbers for each region, year, and racial, age, sex, and income group) for a planning period of up to twenty years.

This particular model was developed by the Davis-McConnell-Ralston Division of Westinghouse Learning Corporation in coopera-tion with Westinghouse Research Laboratories (much of this material was drawn from Schweizer 1973 and Westinghouse Learning Corpo-ration 1972). It is presented here for several reasons. It is an example of the more sophisticated forecasting models used in education and shows the problems relevant to simulation methodology. (The model is described from a "nonmathematical" viewpoint here; see Schweizer (1973) for a more technical description of how the model operates.)

The approach taken by Westinghouse was based on an elaboration of the cohort-survival method using, instead of enrollment data, a de-tailed distribution of a population obtained in a base year (most likely a census year). The model simulates the movement and aging of that population through time, applying to it various population-changing factors, according to a set of assumptions about those fac-tors. A model was constructed using this methodology, but with modifications for including local population-influencing factors. (The term cohort is used to apply to a range of concepts. We first used it to apply to numbers of students enrolled in a grade school in a par-ticular year. In this section, we expand the concept of cohort to mean "age group" and focus specific attention on those factors that can influence cohorts.)

The model classified the total population according to five factors:

1. Geographical location (region)
2. Age
3. Year under consideration
4. Race or income group
5. Sex

The total population is divided into age groups, or cohorts. Diagrams depicting the four basic considerations—aging, mortality, fertility, and migration—that are modeled for each cohort are shown in figure 15.1. The dynamics are incorporated in the model by changing the

## Figure 15.1: The Four Primary Demographic Considerations

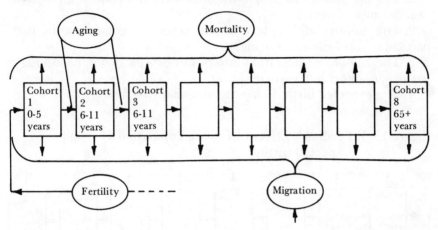

number of people that belong to the cohort each planning period, usually each year. A certain number of people are removed from the cohort to represent those who have aged to the next older cohort, those who have died during the planning period, and those who have migrated from the area. Numbers of people are added to the cohort to represent those who are aging from a younger cohort and those who are migrating into the area. The above modeling procedure is expressed in figure 15.2.

## Figure 15.2: Single Cohort Model

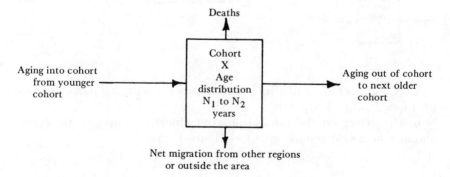

The number of people in a particular population cohort equals the sum of

1. The difference between the cohort population in a particular year and the number of people who will leave this cohort during that year because of aging;

2. The number of people who will enter the cohort during that particular year because of aging;

3. The amount of migration into or out of a particular region for a particular cohort in a particular year;

4. The expected births in a particular year (see figure 15.3);

## Figure 15.3: Feedback Effect of Female Population Through Expected Births

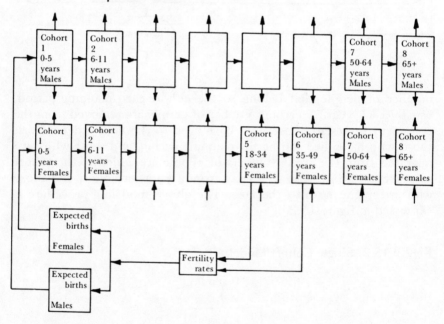

5. The expected deaths in a particular year within a particular cohort (see figure 15.4); and

6. The effect on the total population due to changes in the types and numbers of dwelling units (see figure 15.5).

## Figure 15.4: Interaction of Mortality Rates and Distribution Within Each Cohort

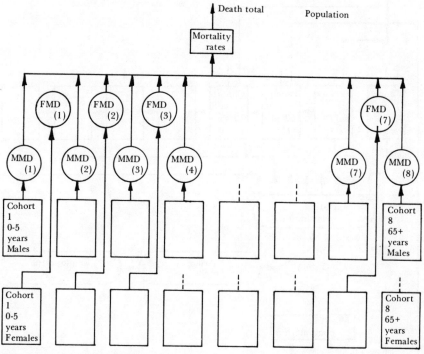

FMD   Female mortality distribution
MMD   Male mortality distribution

The numbers of students enrolled in kindergarten through grade twelve are estimated by determining the fraction of each age cohort that is in a particular grade, a particular region, and a particular year.

The migration term equals the product of three terms:

1. Average school-enrollment change over the past for a particular region and a particular race;

2. The ratio of average family size to average number of school-age children per family; and

3. The ratio of the number in a particular cohort to the total population.

The reasoning behind the formulation of the migration term is as follows. First, the number of immigrating schoolchildren is estimated

## Figure 15.5: Migration Model

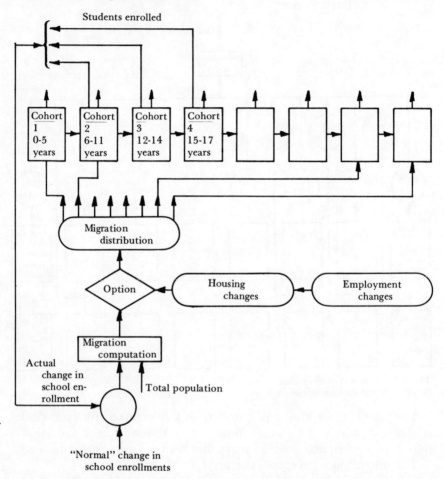

on the basis of past history. This number is then divided by the average number of school-age children per family to determine the number of immigrating families. It is then multiplied by average family size to determine the size of the immigrating population. This population is then allocated to appropriate cohorts by the ratios of the number in a particular cohort to the total population.

This term for migration allows the planner to use one of two options. The first uses the migration term and computes migration from a knowledge of past and present enrollment changes by race, average family size, and average number of school-age children. The second option computes migration based on the type and number of dwelling units being constructed or removed from the area. In a case where the exact number of future dwelling units is unknown, the units for the planning period may be determined by using an estimated rate of change.

In making the population projections, the maximum population, or *saturation* condition, for each region must be determined. In other words, a population projection of a particular cohort in a particular region of a particular race and sex cannot be greater than the maximum expected population of that group. This saturation population for each region is computed from an assumed set of characteristics for the neighborhood. These characteristics include type and number of dwelling units and the average number of people per type of dwelling unit.

## Resource Forecasting

Techniques of resource forecasting are tied closely to enrollment forecasting. Many of the items to be projected are in large part functions of the numbers of students to be served in the future. A number of models have been created to forecast resource demands in both elementary-secondary and higher education organizations. (The following references deal with the development of a resource forecasting model similar to the one discussed here: Sisson 1967, 1968; Stankard 1968; Stankard and Sisson 1968. For a review of efforts to build computer models of education organizations and processes, see Johnstone 1974.) In this section we will discuss a resource-forecasting model developed initially to analyze the implications of converting elementary schools to a year-round calendar.

Resources in this case refer to the things that must be purchased in order to operate the schools. These "things" include teachers, custodial and classroom supplies, and classrooms. Some resource-forecasting simulations have focused on only one or a few of these items (see, for example, a teacher cost model developed by Tracz and Burtnyk 1972), while others attempt to mirror the interrelated complexities of many of these items. In most of the resource-forecasting simulations in education, a number of decision variables have been incorporated. *Decision variables* require explicit decisions on the part of educational administrators. For example, to forecast the number of teachers required, it is necessary to estimate what enrollment will be and also to determine what class size will be. When decision variables are part of computer simulations, the distinction between forecasting and comprehensive planning tends to blur. The focus of planning shifts from estimating future environments to exploring ways to cope with these environments.

The resource-forecasting model under examination here is best described with reference to figure 15.6. It shows that future resource

**Figure 15.6: Resource-Forecasting Program**

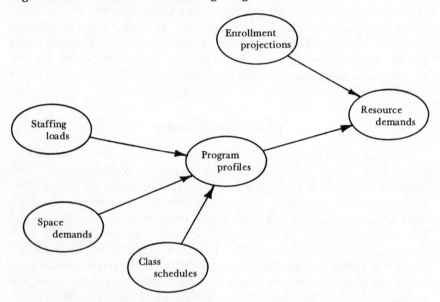

demands are generally a function of estimating the numbers of different types of students and estimating the nature of services (program profiles) that will be provided them. In this model, the services are largely a function of variables associated with how staff is used, how space is used, and how often classes meet.

A much more detailed description of the resource-forecasting program can be inferred by analyzing the output from one instructional program. In one of the school districts where this model has been applied, thirteen different instructional programs were documented in the elementary schools: kindergarten, grades one through seven, and five special education programs. Input data for each program include values for each of the following variables:

1. Class size;
2. The number of days per week that a class meets;
3. The number of time units consumed in each meeting of a class;
4. Hours per time unit;
5. Space utilization, or the number of hours in a calendar year in which space needed by the program can, in fact, be used;
6. The average unit salary of staff during the current year;
7. Construction allowance, or the number of square feet per pupil used in constructing space for that program;
8. Initial construction cost, or the average square-foot construction cost during the current year;
9. Maintenance cost, or the prorated cost per square foot to maintain spaces during the current year exclusive of salaries;
10. Annual inflation rates for salaries, construction costs, and maintenance costs;
11. Enrollment estimates for the next five years; and
12. Space inventory, or the number of spaces currently being used.

Sample output from the kindergarten program is presented in table 15.7.

In addition to modeling programs, this resource-forecasting method also models support services. *Support services* include:

| | |
|---|---|
| Principal | Instrumental music teacher |
| Assistant principal | Vocal music teacher |
| Secretary two | Physical education teacher |
| Custodian one | Art teacher |
| Custodian two | Reading resources teacher |
| Custodian three | Remedial reading teacher |
| Cafeteria worker one | Speech therapist |
| Cafeteria manager | Nurse |
| Librarian | |

Clearly, the distinction between programs and support services has no relation to instruction vs. noninstruction or certificated vs. classified. Rather, the division of elementary school operations in this district was done for computational reasons only. The model builder determined that there were two distinct classes of activities in the elementary schools. Programs were defined as those activities that could be modeled as a predetermined set of children meeting on a relatively fixed schedule. Support services could not be accurately

# Table 15.7: Resource-Forecasting (Kindergarten Program Profile)

Class size: 19
Hours per time unit: 1
Time units per day: 3
Days per week: 5
Space utilization per class (hours/year): 600*
Space utilization (hours/year): 1,200
Staff utilization (hours/year): 1,200

Initial staff unit cost: $11,600
Salary inflation rate: 8%
Construction allowance (per pupil): 56,000 square feet
Initial construction cost per square foot: $23
Construction inflation rate: 15%
Initial maintenance cost per square foot: $0.50
Maintenance inflation rate: 8%

| | Current year | Planning year 1 | Planning year 2 | Planning year 3 | Planning year 4 | Planning year 5 |
|---|---|---|---|---|---|---|
| Enrollment | 2,934 | 3,000 | 3,100 | 3,150 | 3,200 | 3,250 |
| Number of classes | 154* | 158* | 163* | 166* | 168* | 171* |
| Space requirements (hours/year) | 92,653* | 94,737* | 97,895* | 99,474* | 101,053* | 102,632* |
| Total spaces required | 77* | 79* | 82* | 83* | 84* | 86* |
| Space inventory | 77* | 77* | 79* | 82* | 83* | 84* |
| Net spaces required | 0* | 2* | 3* | 1* | 1* | 1* |
| New construction costs | $ 5,924* | $ 56,211* | $ 97,944* | $ 56,318* | $ 64,767* | $ 74,480* |
| Maintenance costs | $ 44,362* | $ 45,360* | $ 46,872* | $ 47,628* | $ 48,384* | $ 49,140* |
| Instructional staff (groups) | 77* | 79* | 82* | 83* | 84* | 86* |
| Instruction staff (costs) | $1,100,354* | $1,213,725* | $1,353,081* | $1,483,437* | $1,626,061* | $1,782,080* |
| Total costs | $1,150,600* | $1,315,295* | $1,497,895* | $1,587,381* | $1,739,211* | $1,905,698* |
| Cost per pupil | $ 392* | 438* | 483* | 504* | 544* | 586* |

*Note:* Instructional staff includes one teacher and one paraprofessional.

*These numbers were calculated by using the model: they were generated *endogenously*. All other numbers were "read into" the model: they were generated *exogenously*.

modeled on this basis and, instead, have been modeled on an average-amount-per-student basis.

To determine the profile of resource demands for support services, data were gathered for each of the following variables:

1. Utilization rate of staff (the ratio of staff in that service to total student population);
2. Unit salary (the unit salary of staff in that service);
3. Utilization rate of space (the ratio of spaces used in that service to total student population); and
4. Unit cost of space (the average 1973-1974 unit cost of space for that service).

The data are presented in tables 15.8-15.12.

## Table 15.8: Support Services Data

| Support staff | Utilization rate | Salary | Inflation rate |
|---|---|---|---|
| Principal | 850 | $16,382 | 1.08% |
| Assistant Principal | 1,200 | 12,616 | 1.08% |
| Secretary Two | 850 | 5,690 | 1.08% |
| Custodian One | 850 | 4,622 | 1.08% |
| Custodian Two | 850 | 4,845 | 1.08% |
| Custodian Three | 850 | 5,933 | 1.08% |
| Cafeteria Worker One | 175 | 2,071 | 1.08% |
| Cafeteria Manager | 850 | 5,009 | 1.08% |
| Librarian | 850 | 10,719 | 1.08% |
| Instrumental music teacher | 5,400 | 9,000 | 1.08% |
| Vocal music teacher | 850 | 9,000 | 1.08% |
| Physical education teacher | 1,275 | 9,440 | 1.08% |
| Art teacher | 1,275 | 9,440 | 1.08% |
| Reading resources teacher | 850 | 9,940 | 1.08% |
| Remedial reading teacher | 850 | 9,940 | 1.08% |
| Speech therapist | 850 | 9,940 | 1.08% |
| Nurse | 850 | 9,000 | 1.08% |

The "essence" of this model (i.e., the functional relationships among variables) is presented in exhibit 15.13. The data and how they are used determine the quality of the simulation.

This particular resources forecasting model is helpful in discussing issues of validation and use. As implied earlier in the chapter, clear statements about the problem areas under study make possible clear statements about what a valid mathematical model will look like. Are

## Table 15.9: Projected Cost and Number of Support Staff

| Support staff | Current year | | Planning year 1 | | Planning year 2 | |
|---|---|---|---|---|---|---|
| | Cost | Number | Cost | Number | Cost | Number |
| Principal | $ 635,524 | ( 37) | $ 724,958 | ( 39) | $ 802,414 | ( 40) |
| Assistant principal | 348,022 | ( 26) | 396,885 | ( 28) | 439,174 | ( 28) |
| Secretary two | 224,593 | ( 37) | 255,747 | ( 39) | 282,607 | ( 40) |
| Custodian one | 183,989 | ( 37) | 209,384 | ( 39) | 231,245 | ( 40) |
| Custodian two | 192,467 | ( 37) | 219,065 | ( 39) | 241,969 | ( 40) |
| Custodian three | 233,832 | ( 37) | 266,296 | ( 39) | 294,294 | ( 40) |
| Cafeteria worker one | 422,583 | (182) | 479,121 | (192) | 527,302 | (197) |
| Cafeteria manager | 198,702 | ( 37) | 226,184 | ( 39) | 249,857 | ( 40) |
| Librarian | 415,791 | ( 47) | 474,061 | ( 39) | 524,462 | ( 40) |
| Instrumental music teacher | 55,544 | ( 5) | 63,312 | ( 6) | 70,026 | ( 6) |
| Vocal music teacher | 352,871 | ( 37) | 402,217 | ( 39) | 444,871 | ( 40) |
| Physical education teacher | 246,479 | ( 25) | 280,969 | ( 26) | 310,789 | ( 27) |
| Art teacher | 246,479 | ( 25) | 280,969 | ( 26) | 310,789 | ( 27) |
| Reading resources teacher | 388,863 | ( 37) | 443,314 | ( 39) | 490,400 | ( 40) |
| Remedial reading teacher | 388,863 | ( 37) | 443,314 | ( 39) | 490,400 | ( 40) |
| Speech therapist | 388,863 | ( 37) | 443,314 | ( 39) | 490,400 | ( 40) |
| Nurse | 352,871 | ( 37) | 402,217 | ( 39) | 444,871 | ( 40) |
| Total cost | $5,276,326 | | $6,011,321 | | $6,645,860 | |
| Cost per pupil | $165 | | $178 | | $192 | |

| Support staff | Planning year 3 | | Planning year 4 | | Planning year 5 | |
|---|---|---|---|---|---|---|
| | Cost | Number | Cost | Number | Cost | Number |
| Principal | $ 893,268 | ( 42) | $ 990,460 | ( 43) | $1,105,337 | ( 44) |
| Assistant principal | 488,781 | ( 29) | 541,840 | ( 30) | 604,558 | ( 31) |
| Secretary two | 314,127 | ( 42) | 347,812 | ( 43) | 387,643 | ( 44) |
| Custodian one | 256,901 | ( 42) | 284,312 | ( 43) | 316,727 | ( 44) |
| Custodian two | 268,850 | ( 42) | 297,571 | ( 43) | 331,534 | ( 44) |
| Custodian three | 327,147 | ( 42) | 362,260 | ( 43) | 403,778 | ( 44) |
| Cafeteria worker one | 583,899 | (204) | 644,236 | (209) | 715,650 | (216) |
| Cafeteria manager | 277,367 | ( 42) | 307,322 | ( 43) | 342,424 | ( 44) |
| Librarian | 583,589 | ( 42) | 646,823 | ( 43) | 721,571 | ( 44) |
| Instrumental music teacher | 77,903 | ( 6) | 86,326 | ( 6) | 96,283 | ( 7) |
| Vocal music teacher | 494,913 | ( 42) | 548,423 | ( 43) | 611,681 | ( 44) |
| Physical education teacher | 345,771 | ( 28) | 383,180 | ( 28) | 427,403 | ( 29) |
| Art teacher | 345,771 | ( 28) | 383,180 | ( 28) | 427,403 | ( 29) |
| Reading resources teacher | 545,639 | ( 42) | 604,711 | ( 43) | 674,542 | ( 44) |
| Remedial reading teacher | 545,639 | ( 42) | 604,711 | ( 43) | 674,542 | ( 44) |
| Speech therapist | 545,639 | ( 42) | 604,711 | ( 43) | 674,542 | ( 44) |
| Nurse | 494,913 | ( 42) | 548,423 | ( 43) | 611,681 | ( 44) |
| Total cost | $7,390,381 | | $8,186,289 | | $9,127,293 | |
| Cost per pupil | $207 | | $223 | | $240 | |

## Table 15.10: Support Spaces Data

| Support space | Utilization rate | Unit cost | Inflation rate | Inventory |
|---|---|---|---|---|
| Administration | 850 | $ 63,000 | 1.12% | 37 |
| Cafeteria | 850 | 117,000 | 1.12% | 37 |
| Library | 850 | 42,500 | 1.12% | 37 |
| Kitchen | 850 | 80,800 | 1.12% | 37 |
| Activity | 280 | 25,300 | 1.12% | 114 |
| Miscellaneous support | 850 | 124,300 | 1.12% | 37 |
| Site | 850 | 180,000 | 1.12% | 37 |

## Table 15.11: Projected Cost and Number of Support Spaces

| Support space | Current year Cost | Number of spaces* | Planning year 1 Cost | Number of spaces | Planning year 2 Cost | Number of spaces |
|---|---|---|---|---|---|---|
| Administration | $ 40,094 | (0.57) | $ 169,955 | (2.15) | $ 90,593 | (1.02) |
| Cafeteria | 74,460 | (0.57) | 315,631 | (2.15) | 168,244 | (1.02) |
| Library | 27,046 | (0.57) | 114,652 | (2.15) | 61,114 | (1.02) |
| Kitchen | 51,422 | (0.57) | 217,974 | (2.15) | 116,189 | (1.02) |
| Activity | 1,315 | (0.05) | 207,193 | (6.53) | 110,442 | (3.11) |
| Miscellaneous support | 79,106 | (0.57) | 335,324 | (2.15) | 178,741 | (1.02) |
| Site | 114,554 | (0.57) | 485,586 | (2.15) | 258,837 | (1.02) |
| Total cost | $387,997 | | $1,846,312 | | $984,160 | |
| Cost per pupil | $12 | | $55 | | $28 | |

| Support space | Planning year 3 Cost | Number of spaces | Planning year 4 Cost | Number of spaces | Planning year 5 Cost | Number of spaces |
|---|---|---|---|---|---|---|
| Administration | $ 127,705 | (1.29) | $ 128,138 | (1.15) | $ 182,869 | (1.47) |
| Cafeteria | 237,167 | (1.29) | 237,971 | (1.15) | 339,615 | (1.47) |
| Library | 86,150 | (1.29) | 86,442 | (1.15) | 123,364 | (1.47) |
| Kitchen | 163,787 | (1.29) | 164,342 | (1.15) | 234,537 | (1.47) |
| Activity | 155,686 | (3.91) | 156,214 | (3.50) | 222,936 | (4.46) |
| Miscellaneous support | 251,964 | (1.29) | 252,819 | (1.15) | 360,804 | (1.47) |
| Site | 364,872 | (1.29) | 366,109 | (1.15) | 522,485 | (1.47) |
| Total cost | $1,387,330 | | $1,392,035 | | $1,986,609 | |
| Cost per pupil | $39 | | $38 | | $52 | |

*While only whole units of spaces are constructed, the decimals are reported. Decisions to automatically "round up" or "round down" a decimal can be built into the simulation.

Table 15.12: Summary of All Programs and Support Services

| | | | | | | |
|---|---|---|---|---|---|---|
| Instructional staff costs | $12,835,434 | $14,849,878 | $16,530,354 | $18,787,824 | $21,094,160 | $24,377,824 |
| Construction costs | 4,414,930 | 1,832,665 | 1,025,178 | 1,596,002 | 1,584,078 | 2,486,869 |
| Maintenance costs | 539,652 | 575,985 | 592,542 | 612,286 | 630,246 | 653,708 |
| Support staff costs | 5,276,326 | 6,011,321 | 6,645,860 | 7,390,381 | 8,186,289 | 9,127,293 |
| Support space costs | 387,997 | 1,846,312 | 984,160 | 1,387,330 | 1,392,035 | 1,986,609 |
| Total costs | $23,454,240 | $25,116,112 | $25,778,048 | $29,773,824 | $32,886,800 | $39,632,256 |
| Total enrollment | 31,933 | 33,761 | 34,631 | 35,726 | 36,707 | 37,957 |
| Cost per pupil | $734 | $744 | $744 | $833 | $896 | $1,018 |

## Exhibit 15.13: Formulas for Calculating Endogenous Variables in the Resource-Forecasting Program

For programs

(1) Space use = ( _____ hours per time unit) $\times$ ( _____ time units per day) $\times$ ( _____ days per week) $\times$ ( _____ weeks per year), e.g., 1 $\times$ 3 $\times$ 5 $\times$ 40 = 600 hours for kindergarten

(2) Number of classes = ( _____ enrollment $\div$ (class size), e.g., 2,934 $\div$ 19 = 154 classes of kindergarten children in the current year*

(3) Space requirements (hours/year) = (number of classes) $\times$ (space use per class), e.g., 154 $\times$ 600 = 92,653 hours for kindergarten in the current year

(4) Total spaces required = (space requirements) $\div$ (space utilization), e.g., 92,653 $\div$ 1,200 = 77 kindergarten classrooms in the current year

(5) Space inventory in a particular year = (space inventory in the previous year) + (net spaces required in the previous year), e.g., 77 + 2 = 79 kindergarten spaces in planning year 2

(6) Net spaces required in a particular year = (total spaces required in that year) $\div$ (space inventory in that year), e.g., 77 $\div$ 77 = 0 spaces in the current year

(7) New construction costs = (net spaces required) $\times$ (class size) $\times$ (construction allowance per pupil) $\times$ (initial construction cost per square foot) $\times$ (inflation rate raised to the power of the planning year), e.g., 3 $\times$ 19 $\times$ 56 $\times$ 23 $\times$ $1.15^2$ = $ _____ for kindergarten in planning year 2

(8) Maintenance costs = (initial maintenance cost per square foot) $\times$ (total spaces required) $\times$ (construction allowance per pupil) $\times$ (class size) $\times$ (inflation rate raised to the power of the planning year), e.g., .50 $\times$ 82 $\times$ 56 $\times$ 19 $\times$ $1.08^2$ = $46,872 in planning year 2

(9) Instructional staff groups = (number of classes) $\times$ (space use per class) $\div$ (staff utilization), e.g., 154 $\times$ 600 $\div$ 1,200 = 77 kindergarten instructional staff groups

(10) Instructional staff costs = (instructional staff groups) $\times$ (initial staff unit cost) $\times$ (inflation rate raised to the power of the planning year), e.g., 84 $\times$ 11,600 $\times$ $1.08^4$ = $1,626,061 for kindergarten in planning year 4

(11) Total costs = (new construction costs) + (maintenance costs) + (instructional staff costs), e.g., $56,211 + $45,360 + $1,213,725 = $1,315,295 for the kindergarten program in planning year 2

(12) Cost per pupil = (total costs) $\div$ (total enrollment), e.g., $1,905,698 $\div$ 3,250 = $586 per kindergarten pupil in planning year 5

For support staff

(13) Number of a support staff position in a particular year = (total enrollment in that year) $\div$ (utilization rate), e.g., 34,636 $\div$ 850 = 40 elementary principals in planning year 2

(14) Total cost of a support staff position in a particular year = (number of a support staff position in that year) $\times$ (unit salary of that staff position) $\times$ (salary inflation rate raised to the power of the planning year under consideration), e.g., 40 $\times$ $16,382 $\times$ $1.08^2$ = $802,414 for elementary principals' salaries in planning year 2

(15) Total cost of all support staff in a particular year = the sum of the total cost of each support staff in that year, e.g., $635,524 + $348,022 + $224,593 + $183,989 + $192,467 + $233,832 + $422,583 + $198,702 + $415,791 + $55,544 + $352,871 + 2($246,479) + 3($388,863) + $352,871 = $5,276,326 in the current year

(16) Cost per pupil of all support staff in a particular year = (the total cost of all support staff in that year) $\div$ (total enrollment that year), e.g., $9,127,293 $\div$ 37,957 = $240 in planning year 5

For support spaces

(17) Number of a new support space needed in a particular year = (total enrollment in

## Exhibit 15.13 *(continued)*

that year) $\div$ (the utilization rate of that space) $-$ (the current inventory of that space), e.g., $31,933 \div 850 - 37 = .57$ administration spaces in the current year

(18) Cost of a new support space needed in a particular year = (the number of that support space needed in a particular year) $\times$ (the unit cost of that space) $\times$ (the rate of inflation raised to the power of the planning year), e.g., $3.91 \times \$25,300 \times 1.12^3 = \$155,686$ for activity rooms in planning year 3

(19) Total cost of support spaces in a particular year = the sum of the individual space types for that year, e.g., $\$90,593 + \$168,244 + \$61,114 + \$116,189 + \$110,442 + \$178,741 + \$258,837 = \$984,160$ in planning year 2

(20) Per-pupil cost of support space in a particular year = (total cost of support spaces in that year) $\div$ (enrollment), e.g., $\$1,387,330 \div 35,726 = \$39$ per student in planning year 3

(21) Total costs captured by the model = (total program staff costs) + (total program space costs) + (total program maintenance costs) + (total support staff costs) + (total support space costs), e.g., $\$24,377,824 + \$2,486,869 + \$653,708 + \$9,127,293 + \$1,986,609 = \$38,632,256$ in planning year 5

---

*The figures given in this exhibit are drawn from tables 15.7-15.12. Apparent "errors" in calculation are due to rounding of figures in some cases within the computer program. In addition, where salary figures are involved, partial fringe benefits were included in the final figures but were not included in the "unit salary" figures.

the data and relationships "appropriate"? For example, "New construction costs" are currently modeled as follows:

$$S = (N) \times (C) \times (A) \times (R)^n.$$

In this equation, $S$ is new construction (total dollar value), $N$ is net spaces required in a year, $C$ is class size, $A$ is construction allowance per pupil, $I$ is initial construction cost per square foot, $R$ is inflation rate, and $n$ is the number of the planning year under consideration.

This means that the total cost of new construction is reported in that year. It may be useful to report out the total dollar value of new construction even though most education agencies finance construction and, therefore, pay for it over a period of time. If it is more useful to know what would actually be paid out in a particular year, this equation could be modified by adding several variables and changing the relationships among them. Additional variables would include: $A$ (cost in the first year of new construction), $B$ (the yearly interest rate on the capital construction loan), and $Y$ (the number of years over which the loan is to be paid back).

Although the precise formula would depend on the nature of the loan, it would take the general form:

$$A = (S)/(Y) + (S) \times (B).$$

In other words, $A$ is equal to principal plus interest. The validity of the model, then, depends on its ability to specify outputs precisely.

As stated earlier, the nature of the simulation depends on the problem for which it was built. This resources forecasting simulation is for "general purpose" use in planning school district programs in future years. It is "general" only in that a number of different policy and forecasting alternatives are examined in successive runs of the simulation. As an example, one district used this simulation to analyze the interactive effects of the following changes in assumptions for next year in its elementary schools:

1. Average school loading is 900, 950, 1,000 instead of 850;
2. One counselor will be added to each school;
3. Enrollment is 3 percent higher than anticipated;
4. Enrollment is 3 percent lower than anticipated;
5. Average class sizes are 25 and 30 instead of 28;
6. All kindergartens are converted from half to full day;
7. Teaching aides are dropped from the kindergarten program;
8. One assistant principal will be assigned to each school instead of only to those schools with more than 950 students;
9. Costs of construction and land inflate at a rate of 10 and 12 percent instead of 15 percent;
10. Wage settlements will be 10 percent instead of an anticipated 8 percent;
11. All portable classrooms will be eliminated;
12. A program for early-childhood handicapped will be added to ten of the elementary schools;
13. The school calendar will be a 45-15 (year-round) plan instead of a traditional plan; and
14. The reading disability program will be lengthened from a semester to a year course.

In developing this and the previously discussed simulations, it has become apparent that more benefits can accrue from computer simulation of a problem than those resulting directly from the "answers." The following list of benefits is adapted from Naylor (1968, pp. 8-9).

1. Simulation makes it possible to study and experiment with the complex internal interactions of a given system whether it be a firm, an industry, an economy, or a subsystem of one of these.
2. Through simulation one can study the effects of certain informational, organizational, and environmental changes on the opera-

tion of a system by making alterations in the model of the system and observing the effects of these alterations on the system's behavior.

3. Detailed observation of the system being simulated may lead to a better understanding of the system and to suggestions for improving it that otherwise would not be obtainable.

4. The experience of designing a computer simulation model may be more valuable than the actual simulation itself. The knowledge obtained in designing a simulation study frequently suggests changes in the system being simulated. The effects of these changes can then be tested via simulation before implementing them on the actual system.

5. Simulation of complex systems can yield valuable insight into which variables are more important than others and how these variables interact.

6. Simulation can be used to experiment with new situations about which we have little or no information so as to prepare for what may happen.

7. Simulation can serve as a "preservice test" to try out new policies and decision rules for operating a system, before running the risk of experimenting on the real system.

8. Simulations are often useful in that they afford a convenient way of breaking down a complicated system into subsystems, each of which may then be modeled by an analyst who is expert in that area.

9. Simulation enables one to study dynamic systems in either real time, compressed time, or expanded time.

10. When new components are introduced into a system, simulation can be used to help foresee bottlenecks and other problems that may arise in the operation of the system.

11. Simulation makes generalists out of specialists. Analysts are forced into an appreciation and understanding of all facets of the system, with the result that conclusions are less apt to be biased by particular inclinations and less apt to be unworkable within the system framework.

## Questions for Review and Discussion

1. In what fundamental ways does the demographic model discussed in this chapter differ from the demographic models discussed in the previous chapter? Are these the differences between simulation and simple extrapolation?

2. How does the process of constructing and using a computer simulation differ from the central ideas of the scientific method, described in the Preface?

3. Equation (7) in exhibit 15.13 calculates new construction costs for instructional space. Why doesn't this equation represent what a school district would actually pay out for new instructional spaces in a year? What could be done to make this equation represent actual costs more accurately?

4. Equation (21) in exhibit 15.13 calculates the total costs captured by the model. What school district costs are not included in this equation?

5. What criteria should be used to determine whether resources should be expended to construct a computer simulation of a problem in education?

## References

Emshoff, James R., and Sisson, Roger L. *Design and Use of Computer Simulation Models.* New York: Macmillan, 1970.

Johnstone, James N. "Mathematical Models Developed for Educational Planning." *Review of Educational Research* 44, no. 2 (spring 1974): 177-97.

Naylor, Thomas. *Computer Simulation Techniques.* New York: John Wiley & Sons, 1968.

Schmidt, J. W., and Taylor, R. E. *Simulation and Analysis of Industrial Systems.* Homewood, Ill.: Richard D. Irwin, 1970.

Schweizer, Phillip F. "A Demographic Simulation Model for Health Care, Education, and Urban Systems Planning." *1973 Winter Simulation Conference,* edited by Austin Hogatt, pp. 320-33. Berkeley: University of California, 1973.

Sisson, Roger. "A Hypothetical Model of a School." ERIC, no. ED030978, 1968.

Sisson, Roger. "Some Results of a Simulation of an Urban School District." ERIC, no. ED012096, 1967.

Stankard, Martin, Jr. "Development of Quantitative Models of the Educational Process." ERIC, no. ED024116, 1968.

Stankard, Martin, Jr., and Sisson, Roger. "On the Modeling of Relationships Between Performance and Resource Management in an Urban School District." ERIC, no. ED025839, 1968.

Tracz, G. S., and Burtnyk, W. A. *Teacher Cost Models.* Toronto: The Ontario Institute for Studies in Education, 1972.

Westinghouse Learning Corporation. "Planning Models for School Districts." *Management Information Systems,* edited by Guilbert C. Hentschke, pp. 35-51. Denver: Department of Education, 1972.

## Related Readings

Higgins, K. R. "A Model Generation for the Faculty Flow Process in a Large-City District." ERIC, no. ED087439, 1973. Personnel Simulation (PER SIM), a computerized model developed to trace the flow of faculty through the processes of entry into, engagement within, and withdrawal from an educational agency, is described.

Geoffrion, A. M. "Academic Departmental Management: An Application of an Interactive Multicriterion Optimization Approach." ERIC, no. ED081402, 1974. This paper describes a mechanism for assisting an administrator in determining resource allocation decisions which only require local trade and preference information. A numerical example of the use of this model coupled with the interaction procedure is provided.

Morrisseau, J. J. "Simulation Models in Higher Education." ERIC, no. ED083890, 1973. This paper discusses cost simulation models in higher education. Emphasis is placed on the art of management, mini-models vs. maxi-models, the useful model, the reporting problem, anatomy of failure, information vs. action, and words of caution.

Rodemacher, R. A. "A Resource Allocation Model for Public School District Planning." ERIC, no. ED087438, 1973. This paper explores the development and use of a general purpose computer simulation model for diverse sizes and levels of school district organization. Part one introduces modeling and simulation theory; part two describes a school submodel; and part three discusses the applicability and mechanics of Optiplanner, a FORTRAN-based computer simulation.

Turk, James H. "Budget ESTimation (BEST)." ERIC, no. ED087440, 1973. A series of computer programs are employed to assist the secondary principal in dealing with budget preparation, teacher requirement estimates, and schedule making.

# PART V

# INFORMATION SYSTEMS

# 16
# Developing Information Systems

A fundamental premise of this book is that systematically developed information is necessary for managerial decision making. Up to this point, ready access to such information has been assumed. It is now appropriate to focus on information, and on the management tasks and responsibilities related to information, especially information handled by computers.

Even a superficial introduction to the basic issues emerging in information science is beyond the scope of this volume. However, educational managers are increasingly required to deal with information handling as an ongoing part of management operations. This is particularly challenging in a field involving highly technical issues and rapid developmental advances. The role of the educational manager in the development and operation of information systems is that of knowledgeable broker among specialists: the information-related goals of educational management are served by highly skilled and specialized technicians.

This chapter discusses a few of the fundamental concepts of information systems and some of the basic activities involved in bringing them to an operational condition. Chapter seventeen deals with the various uses that educational managers make of information and with the implications of information systems in management of other segments of the educational organization.

## Analytical Prerequisites

Although qualitatively different from traditional assets, information can be viewed as an important asset of an educational organization, just as cash, inventories, or buildings. Using inventory management as an analogy may help to clarify what is meant by managing information as an asset. As with inventories, information of the right variety and type should be stored and made available for use in the proper locations, and at the required times and frequencies. Again like inventories, too much information is costly and too little is equally damaging. Information also must be protected from use by unauthorized persons and from physical loss through fire, flood, or power failure.

Unlike inventories, however, information can be physically managed and controlled directly via computers, file folders, or other means used to control inventories indirectly. Although information management is similar in part to many other management operations, there are a range of issues that apply specifically to the study of information systems. Particularly useful for our purposes are: a working definition of information system; an introduction to flow charting; and brief descriptions of how data are organized and coded.

## A System of Information

While the word *system* has been used frequently, little has been said about the characteristics of a system or about determining or constructing a system, especially as it applies to the concept of information. System is a term used in many contexts. In the natural sciences we speak of the solar system, molecular systems, and ecological systems. When discussing the human body, we speak of the circulatory system and the central nervous system. In virtually all contexts, system denotes "an organized or complex whole, an assemblage or combination of things or parts forming a complex or unitary whole, . . . it will be helpful to define systems more precisely as an array of components designed to accomplish a particular objective according to plan." (Johnson; Kast; and Rosenzweig 1967, p. 113)

A system is confined by a boundary. The concept of boundary is described by Chin:

The boundary of a system may exist physically: a tightly corked vacuum bottle, the skin of a person, the number of people in a group, etc. But, in addition, we may delimit the system in a less tangible way, by placing our boundary according to what variables are being focused upon. We can construct a system consisting of multiple roles of a person, or a system composed of varied roles among members in a small work group, or a system interrelating roles in a family. The components or variables used are roles, acts, expectations, communications, influence and power relationships, and so forth, and not necessarily persons. . . . In small groups we tend to draw the same boundary line for multiple systems of power, communications, leadership, and so on, a major advantage for purposes of study.

In diagnosing we tentatively assign a boundary, examine what is happening inside the system and then readjust the boundary, if necessary. We examine explicitly whether or not the "relevant" factors are accounted for within the system, an immensely practical way of deciding upon relevance. Also, we are free to limit ruthlessly, and neglect some factors temporarily, thus reducing the number of considerations necessary to be kept in mind at one time. The variables left outside the system, in the "environment" of the system, can be introduced one or more at a time to see the effects, if any, on the interrelationship of the variables within the system. (Chin 1961, pp. 203-4)

Chin is saying that all inputs and outputs cannot always be included in the system. The selection of which variables to include is difficult. Hussain provides a useful example dealing with computing grade point averages:

If the processor chosen was a computer system, it may well be determined that the incremental cost for other related computations is negligible and should also be processed. So the stated objectives may be restated as being the determination of students on probation and suspension. Extending this further, it may be logical for the information system to register and schedule the student. And so the system expands. *Unless the system is carefully planned, the system becomes overextended and uncontrollable.* (Hussain 1973, pp. 67-68, emphasis added)

Typically, the components of a system will be of four types: input, processing, control, and output. One of the guiding rules used in setting system boundaries is that of minimizing the intersections of the boundary with inputs and outputs, but still including the most relevant activities. This is illustrated in figure 16.1. In this figure two boundaries have been drawn. Many others are, of course, possible. The boundary drawn with a broken line has three inputs (activities coming into the system) and five outputs (activities going out). The boundary drawn with a continuous line has only one input (activity 20-25) and one output (activity 60-90). This reduces the system's relations with its environment to one input and one output and still includes all other interrelated activities. Therefore, it is probably a better boundary than the one drawn with a broken line.

It is often tempting for educational managers to define a system which aligns with their particular responsibilities, and to ignore the potential for a more comprehensive determination of an information system. As Hoag states it, this course

is the natural one for an administrator to take, for he is charged with looking after an organization whose boundaries will usually have been defined. But it is only accidentally a natural course for an analyst. And for him it is often a dangerous course, because administratively determined systems will be too narrow for some problems, leading to bad analysis through unduly restrictive

## Figure 16.1: Boundaries of a System

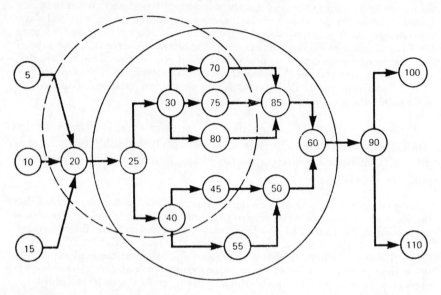

Source: Khateeb M. Hussain, *Development of Information Systems for Education* (Engle-wood Cliffs, N.J.: Prentice-Hall, 1973), p. 68. Reprinted by permission.

criteria, and too broad for others, leading to unnecessarily complicated analyses. (Hoag 1957, p. 445)

Such systems can be further divided into subsystems. When the number of subsystems increases, problems of coordination and compatibility arise. Subsystems should be united and coordinated in order to achieve system effectiveness. The unification of subsystems within a system is referred to as integration. There are at least three different types of integration of information. One is horizontal integration, where a piece of information in a certain stage, say processing, is located in a single place, but is accessible to a large number of potential users. Figure 16.2 shows the concept of horizontally integrating student registration information at a higher education institution with the needs of various units or departments on campus.

An information system may be vertically integrated to the extent that a single administrative unit is responsible for the various stages of information handling. For example, instead of receiving data in machine-readable form from other departments, a data-processing center may assume for itself the responsibility for converting the data to machine-readable form.

## Figure 16.2: Example of a Horizontally Integrated Information System (Higher Education Student Registration)

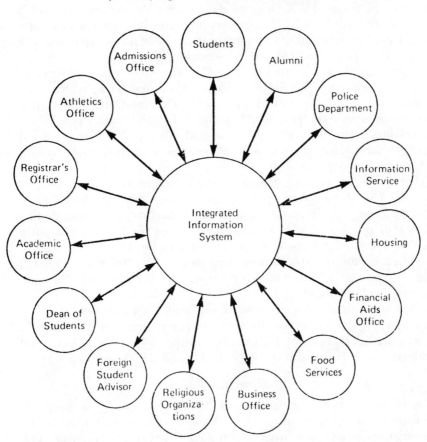

Source: Khateeb M. Hussain, *Development of Information Systems for Education* (Englewood Cliffs, N.J.: Prentice-Hall, 1973), p. 72. Reprinted by permission.

Longitudinal integration refers to linking together pieces of information as they are generated. Longitudinal information is often needed for record purposes and for predicting future values of variables such as student enrollment, staffing patterns, and instructional programs.

What then, are the components of information systems? There are several distinct parts to consider. For example, an information system implicitly requires a user, or someone who identifies the information needed and uses it. After the information is used, it may again become data which, along with other data, is reprocessed. The general form of a system of information is described by Hussain and depicted in figure 16.3. Original data enters the system (1), and is checked and edited (2). If necessary the data is modified to ensure that it is complete and has no apparent errors or inconsistencies. The data is then processed (3) and information is generated (4). The information is then sent to the user (5). The satisfaction or dissatisfaction concerning this information is then fed back, which may modify the needs for information (6). The modified needs then determine new data (7), which is used for the next cycle of reprocessing, again with the checking and editing (2). The modified needs (6) also affect the instructions for processing (8), which in turn determine future processing.

The information once generated (4), in addition to being sent to the user (5), also becomes part of the historic data (9). An example would be the payroll for the month. Social Security and other deductions will be carried over as historic data for the following month. The nature of the historic data needed will be determined by the modified needs for information. This data is used for processing (3) and need not be edited or checked for validity (2) since it has already gone through that stage.

This system has a "wholeness" because it has a common plan and objective. It includes the four basic components: input (1,7,9), processing (2,3), control (5,6,8), and output (4). (For an extended discussion of information systems, see Hussain 1973, pp. 57-94.)

## Flowcharting

A flowchart is a shorthand method for representing the overview or logic of an information system. Flowcharting can be used to describe an information system which does not require computer capabilities. However, for purposes of introducing some basic computer concepts, flowcharting for computer programming is discussed here.

A flowchart looks much like figure 16.3, where boxes, arrows, words, and numbers are used to describe an information system. In information handling, flowcharts are used to "pick apart" complex problems; to aid in synthesizing a system by combining detailed elements into a whole; to program a solution to a problem on a computer; and to aid in documentation and communication among systems personnel and administrators who are responsible for managing complex information systems.

Like mathematical equations and chess moves, flowcharting consists of a series of universally recognizable geometric figures and

# Figure 16.3: Components of an Information System

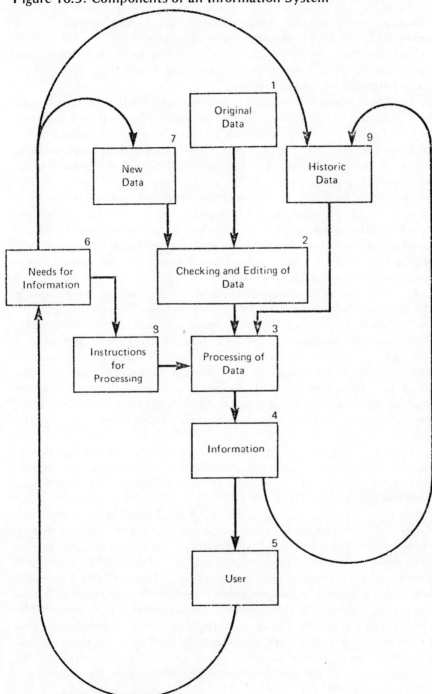

Source: Khateeb M. Hussain, *Development of Information Systems for Education* (Englewood Cliffs, N.J.: Prentice-Hall, 1973), p. 84. Reprinted by permission.

symbols. Some of the more common flowcharting symbols are shown in figure 16.4 and described briefly here.

The *processing functions* are usually written within a rectangle and include such operations as instructions for transferring data, arithmetic instructions, and others.

The *input/output functions* are concerned with making information available to the system (input) and recording processed information (output). There are a variety of ways in which information can be stored or fed into and out of a computer. These include punched cards, magnetic and paper tapes, magnetic drums, and typewriter-like keyboards.

The *decision function* is concerned with alternative routes in a program. The question to be answered is usually written within the symbol and can be related to a specific logic instruction. The logic function is important in that it gives the programmer the means by which the computer can make some basic decisions and to select alternative paths during processing.

Other special symbols are used to show the flow of data through the system and are called connector symbols. The important connector symbols are the terminal, connector, and offpage connector. The terminal connector is used to indicate both the beginning and the end of a particular program flowchart. The connector symbol indicates the continuation of processing at some other point in the program on the same page. The offpage connector indicates that the continuation of processing is on another page. A unique identifying code is entered in the connectors on both pages (both codes are the same).

The use of flowcharting to solve information handling problems can be clarified by describing a commonly occurring problem, preparing the payroll. (This example is adapted from Abrams and Corvine 1966, pp. 250-54.)

An input deck of cards for the company payroll is first produced. There are three cards for each employee. The first card, coded A, contains his names and address, company ID number, and pay rate to two decimal places. The second card, coded B, is the employee's hours rate card and contains the employee ID number and the total hours worked during the pay period. The third card, coded C, contains the employee's ID number and his payroll deductions. The three cards are grouped in A, B, C sequence for each employee. This problem has several parts: computations of the gross pay, the net pay, and the accumulated sums of all categories. The output from this computer run would be either the paycheck or the input for a

Figure 16.4: Flowcharting Symbols

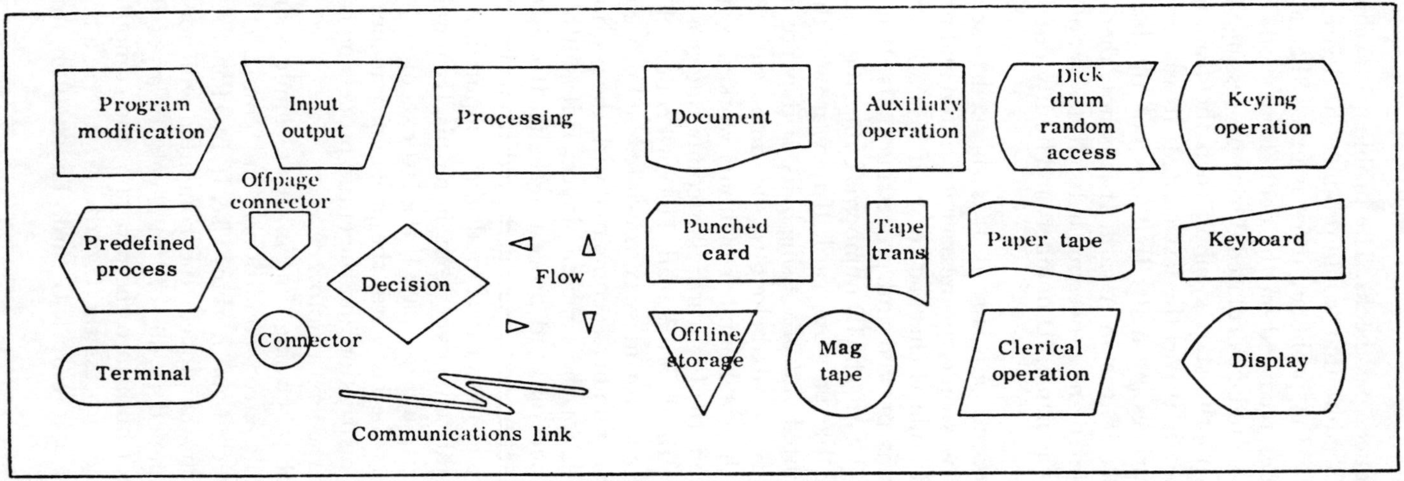

run that produces paychecks. The problem flowchart in figure 16.5 shows one procedure that would produce the desired results.

To simplify the problem, it is assumed that all deductions are fixed quantities recorded on the deductions card. In practice, some deductions have to be calculated during processing. The problem outline begins with the start symbol, then the reading of a card. It is checked to see if it was the last card. If it was, an error message is printed and processing halts. If it was not the last card, it is next checked to see if it is an A card. If it is not, then a different error message is printed and processing halts. If it was not the last card and is an A card, the name, ID number, and hourly rate figures are stored in memory.

Now the second card is read. It is checked to see if it was the last card and if it was, an error message is printed and processing halts. If not, the card code is checked to see if it is a B card and if not, an error message is printed and processing halts. If it was not the last card and is a B card, the ID number is compared with the ID number retained from the previous card. If they are not the same, an error message is printed and processing halts. If they are the same, indicating that the two cards belong to the same employee, the figure on this card for the total number of hours worked is multiplied by the hourly rate from the first card, thus computing gross pay.

Finally, the third card is read. The card code is checked and if it is not a C card, an error message is printed and processing halts. If it is a C card, its ID number is compared with the previous one to ensure that the card is for the same employee. If it is different, a new error message is typed out and processing halts. If it is the correct third card, the deductions on it are deducted from the gross pay to calculate net pay, and the various totals are computed. A new card is now punched for this employee containing his ID number, name, gross pay, deductions, and net pay. If the last executed "read" instruction did not process the last card, the program branches back to the first "read a card" instruction and the entire processing is repeated for the three cards of the next employee.

Much of the processing time in this example is spent checking for various possible error conditions. The computer will always do exactly as directed and nothing else. If, by chance, B and C cards are reversed for any employee, the computer will not detect the error unless programmed to do so. If a check for a possible error in card sequence is not built into the program, the computer would, in the case mentioned, process the C card as if it were a B card and process the B card as if it were a C card. The resulting output would, of

# Figure 16.5: Structure Flowchart of Payroll Problem

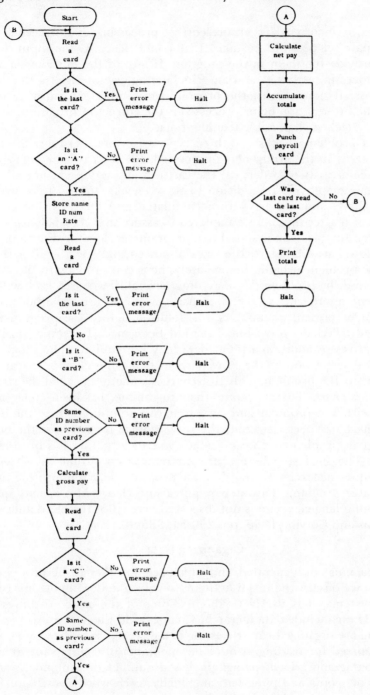

Source: Peter Abrams and Walter Corvine, *Basic Data Processing* (New York: Holt, Rinehart, and Winston, 1966), p. 252. Reprinted by permission.

course, be incorrect. To ensure correct processing, it is necessary to anticipate all possible mistakes that could occur in the input deck and provide for them in the program. If any of the mistakes occur, the processing will halt and an error message can designate the type of error. If none occur, the programmer can be reasonably certain that the information being processed is the correct information, since he has checked all possible trouble spots.

This problem checks for three types of errors: (1) there are not three cards in the group being processed, (2) the cards in any group of three are out of order, (3) the cards in any group are not all for the same employee. In addition to these checks, totals of gross pay, deductions, and net pay are accumulated and these can be cross-referenced after the run is completed to assure that they balance.

After any problem is stated to a programmer, he may draw a problem flowchart similar to the ones discussed, but specifically geared for the problem at hand. Immediately, he is concerned with the ways of solving the problem. He may draw several flowcharts, each with a different approach. As the flowcharts are being drawn, other problems may present themselves for solution before the programmer proceeds. Perhaps provisions have not been made for some possible alternatives or additional input data may be required. The programmer will select one of the flowcharts as being the most practical approach to the problem. This flowchart is sometimes called the *structure flowchart*. To this point, the programmer has been concerned only with the problem and its alternative solutions. Once the best flowchart has been selected, the programmer is ready for the next step. The problem has been stated, and its structure has been analyzed. The final step before programming is to outline the specific techniques necessary to translate the proposed solution into the final computer program. This step requires knowledge of a specific programming language, and is not discussed here. (For further details see Abrams and Corvine 1966, pp. 250-54, 385-90.)

## Organizing Data

Data must be generated and organized in order to be processed. Before we discuss the major activities involved in developing information systems, it is useful to discuss some of the basic attributes of data. These include data hierarchies, codes, and file design.

Data are organized for processing in a way similar to the way a book is organized for reading. A book has a number of chapters, organized into paragraphs. Each paragraph has a number of sentences, composed of words and punctuation. Finally, each word consists of letters. In the case of data organization, there is a data bank consisting of a number of files; each file has many records; each record is composed of data fields; and finally, each data field contains a set of characters. In this way, data is organized into a hierarchy of levels.

A *character* of data is the most basic of the data levels. It can be one of the following types: alphabetic (from A to Z), numeric (from 0 to 9), or special symbols (e.g., $, +). One of the input/output media mentioned earlier is a printer. All of the possible characters that can be printed by a particular printer are called a *character set*.

Many times a single character is insufficient to express attributes. In these cases, characters are combined. Whether single or combined, they form a *data field*. The value in the data field represents the attributes of the data element; for example, the social security number of the teacher, the age of the student, or an amount paid for classroom materials. The data element need not be quantitative. It could represent the name or address of a person, or her teaching assignments. The attribute of a data element must be recorded in the data field assigned to that element.

In order to illustrate a data element, it is necessary to select a medium for storing data. The most common medium is a *data card,* mentioned in the payroll calculation example. This card has space for representing 80 different characters, with each character in one of the 80 columns in the card. A commonly used character set is shown on the data card in exhibit 16.6. Each character in that exhibit is identified by its unique combination of punched holes in the card. When this card is read by special card readers, electrical pulses passing through the holes are recorded and the character corresponding to the card holes is recognized. Data so recognized by machines is referred to as machine-readable data. The transformation of written data into machine-readable data by punching prescribed holes on a card is achieved by using equipment called keypunches.

An example of what has been described was developed by Hussain (1973, pp. 126-35) and is shown in figure 16.7. In this figure three data elements are shown for purposes of illustration: social security number, name, and card type information. Each data element has a specific data field assigned to it. The social security number has a data field of cc (card columns) 1-9; name, cc 11-26; and card identification, cc 79-80. Every set of numbers in a field represents the data element assigned to that field. For example, any set of numbers in cc 1-9 represents a social security number. In this particular illustration the data elements are separated by blank fields.

The format of a data element identifies both the width of the data

Exhibit 16.6: Data Card

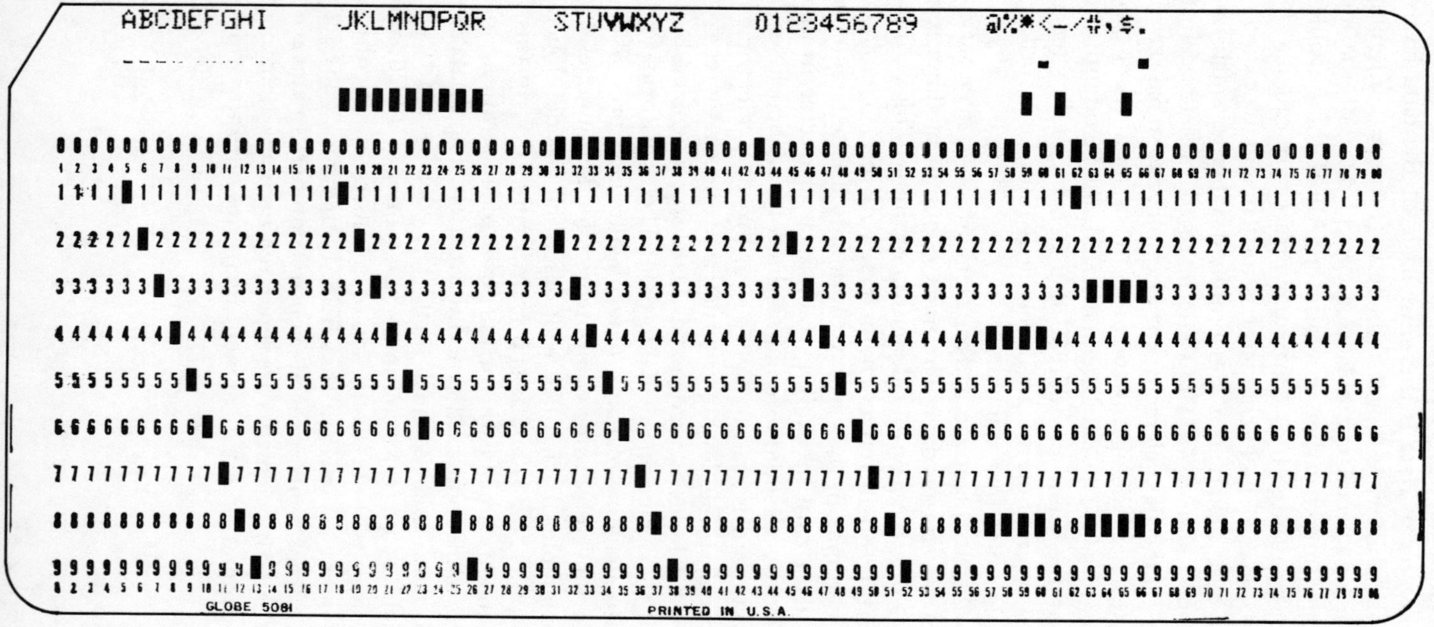

Figure 16.7: Illustration of Data Fields and Elements

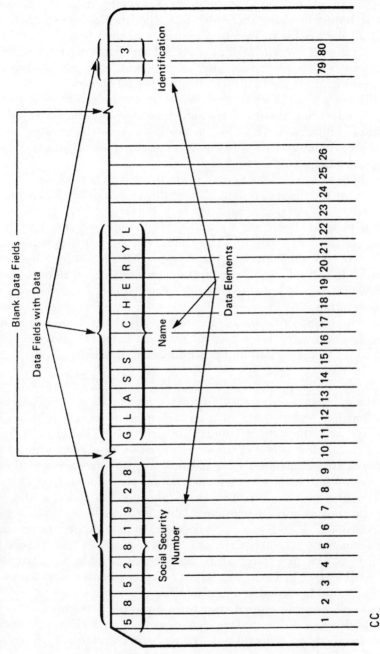

Source: Khateeb M. Hussain, *Development of Information Systems for Education* (Englewood Cliffs, N.J.: Prentice-Hall, 1973), p. 128. Reprinted by permission.

field (i.e., number of cc's for the field) plus the location of a decimal point if required. Once the width of each data field has been identified, all data fields related to an entity can then be collected into what is called a *record*. Within a record are fields that relate to a logical entity or transaction, such as a student, a course offered, or an amount paid. These fields constitute a *logical record*.

A file consists of a set of records. As an example, a student file at a higher education institution would typically contain names, identification numbers, date of birth, academic records, courses being taken, etc. As data in the file change, e.g., as students add and drop courses, the file would be updated.

The highest level of data aggregation is the data base or data bank. This is a set of integrated data files, as shown in exhibit 16.2, wherein a variety of operating agencies in a university have access to a single data base. There are a number of obvious advantages to integrating separate files within an organization. One, it makes possible analyses of the educational organization that cross functional and organizational lines. Also, overlap and redundancy of data is eliminated when data is collected in one place; this reduces the cost of data generation.

One important criticism of a data bank is that the user (an individual administrator) loses control over his data. He must accept a standard set of definitions and procedures for updating.

## Coding Data

In the context of information systems, a code is a set of characters that identifies an attribute of a data element so that it achieves an advantage over the natural language identification (Hussain 1973, p. 414). Information is coded for several reasons. First, codes are often an abbreviated equivalent of a natural language message and therefore occupy less space than uncoded data. This reduces storage space and expense. Second, because they take up less space, codes are easier to convert into machine-readable form, such as keypunched data cards. Third, codes can be processed by a computer faster than natural language counterparts. An example of the advantages of coding is shown in exhibit 16.8. The inventory code for a wooden chair with a straight back, side arms, and green leather upholstery in an office could be coded as 193015181.

Such codes are developed, and for a given file make up a data element dictionary. A file is then identified by a data element number and description, an indication of the physical location (e.g., in which cc's) of each element within which the code can be found. An example from a personnel file is given in table 16.9.

## Exhibit 16.8: Example of Codes

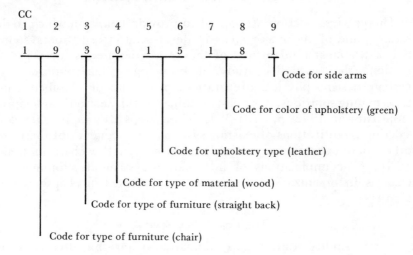

CC

| 1 | 2 | 3 | 4 | 5 | 6 | 7 | 8 | 9 |

1 9 3 0 1 5 1 8 1

Code for side arms

Code for color of upholstery (green)

Code for upholstery type (leather)

Code for type of material (wood)

Code for type of furniture (straight back)

Code for type of furniture (chair)

## Table 16.9: Personnel File Code

| Data element no. | Description | Card column | Comments |
|---|---|---|---|
| 1 | Institutional code | 1-2 | |
| 2 | Campus code | 3-4 | |
| 3 | Identification number | 5-13 | |
| 4 | Check digit | 14 | |
| 5 | Unassigned | 15-16 | |
| 6 | Sex | 17 | |
| 7 | Birthdate | 18-23 | |
| 8 | Place of birth | 24-25 | |
| 9 | Birth place classification | 26 | |
| 10 | Unassigned | 27-28 | |
| 11 | High school state | 29-30 | |
| 12 | High school graduation year | 31-32 | |
| 13 | Unassigned | 33-41 | |
| 14 | Year of first appointment | 42-43 | |
| 15 | Title position in first 1 appointment | 44-45 | |
| 16 | Title position in first 2 appointment | 46-47 | |
| 17 | State of residence in first appointment | 48-49 | |
| 18 | Nature of prior employment | 50-51 | |
| 19 | Year of termination of first appointment | 52-53 | |
| 20 | Year of second appointment | 54-55 | |
| 21 | Title of second appointment | 56-57 | |
| 22 | Unassigned | 58-78 | |
| 23 | Card number | 79 | Should be "1" |
| 24 | File type code | 80 | Should be "4" |

Source: Khateeb M. Hussain, *Development of Information Systems for Education* (Englewood Cliffs, N.J.: Prentice-Hall, 1973), p. 164. Reprinted by permission.

## Developing an Information System

The previous section attempted to provide a basis on which to describe some of the major steps in developing information systems. Six of the most fundamental of these activities are discussed in this section: the feasibility study; determining system requirements; system design; physical preparation; procedure development; and determining solutions. (The basic outline for this section was adapted from Hussain 1973, pp. 181-324.) These steps also apply when considering modifications of existing systems. The sequence of these and other developmental activities is shown in a flowchart in figure 16.10. (The implications of information systems development for changes in organizational structure are discussed in chapter seventeen.)

### The Feasibility Study

The feasibility study is an examination of possible alternatives to the development of an information system. This study determines how the various alternatives are constrained by technology, resource availability, and the existing organizational structure. For each solution that is feasible (i.e., within established constraints), the costs are compared to the benefits. If the costs are greater than the benefits or if the organization cannot afford the resources required, then the development process is terminated. If the opposite is true, then one of the alternatives is selected for implementation.

There are four major phases of the feasibility study: (1) organizing for the study; (2) searching for alternative solutions; (3) analyzing the relative merits of feasible alternatives; and (4) selecting an alternative. The goal implicit in organizing for the study is to assemble a qualified team with a clear set of organizational objectives, policies, and constraints. There is a variety of strengths required of the team, including knowledge of systems techniques, ability to work with other people, understanding of the organization, formal authority within the organization, and experience in system project management. It is unlikely that a single individual will possess all these qualifications, but the team as a whole should. Recently, in a large school district, such a team was composed of the assistant superintendent for management information systems, the controller, the director of accounting, the deputy superintendent (with line authority over school principals), and several outside consultants.

The feasibility study team must ensure that all constraints are specified. Administration must specify the resources that will be available for the project and the organizational changes that are possible

# Figure 16.10: Flowchart of System Development and Redevelopment Process

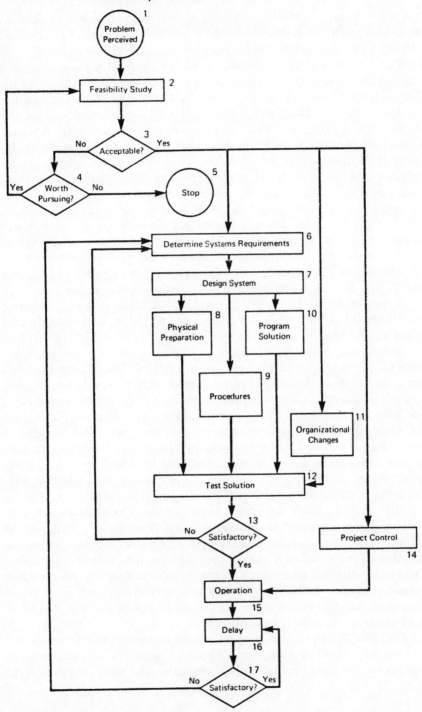

Source: Khateeb M. Hussain, *Development of Information Systems for Education* (Englewood Cliffs, N.J.: Prentice-Hall, 1973), p. 186. Reprinted by permission.

or not possible, including policies regarding displacement of personnel. The team, of course, should be given all the authority to cross departmental boundaries when necessary to collect information.

There is no uniform agreement on the method for searching for alternative solutions to information systems problems (phase two). One school of thought says that the first step is to study the existing system and to collect and analyze all relevant information on the environment (see, for example, Hussain 1973, p. 202). Another school of thought says, in essence, that such an examination of the present system will bias the team's view (see, for example, Heany 1968, p. 165). Instead, it is argued that the team ought to start fresh in its search, and only later examine the current system.

Regardless of the approach taken, one of the fundamental problems is to determine the amount of resources to be devoted to the feasibility study as opposed to the subsequent activities in systems development. For example, spending more on the feasibility study (a short-run cost) may reduce the total cost of the project (a long-run cost). But at some undetermined point, this will not be the case.

There are a variety of criteria against which to evaluate alternative solutions (phase three). In its general form, the feasibility analysis is similar to those discussed in earlier chapters (e.g., alternatives in supply management organization, food service, and student transportation). However, several unique considerations should be mentioned here. Economic feasibility is often considered a relatively simple concept. The expected benefits must exceed or equal the expected costs in order for a project to be economically feasible. However, the costs of information system development are frequently underestimated (Brandon 1966, p. 27). One reason for this is that the user's requirements are almost always understated and invariably increase along with the development of the project. The other reason is that analysts often underestimate costs (Hussain 1973, p. 206).

The analysis must also take into account "organizational constraints." An information system can often necessitate realignment of the existing organizational structure, e.g., setting up a separate division of information systems, and reducing the current responsibility of the division of research, planning, and evaluation. Alternatives requiring major changes in the way people relate to each other could be resisted by those people for a variety of reasons. These should be considered and evaluated as constraints.

The fourth phase, the choice of the solution, usually concerns administrators, who must make the final decision. The information necessary for the administration to make the final decision must include the statement of the objectives and scope of the study, and an identification of alternatives with preference rankings. The following information should be provided for each alternative: (1) resources required, both developmental and recurring, including equipment, personnel, space, etc.; (2) anticipated consequences, including organizational and informational changes, and anticipated problems; (3) limitations; (4) benefits, stated in a variety of terms, including economic, organizational, etc.; and (5) the time schedule, including the priority reassignment of other jobs if applicable. A flowchart showing the various phases of the feasibility study is shown in figure 16.11.

## Determining Systems Requirements

This activity determines the requirements of the system user. It is an extension of the effort in the feasibility phase to identify the problem. In determining system requirements it is necessary to undertake two highly interrelated activities: developing performance specifications and evaluating them.

Performance specifications are precise operational definitions of various aspects of a user's requirements. For example, the *output* of the system must be specified (usually by a mock-up form), including the contents and format of the output document. In addition, the following questions need to be asked about the output: How soon and how often is it needed? To whom is it distributed? Will the output data be retained for future use? If so, for how long?

A number of questions must be asked of the user regarding the *processing* of information. Precisely how should data be calculated and how accurately? For example, should grade point average be calculated to three decimal places? What kind of capacity will be required of the system? For example, for how many students will grade point averages be calculated?

*Input* specifications need to be determined. Where will the information come from, i.e., which office? In what form will that information be? For example, will grades be on grade sheets filled out by teachers? Will those sheets be machine-readable, or will additional processing be required? It is also necessary to determine what procedures will be used to check the validity of the data.

A fourth type of specification required of the user relates to *security*. Who is to have access to the data before and after it has been processed? What procedures will be instituted to prevent unauthorized persons from using the information?

Finally, it is necessary to specify the type of *back-up system* that

## Figure 16.11: Flowchart for Feasibility Study

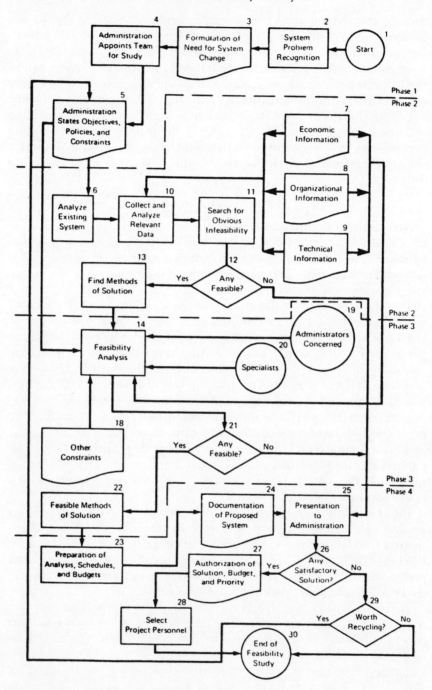

Source: Khateeb M. Hussain, *Development of Information Systems for Education* (Englewood Cliffs, N.J.: Prentice-Hall, 1973), p. 216. Reprinted by permission.

will be instituted. The most basic question to be asked here is whether the educational organization can tolerate serious breakdowns of the system under consideration. If it cannot, then specific measures need to be instituted which enable the organization to "fall back" to an emergency operating system. This can be accomplished, for example, by creating duplicate sets of all data and storing them in a separate place. However, this process is expensive, and should only be undertaken selectively.

Answers to these kinds of questions constitute performance specifications, and are generated by the user with the assistance of systems personnel. Performance specifications developed by individual users must be evaluated by information personnel using the perspective of the entire system under consideration.

The kinds of questions asked about a user's individual performance specifications are listed in exhibit 16.12. Actually, the process of developing and evaluating performance specifications is more a

## Exhibit 16.12: Questions Related to User Specifications

*Related Work*
    What related work is being done?
    How is it being done?
    To what degree is there overlap?
*Preparation and Processing*
    Who originates source data?
    Who prepares documents?
    How often is processing performed?
    How long does it take?
    Where is the processing performed?
    Who performs it?
    What equipment and supplies are used?
    How many copies are prepared? Who receives them?
    Is there unused processing capacity?
    What is the volume of documents (maximum, minimum, and average)?
    What has been the historical growth rate in usage?
*Form and Timeliness of Documents*
    Is document in a useful form?
    What are its limitations?
    Can two or more documents be combined?
    Is greater accuracy needed?
    Can lesser accuracy be tolerated?
    Is faster reporting desired? Is it needed?
*Use of Documents*
    Who receives the document?
    Does the document initiate decision? What decision? By whom?
    Is there a part of the document that is ignored or rarely used?
    What additional information is needed by the user?
    What processing is performed by the user of the document?
    What is the flow of the document?

**Exhibit 16.12** *(continued)*

*Storage and Retrieval*
Is the document retained? How? For how long?
What are the procedures for retention and purging?
How often is data purged and updated?
How often is it retrieved?
What are the procedures for retrieval?
How large is file (in number of records and average size per record)?
What is growth rate for file?
Is there a need for integrating different files? Which files?
*Cost*
What is the cost of processing the document?
What is the change in cost resulting from a change in frequency or accuracy of process-
ing?
How much of present costs of processing will be eliminated by computer processing?
What is the cost of storage and retrieval?

Source: Adapted from G. B. Davis, *Computer Data Processing* (New York: McGraw-Hill,
1969), p. 468.

dialogue between educational administrators and systems people
than a two-step process.

## Design of the System

Having determined the gross specifications from the user's point of
view, it is now necessary to specify the details of the design for the
construction of the system. Conceptually this activity is a continuation of the previous one, with one fundamental difference. In the
previous activity the major responsibility for the task lay with the
user. It was his or her needs that were specified. In the actual design
of the system, the major responsibility lies with the information
systems analyst.

The steps required in this activity include determining operations
procedures for the handling of information; determining machine
(hardware) requirements; designing input and output forms; and
determining programming needs (whereby the instructions for data
handling are prepared for the computer), personnel needs, and procedures for testing.

Even at this stage in development, educational managers are involved, though less heavily. As systems design takes place, detailed
design specification may require adding activities or adjusting time
estimates to complete activities. These clearly will affect the expectations of the users, and hence, educational management.

## Physical Preparation, Procedure Development, and Determining Solutions

The last three stages of information system development are much less under the direction of the educational manager than the previous activities, and for that reason are only mentioned in passing here. Physical preparation deals largely with activities related to equipment and the actual development of forms. Operating procedures are developed with the purpose of describing what jobs are to be done and why. These are used to guide and evaluate personnel performance. Determining a solution deals largely with the variety of programming activities required to bring the system to operational status.

As implied above, educational managers need to be intimately familiar with managerial issues related to the development (and redevelopment) of information systems, while having only a general familiarity with the more technical aspects. Both kinds of knowledge are important, and both have been addressed briefly in this chapter. It is perhaps more important, however, for educational managers to have a basic grounding in the ways that information systems are and can be managed most effectively to achieve the fundamental goals of educational institutions. This is the subject of the following chapter.

## Questions for Review and Discussion

1. Develop a flow chart of the process of assessing the feasibility of computerizing one or more activities in the area of student transportation.

2. In what ways does flowcharting differ from PERT charting (discussed in chapter nine)? Can both charting techniques be used to describe the same activities or projects? What criteria should be used to determine which is more useful in a particular instance?

3. What various offices and agencies in large elementary-secondary school system have occasion to rely on data about characteristics of individual students (similar to that shown in figure 16.2 in the area of higher education)?

4. Relying primarily on the information in chapters one and two, portray (in terms of inputs and outputs) the general form of an accounting system in education.

5. What kinds of problems encountered in educational organizations would prompt an examination of part or all of the institution's information system?

# References

Abrams, Peter, and Corvine, Walter. *Basic Data Processing*. New York: Holt, Rinehart, and Winston, 1966.

Brandon, D. "The Need for Management Standards in Data Processing." *Data and Control Systems* 4, no. 9 (September 1966): pp. 27-29.

Chin, R. "The Utility of Systems Models and Developmental Models for Practitioners." *The Planning of Change*, edited by W. G. Bennis and R. Chin. New York: Holt, Rinehart, and Winston, 1961.

Davis, G. B. *Computer Data Processing*. New York: McGraw-Hill, 1969.

Heany, D. F. *Development of Information Systems*. New York: Ronald Press, 1968.

Hoag, M. W. "What is a System?" *Operations Research* V, no. 3 (June 1957): pp. 440-51.

Hussain, Khateeb M. *Development of Information Systems for Education*. Englewood Cliffs, N.J.: Prentice-Hall, 1973.

Johnson, R. A.; Kast, F. E.; and Rosenzweig, J. E. *The Theory and Management of Systems*. New York: McGraw-Hill, 1967.

# Related Readings

Blackwell, F. W. *Educational Information System Design: A Conceptual Framework*. Santa Monica, Calif.: The RAND Corp., 1970. ERIC, no. ED045096. Discusses, with specific reference to educational institutions, criteria for: (1) establishing information system policies, (2) determining the accuracy volume and retrievability of information to be maintained, and (3) designing and implementing the hardware-software system.

Chervany, Norman Y., and Dickson, Mary W. "Economic Evaluation of Management Information Systems: An Analytical Framework." *MIS: Management Dimensions*, edited by Raymond J. Coleman and M. J. Riley. San Francisco: Holden-Day, 1973. Provides a short and useful description of activities required in developing an information system, along with criteria for determining costs. Includes a bibliography of related readings.

Johnson, Richard A.; Kast, Fremont E.; and Rosenzweig, James E. *The Theory and Management of Systems*. New York: McGraw-Hill, 1973. Provides in the first 130 pages a comprehensive description of systems concepts applied to the management of complex organizations, including specific mention of information systems.

Olsen, Harold A. *The Economics of Information: Bibliography and Commentary on the Literature*. Washington, D.C.: ERIC Clearinghouse on Library and Information Sciences, 1971. ERIC, no. ED074545. Describes the economic framework of the analysis of information. Also indexes many references into fourteen useful categories including several dealing with operation analysis of information systems.

Porter, J. D. *Digital Computer Principles*. Bedford, Mass.: Mitre Corp., 1968. ERIC, no. ED047732. Provides a brief history of computers. Explains basic computer principles and discusses such subjects as input/output, binary logic, storage, and costs.

# 17
# Information Systems
# in Educational Management

This chapter and chapter sixteen are related to each other in much the same way as chapters one and two. In discussing accounting, chapter one emphasized "how to do it," whereas chapter two emphasized "how to use it." In discussing information systems, chapter sixteen emphasized "how to do it," whereas this chapter emphasizes "how to use it." In this chapter, we will examine three areas: information requirements for different types of management decisions, current attitudes of managers about information generation, and the impact of information systems on the behavior of people in educational organizations.

An underlying theme of this chapter needs to be stated at the outset: all useful information for management decisions does not necessarily emanate from a formally structured, computer-based information system. Stated another way, there is important information for management decisions which could not, and sometimes should not, emanate from an organization's formal information system. The formal system is a necessary, but by no means sufficient method for gathering information for decisions. Gardner (1965) provided a classic description of problems inherent in relying solely on computer-based information systems.

As organizations (and societies) become larger and more complex, the men at the top (whether managers or analysts) depend less and less on firsthand experience, more and more on heavily "processed" data. Before reaching them, the raw data—what actually goes on "out there"—have been sampled, screened, condensed, compiled, coded, expressed in statistical form, spun into generalizations and crystallized into recommendations.

It is a characteristic of the information processing system that it systematically filters out certain kinds of data so that these never reach the men who depend on the system. The information that is omitted (or seriously distorted) is information that is not readily expressed in words or numbers, or cannot be rationally condensed into lists, categories, formulas or compact generalizations by procedures now available to us.

No one can run a modern organization who is not extraordinarily gifted in handling the end products of a modern information processing system. So we find at the top of our larger organizations (and at the top of our government) more and more men who are exceedingly gifted in manipulating verbal and mathematical symbols. And they all understand one another. It is not that they see reality in the same way. It is that through long training they have come to see reality through the same distorting glasses. There is nothing more heartwarming than the intellectual harmony of two analysts whose training has accustomed them to accept as reality the same systematic distortions thereof. But what does the information processing system filter out? It filters out all sensory impressions not readily expressed in words and numbers. It filters out emotion, feeling, sentiment, mood and almost all of the irrational nuances of human situations. It filters out those intuitive judgments that are just below the levels of consciousness.

So the picture of reality that sifts to the top of our great organizations and our society is sometimes a dangerous mismatch with the real world. We suffer the consequences when we run head on into situations that cannot be understood *except* in terms of those elements that have been filtered out. The planners base their plans on the prediction that the people will react in one way, and they react violently in quite another way. (pp. 78-79)

Although to some educational managers the above may seem obvious, it is important to underscore the context within which management information systems must be considered.

## Information Requirements for Different Types of Management Decisions

Thus far, management activities requiring data have been referred to as "management decisions," distinguishable only by the subject matter of the decision (e.g., inventory control, enrollment forecasting). It is necessary at this point to discuss some additional distinctions among management decisions which have implications for how information systems are used. One widely used framework applicable to educational organizations was developed by Anthony (1965). His work suggests that management operations in education entail three kinds of activities: strategic planning, management control, and operational control. *Strategic planning* is the process of determining organizational objectives, changes in these objectives, resources used to attain them, and policies that govern the acquisition, use, and disposition of these resources (Anthony 1965, p. 16). This definition conveys a sense of the "big plan," i.e., formulations of long-range plans and policies that determine or change the character or direction of the organization. Examples of such plans in the elementary-secondary education include establishing separate junior high school facilities and programs where none existed before, or phasing out certain course offerings. In higher education strategic plans might deal with establishing a law school at a university or undertaking a major enlargement of the extension or part-time programs of a college.

*Management control* is the process by which managers assure that resources are obtained and used effectively in the accomplishment of the organization's objectives (Anthony 1965, p. 17). This definition conveys three ideas. First, the process involves managers, who get things done by working with other people. Second, the process takes place within a context of objectives and policies that have been determined in the strategic planning process. Third, the actions taken in this process are judged in terms of how effectively they work.

*Operational control* is the process of assuring that specific tasks are carried out efficiently (Anthony 1965, p. 18). Operational control is distinct from management control in at least two ways. It is concerned with tasks, (e.g., scheduling buses, ordering supplies), whereas management control is concerned with individuals. Also, the tasks are specified, so that little or no judgment is required; management control activities are not specified, and management decides what is to be done within the general constraints of the strategic plans. In operational control, the focus is on execution, whereas in management control it is on both planning and execution.

Strategic planning functions are performed by top administrators; managerial control functions are performed by middle-level administrators; operations are performed by the operations personnel. In educational organizations, especially higher education, academic and nonacademic personnel are organized in parallel hierarchies. In higher education, among the academic personnel, the operational functions are performed by the instructional faculty. They are directed and controlled by their department chairmen and academic deans (middle-level administrators) and their top administrators are the academic vice-president and his superior. Among the nonacademic personnel, the secretarial, semiskilled, and unskilled workers constitute the operational personnel and are directed and controlled by their supervisors, directors, and nonacademic deans (middle-level administrators). They, in turn, are supervised by top administrators, who are nonacademic vice-presidents or hold an equivalent rank.

In performing the different functions at the different levels of hierarchy in educational management, there is a need for information relevant to each function. This is shown in figure 17.1. Operational

## Figure 17.1: Information for Different Levels of Management

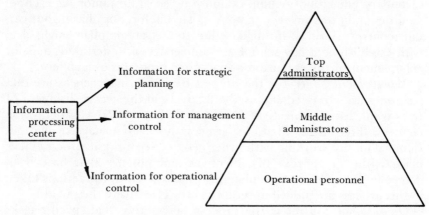

information, for example, is factual reporting of periodic operations. Examples of such information are lists of classes offered, students registered, grade reports, students on each bus route, etc. Periodic financial reports are also generated, such as those specifying how much of each budget has been spent to date. Operational information has the special characteristic of being cyclic. It is needed repeatedly and corresponds to an administrative cycle such as a semester or calendar month.

In one sense management control is the comparison of desired performance with actual performance and action taken to eliminate undesirable deviations. To facilitate control, information is needed on current performance in a form that will facilitate its comparison with desired performance. For example, in examining expenditures of different budgetary accounts, it is useful for management to know which accounts are already 90 percent spent by the end of the first semester of school. With some accounts this is an acceptable position; with others it is not.

The information requirements of top administrators are different from those at the other levels in at least two ways. For one thing, information for goal-setting seldom comes directly from an information system. Rather, it is more a product of the personality and background of top-level decision makers and the environment and constraints of the particular educational organization. Second, top administrators are interested in all levels of institutional operations, but because of human limitations they cannot control all levels of the organization. Therefore, the information that comes to them is very selective. Hussain (1973, p. 113) cites four types of information that filter up to top management from lower levels:

1. Operations that are above or below acceptable levels
2. Problems that cannot be corrected at the operational or control level
3. Variables that have a major effect on institutional goals and plans
4. Undesirable trends (including those inside prescribed control limits)

Examples of the above types of information in elementary-secondary education include increases in district-wide suspension rates throughout the city, significant changes in reading scores, dropout rates, and number of high school seniors going on to college. Examples in higher education include major changes in ratios of students admitted to those enrolling in the freshman class and major changes in the earning rate on endowment.

At this point it is useful to review several of the major ongoing management operations discussed in this book to highlight how the three levels of administration make different decisions regarding each management operation. The relationship between the various management operations and the levels of administration is shown in figure 17.2. Each of these management operations has tasks and information requirements at, for example, the strategic planning level. In the area of financial operations these include (for a public school district) assessing long-range changes in property valuations, tax rates, state aid formulas, and federal grant-in-aid programs. At the managerial control level tasks and information requirements include determining which investment instruments have the current highest yield, reviewing the spending patterns among major budgetary accounts, and monitoring the cash position of the educational organization. At the operating control level tasks and related information requirements include posting accounts, determining trial balances, and receiving and depositing cash.

In the area of supply management some of the tasks and decisions at the strategic level include determining who should have the responsibilities for purchasing various supplies, and how much of the organization's resources should be devoted to supplies vs. other instructional resources. At the management control level, decisions include determining the bid specifications and developing methods for inventory control. At the operational control level, decisions

## Figure 17.2: Management Operations and Levels of Administration

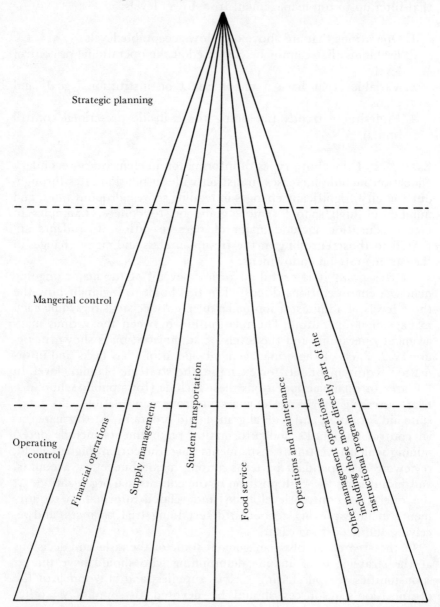

Strategic planning

Mangerial control

Operating
control

Financial operations

Supply management

Student transportation

Food service

Operations and maintenance

Other management operations directly part of the
including those more directly part of the
instructional program

include recording receipts of supplies from distributors and assembling bundles of supplies for distribution to individual school sites.

In the area of student transportation at the elementary-secondary level, strategic tasks and decisions include determining maximum walking distances to school for students and developing general guidelines for determining the amount of resources devoted to field trips. Tasks at the management control level include developing cost analyses of inhouse vs. contracted bus service and developing repair schedules which minimize the total costs of transportation. Tasks at the operational control level include updating lists of students to be picked up on each bus route and scheduling buses for field trips. The same distinctions among types of decisions can be made for each of the other operating systems listed.

As mentioned earlier, automated information systems are more likely to be found at the operational (and, to a lesser degree, managerial) control levels. This is not to say, however, that strategic planning relies on entirely separate sources of information. Rather, it is a blend of information from each of the three levels, as shown in figure 17.3. In moving toward the level of strategic planning, the distinctions between the separate operations become less clear, because the decisions are more fundamental and affect the educational organization more broadly. Actually, from the viewpoint of information systems management (as opposed to overall organizational manage-

## Figure 17.3: Information Needs at Strategic Planning Level

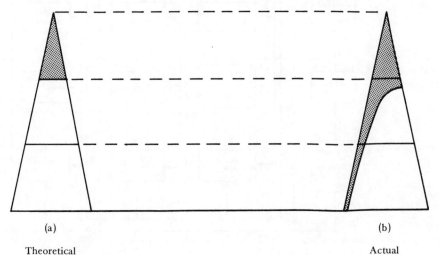

(a)

Theoretical

(b)

Actual

# Figure 17.4: Interrelated Files for Operation, Control, and Planning

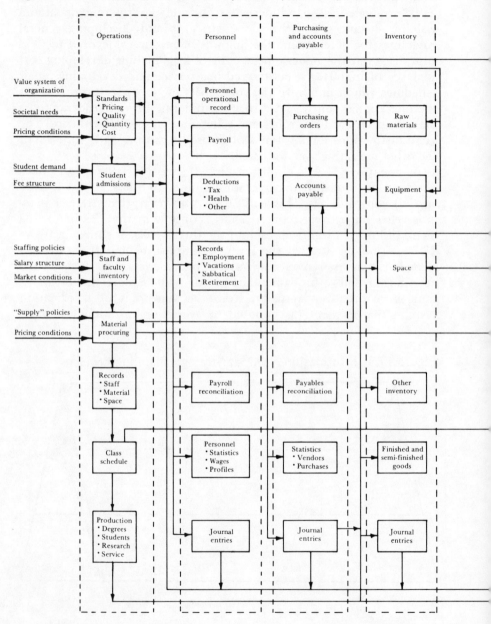

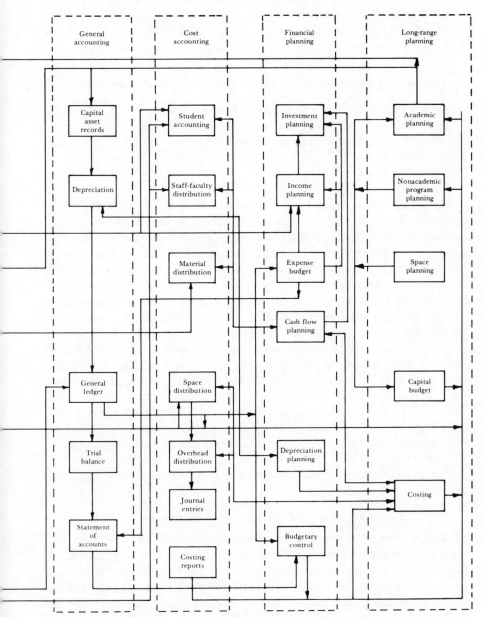

Source: Khateeb M. Hussain, *Development of Information Systems for Education* (Englewood Cliffs, N.J.: Prentice-Hall, 1973), pp. 354-55. Reprinted by permission.

ment), figure 17.2 shows management operations as much more seg-
mented than in fact they are. Accounting operations, for example,
are a part of most other operations. Enrollment forecasting relates to
long-range financial planning, and also to academic planning (new or
enlarged programs, etc.). Figure 17.4 shows how various operations
and information sources overlap in a higher education institution.

### Prevalent Attitudes of Managers about Information Generation

Managerial use of information systems is determined in large part
by management's perception of these systems and what they can or
cannot do. Several common misconceptions of managers are
discussed here.

#### Information Systems Are Neutral

Many managers think that computer-based information systems
are objective and neutral means of gathering and producing data. As
implied in the introduction to this chapter, computer-based information systems produce only certain kinds of information: that which
can be counted or in some other way explicitly stated. Actually,
then, information systems are biased in favor of quantifiable information. More important, information systems cannot be neutral even
as regards quantifiable information, because the educational managers who design and operate the system are as much a part of the
system as the managers who use the information. Neither set of
actors is neutral. Indeed, information systems "encompass the people
who use them and are used by them: their optimisms, their fears,
their biases, their frustrations, and their antagonisms" (Weinwurm
1970, p. 512). For example, an information system that systematically reports out the number of student suspensions for each teacher
in a school is likely to raise questions about discipline policy, suspension practices, teacher classroom control, etc. If this information is
not gathered and made available, the problem is less likely to be addressed.

#### More Information Is Better

Most information systems are designed on the assumption that the
critical deficiency in management operations is lack of relevant information. The problem, however, is often that management suffers
from an overabundance of irrelevant information. Hence, more does
not necessarily mean better. What happens is that criteria dealing
with quality get replaced by criteria dealing with quantity. There are

at least two major issues at stake here. First, how often is an update of that particular report really needed? The quantitative dimensions of these issues are obvious. However, it is very difficult to ascertain the quality of the output of the information system without at the same time examining the specific decisions made by each manager. Two variations on this assumption have been developed by Ackoff (1967, pp. 322-23). Each is discussed separately below.

The manager needs the information he wants. This proposition assumes that managers are aware of each type of decision to be made and have an adequate model of each. To the extent that this is not the case, information systems will generate data that are not useful.

Give a manager the information he needs and his decision making will improve. This proposition assumes that all managers are capable of using the necessary information that is provided them. The degree to which this is true depends largely on a variety of intangibles concerning the quality of management, and very little on the presence of a computer-based information system.

### Centralized Information Systems Utilize Systems Experts More Effectively

Because the purpose of the information system is to improve the operation of the educational organization, not to utilize experts more effectively, there are conditions under which centralized systems may be less effective. The most obvious example is information system development in multicampus state universities. Although a clear need exists for data elements and report formats common among campuses, the cost of centralizing the information system often appears to outweigh the cost of a decentralized operation, holding everything else constant. In elementary-secondary public education, many information system functions are being aggregated at the regional educational agency level instead of at the state level. There is no definitive rule regarding the degree of centralization of an information system in an educational organization. The relationship between costs and benefits will vary from case to case.

There are a variety of current theories about information systems (see, for example, Tolliver 1971). Behind many of them are three important and defensible assumptions. (1) The quality of an information system is dependent on the quality of an analysis of the way decisions are made in the organization. (2) While there are many decisions (especially at the managerial and operational control levels) for which computer-generated data are relevant, indeed vital, there are other decisions for which one can only guess what information is relevant. This is another way of saying that it would be prohibitively expensive to gather and report all information that might be relevant to some decisions. (3) Accuracy in information systems is not an absolute. Rather, the costs of increased accuracy must be weighed against the potential benefits. This is shown generally in figure 17.5, but will vary from operation to operation.

### Figure 17.5: Benefits and Costs of Information System Accuracy

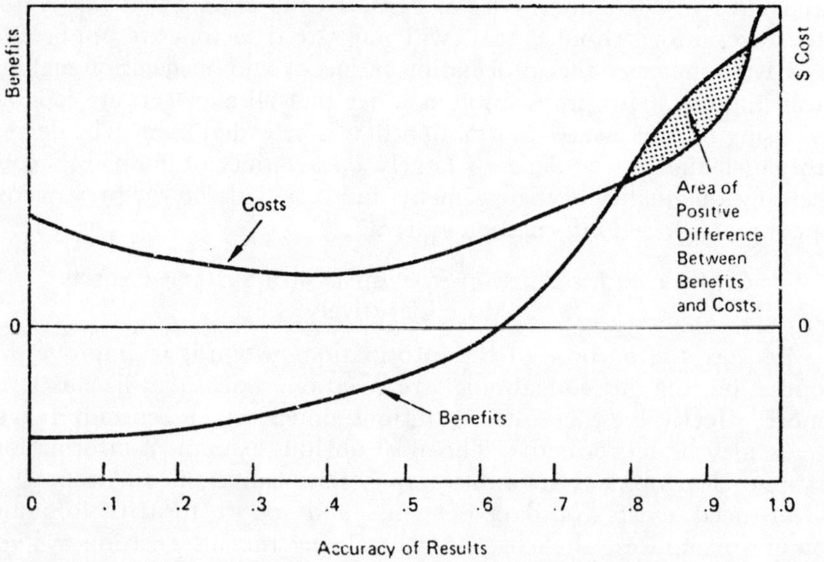

Source: R. H. Gregory and R. L. Van Horn, *Automatic Data-Processing Systems, Principles and Procedures* (Belmont, Calif.: Wadsworth, 1963), p. 518. Reprinted by permission.

## Impact of Computer-Based Information Systems

Computer-based information systems are accompanied by fundamental changes in the ways an organization conducts its business, and educational organizations are no exception to this. At least three affected areas deserve mention here. One deals with the types of educational organizations (and types of operating units within the organization) where automated information handling appears to be more cost effective. A second deals with how computer-based information systems affect the behavior of educational managers. A third deals with changes in management skills necessary for a "data-oriented" organizational environment.

## Where Systems Are Likely To Be Implemented

Educational organizations are not only different from other organized enterprises in several basic respects (as discussed in chapter two), they are different from each other in terms of size, type of student served, etc. Factors like these can indicate in a general way whether a computer-based information system is likely to be implemented.

Service enterprises (as distinguished from manufacturing industries) can anticipate greater sophistication regarding the incorporation and use of information technology (Baum and Burack 1969). Clearly this includes the "knowledge industries," such as schools and colleges. The reasoning is that the service segment of society is growing faster than the manufacturing segment and that management in the service area is becoming increasingly complex holding other factors, such as size, constant.

Large enterprises will develop more formalized information systems than small ones. Size includes the number and combination of variables, as well as volume of business activity, that encourages the implementation of a computer-based system. In large educational organizations, top management cannot digest directly all relevant information without abstracting it through an information system.

Educational organizations with long histories of using information technology are more likely to develop sophisticated information systems because they are more likely to have developed an information and data discipline which encourages a positive attitude toward new areas of application (Mann and Williams 1960, p. 217). This suggests that early implementation efforts will be relatively slow until a critical mass of positive opinion has built up regarding the cost-effectiveness of computer usage.

Applications of information technology not only have an uneven impact on educational institutions, but operations within each educational institution are affected unevenly. For example, information systems development is more likely to take place within organizational units where speed and manipulation of data are crucial factors in the decision-making process. This explains why accounting and financial reporting systems are often the first operations that are automated in education organizations. Related to this is the observation that units or organizational divisions where personnel with a background of formal, technical education are central to success will be more likely to develop automated information systems.

## Impact on the Behavior of Educational Managers

While all students of information systems would argue that information technology is changing the way managers behave, there is little consensus about the precise nature of change, especially as regards education organizations. One apparent trend is that "work pushing" at the managerial and operational control levels has been reduced. Automated systems help to assure that largely routine work will get out. This is the case because machine-paced operations depend less on workers maintaining a standardized rate (see Karp 1970).

The impact of automated information systems on overall job demand for people at the management control level is unclear. Some say that fewer middle management people will be needed to perform supervisory routine tasks, and even that top management is absorbing former middle management functions in the areas of planning, budgeting, and forecasting (see, for example, Karp 1970). Others predict precisely the opposite. "Top executives depend upon the specialization and skills of their middle managers to a great extent. Now that the computer has allowed for an increase in this specialization and these skills, the attributes of middle managers will be in greater demand and their number will increase with computer use. Middle management positions will be upgraded due to increased need and the greater amount of responsibility inherent in the new aspects of these positions" (Jackson 1970, p. 16). While it may be true that in educational organizations middle management positions are being created dealing directly with information systems, it appears that their relationship to top management is more in the nature of staff than line operations. That is, they exercise little direct formal authority over large segments of the work force in the organization.

Although most of the computer applications have been at the operational and managerial control levels, these developments have influenced the behavior of top managers. For example, research conducted by Hofer suggests that such developments have permitted top managers to:

Make some decisions at an earlier date;
Gain time in which to consider some decisions;
Consider more thorough analysis of some situations;
Review several courses of action on many problems;
Obtain additional information from middle managers concerning problems, opportunities, and promising alternatives before making decisions. (1970, p. 18)

Whether these conclusions hold true for the majority of educational organizations is difficult to say at this point.

## Necessary Management Skills

Today's "general" or academic managers in education organizations are required to possess greater technical competence than their predecessors. This is particularly true in the areas of information technology. As educational organizations grow in size and complexity, and as their educational objectives proliferate, educators in different management positions will find their work relating more and more to information demands. What kinds of information-related skills will education managers require? Investigations of business, governmental, and educational organizations conducted by Murdick and Ross (1969) suggest (1) that there are a wide variety of emerging skills and (2) that skill requirements will vary for the type of manager being considered. Table 17.6 shows these requirements via a modified form of linear responsibility charting. Each of the five columns represents different roles most directly affecting the operation of information systems in an educational organization. The general roles of top administration (strategic planning) and middle level administration (managerial control) were discussed earlier in this chapter. Management information system managers are those people who have direct responsibility for the development and operation of an organization's formal information system. Systems designers and computer programmers (alluded to in chapter sixteen) work under the supervision of the MIS managers, and are responsible for what might be termed the operating control level of the information system.

Each of the sixteen rows represents information-related skill areas required, many of which have been mentioned briefly in previous chapters. The numbers in the cells represent the kind of familiarity that the person occupying a given position should have with a given skill area. While this schema represents but one of many possible estimations of skill requirements for managing information systems, it may imply a potential shift in emphasis in training (both preservice and inservice) of educational managers from concrete information about education to more abstract analytic methods related to management. Taken as a whole, table 17.6 portrays the skill levels necessary to provide the information base on which to make competent managerial decisions in educational organizations.

This book has hopefully conveyed the idea that thoroughly analyzed management operations, based on rational decision-making or management science techniques can improve performance in educational organizations. Yet, at the risk of seeming to turn around in the last pages, it must be said that quality of educational management is

# Table 17.6: Skill Requirements of Managers

| 1: Knowledge<br>2: Understanding<br>3: Skill in application<br>4: Analysis and evaluation<br>5: Synthesis<br><br>Analysis, Synthesis, and Design Concepts | Top managers | Operating managers | MIS managers | Systems designers | System computer programmers |
|---|---|---|---|---|---|
| I—Problem solving—the theory and practice of logic, decision making and creative thinking. The use of these and other problem-solving principles in the analysis and design of systems. | 5 | 5 | 5 | 5 | 3 |
| II—Organization principles—classical and contemporary principles of organization design and analysis. An understanding of the structure, decision centers, information flow and other organizational considerations in systems design. | | 2 | 2 | 2 | |
| III—Management—the basic functions of management, with special emphasis on planning and controlling through information systems. Consideration and understanding of facilitating the management process with systems. | | 2 | 2 | 2 | |
| IV—Systems planning—determining systems objectives and planning time, cost and resource allocations. Design proposals. PERT/CPM input/output considerations. | 2 | 4 | 5 | 5 | 1 |
| V—Systems theory—theory of information systems operation and design. Control theory. Integrated and total systems concepts. Planning and control through information feedback systems. | | | 5 | 5 | 1 |
| VI—Systems evaluation—measuring efficiency against goals. Input/output review and review of objectives. | 2 | 4 | 4 | 4 | |
| VII—Human interaction in systems—gaining acceptance and "selling" ADP. The impact of automation on personnel. Getting cooperation. Interpersonal relationships. Applied psychology. | 2 | 2 | 3 | 2 | |
| VIII—Quantitative techniques in systems design—application of operations research and other management science techniques. Formulation of decision rules. Simulation and modeling. | | 1 | 2 | 3 | 3 |
| **Analysis and Design Techniques** | | | | | |
| IX—Systems planning—network analysis technique for logical structuring of planning. Preliminary systems survey. The feasibility study. The cost evaluation and analysis. Analysis of time requirements. Planning quality elements of the system. | | 2 | 3 | 5 | 2 |
| X—Systems analysis and design—analytical techniques and documentation (work measurement, flow charting, forms design, source data automation, etc.) Input-output alternatives. Communications, interviewing, and selling. Principles of systems design. | | 2 | 4 | 5 | 1 |
| XI—Implementation and follow-up—planning site preparation, personnel, organization, other considerations. Training the user. Evaluation and audit. | | 5 | 5 | 2 | 1 |
| **Computer Concepts and Capabilities** | | | | | |
| XII—Hardware characteristics—mainframe capability, peripheral equipment remotes and linkage input-output devices, time-sharing, on-line systems, etc. | 1 | 1 | 2 | 2 | 5 |
| XIII—Software—languages and compiler options (FORTRAN, COBOL, ALGOL, BASIC, TELCOMP, QUIKTRAN, CAL) Standard programs and models. Systems applications. | 1 | 2 | 4 | 4 | 5 |
| **Additional Skill Requirements** | | | | | |
| XIV—Programming | | | 1 | 2 | 5 |
| XV—Quantitative techniques—management science techniques in systems design. | | | 2 | 3 | 4 |
| XVI—Communications—graphics and visual presentations. The oral and written staff report. | | 5 | 5 | 3 | 3 |

Source: R. G. Murdick and J. E. Ross, "Management Information Systems: Training for Businessmen." *Journal of Systems Management* 20, no. 10 (October 1969), p. 38. Reprinted by permission of the authors.

a function of people and not techniques. Clearly there is a relationship between the educational manager and his or her models, systems, and computer technology, just as there is between a surgeon and his tools. This book deals with the techniques, but the "bottom line" of performance in educational organizations depends on the *creative* talent of their managers. This point has been well stated by Harold Enarson, president of Ohio State University, and, because of its importance in a book like this, it is the last thought with which we leave the reader.

Planning is inseparable from management and both involve those elements associated with art: intuition, creativity, discernment, command of the work tools and materials, and appreciation of the interaction of form and function.

There are planners and then there are *planners*—at least two models: the Cook's-tour model, the Lewis and Clark model.

The Cook's tour defines a precise schedule on a well-defined route; it moves in orderly progression amid known landmarks. The aim is to plan to avoid contingencies; the unexpected is to be avoided; all is schedule, order, routine.

I prefer the Lewis and Clark model, with its sense of adventure as it explores new frontiers. They envisioned their goal, assembled the minimum resources, and had the nerve and the courage to take the unexpected in stride. They knew that success depended upon painstaking completion of the smallest of plans—building of the campfires, fording of the stream, delicate negotiations with the Indians. Their epic success was a triumph of small, daily successes—all within the context of a goal and clear sense of direction. The Cook's tour provides the illusion of planning in a world of imagined stability. The Lewis and Clark tour is an adventure into the unknown. Can there be any choice for us? (1975, p. 37)

## Questions for Review and Discussion

1.  List examples of strategic planning, management control, and operational control tasks for each of the following management operations: food service and operations and maintenance.

2.  How can the prevalent attitudes of managers about information generation affect the operation of information systems in educational organizations?

3.  How would education managers at the operational control, managerial control, and strategic planning levels differ in their use of the information files shown in figure 17.4?

4.  To what extent do training programs in educational management currently impart skills such as those listed on table 17.6? How can educational managers acquire these skills?

5.  How would Enarson's "Lewis and Clark" model apply to the management operations discussed in this book?

# References

Ackoff, Russell L. "Management Misinformation Systems." *Management Science* 13, no. 4 (December 1967): B147-B156.

Anthony, Robert N. *Planning and Control Systems: A Framework for Analysis.* Boston: Harvard University Press, 1965.

Baum, Bernard, and Burack, Elmer. "Information Technology, Manpower Development, and Organizational Performance." *Academy of Management Journal* 12, no. 9 (September 1969): 279-91.

Enarson, Harold L. "The Art of Planning, or Watching You Get It All Together." *New York Times* (October 4, 1975): 37.

Gardner, John. *Self Renewal: The Individual and the Innovative Society.* New York: Harper & Row, 1965.

Gregory, R. H., and Van Horn, R. L. *Automatic Data-Processing Systems, Principles and Procedures.* Belmont, Calif.: Wadsworth, 1963.

Hofer, Charles W. "Emerging EDP Pattern." *Harvard Business Review* 48, no. 2 (March/April 1970): 16-18.

Hussain, Khateeb M. *Development of Information Systems for Education.* Englewood Cliffs, N.J.: Prentice-Hall, 1973.

Jackson, Robert S. "Computers and Middle Management." *Journal of Systems Management* 21, no. 4 (April 1970): 15-18.

Karp, William. "Management in the Computer Age." *Data Management* 8, no. 12 (December 1970): 24-29.

Mann, Floyd C., and Williams, L. K. "Observations on the Dynamics of a Change to Electronic Data Processing Equipment." *Administrative Science Quarterly* 5, no. 1 (September 1960): 217-56.

Murdick, Robert G., and Ross, Joel E. "Management Information Systems: Training for Businessmen." *Journal of Systems Management* 20, no. 10 (October 1969): 36-39.

Tolliver, Edward M. "Myths of Automated Management Systems." *Journal of Systems Management* 22, no. 3 (March 1971): 29-32.

Weinwurm, George F. "Managing Management Information." *Management International Review* 10, no. 1 (January 1970): 43-47.

# Related Readings

Brandon, Richard H. *Management Planning for Data Processing.* New York: Brandon/Systems Press, 1970. Treats the range of topics discussed in chapters sixteen and seventeen at a very elementary, easy-to-understand level.

Diebold, John. *Business Decisions and Technological Change.* New York: Praeger, 1970. Critically examines how change brought about as a result of technological innovation has posed great opportunities for and threats to business enterprises. Examines a variety of industries, and concludes with a discussion on information and communication technologies in education.

Fletcher, Allan, ed. *Computer Science for Management.* New York: Brandon/Systems Press, 1967. Concerned less with management issues related to information systems than with communicatig to managers the technical issues which confront data-processing personnel.

Foy, Nancy. *Computer Management: A Common Sense Approach.* Philadelphia: Auerbach, 1972. Particularly useful discussion about how to analyze the options of leasing vs. buying computers. Discusses specifically how to use service bureaus and consultants.

Henderson, Diane. "More Yearning for the Educational Dollar." *Journal of Systems Management* 24, no. 3 (March 1973): 22-26. Describes how user requirements for information were determined at a university. Integrates analysis of requirements for computer-based information with those in print and nonprint media.

Knutsen, K. Eric, and Nolan, Richard L. "Assessing Computer Costs and Benefits." *Journal of Systems Management* 25, no. 2 (February 1974): 28-34. While acknowledging that costs and benefits of computer-based information systems are hard to predict, the authors describe several useful procedures to deal with the problems.

Lucas, Henry C., Jr. *Computer-Based Information Systems in Organizations.* Chicago: Science Research Associates, 1973. A basic and, at the same time, comprehensive description of the MIS development topics discussed in chapter sixteen plus problems and potential of EDP usage. Includes a discussion of "online" (real time) and computer timesharing systems.

# Index

Accounting, 3-4, 198

Accounts: proprietary, 28; budgetary, 28; dimensions of, 20-27. *See also* T accounts

Achieved availability, 206

Administrative delay time, 207-208

Alternatives, analysis of: in supply management, 100-112; in transportation, 144-169; in food service, 188-198

Analytical solution, 136

Asset, 3, 5, 15

Audit, 4, 9-12, 200

Bounded solution, 328

Budgeting: using PERT, 233-256; using linear responsibility charts, 261-274; by program, 241; by site, 312-320; calendars, 234-235; for transportation, 145-149, 155-159; for operations and maintenance, 218-225. *See also* Planning, Resource allocation procedures

Carrying costs, 91-93

Cash flow, *see* Cash planning

Cash planning, 53-66; forecasting cash flows, 64-66. *See also* Investment instruments

Certificates of deposit, *see* Investment instruments

Classroom scheduling, 276-293; types of schedules, 279-285; impact on building utilization, 285-288; use of computer in, 288-293

Cohort survival method, 365-368

Co-insurance clause, 83-84

Computer applications: in classroom scheduling, 288-292; in transportation routing, 137-144; in supply management, 115; in unscheduled maintenance, 225-226. *See also* Computer simulation

Computer simulation, 382-386, 401-402. *See also* Resource forecasting, Flowcharting

Conflict matrix, 276-277

Conservatism, use in accounting, 6

Consistency, use in accounting, 10

Constrained optimization, 53, 58. *See also* Optimization

Constraints: changing, 339-340; organizational, 426; in food service, 198-203. *See also* Linear programming (general form)

Control: managerial, 435ff; operational, 435ff; internal, 35-36

Corrective maintenance cycle, 207-208

Cost allocation, 25-51; for food service, 152-155, 155-169, 179, 181

Cost analysis, 45, 171-186, 210, 219-228

Cost center, 172, 193

Costs, 50-51, 82-83, 91-93, 129, 160. *See also* Cost analysis, Cost allocation, Fixed costs, Variable

costs, Direct costs, Indirect costs, Ordering costs, Carrying costs
Cost-volume relationships, 176-178. *See also* Fixed costs, Variable costs
Credit, 13-19
Critical path, *see* PERT
Cubberley, Ellwood P., 298-299

Data, 418-424; character, 419; field, 419; logical record, 422; bank, 422; coding, 422-424
Debit, 13-19
Decision variables, 391-392; in linear programming, 133
Direct costs, 47-49, 160-169; of food service, 185-186; for transportation, 159-166
Discounting, 210. *See also* Life-cycle costs
Double-seating, practice of, 142

Economic order quantity, 93-95, 100
Electronic data processing, *see* Computer applications, Computer simulation
Enarson, Harold L., 449
Encumbrance, 29
Endogenous factor, 385
Endowment fund, *see* Fund
Enrollment forecasting, 361-380; assumptions in, 362-365; cohort survival, 365-368; curve fitting, 369-373, 378-381; using census based data, 372-377, 386-391
Enterprise, use in accounting, 4, 8-9
Equity, use in accounting, 6
Exogenous factor, 385
Expected value, *see* Uncertainty
Expenditure, 7, 27

Facilities: utilization, 285-288; planning, 391-401; food service, 188-190
Feasible solution, 137, 328, 329
Feasibility study, information systems, 424-427
Fertility, 364
Financial condition, use in accounting, 6

Financial statement, 9, 11, 37-41
Fixed costs, 45-46. *See also* Cost-volume relationships
Flowcharting, 412-415
Food service, 171-201
Forecasting, *see* Enrollment forecasting, Resource forecasting
Full absorption costing, 180
Full disclosure, use in accounting, 10
Full repairable item, 217
Fund, 8, 20; revolving, 8; sinking, 8; endowment, 8; matching, 8. *See also* Fund balance
Fund balance, 6

Gardner, John, 433-434

Haig, Robert, 305
Heuristics, 136

Incremental cost, 91
Indirect costs, 47-49, 160-169; for food service, 185-186
Inequalities, graphing, 328
Information systems: feasibility, 424-427; requirements, 422, 430, 434-442; design, 430; managerial attitudes, 442-444; impact on managers, 444; skill requirements, 447-449
Inherent availability, 206
Insurable value, 82-83
Insurance, *see* Risk
Inventory, average value of, 92. *See also* Economic order quantity
Investment instruments, 61-64; treasury bills, 62-63; repurchase agreements, 63-64; savings accounts, 64; certificates of deposit, 64

Job descriptions, 258-260; of assistant superintendent for business, 259-260; in budgeting, 267-273; in food service, 197-198

Least squares, 368-372, 378-380
Liability, accounting use of, 6
Life cycle cost, 210-214
Linear programming: general form, 323-357; applied to transporta-

tion, 129-135; graphic solution, 328-333; goal programming, 340-352

Linear responsibility charting, 258, 261-274; applied to skill requirements, 447-449; applied to supply management, 114

Logical record, 422

Logistics, 89-90; supply time, 207

Maintainability, 206-210

Maintenance, *see* Operations and maintenance

Maintenance downtime, 209

Master schedule, 290

Matching, *see* Fund

Materiality, use in accounting, 10

Mean active maintenance time, 209

Mean corrective maintenance time, 207

Mean preventative maintenance time, 209

Menu planning, 190-193

Model, mathematical, 383-384

Modes of maintenance, 214-215

Mort, Paul, 305

Nonrepairable item, 217

Numerical solution, 136

Objective function, *see* Linear programming (general form)

Operational availability, 205-206

Operations and maintenance, 205-228; theoretical foundations, 205-214; operating policies, 214-218; unscheduled, 225-228. *See also* Budgeting

Optimization, 53-54; in scheduling, 278; in supply management, 90-91; in transportation, 130, 133, 137. *See also* Suboptimization, Linear programming (general form), Optimum solution

Optimum solution, 331

Ordering costs, 91

Organization charts, 260-261

Overhead, *see* Indirect costs

Parameter, 327, 385

Partially repairable item, 217

PERT, 235, 237-256, 264, 267, 273-274; critical path, 245-247; estimating duration of activities, 253-256; used with linear responsibility charts, 264-266

Planning, 361, 434, 449; information needs, 435-442; for food service, 188-203. *See also* Resource forecasting, Cash planning

Policies: purchasing, 195; repair, 215-218; risk management, 80; maintenance, 214

Present fairly, use in accounting, 9

Present value, *see* Life cycle cost

Probability, 68-71; objective, 68; subjective, 69; independent, 69-71; dependent, 69, 71; joint, 69-71; marginal, 69; conditional, 69-71. *See also* Uncertainty

Productivity, maintenance, 224

Programs, instructional, 392-395. *See also* Budgeting

Purchasing, policies in food service, 195. *See also* Supply management

Reorder point, 96-100

Replacement cost, 82-83

Reporting, financial, 32, 33

Repurchase agreements, *see* Investment instruments

Resource allocation formulas, 295-320; in state-level financial assistance, 296-312. *See also* Linear programming

Resource forecasting, 391-401; cash, 64-65

Revenue, 7, 25-26, 54-57

Revolving fund, *see* Fund

Risk, 76-84; methods for controlling, 76-80; policies governing management of, 80-84

Roster scheduling, *see* Classroom scheduling

Safety stock, 97

Scheduling, *see* Classroom scheduling

Simulation, *see* Computer simulation

Sinking fund, *see* Fund

Slack, 246

Standard costs, 171-172, 176
Standard deviation, 255-256
State financial aid to school districts,
    296-312; flat grant, 297-299;
    foundation program, 299-301;
    weighted-pupil measures, 305-
    307; percentage equalizing, 307-
    309; power equalizing, 309-310
Stockout, 96
Strategic planning, 434. *See also* Plan-
    ning
Strayer, George, 305
Suboptimization, 152-155
Supply management, 90-126; theoreti-
    cal foundations, 90-100; organi-
    zational alternatives, 100-112; in-
    formation system requirements
    of, 112-126
System, 383, 408-412. *See also* Infor-
    mation system

T accounts, 13. *See also* Accounts
Transaction, financial, 15
Transfer prices, 49
Transformation functions, 263

Transportation, 128-169; theoretical
    foundations, 128-136; route
    scheduling, 137-144; buy-or-
    make option, 144-152, 155-169;
    suboptimization, 152-155
Traveling salesman problem, 135-136
Treasury bills, *see* Investment instru-
    ments
Trial balance, 19

Unbounded solution, 328
Uncertainty, 53-54, 71-76; conditional
    values, 71-74; expected values,
    74-76. *See also* Probability, Risk
Utilization, building, *see* Classroom
    scheduling

Variable, 385. *See also* Decision vari-
    ables
Variable costs, 45-46. *See also* Cost-vol-
    ume relationships
Variance, analysis of, 175
Volume, *see* Cost-volume relationships

Workloading standards, 219